MW00655441

The Pentateuch And Book Of Joshua
Critically Examined

You are holding a reproduction of an original work that is in the public domain in the United States of America, and possibly other countries.You may freely copy and distribute this work as no entity (individual or corporate) has a copyright on the body of the work.This book may contain prior copyright references, and library stamps (as most of these works were scanned from library copies).These have been scanned and retained as part of the historical artifact.

This book may have occasional imperfections such as missing or blurred pages, poor pictures, errant marks, etc. that were either part of the original artifact, or were introduced by the scanning process. We believe this work is culturally important, and despite the imperfections, have elected to bring it back into print as part of our continuing commitment to the preservation of printed works worldwide. We appreciate your understanding of the imperfections in the preservation process, and hope you enjoy this valuable book.

CRITICAL EXAMINATION

OF THE

PENTATEUCH AND BOOK OF JOSHUA.

LONDON
PRINTED BY SPOTTISWOODE AND CO.
NEW-STREET SQUARE

O

THE

PENTATEUCH AND BOOK OF JOSHUA

CRITICALLY EXAMINED.

BY

PROFESSOR A. KUENEN OF LEYDEN.

TRANSLATED FROM THE DUTCH AND EDITED WITH NOTES

BY THE

RIGHT REV. J. W. COLENSO, D.D.

BISHOP OF NATAL.

DIVINITY SCHOOL
LIBRARY.
HARVARD UNIVERSITY

LONDON:

LONGMAN, GREEN, LONGMAN, ROBERTS, & GREEN.

1865.

Sem 1140

Bi 808.65

HARVARD
UNIVERSITY
LIBRARY
AUG 11 1960

PREFACE.

———◦◦———

HAVING been detained in England longer than I expected,
yet under circumstances which prevented my setting myself steadily down, with the prospect of being able to
complete the Fifth Part of my work on the Pentateuch
before returning to my diocese, I have thought that I
might render a service to those now engaged (as I trust)
in England in the study of the criticism of the Old Testament, by translating and publishing that portion of Professor KUENEN'S, work, which concerns the Pentateuch
and Book of Joshua—the special subjects of my own enquiries. It is much to be regretted that the great Continental scholars, who for more than half a century have
been labouring diligently in the field of Biblical criticism,
are almost unknown, except by name, to the generality
of English readers. Translations, indeed, have been published of a few of those authors who have written most
strongly in defence of the traditional views—HÄVERNICK,
HENGSTENBERG, KEIL, &c.—for the benefit of English
students. But I am not aware that, except Mr. HEYWOOD'S

edition of VON BOHLEN, and PARKER'S of DE WETTE'S
Introduction, a translation has been published of any
one of the very important critical works of DE WETTE,
GESENIUS, HUPFELD, EWALD, KNOBEL, HITZIG, &c., which
have long been held in high repute among the scholars
of Europe. A single glance at the list appended, of the
works quoted by Professor KUENEN in the course of his
' Enquiry,' will show how extensive this literature is, and
how entirely, at this time, those of the clergy and laity
of England, who are not conversant with German or
Dutch, in which languages these criticisms are almost
all written, must be living outside those learned discussions, and to be unable to take any active part in them,
or to form any satisfactory judgment about them. Hence
it is, I believe, in great measure, that such an outcry has
been raised against my recent publications. Not only has
the study of Hebrew been so completly neglected among
us, that not a few of our bishops and clergy are necessarily
unacquainted with the facts about which such discussions
are raised : but many, who would desire to be informed,
have had no opportunity, till very lately,—as by the publication of Dr. KALISCH'S Commentaries on Genesis and
Exodus, and Dr. DAVIDSON'S admirable ' Introduction,'
in addition to the two works above-named,—of reading
a single work which could throw light upon the points
involved, or assist them in judging of the nature and
method of these investigations. I hope, however, that
the work now presented to the English reader may lend
some help in relieving this difficulty.

I have selected Professor KUENEN's work for translation for the following reasons.

(i) It is the *most recent* publication on the subject; and the author has kindly, at my request, revised entirely his own work, and made some important corrections and improvements expressly for this edition.

(ii) It embodies, as will be seen by the list of authors appended, the results of Continental Criticism generally up to the present time, and so provides, in a compact form, a mass of most valuable information for the scholar.

(iii) Professor KUENEN's work,— whether from the peculiar quality of his own mind, or it may be from the fact that the Dutch habits of thought and expression are more closely allied to the English than is frequently the case with the German,—while it is a splendid instance of clear and scholarly criticism, and thoroughly complete as far as it goes, is also distinguished by its brevity and conciseness; and on that account, though not so well adapted for *popular* use, it is yet likely, I believe, to be the more acceptable to English students, who only wish to know what the facts really are, and are capable of drawing their own inferences.

(iv) Lastly, although my own researches have led me to different conclusions, on certain points, from those of Professor KUENEN, (as is shown by some of the editorial notes), yet on many points this work will be found to agree substantially with the statements of my own four volumes; and I am able therefore to lay it before the English reader, as a proof that these statements are not so unfounded and shallow as some, high in authority, have pronounced them to be, and as an example of honest and most laborious research, aided by profound learning, and sustained by the sincere love of truth, which may suspend the harsh judgments of some, at least, of my gainsayers.

It will be seen that Professor KUENEN dates the *oldest* portions of the present Pentateuch (152) from about the end of the time of the *Judges*, or under *David's* reign, and the Book of Deuteronomy (154) from the age of *Manasseh*; whereas I have suggested that the oldest portions were probably written about the age of *Samuel*, and Deuteronomy under *Josiah*,—so that in these results, at least, we agree almost entirely. I hope in my Fifth Part, should I be permitted to complete it, to produce more fully the reasons which lead me still to maintain the former of these conclusions, as I adhere also, for the reasons which I have given at length in my Third Part, to the latter.

But there is one point in Professor KUENEN'S results to which I desire to draw the reader's special attention. He has shown, as I have in my Part III, that the Book of Deuteronomy was undoubtedly written in the later times of the kingdom of Judah. And, indeed, if there is any point which may be considered as settled by the almost unanimous judgment of the great critics of the Continent, it is this,—though opinions may still range within a century, as to the *exact* period in the later history, when the Book was written. But I have not yet, in my published volumes, given any account of the composition of the Book of *Joshua*. The reader will here find this subject fully discussed in chapters XXIV—XXIX and the notes appended; and he will see that no doubt exists among scholars that *a large portion of the Book of Joshua was written by the same hand as that which wrote the Book of Deuteronomy*. Now, this result is of the utmost importance; for, if this be true, then it follows at once, that Moses, at all events, did *not* write the Book of Deuteronomy.* Nay, in the last chapters of Joshua, which describe the events of his old age, we have the plainest signs of the hand of the Deuteronomist, who must have lived, therefore, not only after the time of Moses, but also after the time of Joshua, and who wrote, in fact, as Professor KUENEN shows, in far later days, about the age of Manasseh, or after it.

In introducing to the English Student the work of an eminent Dutch critic, it will be a sincere pleasure to me to contribute in any degree to the renewing that literary intercourse on theological subjects, which was in former times so frequent between the two countries. Erasmus,

---

* In addition to the linguistic evidence produced by Professor KUENEN in (46), and by myself in Part III. chap. 1, to show that the Deuteronomist was a very different person from the writer (or writers) of the main portion of the other four Books of the Pentateuch, it may be noted that of the two Hebrew words for 'heart,' לֵב, *lev*, and לֵבָב, *levav*,—

the former occurs *sixty-two* times in Genesis, Exodus, Leviticus, Numbers, and only *four* times in Deuteronomy, viz. iv.11,xxviii.65,xxix.4(3), 19(18),—

the latter occurs only *eight* times in Genesis, Exodus, Leviticus, Numbers, viz. G.xx.5,6, xxxi.26, E.xiv.5, L.xix.17, xxvi.36,41,N.xv.39, and *forty-six* times in Deuteronomy.

the friend of Colet, exercised a considerable influence on the religious movement of England during the Reformation period. At a later time the works of Episcopius became an armoury for our own Arminian divines. The Commentaries, as well as the *de Veritate*, of Grotius enjoyed among us a lasting reputation; and Le Clerc, the friend of Tillotson and Tenison, was acknowledged here, as well as elsewhere, to be the first Biblical critic of his age. The cessation of literary communication between the Netherlands and the rest of Europe is undoubtedly attributable to the disuse of the Latin language as the ordinary means of communication among the learned. A country like Holland, of no very great area, and with a language little known beyond its own boundaries, has in consequence experienced an isolation disproportioned to the real merits of its writers.

The recent isolation of England in matters theological has been owing to other causes—to a certain insular self-sufficiency—to an unreasoning conservatism—to an unpainstaking Scripturalism on the one hand, and to the influence of an exaggerated Episcopalianism on the other. Nevertheless it is possible that, in relation to the present discussion, a foreigner may obtain in some quarters a more candid and impartial hearing than is as yet readily accorded to an English Bishop. Undoubtedly the conclusions of some of the most eminent of the Dutch theologians on the subject of the Scriptures would be little in accordance with the opinions usually current among ourselves. But I trust that the present work will be examined with the attention which it deserves,—with an attention which might be withheld from a German author, because Lessing, Strauss, and Baur have been Germans, or from a French one, because a Voltaire, a Rousseau, and a Renan have lived in France. In that case I shall feel myself amply rewarded for any labour bestowed on its translation.

As to the ultimate verdict, which will be given generally in England on the evidence concerning the authorship and composition of the Pentateuch, I retain the fullest confidence. Nor have I the least fear that any damage will ensue to the cause of true religion, when these books shall be popularly known to have been the literary growth of ages, and the production of numerous authors, whom it is now impossible to identify with complete historical certainty. So far as Christianity itself was derived from, and presupposes, Judaism, it has every thing to gain, towards a true appreciation of itself, from a clear insight into the mode in which the Hebrew records were deposited, not only gradually in time, but under various influences of parties and opinions. And, in regard to the books commonly attributed to Moses, many a stumbling-block to piety will be removed, many an intellectual difficulty will disappear, much strain upon the conscience will be relieved, when it is understood that the great Jewish Lawgiver is not responsible for all which they contain— much less the Gospel or the Author of the Gospel—that statements irreconcileable, or conflicting with each other are explained by their having been derived from different sources—that no inspired penman guarantees the truth of

narratives incredible to Science, or delivers as Revelation
in its highest sense all which patriarchs and tribes, kings
and peoples, have conceived concerning the Divine Being,
His dealings with mankind, and their obligations towards
Him and towards each other.

J. W. NATAL.

LONDON: *Jan.* 24, 1865.

CONTENTS.

———•◦•———

LIST OF AUTHORS

QUOTED OR REFERRED TO IN THE FOLLOWING WORK.

———◦◦◦———

ASTRUC, *Conjectures sur les mémoires originaux, dont il paraît que Moïse s'est servi pour composer le Livre de Genèse* (1753).

BACHMANN, *die Festgesetze des Pentateuchs* (1858).

BAUMGARTEN, *Theologischen Commentar zum A.T.*

BAUR, *Geschichte der A.T. Weissagung.*

BERTHEAU, *die sieben Gruppen Mosaischer Gesetze in den drei mittleren Büchern des Pentateuchs* (1840).

  „   *Richter und Rut.*

  „   *die Bücher der Chronik.*

BLEEK, *Einleitung in das A.T.* (1860).

BOEHMER, *Liber Genesis Pentacheuchicus.*

  „   *das erste Buch der Thora, Uebersetzung seiner drei Quellenschriften und der Redactionszusätze, mit kritischen, exegetischen, historischen Erörterungen* (1862).

BUNSEN, *Bibelwerk.*

CREDNER, *der Prophet Joël.*

DELITZSCH, *die Genesis ausgelegt* (3rd Ed. 1860).

  „   *Symb. ad psalm. illustr. isagogica.*

DIESTEL, *der Segen Jakob's in G.xlix historisch erläutert* (1853).

DRECHSLER, *die Einheit und Aechtheit der Genesis* (1838).

EICHORN, *Einleitung in das A.T.* (4th Ed. 1823).

EWALD, *Geschichte des Volkes Israël* (2nd Ed.)

  „   *die Alterthümer des Volkes Israels* (2nd Ed. 1854).

GEER, *de Bileamo, ejus historiâ et vaticiniis* (1816).

GEIGER, *Urschrift und Uebersetzung der Bibel.*

GEORGE, *die älteren Jüdische Feste, mit einer Kritik der Gesetzgebung des Pentateuch* (1835).

GRAF, *der Segen Mose's, D.xxxiii erklärt* (1857).

  „   *der Prophet Jeremia erklärt* (1862).

HARTMANN, *Historisch-kritische Forschungen über die Bildung, das Zeitalter, und den Plan der fünf Bücher Mose's* (1831).

HÄVERNICK, *Handbuch der historisch-kritischen Einleitung in das A.T.* (Part I, 2nd Ed., by KEIL, 1853–1856, Part II, 1839–1844, Part III, completed by KEIL, 1849).

HENGSTENBERG, *Beiträge zur Einleitung ins A.T.* (1831–1839).

  „   *die Geschichte Bileam's und seine Weissagungen* (1842).

  „   *Christologie des A.T.*

HERZFELD, *Geschichte des Volkes Israël, von der Zerstörung des ersten Tempels bis zur Einsetzung des Mackabäers Schimon.*
HITZIG, *Begriff der Kritik.*
„   *die Psalmen.*
„   *der Prophet Jeremia.*
HUPFELD, *die Quellen der Genesis, und die Art ihrer Zusammensetzung* (1853).
„   *de primitivâ et verâ Festorum apud Hebræos ratione ex legum Mosaicarum varietate eruendâ* (1852–1858).
„   *die Psalmen.*
ILGEN, *die Urkunden des Jerusalemer Tempelarchivs* (1798).
JOST, *die Geschichte des Judenthums und seiner Secten* (1857).
KAMPHAUSEN, *das Lied Mose's, D.xxxii.1–43, erklärt* (1862).
KEIL, *Handbuch der historisch-kritischen, Einleitung in die kanonischen und apokryphischen Schriften des A.T.* (2nd Ed. 1859).
„   *Josua.*
KNOBEL, *die Genesis* (2nd Ed.)
„   *Exodus und Leviticus.*
„   *Num. Deut. und Josua.*
KUEPER, *Jeremias librorum sacrorum Interpres atque Vindex.*
KURTZ, *Beiträge zur Vertheidigung und Begrundung der Echtheit des Pentateuches.*
„   *Geschichte des A. Bundes* (1853, 1855).
„   *die Einheit der Genesis* (1846).
„   *die Söhne Gottes in 1 Mos.vi.1–4, und die sündigenden Engel in 2 Pet.ii. 4,5, und Jud.6,7.*
LAND, *Disputatio de carmine Jacobi, G.xlix.* (1857).
LENGKERKE, Von, *Kenaän.*
MASIUS, *Josuæ Imperatoris historia illustrata* (1574).
MAURER, *Commentar.*
MICHAËLIS, *Mos. Recht* (Dutch Tr.)
MOVERS, *über die Textbeschaffenheit der Chronik.*
OORT, *de pericope N.xxii.2–xxiv, historiam Bileami continente* (1860).
POPPER, *der Biblischen Bericht über die Stiftshütte* (1862).
RANKE, *Untersuchungen über den Pentateuch* (1834–1840).
RAUMER, Von, *Palästina* (3rd Ed. 1850).
RENAN, *Études d'histoire religieuse* (2nd Ed. 1857).
RIEHM, *die Gesetzgebung Mosis im Lande Moab* (1854).
RUTGERS, *het tijdvak der Babyl. ballingschap chronologisch onderzocht.*
SAALSCHUTZ, *das Mosaische Recht* (2nd Ed. 1853).
SCHOLTEN, *Historisch-kritische Inleiding tot het N.T.* (1864).
SCHRADER, *Studien zur Kritik und Erklärung der Biblischen Urgeschichte, G.i.–xi.* (1863).
SCHULTZ, *das Deuteronomium erklärt* (1859).
SPINOZA, *Tract. Theol. Polit.*
STÄHELIN, *Kritische Untersuchungen*
STARK, *Gaza und die Philistaische Küste* (1852).
THENIUS, *die Bücher Samuels* (2nd Ed. 1864).
„   *die Bücher der Könige.*
TUCH, *Commentar über die Genesis.*
VATER, *Commentar über den Pentateuch* (1802–1805).
VATKE, *die Religion des A.T.*
WETTE, De, *Beiträge zur Einleitung in das A.T.*
„   *Einleitung in das A.T.*
WILLES, Von, *Bijdragen tot bevordering van Bijb. uitlegkunde.*
ZUNS, *die gottesdienstlichen Vorträge der Juden.*

THE PENTATEUCH

AND BOOK OF JOSHUA

CRITICALLY EXAMINED.

B

CHAPTER I.

NAME, DIVISION, AND CONTENTS OF THE PENTATEUCH.

1. THE usual name for the Pentateuch among the Jews is
'Thora'='Law,' or 'The Five Parts of the Law,'—a name which
is based on the idea that the laws are the main point in the
Pentateuch, and the history stands merely in connection therewith. We read frequently in the O.T. of *the Book of the Law*,
2K.xxii.8, *the Book of the Law of Moses*, Jo.viii.31,xxiii.6, 2K.
xiv.6, Neh.viii.1, *the Book of the Law of Jehovah, by the hand
of Moses*, 2Ch.xxxiv.14, *the Law of Moses*, 1K.ii.3, 2K.xxiii.25,
2Ch.xxiii.18,xxx.16, Ezr.iii.2,vii.6,&c., *the Book of Moses*, 2Ch.
xxv.4,xxxv.12,&c. These expressions imply that Moses *gave*
the Law, or, perhaps, *committed it to writing*; but they must
not at once be regarded as being names for the Pentateuch, *such
as we now possess it*. The last collector of the Psalms probably
knew of the division of the Thora into five Books; since he
divided the whole collection of Psalms into *five* Books,—
corresponding to the five Books of the Pentateuch,—and not into
three or *four*, as he might otherwise have done.

2. By the Greeks the Thora is usually called ἡ πεντάτευχος
(βίβλος),—by the Latin Christians, *Pentateuchus*. The five
Books, to which these appellations refer, were denoted by the
Jews by means of the words with which they begin in Hebrew.
In the Septuagint translation they bear names, which indicate
their chief contents, and which have been rightly adopted in
many later translations, and have come generally into use.[1]

3. If the Pentateuch, as a whole, contains the history of the foundation of the theocracy, the First Book, *Genesis*, is occupied with the preparation for it. First, we have related the creation of Heaven and Earth, and the fates of the first human beings, i–iv; then follows the history of their descendants as far as and including Noah, v–ix. Some particulars are then mentioned about Noah's sons and their progeny, x.1–xi.9 ; after which the narrative confines itself to Shem's descendants, xi.10–26, and so comes to Abraham, the history of whose life is recorded at length, xi.27–xxv.11. Thereupon there follows first a short notice about Ishmael, xxv.12–18,—then a more full account of the events of Isaac's life, and of his two sons during their father's life-time, xxv.19–xxxv.29. In like manner, a short genealogy of Esau, xxxvi, is followed by a more ample narrative of Jacob's life, in which the history of Joseph, and the removal of Jacob's family to Egypt, fill an important place, xxxvii–l.[2]

4. The Second Book, *Exodus*, describes for us first the oppression of Jacob's offspring in Egypt, i,—then the birth, the earliest adventures and calling of Moses, ii–iv, his appearance before Pharaoh, the miracles wrought through him, and the deliverance of Israel out of the Egyptian slavery, v.1–xiii.16, with which the laws about the Passover, the Feast of Unleavened Bread, and the dedication of the firstborn, xii.1–28,43–49,xiii.1–16, stand in close connection. Next is described the march to Sinai, xiii.17–xix.2, in the course of which the crossing of the Red Sea, xiv,xv, the manna and the quails, xvi, the miracle of Rephidim, the fight with Amalek, xvii, and the visit of Jethro, xviii, claim our attention. During the sojourn of the people at Sinai, E.xix.1–N.x.11, we have first, after suitable preparation of the people, E.xix.3–25, the promulgation of the Decalogue, xx.1–17 ; and then a number of laws are communicated to Moses, xx.18–xxiii, on the basis of which the Covenant between Jehovah and Israel is concluded, xxiv.   Next, Moses receives the description of the Tabernacle and its belongings, xxv.1–xxxi.17 ; and in

accordance with these the Sanctuary is afterwards built, xxxv–xl. Before this, however, we find an account of the apostasy of the people and its consequences, xxxi.18–xxxiv.

5. The Third Book, *Leviticus*, contains the sequel of the Sinaitic Legislation, and scarcely any incidents of an historical kind. We find here a directory for sacrifices, i–vii, provided with a separate subscription, vii.38, with which the account of the consecration of Aaron and his sons, viii–x, is closely connected. Thereupon follow the laws concerning clean and unclean beasts, xi, and bodily defilement, especially leprosy, xii–xv,—the ordinances about the Day of Atonement, xvi, about the sacrificing at the holy place, and the expiatory power of blood, xvii,—a collection of ordinances and punishments, referring principally to civil life, xviii–xx,—prescriptions about the holiness of the priest, xxi,xxii, and about the Feasts, xxiii,—directions as to the golden candlestick and shew-bread, xxiv.1–9, as to the punishment of blasphemy, and the punishment of death, generally, xxiv.10–23,—the law about the year of Jubilee, xxv, and vows, xxvii, the last preceded by a long threatening address, xxvi, which, as well as xxvii, is supplied with a subscription, xxvi.46, xxvii.34.[3]

6. The Fourth Book, *Numbers*, is also, like the second, composed, partly of historical, partly of legislative, matter. The result of the numbering of the people, carried out at Sinai, is recorded in i,—then the arrangement of the Camp, ii. Next, we find directions about the Levites and their duties, iii,iv,—instructions about the cleansing of the Camp, v.1–4, the trespass-offering, v.5–10, the offering of jealousy, v.11–31, the law of the Nazarite, vi.1–21, the priestly blessing, v.22–27. Hereupon there follows an account of the offerings of the tribe-princes at the dedication of the Tabernacle, vii,—the dedication of the Levites to the service of the Sanctuary, viii,—the celebration of the Passover in the second year after the Exodus, ix.1–14,—the cloud and the pillar of fire, v.15–23,—the holy trumpets, x.1–10. Next

we find the narrative of the march from Sinai, x.11–28, with a few historical incidents, *v.*29–36,—then that of the events of Taberah and Kibroth-hattaävah, xi,—of Miriam's leprosy, xii,—of the sending-out of the spies and its results, xiii–xiv. After the promulgation of a five-fold set of ordinances of different kinds, xv, the account is carried on of the desert journey of the Israelites, the rebellion of Korah, Dathan, and Abiram, and the confirmation of Aaron's priestly authority, xvi, xvii. Again there follow directions about the revenues of the priests, xviii, and the purification of the unclean, xix.

7. The following six chapters, xx–xxv, are all of an historical nature, and contain the account of Miriam's death,—of the murmuring of the people at Meribah and Kadesh,—of the sending-out of messengers to Edom,—of Aaron's death,—of the march around Edom to the other side of the Jordan,—of the wars against Sihon and Og,—of Balaam's prophecies,—of the idolatries of the people at Shittim. Thereupon a second numbering of the people takes place, xxvi; Moses receives instructions about the succession of inheritance through daughters, xxvii. 1–11; and Joshua is appointed to be his successor, *v.*12–23. The following three chapters, xxviii–xxx, serve for the completion of the laws about feasts in L. xxiii, and about vows in L. xxvii. Then the Midianites are punished, and, on the occasion of this war against them, ordinances are laid down about booty, xxxi. Hereupon follows an account of the settlement of certain tribes in the trans-Jordanic lands, xxxii,—a list of the stations of the march through the wilderness, xxxiii. 1–49,—an injunction as to the extirpation of the Canaanites, *v.*50–56,—the definition of the boundaries of Canaan, xxxiv,—the direction about the Levitical cities, xxxv. 1–8, and the free cities, or cities of refuge, *v.*9–34,— lastly, a more minute direction, xxxvi, about the inheritance of daughters, xxvii. 1–11. The whole is concluded with a subscription, xxxvi. 13.

8. The Fifth Book, *Deuteronomy*, contains, first, a hortatory

address of Moses to Israel, i.1–iv.40, in which he reminds them of the favours they had enjoyed. Next, after a short account of the free cities beyond the Jordan, v.41–43, and a diffuse subscription, v.44–49, we have a second discourse, in which the people are exhorted to confidence in Jehovah, and the Law, for a great part, is repeated, v–xxvi. Then follows the ratification of the covenant between Jehovah and Israel, xxvii,xxviii, whereby blessing or cursing is set forth as the consequence of the faithfulness or unfaithfulness of the people, and Moses admonishes the people again, xxix,xxx. Thereupon the Lawgiver takes leave of the people, and the ' Song of Moses ' is imparted to us, xxxi,xxxii. The Book is closed with the ' Blessing of Moses,' xxxiii, and the account of his death, which ends with the reverential recognition of his great services, xxxiv.

CHAPTER II.

THE TESTIMONY OF THE PENTATEUCH AS TO ITS OWN ORIGIN.

9. In this investigation as to the origin and age of the Pentateuch, we shall set aside at once the Jewish and Christian traditions on these points, and consult immediately the sources themselves. The Books of the Pentateuch give evidence in two different ways as to their origin,—*directly*, in those places, where mention is made of committing to writing the whole or certain parts of it,—*indirectly*, through the nature of the contents and the Legislation itself. We shall consider, first of all, only the *direct evidence.*[4]

10. In the Books of *Genesis* and *Leviticus* no mention is made of any portion of these Books being committed to writing.

In E.xvii.14 Moses receives from Jehovah a command, to

write the attack of Amalek for remembrance 'in the Book,' that is, in the book which he employed for that purpose.[5]

In E.xxiv.4 Moses *writes* 'all the words of Jehovah,'—that is, the laws of the *Covenant*, xx.22-xxiii.33,* with or without the Decalogue, xx.1–17; and, on this account, the laws here said to be recorded by him are named the ' Book of the Covenant,' xxiv.7.

In E.xxxiv.27 God commands that Moses shall *write* ' these words,' that is, the commands imparted in *v.*10–26.[6]

In N.xxxiii.2 we read that Moses *wrote* the 'goings-out' of Israel, which are then summed up, *v.*3–49.

Since, thus, in the first four Books of the Pentateuch, only the writing-down of certain passages of small extent is ascribed to Moses, this very fact makes it probable that all the rest, in the author's opinion, was *not* from the hand of Moses. In one or two places, the very notice itself, that Moses committed to writing this thing or that, must be distinguished from that which he wrote; so that this last, even according to the narrative itself, is *not* preserved for us.

11. In the Book of Deuteronomy it is related, xxxi.9, comp. *v.*24–26, that Moses wrote ' *this* Law,' and handed it over to the Priests. Yet, before this, Moses makes mention in his addresses of ' *this* Book,' xxix.20,27, ' *this* Book of the Law,' xxix.21,xxx.10, comp. xxxi.26, 'the Book of *this* Law,' xxviii.61, ' the words of *this* Law, written in *this* Book,' xxviii.58,—as if the Law had been already committed to writing *before* the point of time, which its own contents indicate as the time of its being written. This contradiction is explained by the supposition, that Moses, according to the narrator's view, had first written down his discourses, and then read them off, so that he was able to refer to them in the course of his speech. The account contained in xxxi.9, that 'Moses wrote this Law,' is thus

---

* There is reason, as I believe, for supposing that the *conclusion* of E.xxiii, *viz.* *v.*20–33, is one of the Deuteronomistic interpolations to which I have referred in *Pent.*III.566. *Ed.*

brought in *after* the proper place for it, and ' the Book,' written by Moses, consisted of i.6–iv.40,v.1–xxix.1 (or xxx.20).[7]

12. Further, the expression 'this Law' can only refer to the Book of Deuteronomy, or some portion of that Book, and by no means, as is maintained by some, to Genesis, Exodus, Leviticus, Numbers, or, perhaps, 'the whole Pentateuch. This appears, both from the use of the defining pronoun, 'this,' and from passages such as i.5,iv.8,xxvii.1,3,8,26, comp. xxix.9,12,14,15, where it is expressly said that Moses sets before them 'this Law' *this day*,[8] and the Covenant, made in the land of Moab, is distinguished from that at Sinai, xxix.1. Hence this only follows from the passages above-quoted, xxxi.9, comp. *v.*24–26, —*viz.* that the Book of Deuteronomy, for by far the greatest part of it, professes to be a Mosaic writing, without our being justified in extending this testimony to the first four Books also of the Pentateuch.

13. From the above it appears that the Mosaic origin of the five Books in their entirety is nowhere taught in the Pentateuch, and even, as regards the first four Books, it is rather negatived than affirmed by their own testimony. The following investigation, however, will extend not merely to those passages, whose author is not named, but also to those which are ascribed to Moses, including the whole of Deuteronomy. The possibility always exists that he may be erroneously indicated as the author of these sections, or that they may have been ascribed to him through a not unusual literary fiction.[9]

CHAPTER III.

14. THE contents of the Pentateuch exhibit by no means the appearance of accounts recorded by eye-witnesses or contemporaries. This is true not merely of the historical narratives in Genesis, but also of the stories about the Mosaic time. Least of all does it appear that Moses himself is here relating the events, in which he played so important a part. Mention is made throughout of Moses in the third person,—sometimes in quite an objective way, E.vi.26,27,xi.3, D.xxxiii.4. Judgments as to the character and services of Moses, such as are found in N.xii.3,6–8, are just as intelligible, on the supposition that they proceed from others, as they are objectionable, supposing that he himself wrote them.[10] The view, that in all these passages Moses himself is speaking, is quite as unnatural as the generally rejected notion, that he was the author of D.xxxiv.

15. Again the contents of the Pentateuch are in some places very *incomplete*, even with respect to such details as must have been known to Moses and his near contemporaries. Especially, here comes into consideration the large interval of 400 * years, during which the Israelites sojourned in Egypt, E.xii.40, comp. E.ii.1,vi.16–25, N.xxvi.59,[11] and the wanderings of the people in the wilderness from the second to the fortieth year after the Exodus, N.xv–xix.[12]

16. Some narratives of the Pentateuch leave much to be desired in respect of clearness. This is true, *e.g.* of N.xx.1–3,[13] xxi.1–3,[14] and of many other passages, which will come to be

---

* In Part I.xv. I have shown, as I believe, that the duration of the sojourn of the Israelites in Egypt is meant in the narrative to be 215 or 210 years, not 400 or 430. *Ed.*

considered below, Chap.IV,V.   If we had before us the accounts
of contemporaries, we should not find ourselves so frequently in
uncertainty as to the meaning of their contents.

17. Lastly, we find at least once in the Pentateuch, N.xxi.14,
a reference to a document, from which the narrator derived some
particulars, *the Book of the Wars of Jehovah.*   This very book
must, as appears from the title which it bears, have been written after the time of Moses, and, *à fortiori,* this must have been
the case with the narrative, which makes reference to it.[15]
In connection with this extract, it is further most probable that
also other, especially poetical, passages, N.xxi.17,18,27–30,E.xv.
1–18,G.xlix.1–27, have been taken-over from similar collections,
e.g. from the ' Book of Jasher,' Jo.x.13, 2S.i.18.

CHAPTER IV.

DIFFERENT NARRATIVES CONCERNING THE SAME FACT.

18. IN a document, which from first to last is the work of
one hand, we expect as a rule to find no repetitions, unless special occasion should arise to mention the same fact a second
time ; and in this case the two accounts would agree in the main,
and only vary from one another in points of secondary importance.   Such variations are then easily explained from the purpose
which the writer had in view, and the circumstances which made
the repetition necessary.[16]

19. In the Pentateuch, however, we find not unfrequently
two accounts about the same fact, and between the two accounts
such a difference is perceived, that we cannot possibly ascribe
them to the same writer.[17]   This is true not only in Genesis—
where, if need be, it might be explained as arising from the

difference of the written records, used by the one author, Moses, or one of his contemporaries,[18]—but also in Exodus [19] and Numbers.[20]   With respect to these Books it is only possible for us to resort to a like supposition, if we place the compilation of the Pentateuch,—as a whole, at all events,—some time after Moses. This seems to be the more justified, since the phenomena, noticed above in Chap. III, lead also to the same conclusion.

CHAPTER V.

ACCOUNTS COMPILED FROM DIFFERENT DOCUMENTS.

20. Some narratives of the Pentateuch manifestly do not proceed from one and the same hand, but have been compiled out of different documents or records, which related probably the same fact, but not exactly in the same manner.   Such a difference between the documents, which the narrator had at his disposal, may certainly have been got rid of in the process of retouching.   But, that it still exists in many narratives of the Pentateuch, as well as of other historical books of the Old Testament, is quite in accordance with the character of Eastern historical writings,[21] and is a proof of the fidelity, with which the narrators are wont to repeat the identical words of their predecessors.   Since this phenomenon presents itself, not merely in Genesis,[22] but also in passages, where events out of the Mosaic time are related,[23] the inference drawn at the end of Chap. IV holds good here also.

CHAPTER VI.

DIFFERENT VERSIONS OF THE SAME TRADITIONAL MATTER.

21. If from the facts above cited, Chap.IV,V, it appears that the narratives of the Pentateuch do not all proceed from one hand, we are now prepared to explain also other phenomena, from the difference between the narrators. We find, for instance, in Genesis, Exodus, and Numbers, a number of narratives, which in the main agree with each other, but differ from one another in details of more or less importance. As often as in the one account we meet with no trace of acquaintance with the other,—as often, therefore, as the hypothesis, that they are not from one and the same hand, can be proposed,—we are also justified in appealing to it.

22. The historical matter, then, which lies at the basis of the stories of Genesis, was not at once committed to writing, but remained a long while preserved in the traditions of the people. So, too, with respect to the narratives in Exodus and Numbers, the same is, at least, made probable through Chap.III,IV,V.   It lies in the nature of such a tradition, that it does not continue like unto itself, but assumes different forms in different regions and different times.   The variations become still greater, when at length they are committed to writing by different authors. Whether, however, the agreement between two narratives is so great that we must regard them, notwithstanding the points of difference, as versions of one and the selfsame tradition, can only appear from a close critical enquiry, in which, naturally, attention must be directed not only to the contents, but also to the form, of the narratives.[24]

CHAPTER VII.

THE GEOGRAPHICAL AND HISTORICAL POINT OF VIEW OF THE NARRATORS.

23. EVERY historical work of any extent, however objective it may be, must necessarily either exhibit plainly, or at least betray, the point of view of the writer. This remark holds good also with respect to the Pentateuch, although the writers usually confine themselves to the mere mention of facts, and, consequently, the number of passages, from which we can learn their geographical and historical position, is comparatively small.

24. As to the first point, the narrators in the Pentateuch lived in the land of Canaan. They use a language marked by idioms, which can only have been formed in Canaan.[25] They take pleasure in explaining the origin of names of places in Canaan, in which Israel could have had no interest during the sojourn in Egypt and in the wilderness.[26] And, sometimes, they are circumstantial in defining the position of places, which, during the march through the wilderness, were *well known* to every Israelite.[27]

25. With respect to the historical point of view of these narrators, they lived *after* the conquest of Canaan through Joshua. They make remarks, and mention particular circumstances, which in Moses' time needed not to be made or mentioned;[28] they employ names, which did not come into use till after the time of Moses.[29] Sometimes they refer back to events of the time of Moses as events long past;[30] or they imply a knowledge of facts, which did not occur till after the time of Moses.[31]

26. It is not unnatural that the poetical passages inserted in the Pentateuch, *e.g.*, the 'Blessing of Jacob,' G.xlix, the 'Hymn of Moses' after the passage through the Red Sea, E.xv, the 'Song'

and the 'Blessing' of Moses, D.xxxii.1–43,xxxiii, and, in some measure, also the Blessings of Balaam, N.xxiii,xxiv,—should betray much clearer signs, than the purely historical portions, of the time of their preparation. Now in all these passages may be remarked traces of the time after Moses.[32] And, as these are probably older, but certainly not later, than the narrative in which they are inserted,[33] it follows that in this way the result of our enquiry with respect to the historical portions is fully confirmed.

CHAPTER VIII.

THE LEGISLATION CONTAINED IN THE BOOKS OF EXODUS, LEVITICUS, AND NUMBERS.

27. THE Legislation contained in the Books of Exodus, Leviticus, and Numbers, professes, as a whole, to be Mosaic. The particular laws were communicated by Jehovah to Moses, usually with the specification of those to whom they were to be delivered, whether to the people of Israel or to Aaron (afterwards Eleazar), as the representative of the priesthood.[34] It is not said that Moses himself committed the laws to writing. Only with respect to the laws of the so-called 'Book of the Covenant,' E.xx.22–xxiii, we find it recorded that Moses wrote them, E.xxiv.4, comp. xxxiv.27, and (10) above. Yet the nature of the case would lead us to conclude that the other ordinances also, *if Moses really uttered them, as they now lie before us,* must have been committed to writing by him, or, at all events, under his immediate superintendence. On that supposition, he may not have thought it good to trust them to the memory of the Israelites, but must at once have provided for their being preserved in writing.

28. In the three Books just named we do not find by any means a *system* of Legislation, in which each subject is treated entirely by itself, and similar subjects are considered in succession.   On the contrary, it is not seldom that the prescriptions about one and the same matter are found scattered about in two or three Books.[35]   In point of fact, however, the giving such a system was not the design of the writer, who gave to the Books of Exodus, Leviticus, and Numbers their present form.   He ranges the laws *chronologically, i.e.* according to the time of their being uttered; and distinguishes thus—

(i) The laws revealed before the arrival of the people in the wilderness of Sinai,—

(ii) The Sinaitic Legislation,—

(iii) The laws uttered after the departure from Sinai, during the march through the wilderness, and especially in the plains of Moab.[36]

29. Nothing seems more simple than to accept this whole hypothesis, and to see in the middle three books of the Pentateuch, the *journal*, as it were, of the Divine revelations to Moses.   Yet against it there arise serious objections.   The chief of them is derived from the result of our enquiry with respect to the historical narratives contained in these Books.   If *these* do not proceed from one hand,—still less, from one out of the time of Moses,—there arises a doubt whether the present arrangement of the laws is, perhaps, so entirely grounded upon the course of the history.   And this doubt is completely confirmed, both by the order itself, and by the contents and form of the laws.

30. In the first place, it is confirmed by the *order* of these laws.   It is in the highest degree improbable that in that night, in which Israel left Egypt, such ordinances about the Passover and the firstborn were uttered, as we find recorded in E.xii,xiii, [37]—that by far the greater number of the laws, E.xii–N.x.10, were promulgated during the *single* year's sojourn at Sinai, — that in the time of the thirty-

seven years' wanderings, so singularly suited (as it would seem) for the organisation of the people, only those few laws fall at most (see note[12]), which we find recorded in N.xv,xviii,xix, —that, finally, Moses, between the sixth and eleventh months of the fortieth year after the Exodus, (*i.e.* on the journey from mount Hor to the plains of Moab, and in the midst of the wars against Sihon, Og, and Midian,) should have found time for holding a census, N.xxvi, and for the proclamation of the laws contained in N.xxvii–xxxi,xxxiv–xxxvi.

31. Supposing, however, that we might be able to get over these difficulties, yet the *contents* and *form* of the laws do not allow us to regard them as being all without distinction Mosaic. For the proof of this, however, it is not right to appeal to the fact, that by far the greater part of the laws are designed for the people after they should have been settled in Canaan. For, in any case, if Moses published any laws, he must of necessity have had his eye upon the requirements of Israel, after they should have conquered their extensive places of settlement.

32. It is another question, however, whether Moses in the wilderness found occasion and opportunity to descend so minutely into details, as happens in most of the laws, with reference to so many points, not always of equal importance.[38] It is much more probable, and more in accordance with the nature of his important task, that he indicated in each province of legislation the direction in which he wished the people to move, and left to experience the development of the details. It is much more probable that he regulated practically the religions, political, and moral condition of the people, than that he wrote out at full length the prescriptions concerning it, which were, to a great extent, impracticable in the wilderness, and did this, too, in a time when, it is true, the art of writing was known, but it was as yet very little exercised.[39]

33. But that, which gives decisive weight to these probable reasons, is the fact, that there exists discrepancy between some

c

of the laws, contained in the Books of Exodus, Leviticus, and Numbers. Two cases may here be conceived, and in fact actually do present themselves :—

(i) The discrepancy, though really existing, may be of such a kind as to seem to be capable of exegetical explanation, through interpretation of the law ;

(ii) The one ordinance may distinctly exclude the other.[40] In any law-book, however, which from beginning to end proceeds from one hand, and dates out of one period, the first case would be as little likely to occur as the second. Inasmuch, then, as *both* occur in the Books in question, the Legislation contained in them cannot be in its entirety Mosaic, but must be regarded as the work of different persons and different times.[41]

34. That this is, in fact, the case, appears also from those laws, which are plainly seen to be appendices to former ordinances, designed to fill up some deficiency in them. Since, however, such defects are in most cases only revealed by experience in after years, this phenomenon also points to a *gradual* origination of the present Legislation.[42]

35. Lastly, this is also rendered probable by the obvious difference of expression between some of the laws,—a difference which speaks the more strongly for a difference of authorship, inasmuch as the legislative style, from the nature of the case, is simple, and is usually marked by a certain fixedness and the use of standing formulæ.[43]

CHAPTER IX.

CONNECTION BETWEEN THE HISTORY AND LEGISLATION IN THE BOOKS OF EXODUS, LEVITICUS, AND NUMBERS.

36. THE connection between the historical accounts and the Legislation contained in the Books of Exodus, Leviticus, and Numbers, is not so simple as to admit of being set forth in a few words. Rather, different cases must here be distinguished :—

(i) Some laws are provided with historical introductions, which are so closely connected with them, that the historical narratives can be no more thought of without the laws, than the laws without the narratives;[44]

(ii) Some laws are so closely connected with historical narratives, and *vice versâ*, that both must have been always bound together ;[45]

(iii) On the other hand, the connection between the History and the Legislation is sometimes so loose or even interrupted, that we may very well suppose that both have originated independently of each other. The original connection, now interrupted by the insertion either of an historical narrative or of one or more laws, is, here and there, still very plainly to be discerned.[46]

37. From the above it follows that those, who see in the Legislation of Exodus, Leviticus, and Numbers a whole, with which the historical narratives have been *afterwards* connected, explain the facts only partially, and especially can give no account of those laws which have been summed up above in (36) under (i) and (ii). This general judgment is applicable in particular to BERTHEAU, whose hypothesis, however, remains in any case still worthy of being mentioned.[47] He finds, in the Books of Exodus, Leviticus, and Numbers, *seven* groups of Mosaic laws,—in each of these groups, *seven* series,—in each series, *ten*

c 2

commands.[48] The seven groups, or four hundred and ninety commands, made formerly a continuous whole, a codex of pure legislative contents ; but, when the Pentateuch was compiled, the historical narratives were inserted between the 'groups,' and, in some cases, even between the 'series' of one 'group.' [49]

38. Besides the facts mentioned above in (36.i,ii), this hypothesis is negatived—

(i) By the great number of laws, which BERTHEAU is obliged to separate from his 'groups' as 'additional laws,'—not unfrequently, as it seems, without any sufficient reason,[50]—

(ii) By the laws which conflict with each other, see note [40],—

(iii) By the occasionally artificial assignment of the ten commands to one 'series,' and the seven 'series' to one 'group.' [51]

Nevertheless, it must be admitted that further traces also are found in the Pentateuch of that custom of connecting ten commands into one whole, of which the Decalogue gives the first example. And these are sometimes happily exhibited by BERTHEAU.[52]

CHAPTER X.

THE DEUTERONOMISTIC LEGISLATION.

39. IT is not accidental or arbitrary that we have treated separately in Chap. VIII,IX, of the laws contained in the Books of Exodus, Leviticus, and Numbers, and that we come now first to speak of those in Deuteronomy. The fact is, that there exists between the two Legislations a difference, which at once strikes the eye, and can the less be denied, inasmuch as it is plainly recognised in the last-named Book itself.[53]

40. The phenomena, which have been considered in Chap. VIII,

are sufficient to show that the Legislation contained in the Books of Exodus, Leviticus, and Numbers, by no means proceed from one hand or out of the same time. Also the historical narratives of Exodus and Numbers must be ascribed to different writers, Chap.IV–VI. From this it follows that the relation of the Book of Deuteronomy to the preceding three Books can only then be established with complete certainty, when the portions of these Books have been properly separated, and their chronological order determined as far as possible. Nevertheless, it seems advisable to make at once a preliminary comparison of the Book of Deuteronomy with Exodus, Leviticus, and Numbers, in order that after such a comparison the method, which we shall follow in our enquiry as to the composition of the Pentateuch, may be set forth in Chap.XI.

41. The Book of Deuteronomy, then, supposes, generally, the existence of a Legislation, *similar* to that which is contained in Exodus, Leviticus, and Numbers. Not only were the addresses, of which the Book consists, delivered according to its own datum, i.1,2, nearly forty years after the Sinaitic Legislation, and so reference is made in them to the events in the wilderness, and to the laws there given, as to things past; but it plainly appears, also, that these laws and this history were already recorded before Deuteronomy was written. It does not immediately follow from this, that the writer of Deuteronomy had before him the Books of Exodus, Leviticus, and Numbers, *in the same form in which we now possess them.* It would seem, however, that the legislative and historical documents, which he uses and to which he refers, agreed very closely with the said Books, and were to a great extent identical with them.[54]

42. With respect to the historical documents this is generally allowed. Yet there, also, where the Deuteronomist produces laws which occur in the other Books, he employs the same expressions which were used in them, and in such a way that we cannot, conversely, suppose that these latter have been borrowed

from Deuteronomy.[55] It cannot, therefore, be a matter of surprise
that most enquirers assign the priority to the Books of Exodus,
Leviticus, and Numbers, as a whole; and, although we shall see
below, Chap.XXI,XXII, that their view does not by any means
explain all difficulties, yet this deserves certainly the preference
above the view of DELITZSCH, Von BOHLEN, GEORGE, and VATKE,
who place the recording of nearly all the laws in Exodus, Leviticus, and Numbers (E.xx–xxiii alone excepted) later than that of
the Deuteronomistic Legislation.[56]

43. Now that our preliminary investigation has taught us,
that not even the Legislation, any more than the historical
narrative, contained in Exodus, Leviticus, and Numbers, proceeds
from the time of Moses, it is plain already, if only for this
reason, that the Book of Deuteronomy also cannot be Mosaic.
Nevertheless, it seems to be most important to set clearly in the
light the agreement and the difference between these four Books,
so that it may be seen what is the tendency of the Deuteronomistic Legislation, what distinguishes it from that of the preceding three Books, and whether it has proceeded from one
hand with these, or at least out of one and the same age. Such
a comparison leads us to the following conclusions.

44. First, the Deuteronomistic Legislation is addressed to
different persons from those, for whom most of the laws
in Exodus, Leviticus, and Numbers are designed. So far as
these last have reference to worship and all matters connected
therewith, they are intended for the priests and Levites, whose
labours they regulate, and to whom they give the necessary
instructions about their duties and their relation to the people.
This is true, e.g. of the laws in E.xxv–xxxi, L.i–vii,xii–xvii,xxi,
xxii, &c. It is true that duties are here enjoined upon the
people also; but they occur together with the ordinances, which
concern the priest alone, and are combined into a whole with
them. On the contrary, the Deuteronomistic Legislation, which
throughout is set before Israel itself by Moses, is intended

also for the whole people. Such prescriptions, as only concerned the priests and Levites, are not repeated in Deuteronomy, though they are implied in it.[57]

45. Again, the Deuteronomistic Legislation is distinguished most plainly by its form from that of the preceding Books. Although in these also there is no want of exhortations to obedience to Jehovah, and of earnest warnings against unfaithfulness towards Him, yet usually the ordinances are given simply and in the legislative form. On the contrary, the Book of Deuteronomy is entirely hortatory in tone and tendency.[58]

46. Further, the Deuteronomistic Legislation is distinguished from that of the Books of Exodus, Leviticus, and Numbers, by its peculiar style, especially by the use of a number of expressions, which continually recur, and are manifestly connected with ideas and images, which are foreign to the preceding Books. This phenomenon argues as strongly *for* the unity of the Book of Deuteronomy, as *against* the view, that it can be ascribed to the author or authors of the preceding Books.[59]

47. Lastly, if these phenomena point already to a difference of authorship and age for this Book, compared with the other three, such a difference is absolutely demanded by the different contents of the two Legislations. While, for instance, many ordinances, contained in Exodus, Leviticus, and Numbers, are simply repeated in Deuteronomy, others are omitted, others again undergo more or less important variations, and, lastly, some entirely new laws are added to those of the preceding Books.

48. It is true, it cannot be maintained that the silence of Deuteronomy, with respect to this or that law contained in Exodus, Leviticus, and Numbers, implies that it was abrogated. On the contrary, there are evidently many prescriptions implied in Deuteronomy, as actually in existence, of which no mention whatever is [anywhere] made. Yet, where a subject, which is

treated of in the previous Legislation, is expressly mentioned by the Deuteronomist, yet some prescriptions about it are omitted, there the omission of them is equivalent to their abrogation.[60]

49. Again, the variations, which the preceding Legislation undergoes, are not of such a kind that they can be explained on the supposition, that the Book of Deuteronomy was intended for the people, when they should be already settled in Canaan. For, on the one hand, the preceding Legislation was also intended for this same purpose, and was—at least, a great part of it—first committed to writing in Canaan (Chap.VIII). On the other hand, the Deuteronomistic ordinances not unfrequently differ so much from those, which occur in Exodus, Leviticus, and Numbers, that both cannot possibly have been promulgated in the same age; but they must be separated from each other by so great an interval, that during it the condition of the people may have undergone important changes. This is especially true of the Deuteronomistic prescriptions about the priests and Levites, and their revenues.[61]

50. Lastly, as regards the laws, which occur for the first time in Deuteronomy, it is not strange in itself that this Book contains new ordinances. But, when we take into consideration that they refer, almost without exception, to circumstances or persons, which are presented to us first in a later age of the Israelitish history, we must recognise in this also a proof of the later origin of the Deuteronomistic Legislation as a whole.[62]

51. In opposition to all these phenomena, appeal is made both to the testimony of Deuteronomy as to its Mosaic origin, and to the point of view assumed by the whole Deuteronomistic Legislation, in which the Conquest of the land of Canaan is continually represented as future, and several prescriptions are given, which had no meaning except in the time of Moses, e.g. vii,xi.29,30,xix.1,&c.xxv.17,&c.xxvii.2,&c. Yet neither the one reason nor the other should be allowed to move us to do

violence to the plain sense of the ordinances explained in
notes [59-61], or to deny the consequences which necessarily flow
from it. Rather we must try so to explain the testimony of
the Book itself, and the point of view of its Legislation, that all
other phenomena, which conflict. with them, may find adjust-
ment at the same time.[63]

CHAPTER XI.

THE METHOD TO BE PURSUED IN INVESTIGATING THE COMPOSITION OF THE PENTATEUCH.

52. THE phenomena, exhibited in Chap.III–X, are of such a
kind, that they must at once be considered as being irreconcilable
with the tradition of Mosaic origin of the whole Pentateuch.
But this (negative) result is unsatisfactory, and is only of value
so far as there ensues from it the right and the duty to inves-
tigate closely the age and the composition of the whole work.
First, however, we must define the course of this enquiry, and
the principles from which it starts. Generally, this rule applies
to it, that we must follow the indications given in the Pentateuch itself, and these alone, in order to arrive by this purely
historical way at a result, which shall rest upon an objective
foundation.

53. From this rule those depart, who try to meet the difficulties against the Mosaic origin of the Pentateuch by means of
the supposition that *glosses* of a later time are inserted in it.[64]
If, in this way, some of the difficulties named in Chap.VII are
got rid of, yet the others remain still in their full force.
Besides, these 'glosses' are assumed, not because exegetical
enquiry indicates them to be such, but in order to bring the

facts of the case as much as possible into agreement with the
tradition, to which latter in this way an authority is ascribed,
which does not belong to it, so soon as it is seen that it does not
in all parts deserve credence.[65]   For the same reason we
should beware of holding the laws of the Pentateuch for Mosaic,[66]
so long as the opposite is not proved for each particular law.
In this manner, also, a value is continually ascribed to the
tradition, which it ought only then to possess, when it appears
to be thoroughly accurate throughout.

54. Others see in the Pentateuch a collection of a very great
number of *fragments*, out of different times, and belonging to
different authors, which were put together in a far later age, about
the time of the Babylonish captivity.   Yet this hypothesis,
which was formerly defended, especially by VATER and HART-
MANN,[67] makes the Pentateuch the work of accident, and thus
ignores the unity and the connection, by which it is distinguished.
For instance, it is undeniable, that the Pentateuch is a *whole*,
—not, indeed, the work of one hand, for the contrary appears
from Chap.III-X, but yet a work put together out of different
portions after a *definite plan*.[68]   The very possibility of such
a combination excludes at once the fragmentary hypothesis.

55. On the contrary, *our* investigation leads us, as it were, of
itself to the conjecture, that the Pentateuch is composed, in
some way or other, out of various primary documents, whose
contents are partly of historical, partly of legislative, partly of a
mixed, nature.[69]   This must have been assumed as probable,
even if there appeared no other indication of the existence of
such documents than the phenomena discussed in Chap.III-X.
But these phenomena themselves make it probable that the
documents of the Pentateuch may be made out yet more distinctly.   The comparison of the laws and historical narratives
with one another shows not merely variation, but also agreement
and connection.   As the first implies that the Pentateuch is not
all from one hand, so the latter indicates that in it are included

documents of greater or smaller extent, having connection with each other.

56. We have, therefore, now to give attention, first of all, to the points of agreement, in order to be able with their help to restore, even now, as far as possible, the original connection of the documents. In order to this, we shall be guided by the following principle. Narratives and laws, which stand manifestly in connection with each other, (*i.e.* which, negatively, do not contradict each other, and, positively, refer to each other,) and are distinguished besides by similarity of ideas, sentiments, and forms of expression, belong to the same document. When the one or the other of these characteristics is wanting, the earlier connection must either be distinctly denied, or be regarded as more or less doubtful.[70]

57. In tracing, then, the points of agreement between the laws and narratives in the Pentateuch, we have, first of all, to give attention to the use of the Divine Names in the Book of Genesis and in the first chapters of Exodus. For instance, it has been observed long ago, that some sections agree in this respect with one another and vary from others. The more weight we ascribe, and shall further ascribe, to this phenomenon, the more important it is to make ourselves acquainted with its true nature.

CHAPTER XII.

THE USE OF THE DIVINE NAMES IN GENESIS AND THE FIRST CHAPTERS OF EXODUS.

58. THE Israelites employ various names to designate the Supreme Being, of which the most common are *Elohim*, 'God,' and *Jehovah*, 'LORD,'—[*not* 'Lord,' which is used in the E.V.

for the Hebrew *Adonai*.] Between these two names there
exists a difference of meaning,[71] which naturally influences
also the use of them. There are cases where Elohim must,
and Jehovah cannot, be used.[72] There are other cases again,
in which one of these two names is, at all events, more suitable
or proper.[73] Yet it happens very frequently, that either the
one or the other name may be just as fitly used; and in such
cases, therefore, the writers employ them at their pleasure, or
are guided in their choice by subjective considerations.[74]

59. It has long been remarked that in the Book of Genesis
and the first chapters of Exodus the names *Elohim* and *Jehovah*
are used interchangeably, and that, too, in a way, which is very
plainly distinguished from the custom followed by the writers
of the other historical Books of the O.T. In some narratives
the name *Elohim* only occurs, in others only *Jehovah*; in a
third class of narratives both names are met with.[75] And efforts
have been made to explain generally this difference from the
different meaning of the two names, or, in other words, to give
objective reasons for the use of each Divine Name.

60. But these attempts, however acutely, and however confi-
dently, too, their authors have gone to work, must be regarded
as unsuccessful, and are already given up by some, at least, of
their earlier advocates.[76] It is just as impossible to see in the
use, either of Elohim, or of Jehovah, a peculiarity attaching to
the *persons*, who are introduced in the narratives as speaking,
whose example the narrator may be supposed to have followed
in his own practice.[77] Still less can we imagine here a mere
accidental circumstance, or a desire on the part of the writer to
introduce a certain *variety* in his narrative. Little care throughout is shown to secure this last; and a phenomenon, which continually presents itself afresh, cannot be accidental, but must
at least have its distinct ground in the subjectivity of the
writer.[78]

61. All these and other similar explanations are, again,

excluded by an express testimony of the Pentateuch itself, E.vi. 2,3. From this place it appears that according to the writer, whose words we there have before us, the name Jehovah was first revealed to Moses, at least was unknown to the patriarchs, to whom God (*Elohim,v.*2) appeared ' by El-Shaddai,' *i.e.,* as God Almighty.[79] Guided by this conviction, the writer could not put the name Jehovah, during the patriarchal age, in the mouth either of God Himself or of any of the patriarchs; rather, most probably he restrained himself in the use of this name, while occupied in his narratives with this age.[80] Generally, it appears most plainly from his words, E.vi.2-9, that he not only treated of the history of the patriarchal times, but designed also to relate the exodus out of Egypt and the foundation of the theocracy in Israel.[81]

62. It may be assumed, further, as most probable, that we still possess in the Pentateuch the narratives, to which E.vi.2-9 refers, entirely or in part. But it would be too hasty, if we proposed to recognise the hand of the writer of E.vi.2-9 every-where, from G.i to E.vi, where the name Jehovah is omitted. We shall only be justified in assuming this in cases, where the narratives, which betray themselves by this peculiarity, agree also in ideas, expressions, and forms of speech, with E.vi. 2-9.[82] Such an agreement is the only means of tracing-out, even in E.vi-D.xxxiv, and perhaps also in other books of the O.T., the different portions of the *Elohistic Document,* by which name we shall denote here provisionally the writing to which E.vi.2-9 belongs.[83]

63. Further, it appears at once, without any further investi-gation, that very many accounts in Genesis, *e.g.* iv,xii-xvi,xxiv, &c., did not belong to the Elohistic Document, since in them the name Jehovah is continually used, not only by the writer himself, but by the persons whose words he reports. The writers of these historical narratives—which we may name provisionally *Jehovistic*—did not, therefore, adopt the view which is expressed

in E.vi.2,3, or, perhaps, they used the name proleptically even in those narratives, which have relation to the time when that name was not yet known.

64. From G.iv.26 it appears distinctly that one of these writers, at all events, derived the use of the name Jehovah even from the time before the Flood,[84] so that he had no inducement to omit this name. This fact may, perhaps, show that the Jehovistic sections are not distinguished by accident from the Elohistic, and that the different use of the Divine Names has its ground in the different ideas of the writers as to the age of these names. The critical analysis of Genesis, which starts from this difference of usage, is based, consequently, on the testimony of the Pentateuch itself, and is by no means, as some have maintained, an arbitrary hypothesis.[85]

CHAPTER XIII.

THE REMAINS OF THE ELOHISTIC DOCUMENT IN G.I–E.VI.

65. THE Elohistic document, whose existence is indicated by E.vi.2–9, no longer exists *in its original form*, but—for the present, at least, from G.i. to E.vi, to which chapters we at first confine ourselves,—is combined into a whole with notices derived from other sources. Whether, when thus combined with other narratives, it remained *entire*, cannot be determined *à priori*, but must appear out of the enquiry itself. In conducting this investigation, therefore, we must proceed from the incontestably certain to the most probable and the more or less certain. And thus we state first that G.xvii,xxxv.9–15,—to which accounts E.vi.2–9 directly refers,—belong to the Elohistic document.[86]

66. Through this discovery our knowledge of its peculiar

characteristics is considerably extended, and we thus see ourselves in a position to assign to it also the following passages as
its incontestable* property :[87]—

G.i.1–ii.3	xix.29	xxxvi.1–9	E.i.1–7
v (except v. 29)	xxiii	xlvi.6,7	ii.23–25
vi.9–22	xxv.19,20	xlvii.28	
ix.1–17,28,29	xxviii.1–7	xlix.29–33	
xi.10–32	xxxv.27–29	l.12,13	

67. The passages of the Elohistic document, above indicated,
do not form with one another a whole, but imply the existence of other accounts, with which they must at one time have
been connected.[88] A continuation of the investigation shows that
these accounts for a great part still exist in Genesis, but blended
with other, non-Elohistic, narratives in such a manner, that they
cannot now be separated from them with perfect certainty. A
great deal of G.vii,viii, is taken from the Elohistic document [89];
and so xii.5,xiii.6,xvi.3,15,16,xxi.2,5,xxv.7–10,19,20,xxxi.17,18,
xxxvii.1,xlviii.3–6, are easily to be distinguished as remnants of
it.[90]

68. If we connect these passages with those above-named, then
it appears that we most probably still possess in its entirety the
Elohistic document, so far as it contained the history from the
Creation of the world up to and including Isaac's marriage,[91]—
yet that of the sequel, especially of the history of Jacob, Joseph,

* I doubt if this epithet applies to vi.15,16, (see P.IV,47); and certainly xi.28–
30 is *Jehovistic*, comp. v.29 with iv.19—v.30 ' Sarai was *barren*,' with xxv.21,xxix.
31, and, observe, that this notice of Sarai's barrenness is out of place here; the
fact is mentioned afterwards by the Elohist in xvi.1 that Sarai ' bare not to
Abraham.' Comp. also v.30, 'there was no child *to her*,' with the Jehovist's
language in xviii.10,14, whereas the Elohist dwells continually upon the promise
made *to Abraham*, xvi.1, ' Sarai, Abraham's wife, bare not *to him*,' xvii.16, ' I will
give out of her *to thee* a son,' xvii.19, ' Sarah, thy wife, shall bear *to thee* a son,'
xvii.21, ' whom Sarah shall bear *to thee*,' xxi.2; ' and bare *to Abraham* a son,' v.3,
' the son that was born *to him*,' v.5, ' his son Isaac was born *to him* :' comp. also
xvi.15,16. *Ed.*

and Moses, some portions are not inserted in G.i–E.vi, perhaps, because they have been superseded by more ample accounts, derived from other sources, which obtained a place in Genesis.[92]

69. The larger and smaller sections of the Book of Genesis, which have been above assigned to the Elohistic document, are reckoned to it by nearly all enquirers.[93] Yet many of them are of opinion that other passages also of Genesis belong to it, and believe that they discover them, first, in nearly all passages of a genealogical character, and besides also generally, wherever *Elohim* is used as the proper Name of God. Yet against this view there exist serious objections, set forth formerly by ILGEN, and of late, especially by HUPFELD.[94]

70. For instance, the genealogical lists, about which this difference of opinion circles, *viz.* G.x.1–7,13–32,xxii.20–24,xxv.1– 6,12–18,xxxv.23–26,xxxvi.8–43,xlvi.8–27, are, in the first place, distinguished by their form very plainly from the registers, which we have learned to know as portions of the Elohistic document, G.v,xi.10–32, and, secondly, they do not fit into the chronology of this document, or they occur elsewhere in it, or they seem to lie outside its plan.[95]

71. Again, the sections, wherein *Elohim* is used as the proper Name of God, which formerly by TUCH and STÄHELIN, and latterly also by BLEEK, were assigned to the Elohistic document (*Grundschrift*), *viz.* G.xx.1–17,xxi.6–32,xxii.1–13,19,xxv.24–34, xxviii.10-12,17–21ª,22,xxix–xxxv (partly), xxxvii.2–36,xxxix–1 (partly), are, to a great extent by DELITZSCH and KNOBEL, but especially by HUPFELD, rightly derived from other sources. It seems, in fact, that some of these passages conflict with the Elohistic accounts, and that in others ideas and sentiments are met with, different from those of the Elohistic document, while, in addition, the characteristics of the latter are looked for in vain in them.[96]

72. Since, however, these narratives likewise are distinguished by the use of the name *Elohim*, or stand in uninterrupted con-

nection with Elohistic narratives, it follows from this that, besides the author of the Elohistic document, yet one or more other Elohists must have contributed additions to our present Book of Genesis.[97]   In E.i–vi also are inserted accounts, which have been derived from these.[98]   Henceforward, then, in order to avoid all confusion, we shall indicate the Elohistic document, which we have hitherto learned to know, by the name first introduced by Ewald, on the ground of G.v.1,vi.9,&c. (note [2]) *viz.* 'Book of Origins,' while we shall include all other accounts, which are distinguished by the use of Elohim, under the general description, Elohistic Narratives or Documents.[99]

CHAPTER XIV.

THE BOOK OF ORIGINS, AND THE PASSAGES BELONGING TO IT, FROM E.VI TO D.XXXIV.

73. It has been inferred (see note [61]) from E.vi.2–9, that the author, whose words we have here before us, related not merely the history of the patriarchal age, but also the Exodus from Egypt and the foundation of the theocracy.   This result of the critical analysis of G.i–E.vi leads us to cherish the expectation, that this account may still have been preserved, wholly or in part, in E.vi–D.xxxiv.   In this expectation we are not disappointed.   Yet the separation of the Book of Origins, from the connection in which it now stands, is coupled with great difficulties, in consequence of which great difference of view still remains on this point.

74. The *historical* notices of the Book of Origins, as to the fortunes of the people until their arrival in the wilderness of Sinai, are most probably superseded by the more circumstantial

narratives of the other documents. At all events, only the
following can be assigned to it with a certain amount of confidence, E.xii.37,40,41,51,xiii.20,xv.22,23ᵃ,27,xvi.1,xvii.1,xix.
1,2ᵃ,[100] while we shall see hereafter that E.vi.10–12,vii.1–7,
xvi, though in another sense than the verses above-named, may
also be brought to it.

75. With respect to the historical portions of the Book of
Numbers, the judgment about them depends very much upon
the result of the enquiry, as to the origin of the laws contained
in the three Books, Exodus–Numbers; they can only, therefore,
be considered below. According to the almost universal view,
however, most of these laws must be regarded as portions of the
Book of Origins. Particularly, the following passages are
assigned to it, among which are some, which may be reckoned
among the historical passages, but which, both on account of
their connection with the actual laws, and on account of their
legislative character, take their place most properly here:
E.xii.1–20,43–50, xiii.1, 2, xxv.1–xxxi.17, xxxv–xl, L.i–vii,viii–x,
xi–xvii, xxi–xxv, xxvii, N.i.1–x.10, xv, xviii, xix, xxvi, xxvii.1–11,
xxviii–xxx,xxxi,xxxiv–xxxvi.[101]

76. That this view, *in its main features*, is not wrong,
appears—

(i) From the fact that all these laws have the closest mutual
connection, and refer continually to each other, so that there is
no doubt that they do indeed belong together;[102]

(ii) From the agreement in language and ideas, which we
observe between these laws and those narratives of Genesis,
which have been assigned to the Book of Origins.[103]

77. Serious objections, however, arise against this view, from
different sides, which prevent us from subscribing to it at least
in the above form, in which it is usually put forward. These
are the following :—

(i) Among the laws above enumerated, there occur some,
which make up with one another one whole, and treat of one

definite subject, thus forming, as it were, separate law-books or collections, of greater or smaller extent, (*e.g.* L.i–vii,xi,xiii,xiv, xv,) provided with subscriptions, (*e.g.* L.vii.37,38,xi.46,47,xiii.59, xiv.54–57,xv.32,33.) It is, therefore, not only possible, but even by no means improbable, either that the author of the Book of Origins met with these and like collections already existing in writing, and inserted them into his work, or that another writer, labouring in his spirit and after his example, added to it some, at least, of these smaller collections.

(ii) It is not in itself probable that *one* man can have comprehended all the different subjects treated of in this Legislation, so that he was *e.g.*, in the condition to legislate with respect to sacrifices, clean and unclean animals, leprosy and its cure, vows, &c., and to lay down upon these subjects such exact and ample definitions, as we find in these Books, especially in Leviticus and Numbers.

(iii) Some of the laws above-named, especially some of those, which occur in Numbers, appear as *appendices* to the laws, or collections of laws, inserted in Exodus and Leviticus; see the examples cited in note [42], and further comp. N.xv.1–16 with L.i–vii, and N.xxviii,xxix, with L.xxiii. If the latter had proceeded from the same hand with the former, they would probably have been introduced at the proper place, whereas, as it is, they have rather the appearance of later additions.

(iv) Between some of the laws above-mentioned there exists contradiction (notes [40,41]), which can only be explained on the supposition, that one is a later variation of the other. With this circumstance, however, the unity of authorship falls away; though it remains generally undeniable that the two laws, (*e.g.* N.xxviii.27–30 and L.xxiii.18) stand in connection with each other, breathe one and the same spirit, and also agree with each other in form and style.

(v) The history of religious worship in Israel forbids us to assign a high antiquity to some of the above-named laws, in

particular to those which lay stress on the worship being per-
formed *at one place.* This important point, before touched
upon,[40.11] can only be fully developed below (Chap.XIX).
If, on the other hand, the character of the narrative in the
Book of Origins, especially when we compare it with the other
Elohistic or Jehovistic passages, pleads for a comparatively high
antiquity of that Book (Chap.XVI,XXI), it follows that the ·
laws just-named, however closely bound and connected with the
Book of Origins, yet were not recorded by the author of that
Book.

78. Thus, with respect to those laws of Exodus–Numbers,
which are ascribed by most interpreters to the Book of Origins,
this remarkable phenomenon presents itself, that, on the one
hand, numerous indications plead for their common origin, while,
on the other hand, the contents of these laws and the course
of the history do not allow us to regard them as contemporary.
This contradiction can only be explained by the supposition,
that all these ordinances originated in a circle, in which, for a
considerable time together, the same spirit lived on, and was
propagated, as it were, from age to age. By far the greater
number of these laws, however, have reference to religious
worship and the duties of the priests and Levites, while some
betray an unmistakable hierarchical tendency. Thus, then,
we certainly are not far from the truth, if we suppose that
*these laws contain the tradition preserved by the priests and
Levites, and committed to writing, with respect to the Legislation of Moses,** so far as this regulated the religious worship*

---

* This seems to me to be here assumed without sufficient reason. That these laws
have been registered, in one and the same spirit, by the priests of successive ages
—perhaps, of one or two ages only, or perhaps of more—is very reasonable. But,
unless this work is ascribed—and it is not, see (158)—to the time *immediately or
shortly after the time of Moses,* it is difficult to conceive that any such 'traditions'
could have been preserved among them. It is admitted, see Chap. XIX, that we
have no sign whatever of the Levitical ceremonies having been in operation during
the time of Samuel, or for some time previously: in fact, the history of Eli in
1S.i,ii,iii, is directly at variance with the Levitical laws in many particulars.

and all things connected therewith. Through this hypothesis is explained the relative unity of the whole Legislation in respect of religious worship, without any necessity for denying the successive origination of particular laws, for which such strong proofs are produced.[104]

79. The Deuteronomistic Legislation distinguishes itself so manifestly from the laws contained in Exodus–Numbers, that it cannot be supposed to have been either written by the author or authors of the Book of Origins, or adopted by them into their work.

80. There now remains, therefore, only this question to be considered, *viz.* in what relation those other laws in Exodus–Numbers, which have not been named above, stand to the Book of Origins. These laws are the following, E.xiii.3–16, xx.1–17,xx.22–xxiii.33,xxxiv.11–27, L.xviii–xx, besides the prophetical passage, L.xxvi. That none of these passages were *written* by the author or authors of the Book of Origins, follows from their form as well as from their contents.[105] But inasmuch as both the Decalogue, E.xx.1–17, and the Book of the Covenant, E.xx.22–xxiii.33,—as will hereafter be seen,[209,235-242] are older even than the oldest portions of the Book of Origins, the question presents itself whether they were adopted into that Book, or were, perhaps, united with it *afterwards,* when the whole Pentateuch was finally compiled.

81. From E.xxv.16,22,xl.20, it appears that the Book of Origins once contained the Decalogue.[106] And it is not

During the reign of David and Solomon we have not the least reason to suppose that any such laws were in force. How, then, if the commands of these laws were neither preserved in writing nor handed down by practice, could the priests have preserved any such 'traditions' through the lapse of several centuries? It is conceivable that when the Tabernacle or the Temple was established on Mount Zion, and the hierarchical spirit was introduced by Zadok, some such a 'directory' for public worship may have been needed, and may have been gradually elaborated, based, of course, on their previous practice, which may in part have been derived from the Mosaic age. But this can hardly be called a 'tradition of the Legislation of Moses' in respect of these matters. *Ed.*

improbable that the whole Book of the Covenant was also inserted into it. It is true, some contradictions are found to
exist between the laws of the Book of the Covenant and of
the Book of Origins, notes [40,ii-iv,41]. But the Book of the Covenant was, perhaps, so ancient and venerable, that the author of
the Book of Origins thought good to insert it entire. At the
final compilation of the Pentateuch, the Decalogue may have
been omitted, in that form in which the Book of Origins imparted it. So, too, the insertion of E.xiii.3–16,xxxiv.11–26,
must be ascribed to the Jehovistic narrator,[107] and that of
L.xviii–xx,xxvi, to the compiler of the whole Pentateuch.[108]
See below, Chap. XXI,XXII.

82. When, after our investigation concerning the laws of
Exodus-Numbers, we return once more to fix our attention on
the historical narratives contained in Exodus, our judgment with
respect to them must necessarily be somewhat modified. Since,
for instance, we have seen that mention can be made in a
double sense of the Book of Origins, it becomes probable that
some historical narratives in Exodus,—which certainly do not
belong to the original Book of Origins, but yet have great
agreement with it, [100]—must be regarded as passages afterwards added to it, particularly, E.vi.10–12,vii.1–7,xvi.

83. It now remains to be examined whether in the Books of
Numbers and Deuteronomy there still remain *historical* portions
of the Book of Origins. That in D.xxxii.48–52,xxxiv.1–9, we
have before us the conclusion of what the author of the Book
reported about Moses and his time, is highly probable.[109] It is
very difficult, however, to define what narratives in Numbers
are from his hand. The succinctness of his accounts in Genesis,[91]
and in Exodus,[100] makes it probable that he recorded with the
like brevity the adventures of the people, after their departure
from Sinai. In accordance with this, HUPFELD, *Q.d.G.* p.86,
seems to assign to him only N.xxxiii.1–49 (list of stations of
the march through the wilderness), which, however, this

writer cannot have guaranteed himself, but (as appears from *v.2*) regarded [? or treated] as the work of Moses.

84. Yet, supposing that we have rightly assigned to the Book of Origins the Legislation contained in Numbers,* we must then of necessity ascribe to it also all the historical passages, which are more or less closely connected with the Legislation in question, *e.g.* N.x.11-28,—part of N.xiii,xiv,—part of N.xvi,xvii,—N.xx.1-13,22-29,xxvii.12-23,—N.xxv,—part of N.xxxii.[110] These narratives, however, must then be regarded not as original portions of the Book of Origins, but as passages afterwards added. They tend to show that in the priestly circle, in which the tradition as to the Mosaic *Legislation* was preserved, and gradually committed to writing, the *History* also of the Mosaic time was studied. How closely the one is connected with the other, but, at the same time, how the History at times is made entirely subservient to the Legislation and to the priestly requirements, appears especially from N.xxxi,[111] and also, though not so distinctly, from N.xvi,xvii.[112]

CHAPTER XV.

GENERAL SURVEY OF THE PLAN AND CONTENTS OF THE BOOK OF ORIGINS.

85. ALTHOUGH we may not be able to succeed in recovering again in its integrity the Book of Origins in the Pentateuch, (and especially in the last four Books of the Pentateuch),

* The note on p. 36 applies to the *historical*, as well as to the *legislative*, portions of Exodus–Numbers. If no portions of the Mosaic Legislation were handed down either in *writing* or in *practice*, it is difficult to believe that any traditionary recollections of that Legislation, or of the details of the History connected with it, could have existed after the lapse of some centuries. *Ed.*

so as to sever the original portions of that Book from the later additions, yet we are able to form a judgment with perfect certainty about the plan or object of the whole. For that purpose, we must collect together, and combine into one image, the features scattered here and there.

86. First of all, then, we consider it as certain, that the writer of the Book of Origins was a priest or, at least, a Levite.* The legislation about Divine Worship inspires him with so great an interest, that he not only imparts it diffusely, when he treats of the history of Moses and the Mosaic time, but also prepares for imparting it, while he is still occupied with the pre-Mosaic annals. From this point of view must be regarded the explanations of the hallowing of the Sabbath, G.ii.1–3, his imparting of the so-called Noachian commands, G.ix.4–6, and the institution of circumcision, G.xvii. So great an interest is easily explained through the very natural supposition, that the writer employs himself by preference in that domain to which the labours of his life were devoted.

87. In order, then, to place the Mosaic Legislation in the true light, the writer represents it as the result of a continual development. After the creation of heaven and earth, i.1–ii.3, the human race is propagated in *ten* generations, v.1–28,30–32, to Noah, who, when the corrupt race was destroyed by the Flood, vi–viii, was alone saved with his own family. If *Elohim*

---

* This seems to be said chiefly on the assumption that the Levitical laws in Exodus-Numbers are due to this writer. But it does not appear that this has been by any means *proved* with sufficient certainty to enable us to build upon it. Rather, as observed elsewhere, the entire absence of any reference to Levitical practices, and of the very name of priest, altar, sacrifice, in the portions of Genesis assigned to the B.O., seems a very strong argument *against* the author's being a Priest or Levite, except such a priest as Samuel, who was rather a prophet and politician.

The observance of the Sabbath, abstinence from blood, practice of circumcision— to which Prof. KUENEN refers—have no direct connection whatever with Levitical or priestly ceremonies. Doubtless, the laws in Exodus-Numbers were written by a priest. But it seems very strange that one so intensely interested in priestly matters, as this writer must have been, should have written so much of Genesis without making the slightest reference to them. *Ed.*

blessed the whole human race in Adam, i.28-30, He concludes
a yet closer covenant with Noah and his descendants, ix.1-17.
Without, however, troubling himself about Noah's progeny in
general, the writer limits himself to the holy line, which is
propagated from Shem to Abram, xi.10-32, again in *ten* generations. After briefly mentioning, xii.4ᵇ,5,xiii.6,11ᵇ,12ᵃ,xvi.3,5,16,
the removal of the last-named to Canaan, his separation from
Lot, and the birth of Ishmael,—in accordance, again, with the
writer's plan to limit himself to the holy line,—he tells us how
Elohim revealed himself to Abram as El-Shaddai, institutes
circumcision, changes the names of Abram and Sarai, and
announces to them the birth of a son, xvii. With merely a
single word he mentions Lot's deliverance, xix.29, but dwells
longer upon the birth of Isaac, xxi.2-5, Sarah's death and
burial, xxiii, and Abraham's decease, xxv.7-11.

88. He then carries on the history of Isaac, xxv.19,20.* As far
as we can make out from the fragments of it yet in existence, he
pursues also the same plan in the treatment of this, *i.e.* he says
very little about Esau and his descendants, xxvi.34,35,xxvii.46,
xxviii.8,9,xxxvi.1-9,† while all which relates to Jacob is treated
by him more fully and as his special object, xxviii.1-7, &c.⁹¹
At all events, with him the covenant is renewed, xxxv.9-15,
and after Isaac's death, *v.*27-29, he becomes the chief person, ‡
xxxvii.1,2; his removal to Egypt, xlvi.6,7, his adoption of
Ephraim and Manasseh, xlviii.3-6, and his death, xlix.29-33,
are, however, the only events, of which the account has been
preserved to us out of the Book of Origins. § Also the notices

* But he first gives ' the generations of Ishmael,' in xxv.12,17, according to
Prof. KUENEN (note ⁸⁵·¹ʸ), but, as I believe, at greater length in xxv.12-17 : see
note ³⁴. *Ed.*

† I believe that he gives 'the generations of Esau,' also, at greater length in
xxxvi.9-19,31-43: see note ³⁶. *Ed.*

‡ Yet in xxxv.29 *Esau* is named first, and the writer does not pass him over
lightly, but goes on to enumerate his progeny in xxxvi, before he proceeds to speak
of Jacob's ' generations.' *Ed.*

§ I imagine that the account of Rachel's death and burial in xxxv.16-20 is also

about Israel's sojourn in Egypt, E.i.1–7,ii.23–25, are scanty, yet sufficient to prepare for a new and higher stage of God's revelation: *Elohim*, the El-Shaddai of the patriarchs, makes himself known to Moses as Jehovah, while He announces at the same time deliverance to Israel, and the fulfilment of the promises given to their forefathers, E.vi.2, &c.

89. How Jehovah brought the promise to pass, put an end to the Egyptian slavery, led the people to Sinai, and there concluded a new and more glorious covenant with Israel, which was grounded upon the Decalogue,[*] and coupled with a complete refutation of Israel's relation to Jehovah, is related in the sequel of the Book of Origins. Yet, certain as this is in the main,[†] it is just as difficult to indicate in particulars how the writer acquitted himself of the task. At all events, we have seen that we no longer possess this portion of the document in its original form. As we have perceived that to the history of the patriarchs, preserved to us in Genesis, contributions have been made by writers, who agree with the author of the Book of Origins in the use of the name *Elohim* and in other peculiarities, so in the treatment of the history of Israel during the Mosaic time he had his followers also, inspired with the same spirit as himself, and not unlike to him in their mode of writing.

90. But, while from G.i–E.vi we can distinguish easily the Book of Origins from the other Elohistic pieces,[94-98] the Legislation and the History of the Mosaic time contained in that Book have been—not only supplemented, but also—retouched, by later

due to the Elohist: note the sudden change from 'Jacob,' v.14,15,20, to 'Israel,' v.21,22ᵃ, and the return to 'Jacob' in v.27–29, which is certainly Elohistic, or, rather, in v.22ᵇ–29, all of which I ascribe to the Elohist. It should be observed also that this account of Rachel's death and burial is referred to verbally in xlviii.7, which contains 'Padan,' comp.xxxv.9, and appears to me to be plainly the continuation of the Elohistic passage, v.3–6. *Ed.*

[*] It appears to me that this statement is very doubtful. *Ed.*

[†] I will merely here mention that, to my own mind, it has not been at all satisfactorily *proved* that the Book of Origins contained any account of a covenant *grounded on the Decalogue*, or any laws regulating the priestly and Levitical duties. But the whole subject, as KUENEN says, require yet further investigation.[48] *Ed.*

writers, so that we cannot show the original writing, at least in the present state of the enquiry. But the more close appears to be the relation between the author of the Book of Origins and his followers,[103] so much the more probable* is it that he treated in his Legislation nearly the same subjects as they, *viz.* the place of common worship, sacrifices, Levitical cleanliness, the feasts, the duties and rights of the priests and Levites,—all of these. being subjects, which appear here for the first time, and according to the view of our writer [?], distinguish the Mosaic time from the patriarchal.[113] Thus it would seem that in this also the law of the gradual development has been maintained.[114]

91. But the author of the Book of Origins did not suppose, any more than his followers, that his task was completed with the communication of these laws and of the history of the Mosaic time. We shall see hereafter, Chap.XXIV,XXV, that the Conquest of Canaan, also, and the settlement of the tribes in that land, were treated by him, as E.vi.8 already leads us to suspect.[81] It was only through this settlement that the promises given to the patriarchs were fulfilled, G.xvii.8,xxviii.4, xxxv.12. With a view, therefore, to this was the whole Law also given; only by reporting this did the Book of Origins become a well-connected and rounded whole.[115]

---

* This assumption seems to me very doubtful, when it is considered that the original Elohist makes not the slightest reference to priest, altar, or sacrificial act, throughout the Book of Genesis. The only act of worship, which he mentions, is Jacob's setting up a pillar and pouring oil upon it, xxxv.14. In fact, the later Elohist in Genesis does introduce *dreams* and *sacrifices*, and this alone distinguishes him so much from the more ancient Elohist, that it would compel us to recognise the difference of the two writers, in spite of their both using persistently Elohim. *Ed.*

CHAPTER XVI.

THE JEHOVISTIC PORTIONS OF GENESIS.

· 92. BESIDES the two kinds of Elohistic passages, described above in Chap.XII,XIII, we meet with a series of narratives in Genesis, which are from the very first plainly distinguished from the Elohistic, by the use of the name Jehovah, and by many other peculiarities.   Most of these passages agree with one another in phraseology and sentiment, and stand evidently in connection with each other, so that we assign them without any hesitation to one author, the Jehovist.   Others, again, fit exceedingly well into the course of the history, as this is told by the Jehovist, and have certainly been inserted into it by him, but yet seem not to be from his hand, since they differ from him in phraseology and other characteristics.

93. To the first class of narratives we assign—

ii.4ᵇ–iv.26	xv	xxviii.10–22, partly
v.29	xvi, except v.3,15,16	xxix–xxxiii, a great
vi.1–8	xviii	deal, e. g. xxix,
vii and viii, partly—	xix, except v.29	xxxii.3–xxxiii.17
as vii.1–5,16ᵇ,	xxii.14-18,20–24	xxxv.23–26 [see note ᵃ⁵]
viii.20–22	xxiv	xxxvi. 8–43 [see note ᵃ⁵]
ix.18–27	xxv.1–6,12–18,21–	xxxvii.25ᵇ–27,28ᵇ
x.1–xi.9	34,* except, per-	xxxviii
xii, except v.4ᵇ,5	haps, v.12,17,26ᵇ	xxxix, comp. note ᵃ·ᴵᴵ
xiii, except v.6,11ᵇ,	xxvi.1–33	xl–xlviii, partly
12ᵃ	xxvii.1–45	l.1–11,14 ¹¹⁶

94. To the second class must be brought xiv,xxxiv,xlix.1– 28,¹¹⁷ and, perhaps, generally, all the genealogical passages named

* But see note ᵃ⁴. Ed.

above, x.1–7,13–32,xxii.20–24,xxv.1–6,12–18,xxxv.23–26,xxxvi.
8–43,xlvi.8–27, comp. note [95]; although their agreement with
iv.17–26 seems to show that they have not been inserted by the
Jehovist without change, but have been in some respects
modified.[116]

95. All the narratives above mentioned are plainly distinguished from the Elohistic portions of Genesis, especially from
those which have once belonged to the Book of Origins.

(i) Whereas the author of the last-named document holds
generally in view, and brings out strongly, Chap.XV, the difference between the Mosaic time and the ages that preceded
it, the Jehovist makes no such distinction. As he uses the
name Jehovah from the very beginning, and makes the worship
of Jehovah to begin already in the second generation after Adam,
iv.26, so, too, he mentions at the Flood *clean* and *unclean* animals, vii.2,[?8,] and makes repeated mention of sacrifices and
altars, iv.3–5,viii.20,21,xii.7, &c.

(ii) Whereas the author of the Book of Origins mentions
only the chief features of the history, note [91], the Jehovist enters
more into particulars, sketches, *e.g.* the character of the Patriarchs, especially that of Abraham, whom he represents as the
model of faith, xii.1,xv, unselfishness, xiii.8,9,xiv.22–24, and
obedience, xxii.1–18, and that of Jacob, whose craftiness he
brings out in different little traits, xxv.26,29–34,xxvii,xxx.
35–43.

(iii) Whereas the Book of Origins, in its accounts of the revelations of God to Noah and to the Patriarchs, observes great
simplicity and and a certain uniformity, ix.1–17,xxxv.9–15, and
abstains, comparatively speaking, from anthropomorphism, the
Jehovist makes mention of revelations of God through angels,
xvi,xviii,xix,&c.—dreams, xxviii.11,&c.—voices from heaven,
xxii.11,12,—once even of prophetical prediction of the future,
xlix.1–28,—and his representation of God is, generally, very
anthropomorphic, vi.6,7,xi.5,6,xv.9,10,&c.

(iv) Whereas out of the Book of Origins we feel,* as it were, the breath of a pure, priestly, spirit, (86), the Jehovistic passages exhibit a distinct prophetical character, which appears clearly both in the general conception of the history,[119] and in the hortatory tendency of some narratives,[120] and in some expressions of ideas.[121]

These points of difference raise it beyond all doubt that the author of the B.O. lived at an earlier age than the Jehovist, which conclusion is fully confirmed through the further development of the religious convictions of the last, especially of his anthropology.[122]

96. Most of the above-mentioned peculiarities are shared by the later Elohistic passages, note [96], in common with the Jehovist[123]; although, on the other hand, they agree with the Book of Origins in some points, in which the Jehovist differs from it.[124] On this account, and also on the ground of a careful comparison of the Jehovistic with the later Elohistic passages, it has been thought that a higher age must be assigned to these last than to the former.[125]

CHAPTER XVII.

THE JEHOVISTIC PORTIONS OF THE LAST FOUR BOOKS OF THE PENTATEUCH.

97. THAT the Jehovistic writer, from whom, according to Chap.XVI, a considerable portion of the Book of Genesis has been derived, committed also to writing the history of Moses and of the Mosaic time, may be considered as probable à

---

* This assumes that the greater part of Leviticus belongs to the B.O., which at present we consider very doubtful: see note on p. 40. *Ed.*

priori [126]; and it appears also most plainly from the last four Books of the Pentateuch, especially from Exodus and Numbers. When, however, we indicate as *Jehovistic sections* or fragments, E.i.8–ii.22,iii.1–vi.1,vii.8–xi.10,xii.29–36,38,39,42,xiii.3–16,17– 19,21,22,xiv.1–xv.21,23 [b]–26,xvii.2–16,xviii,xix.2 [b]–25,xx.18–21, xxiv,xxxi.18–xxxiv.35, L.xxvi, N.x.29–xii.16,xiii and xiv (partly), xvi(partly),xx.14–21,xxi–xxiv,xxxii(partly),xxxiii.50-56,D.xxxiv. 10–12, this must by no means be understood as if we ascribed all these to the author of the second account of the Creation, ii.4 [b]–iv. The appellation has, chiefly, a negative reference, and serves to separate the above passages from the Book of Origins, and its later additions, to which they certainly cannot be assigned.[127]

98. Yet it expresses at the same time the persuasion, that the sections above-named—though derived from different sources and in part compiled from different prime-documents,[128]— breathe generally the same spirit as the narratives of the Jehovist in Genesis,[129] whose hand may be distinctly recognised in some of them.[130] With respect to some of these passages the hypothesis is justified that the Jehovist wrote them, making use of different and, some of them, very old documents, which he put together, and here and there filled up from tradition.[131] With respect to others, we cannot go further than to maintain that they betray acquaintance with his narratives,—whereupon it remains doubtful whether they were inserted by him into his work, in the form in which we now possess them, or perhaps were taken over out of writings similar to his own, when the whole Pentateuch was compiled.[132]

CHAPTER XVIII.

THE RELATION OF THE JEHOVISTIC PASSAGES TO THE BOOK OF ORIGINS AND THE LATER ELOHISTIC NARRATIVES.

99. AFTER it had been long thought that the different portions of the Pentateuch were connected into one whole by a compiler,[133] the feeling gained ground more and more, in consequence of the appearance of TUCH's Commentary, that the Book of Genesis consisted of—

(i) The Elohistic document or the so-called (Urschrift) *prime-record*,—

(ii) Its completion by the Jehovist, who was at the same time the Compiler of the Book.[134]

100. This *supplement*-hypothesis was at once applied by others also to Exodus, Leviticus, and Numbers.[135] It underwent a not unimportant modification, when it began at length to be seen that Elohistic passages were also met with,—at all events, from G.i to E.vi,—which did not belong to the prime-record or Book of Origins. At present, then, this hypothesis is put forward in this form, that the Jehovist is supposed to have filled-up the prime-record, partly with narratives from his own hand, partly with accounts which he took over from other documents [136] (DELITZSCH, KNOBEL, VAIHINGER,) while the views held with reference to his sources, and the extent of his own labours as a writer, are still considerably divergent.[137]

101. The *supplement*-hypothesis, then, contains properly two propositions, which, however, are closely connected with each other :—

(i) The Jehovistic accounts never existed independently, but were designed from the first to supplement the prime-record.

(ii) The Jehovist was the compiler of the first four Books of the Pentateuch.

The first of these propositions, however, is contradicted by the facts themselves; and so, too, the second cannot be admitted. At all events, although it may be allowed that the first four Books of the Pentateuch, in the form in which we now possess them, are an edition of the Book of Origins, enlarged and supplemented with distinct (Elohistic and Jehovistic) additions, yet it by no means follows from this that these additions—particularly those, in which the Jehovist's own hand, that of the author of G.ii.4[b],&c, may be recognised,—were originally *intended* to serve as such.

102. For (i) it is just as conceivable that the narratives of the Jehovist formed at first an *independent* Jehovistic prime-document. That such a document can no longer be compiled out of the first four Books of the Pentateuch, may very well be a consequence of the Jehovistic passages having been inserted by the compiler of these Books in an incomplete form.[138]

(ii) Some Jehovistic passages or groups of passages can in no sense be regarded as incomplete by themselves; yet this must have been the case, if they were originally composed merely to supplement the prime-record.[139]

(iii) That something is wanting in other Jehovistic accounts, may, perhaps, be ascribed rather to the omission of what is superfluous by the side of other narratives, than to an original, and, so to say, intentional incompleteness of the accounts themselves.[140]

(iv) Not unfrequently, there exists between the Book of Origins and the Jehovistic accounts such obvious discrepancy, that these last cannot in any wise be thought to have been written with the object of supplementing that book, but rather must be supposed to have existed independently of it, and to have been connected with it by a third writer—the compiler of the Pentateuch.[141]

E

103. If it appears from the foregoing with a high degree of probability that we owe the Pentateuch, in the form in which we now possess it, to a compiler, we are not able as yet to settle anything more definitely with reference to his age and activity. We must first enquire what antiquity should be assigned to the historical and legislative documents of the Pentateuch.[142] In this enquiry we shall have to give attention not only to the indications existing in the documents themselves, but also to the History of Israel and the Religion of Israel,[143] and to the Israel-itish literature, generally, in its connection with the Penta-teuch.[144] Especially, it will thus appear, whether, with the majority of enquirers, we must assume a *double* compilation—one, earlier, of the four Books, Genesis–Numbers, another, later, when Deuteronomy was connected with these Books,—or, perhaps, only a *single* compilation, by some one, who had both the prime-documents of Genesis-Numbers, and the Deuterono-mistic Legislation in his hands.[145]

CHAPTER XIX.

THE PENTATEUCH, AND THE HISTORY OF ISRAEL AND OF THE ISRAELITISH RELIGION.

104. WITH respect to what the History teaches as to the antiquity of the Mosaic laws, the views of critical enquirers are very divergent. In great measure this difference of view must be ascribed to the defective method of many of these enquiries. It will, therefore, be necessary that we first give an account of the way, which it seems best to pursue in our own enquiry.

105. (i) First of all, we should be on our guard against con-

founding the life-time of the Israelitish historian with the time about which he is treating ; and this is the more necessary, since the interval between the two may sometimes be very considerable. Every historical writer stands exposed to the danger of transferring to an earlier time the modes of thought and other peculiarities of his own time, and so of exhibiting somewhat incorrectly the facts and persons, about which he is treating. With reference to the point, about which our present enquiry circles, this must the more be taken into consideration, since the historians, whom we shall consult, all knew the Pentateuch, and were persuaded—at least, nearly all of them—of its Mosaic origin, Chap.XX. Hence it follows that more weight must be ascribed to those facts, which conflict with the ideas of the historian himself, than to such as agree with them.[146]

106. (ii) Not every action, which is at variance with the Mosaic Law or with some part of it, can be regarded as evidence against the existence of the Law. All depends here upon the character of the persons, who appear as acting. If it is sufficiently certain from other quarters that they belonged to the number of *pious* Israelites, those well-disposed to the theocrary—if also, in addition, their transgression of a prescription of the ,Law does not stand alone, but may be paired with numerous similar instances,—then arises the high probability, that *they did not know the Law,* by which posterity tested their deeds.

107. (iii) Just as little can every action, which may be in accordance with the Law, be regarded as a proof that the Law itself was known and recognised. Those who are of opinion that many of its prescriptions were first committed to writing, in the form in which we now possess them, long after Moses, admit at the same time, that these prescriptions were not later *inventions,* but were in agreement with existing customs, and were developed out of them. Hence any action, which agrees with the Law, only then gives evidence of the existence of the Law, when it appears that it has taken place—not on the ground

of custom, but—in consequence of the prescriptions of the Law.

108. Our enquiry divides itself into two Parts. In the *First*, we shall treat of what the History teaches us in regard to the observance of the Mosaic Law with respect to (i) Holy Places, (ii) Holy Persons, (iii) Holy Seasons, (iv) Holy Actions, (v) Civil and Political Life.[147]   In the *Second*, we shall consider the cases, where express mention is made of the *Law of Moses*, either by persons who are introduced as speaking, or by the historian where he is treating, not about his own lifetime, but about earlier times.[148]

PART I.

(i) *Holy Places.*

109. During the time of the Judges, the Tabernacle stood at Shiloh, Jo.xviii.1,xix.51,xxi.2,xxii.19,29, or, at least, a national Sanctuary stood there, Ju.xxi.12,19, 1S.i, &c., as we find one during the reign of Saul at Nob, 1S.xxi.*   While thus, according to the prescriptions of the Pentateuch (see *e.g.* L.xvii.1–9,D.xii), sacrifices might only be offered at Shiloh,—or, later, at Nob,—we read that altars were built and sacrifices offered at *Bochim*, Ju.ii.5, *Ophrah*,vi.24,25,viii.27,*Zorah*,xiii.19,[149] perhaps at *Mizpeh*,xx.1, but certainly at *Bethel*, xx.23,26–28,xxi.2,4.   To these facts the more significance should be assigned, since the offerings were made either by the whole people, or by men such as Gideon and Manoah.

110. So Samuel offers at *Mizpeh*, 1S.vii.9, builds an altar at *Ramah*, vii.17, and celebrates a sacrificial feast there upon a 'high place,' ix.12, as afterwards at *Bethlehem*, xvi.5.[150]   Just so

---

* There is no proof that '*the* Tabernacle' was ever at Nob, as some suppose. There were 'priests' there, an 'ephod,' 'shewbread'; but there is no sign in the narrative of the Tabernacle of Shiloh having been removed to Nob.   *Ed.*

sacrifices are offered in his presence, xi.15, or by Saul at his express command, x.8,xiii.9, at *Gilgal.* It is recorded to the praise of Saul that he 'built an altar to Jehovah,' xiv.35.[151] Absalom asks and obtains from his father David permission to celebrate a sacrificial feast at *Hebron,* 2S.xv.7,8. David himself had a place in the neighbourhood of Jerusalem, where he used to pray and certainly also to sacrifice, xv.32. Under his reign sacrifices were offered both on the hill *Zion,* vi.17,18, and at *Gibeon* on the 'high place,' where, according to the Chronicler, 1Ch.xvi.38-40, the Tabernacle of Jehovah must have stood.[152] He sacrificed on the threshing-floor of Araunah at *Jerusalem,* 2S.xxiv.25, comp. 1Ch.xxi.21,22,28-30,[153] as did Solomon upon the 'high place' at Gibeon, 1K.iii.2-4.

111. The kings of Judah, Asa, 1K.xv.14, Jehoshaphat, xxii.43, Joash, 2K.xii.3, Amaziah, xiv.4, Uzziah, xv.4, Jotham, xv.35, Ahaz, xvi.4, allowed the worshipping of Jehovah upon the 'high places,' to continue.[154] Hezekiah was the first, who made attempts to do away with this worship, xviii.4 ; and how strange his endeavour after unity of worship appeared to his contemporaries, may appear from the language of the Assyrian ambassadors, 2K.xviii.22, Is.xxxvi.7,—'If ye say unto me, We trust in Jehovah our God, is not that He, whose high places and whose altars Hezekiah hath taken away, and hath said to Judah and Jerusalem, Ye shall worship before this altar in Jerusalem ?' Under Manasseh, accordingly, there followed a reaction, 2K.xxi.3 ; Josiah first succeeded in making the Temple the only sanctuary of the people, at least during his own life-time, 2K.xxiii. His successor, probably, followed in this respect a system of government different from his own, 2K.xxiv. After the Captivity, the Temple at Jerusalem was the only place of sacrifice, and is recognised as such by all (Ezra, Nehemiah, *passim*).

All these facts, viewed in their natural connection, lead to the

supposition, that the Mosaic prescription,* by which the worship
was attached to one single Sanctuary, was not in existence, at all
events, before Hezekiah's reign, and was first introduced under
Josiah, a century afterwards.[155]

(ii) *Holy Persons.*

112. In the Pentateuch the priests alone are considered
fitted for proper sacrificial acts, E.xxviii,&c.; and the Israelites,
generally, and the Levites in particular, were threatened with
death, if they presumed to take upon themselves priestly duties,
N.xviii.3,7, comp. xvi,xvii. Also to Aaron's descendants was
especially assigned the duty of blessing the people, N.vi.22–27.
With these and other prescriptions, which will be considered
below, the actual state of things, during many ages, was in very
little accordance. It seems, indeed, that already, during the
time of the Judges, the Levites were considered to be *exception-
ally* called to the service of the Sanctuary, Ju.xvii.13,xix.18,†
and that Aaron's descendants were priests at Shiloh, 1S.i,&c.

---

* Probaby, the attempt to establish one Sanctuary for Israel had been first made
in Hezekiah's time, when such an attempt became for the first time reasonable and
practicable, since it chiefly affected the Kingdom of Judah, the people of the sister
kingdom having been already carried into captivity. And this particular Mosaic
prescription may have been first introduced in a still later age, *e.g.* in that of Josiah,
in order to commend and enforce the practice, formerly introduced by Hezekiah,
but discontinued under Manasseh and Amon. *Ed.*

† This *may* be indicated—but it is not necessarily—by the passages referred to.
In Ju.xvii.13,—'Then said Micah, Now know I that Jehovah will do me good, seeing I
have the (=this) Levite [not ' *a* Levite,' E.V.] for a priest,'—the stress seems rather
to be laid on the fact of Micah's having a *priest* at all—having a family altar—having
established regular family-worship—in his house. If, for instance, a vagrant
Simeonite had come to him, instead of a Levite, and he had said, as above, ' Now
know I that Jehovah will do me good, seeing I have the (=this) Simeonite for a
priest,' we should not have supposed that this pointed to any special fitness of the
Simeonites for the service of the Sanctuary. So in Ju.xix.18, the Levite *might* be
' going to the house of Jehovah' to *minister*; but it is quite as likely that he might
be going, as Elkanah did, 1S.i.3,7,21, merely to *worship*. *Ed.*

But we see nothing of any *exclusive* fitness of the last-named for the office of priest.

113. *Gideon* and *Manoah* sacrificed, Ju.vi.26,xiii.19. In Micah's house, and afterwards at Dan, a *Levite* undertakes the office of the priest, Ju.xvii,xviii.[156] Whether *Samuel* was a *Levite* is doubtful[157]; but certainly he was no *priest*, and yet he performs priestly acts, 1S.vii,&c. *Saul* himself sacrifices, 1S.xiii.9,[158] as does afterwards *David*, who besides blesses the people, 2S.vi.17,18,xxiv.18,19,25.

114. Under David's reign we see Zadok and Abiathar, 2Sx.v. 24,29,(Abimelech, 2S.viii.17) clothed at the same time with the priestly dignity, in contradiction to the Law, which knows only one High Priest, L.xxi.10, comp. N.xx.22–29,&c. Further, David orders that the Levites shall enter into office in their twentieth year, 1Ch.xxiii.24,27, while the law requires an age of *twenty-five* or *thirty*, note [40.viii]. At the dedication of the Temple, Solomon evidently fills the chief place, 1K.viii, at variance with what is recorded in L.viii–x about the dedication of the Tabernacle.[159] It is further noticeable that not a trace of the account contained in 2Ch.xxvi.16–21 appears in the older historian, 2K.xv.1–5.[160] Lastly, as to what concerns the Nazariteship, the two examples of it, which the history affords us in the case of Samson and Samuel, Ju.xiii–xvi, 1S.i, must for various reasons have preceded the establishment of the law laid down in N.vi.[161]

(iii) *Holy Seasons.*

115. The laws of the Pentateuch on this subject, *e.g.* E.xii, xxiii, L.xxiii, D.xvi, &c., prescribe,—besides the Sabbath, the Sabbatical Year, and the Year of Jubilee,—the celebrating of the three well-known High Feasts, of the New Moon of the seventh Month, and of the Great Day of Atonement. Since the Old-Testament historians neither wrote nor wished to write a com-

plete History of their Religion, they mention only now and then
the celebration of these Feasts. From the writings of the Prophets,
as well as from the historical Books, it appears that the Sabbath,
although not always observed, was yet known, Am.viii.5, Hos.ii.
11, Is.i.13, Jer.xvii.21-27, Ez.xx.12-24,&c., 2.K.iv.23,xi.5,7,9,
1Ch.ix.32,xxiii.31,&c. Of the Sabbatical Year no mention is
made, unless it is treated of in Jer.xxxiv.8-22, in which place
others find the mention of a year of Jubilee,[162] which also
Ezekiel notices, xlvi.17, but no one before him. The Day of
Atonement is mentioned only in the Pentateuch. Even Ezekiel,
xlv.18,&c., prescribes that on the first and seventh day of the
first month the Sanctuary shall be ' reconciled' (purged of sin),
without saying a single word about the atonement of the tenth
day of the *seventh* month. That the first day of the month—
not, however, distinctly of the *seventh* month—was celebrated,
appears from 1S.xx.5, comp. Hos.ii.11,v.7, Is.i.13,14.[163]

116. During the time of the Judges a yearly feast was celebrated at Shiloh, Ju.xxi.19,20, 1S.i.3,7,21. Yet the manner, in
which this is mentioned, raises the suspicion that, besides this, no
other yearly feasts were known, or, at least, were celebrated at
the sanctuary.[164] In this suspicion we are confirmed by the accounts as to the feast kept by Solomon, 1K.viii.2,65,66, and the
feast instituted by Jeroboam I, 1K.xii.27,32,33,[165] and, further,
by the copious testimonies of 2K.xxiii.21-23, 2Ch.xxx.26,xxxv.
18,19, Neh.viii.18.[166] Although these facts can by no means be
considered sufficient to give us a just insight into the gradual
formation of the Israelitish feast-calendar, they are, however,
utterly irreconcilable with the supposition, that the feasts
were from the very first so regulated by Moses, as we should
infer from the present Pentateuch.

iv. *Holy actions.*

117. It would seem that circumcision was always made account of in Israel, Jo.v.2–9, Ju.xiv.3,xv.18, 1S.xiv.6,xvii.26,36, Jer.iv.4,&c.   Mention is also made continually of sacrifices, and in particular of burnt-offerings and slaughter- or thank-offerings. On the contrary, sin-offerings are named once only by Hosea, iv.8, and mention is first made of trespass- and sin-offerings by Ezekiel, xl.39,xlii.13,&c., and the writers in and after the Captivity.[167]   The offering of Jephtha's daughter, Ju.xi.30–40, shows that very undeveloped ideas prevailed about the mode of honouring Jehovah, which, consequently, were also zealously opposed by the later writers of the Pentateuch.[168]   The ban of extermination (חֵרֶם) was applied by the whole people, and even by Joshua himself, Ju.xx,xxi, Jo.vii, in a way which conflicts with the directions of the Law, D.xiii.13,14,xxiv.16.[169]   The expiatory sacrifice, also, offered by David on the demand of the Gibeonites, 2S.xxi.1–14, is at variance with the law in N.xxxv. 9–34, D.xxiv.16; which gives us the more right to deny the existence of this ordinance in David's time, since he acted by the advice of the (priestly or prophetical) oracle, 2S.xxi.1.[170]

(v) *Civil and Political Life.*

118. Also in the domain of Civil and Political Life we meet with phenomena, which are wholly irreconcilable with the supposition, that the Pentateuch existed from the time of Moses onward.   At once the *rudeness*, which was in many ways peculiar to the time of the Judges, awakens surprise, in connection with the humane spirit, by which many laws, especially those of Deuteronomy, are marked.[171]   The account in R.iv.1–10, about the redemption of Naomi's land, and the marriage of Ruth with Boaz, affords no evidence for the existence of the laws in L.xxv. 25, D.xxv.5–10.[172]   That neither the people of Israel, when they

desired a king, nor Samuel at the inauguration of the kingdom, knew of D.xvii.14-20, appears plainly from 1S.viii,x.17–27,xii.[173] Also in Solomon's time this law was certainly not known.[174] David makes an ordinance about the division of booty, 1S.xxx. 21–25, which excludes the existence of N.xxxi.[175]   From these facts we draw the inference, that the Civil Legislation also of the Pentateuch, as well as the law about Religion, was gradually formed.

PART II.

Actual traces of the existence of the Book of the Law.

119. As Moses in the Book of Deuteronomy makes mention repeatedly of 'the Book of this Law,' and of 'this Book of the Law,' notes [7,8], so also 'the Law,' the 'Law of Moses,' 'the Book of the Law,' &c. is mentioned in the Book of Joshua, both by Joshua himself, xxii.5,xxiii.6,xxiv.26, and by Jehovah speaking to Joshua, i.7,8, and by the historian, when treating about Joshua's time, viii.31,34. These expressions, however, can only be regarded as evidences of the close connection between the Pentateuch and the Book of Joshua, and by no means as actual traces of the existence of the Book of the Law. David's words to Solomon, 1K.ii.3, comp. 2S.xxii.23, would have to be regarded as such, if it were certain that they were thoroughly authentic.   But it is evident that the writer's own point of view has exercised an influence upon this reproduction of them.[176]   The same is true of passages such as 1Ch.xxii.12, 2Ch.vi.16,xv.3,xix.10,[177]—even 2Ch.xvii.9.[178]

120. On the contrary, 2K.xi.12, 2Ch.xxiii.11, is an actual proof that at the coronation of Joash (878 B.C.) in the Temple at Jerusalem, there existed a Book called, on account of the ordinances (? the Decalogue) contained in it, 'the Testimony,' without anything else appearing which may throw light upon the age, origin, or contents of that writing.[179]   Just as little can we with perfect certainty decide what 'Book of the Law'

was found by Hilkiah, and made by Josiah the basis of his Reformation, 2K.xxii.8,&c., 2Ch.xxxiv.14,&c. Only it seems that we may conclude that the Book in question was by no means a complete copy of the present Pentateuch, much less the autograph of Moses, but either the law of Deuteronomy or a portion thereof.[180]

CHAPTER XX.

THE PENTATEUCH AND THE LITERATURE OF ISRAEL.

121. IF we desire to arrive at certainty concerning the use made of the Pentateuch by the Israelitish writers, we must proceed from the certain to the uncertain, or, in other words, we must first consult the *Prophetical Writings*, whose age may be considered to be known with accuracy,—then the *Historical Books*, about which we are more or less in uncertainty,—lastly, the *Psalms* ascribed to David and his contemporaries, and the *Proverbs* assigned to Solomon, whose age, frequently, cannot be at all determined.

We should observe, further, that the historical facts, with which we are made acquainted through the Pentateuch, may have been known to the writers in question from other sources also,—either from tradition, or from the prime-documents used for the compilation of the Pentateuch,[181]—and that, consequently, the mention of an usage or a custom, elevated by the Pentateuch into law, cannot by any means be admitted as a proof, that the Pentateuch itself existed and was known to the writer.[182]

Lastly, we must consider that the agreement between a passage of the Pentateuch and a Prophetical expression can only then be regarded as a sign of the Prophet's acquaintance with the Pentateuch, when it is certain that the *contrary* has not occurred, *viz.* that the writer of the Pentateuch has not followed the Prophet.

THE PROPHETS.

122. We shall fix our attention, first, upon the relation of the Prophets to the Law generally; secondly, upon those passages in their writings in which it has been thought an acquaintance may be observed either with Mosaic laws, or with historical narratives contained in the Pentateuch.

With reference to the relation of the Prophets to the Law in general, we may notice the following.

Malachi is the first of the Prophets, who mentions Moses by name as the lawgiver of Israel, iv.4. After him, the author of the book of Daniel does the same, ix.11,13. The older Prophets mention him, indeed, but only as the deliverer of Israel from Egyptian slavery, Hos.xii.13, Mic.vi.4, Is.lxiii.12, or as a Prophet, together with Samuel, Jer.xv.1.

123. The older Prophets, Joel, Amos, Hosea, the author of Zech.ix–xi, Isaiah, Micah, Nahum, who flourished before the Chaldee period, are defenders of the Jehovah-worship, and in general of the religious and moral principles, which lie also at the foundation of the Pentateuch, and in consequence of these they are zealous against idolatry and immorality. Yet it is far from being true that they do so, *because the Law forbids such transgressions.* On the contrary, they show themselves independent of its prescriptions to such a degree, that they very seldom indeed refer to the Law,[183]—they speak of their own utterances and those of other Prophets as 'the Torah (Law or instruction) of Jehovah,' just as much as the directions laid down by Moses,[184]—and, what especially ought not to be passed by, they do not indeed reject altogether the Ceremonial Legis-

lation, but they place it infinitely lower than the Moral Law, and seem to regard it as the work of the priests.[185]

124. The same phenomena may be observed, also, in the writings of the later Prophets, Zephaniah, Jeremiah, Habakkuk; although in other respects the references to the Law are more numerous with them.[186] Not one of the Prophets before the Captivity reveals the consciousness of standing under the authority of a venerable Law, handed down in writing by Moses. This fact cannot be explained as arising only from the peculiarity of the prophetical point of view. It requires also the supposition, that the Pentateuch, in the form in which we now possess it, with its claims to divine origin and high antiquity, was not known and recognised by them.[187]

125. These remarks with reference to prophetism before the Captivity find their confirmation in the history of the following age. Ezekiel combines great familiarity with the priestly portion of the Law with a certain degree of independence in respect of its prescriptions.[188] The later Isaiah, where he is not occupied with the future, but treads the domain of the actual present, agrees thoroughly with the requirements of the Law, without subjecting himself slavishly to it.[189] The same is true in a greater or less degree of Haggai and Zechariah, ch.i–viii.[190] While Ezra and Nehemiah introduce the Pentateuch in its entirety as the Jews' rule of faith and life, Malachi laboured, as a Prophet, entirely in the selfsame spirit, and ends his prophetical address by a reference to the *Law of Moses*, and an admonition to obedience of its prescriptions, iv.4. After him, prophetism, already languishing for some time, dies out entirely, and the place of the Prophets was taken by the Scribes,— a proof that a free activity, like that of Israel's 'men of God,' was inconsistent with the domination of the letter of the written Law, or, in any case, was rendered superfluous by it. [191]

126. Secondly, observing the rules above laid down (121),

we arrive at the following results with respect to the use, which the older Prophets make of the laws and narratives of the Pentateuch.

JOEL gives no indication that the Pentateuch was known to him.[192]

AMOS follows a tradition, about the destruction of Sodom and Gomorrah, iv.11, and the sojourn of the Israelites in the wilderness and conquest of Canaan, ii.9,10,v.25,26, which agrees in the main with the accounts of the Pentateuch, without its appearing that he has drawn from those accounts.[193]

HOSEA knew probably, xii.4,5,13, the Jehovistic narratives of Genesis,—in particular, xxv.26,xxvii.43,xxix.18,&c.xxxii.24,&c. xxxv.1,&c.[194]

The author of Zech.ix–xi treats of no subjects, which bring him into relation with the Pentateuch.

MICAH shows some acquaintance, vi.5, with the Jehovistic accounts about Balaam, N.xxii–xxiv, while in vi.4,vii.15,20, he expresses ideas about the relation of Jehovah to the patriarchs and the exodus out of Egypt, which agree with the narratives of Genesis and Exodus, but are too general for us to be obliged to derive them from those narratives.

ISAIAH, i.9,iii.9, had read the Jehovistic account of the destruction of Sodom, G.xix, and also, as appears from x.26,xi.11,15,16, xii.2,xxx.29, the accounts about the march out of Egypt, the passage through the Red Sea and the Song of Moses, E.xii–xv.[195] On the other hand, the agreement between Is.xxx.17 and L.xxvi.8, D.xxxii.30, may be explained either from the expression being proverbial, or from the writers of the Pentateuch having imitated Isaiah.[196]

NAHUM and HABAKKUK present no distinct signs of acquaintance with the Pentateuch.[197]

ZEPHANIAH, iii.3, knew the ' Blessing of Jacob,' G.xlix,* the

---

* The references are supposed to be made to G.xlix.9 ('lions'), 27 ('wolves'); but these seem very doubtful. *Ed.*

accounts about the destruction of Sodom and Gomorrah, ii.9, and the Book of Deuteronomy.[198]

JEREMIAH was very well acquainted with Deuteronomy, with the Book of the Covenant, E.xx.22–xxiii, and other Jehovistic portions of the Pentateuch, but less, it seems, with the laws assigned above (Chap.XIV) to the Book of Origins.[199]

EZEKIEL, finally, knows and uses all parts of the Pentateuch, and may have had before him a law-book having close resemblance to the present.[200]

THE HISTORICAL BOOKS.

127. The Book of JOSHUA cannot be taken into account in this enquiry, on account of its connection with the Pentateuch.[201]

The Books of JUDGES and RUTH owe their present form to an author, who knew the Pentateuch, and, in particular, the Book of Deuteronomy.[202]

In the Books of SAMUEL the passages, which are supposed to imply that the compiler knew the Pentateuch, especially Deuteronomy, are few in number and of doubtful cogency.[203]

The writer of the Books of KINGS was not only very familiar with the Pentateuch in all its parts,[204] but he also refers expressly to it, 2K.xiv.6, comp. D.xxiv.16,—further, 2K.xxi.8, xxiii.25, where Moses is named as lawgiver,—lastly, 2K.x.31, xvii.13,34,37.

Still more numerous are the references in the Books of CHRONICLES, whose author continually and designedly points out, how far the particulars mentioned by him agree with the Pentateuch, 1Ch.xvi.40, 2Ch.xii.1,xiv.4,xxiii.18,xxv.4=2K.xiv.6, 2Ch.xxx.16,xxxi.3,4,21,xxxiii.8,xxxiv.19,xxxv.26.

The Books of EZRA and NEHEMIAH are written in the same spirit, the references to the Law being as numerous in them as in the Chronicles, Ezr.ii.63,iii.2,vii.6,&c., Neh.i.7,&c.

128. The assertion of DELITZSCH,[205] that the Literature of the Davidic and Solomonic time implies the existence of the Law in its present form, rests upon the opinion that a great number of the Psalms, the Proverbs, the Canticles, and the Book of Job, date from that time. We must regard this assertion, however, as unproved and unprovable, since the inscriptions of the Psalms can make no pretence to credibility, and many—if not all—of the Psalms, which are ascribed to David and his contemporaries, betray a later origin,—the Proverbs, if not all, yet for the most part, were committed to writing after the time of Solomon,—the Canticles were composed about the year 800 B.C., and the book of Job, probably, in the seventh century B.C.

129. Add to this, that the points of agreement with the Law, which are observed in the above writings, are sometimes very far-fetched, and want all proper power of proof.[206]   On the contrary, it is incontestable that those Psalms, which, according to the most probable and generally received view, were written after the Babylonish Captivity, betray much greater acquaintance with the Pentateuch than those, which with some certainty may be pronounced to have been written before the carrying away of the people.[207]   In general, however, this observation holds good of the Psalms, that the time of their composition is too uncertain for them to render us any service in defining the age of the Pentateuch.   Rather, on the contrary, the use made of the Pentateuch in some Psalms, in connection with the phenomena which we remark in the Prophetical Books, must be regarded as a help for fixing the time, in which the Psalms themselves were composed.

130. The investigation, which has been conducted in Chap. XIX, XX, has resulted in this :—

(i) It has confirmed the conclusion, derived from the Pentateuch itself, as to the gradual development of the Legislation;

(ii) It has marked for us the life-time of Hosea ($\pm$780 B.C.), as the *terminus*, before which many of the Jehovistic accounts of the book of Genesis must have been committed to writing;

(iii) It has pointed out to us some criteria, according to which we may be able to define the relative ages of the different laws;

(iv) It has led us to the conviction that no single proof, which will bear to be tested, can be produced for the existence of the Pentateuch in its present form before the beginning of the Babylonish Captivity.

We must now make use of these results for determining the time, at which the primary documents of the Pentateuch originated, and the Pentateuch, as a whole, attained its present form.

CHAPTER XXI.

THE AGE OF THE PENTATEUCH.

131. In order to attain certainty as to the age of the primary documents of the Pentateuch, we shall first have to enquire, to which of the legislative documents, and to which of the historical, the priority ought to be assigned, or, in other words, we must determine the *relative* ages of these documents. Not till then, in connection with the results attained in Chap. XIX, XX, can an attempt be made to point out as accurately as possible the time in which they were written.

132. If, for the present, we leave out of consideration in our enquiry the Decalogue, about whose high antiquity scarcely any doubt [?] is entertained, comp. notes [241, 242], the *Book of the*

Covenant, E.xx.22–xxiii, first of all, claims our attention. We must regard it as being *the oldest collection of laws which has been preserved to us.* The reasons for this are the following : —

(i) The historian assigns to Moses himself the writing the Book of the Covenant, E.xxiv.4,7, whence it follows that this collection of laws not only was in existence in this writer's time, but was also considered very old [208];

(ii) The directions of the Book of the Covenant, compared with the prescriptions of the Book of Origins and with the Deuteronomistic Legislation, are characterised by simplicity and originality. This is true, in particular, of the laws about the honouring Jehovah by sacrifices, E.xx.24–26, the dedication of the firstborn, xxii.29[b],30, and the firstlings, xxii.29[a], the celebration of the Sabbath, xxiii.12, of the Sabbatical Year, xxiii.10,11, and of the three High Feasts, xxiii.14–17, cleanness, xxii.31, the liberation of Hebrew slaves, male and female, xxi.2–11.[209] The reference to an *earlier* law in xxiii.15, 'as I have commanded thee,' appears, indeed, to stand opposed to this conclusion. But this notice cannot in any case render doubtful the result derived from the laws themselves.[210]

133. After the Book of the Covenant there come into consideration the few laws, which, as we have seen above (Chap. XIV, XVII), were adopted by the Jehovist into his narrative, E.xiii. 3–16, xxxiv.10–35, or, at least, do not belong to the Legislation of the Book of Origins, L.xviii–xx. As far as regards E.xxxiv, it is not a matter of doubt that the prescriptions there given were taken over by the narrator out of the Book of the Covenant, and, to a large extent, out of E.xiii.11–16, and are consequently younger than these laws.[211] But the determination of the relative ages of E.xiii.3–16 and L.xviii–xx is accompanied with great difficulties. We consider that we can only establish this point, that they are younger than the Book of the Covenant, and, on the other hand, older than the Deuteronomistic Legislation, while they may be contemporary with the Book of Origins.[212]

134. Peculiar difficulties are attached to the determination of the age of the Book of Origins, compared with the remaining historical and legislative documents,—difficulties, which are closely connected with the modifications, which that book underwent in course of time (Chap.XIV.) We have seen already that the historical narrative of the Book of Origins, which we possess in Genesis and the first chapters of Exodus, are characterised by great simplicity; and we considered that we must on this account ascribe to them a higher antiquity than to the other (Elohistic and Jehovistic) narratives about the time from the Creation of the world to Moses.[213] Meanwhile, however, it must be taken into account, that the Jehovist already in Genesis does not always relate independently, but introduces older documents or loose accounts of small extent, unchanged or with slight variations, notes [117,118]. From this it follows that the author of the Book of Origins surpasses certainly in age the younger Elohist and the Jehovist, but that the *sources* of the last-named may be older than he.[214]

135. This remark is applicable also to the Books of Exodus and Numbers—even more here than to Genesis—(i) because the historical narrative itself of the Book of Origins, as we have seen, notes[108-112], do not proceed in their entirety from the first author of that Book, but have come down to us in a later edition,—(ii) because the Jehovist here, even much more than in Genesis, has had recourse to older documents.[215] Hence it must follow that the historical record of the Book of Origins, which in Genesis must have preceded the later Elohistic and the Jehovistic, in Exodus and Numbers is contemporary with the last-named.

136. As regards the Legislation of the Book of Origins, its relation to the Book of the Covenant and to E.xiii.3-16, L.xviii-xx, has been already indicated, notes [210-212]. Its position with regard to the Deuteronomistic Legislation cannot be explained in a few words. For, although, as we have seen in Chap.X, the Book of Deuteronomy implies the existence not only of the

Jehovistic historical narrative, but also of the accounts of the Book of Origins,—not simply of the Covenant Book, and E.xiii. 3–16, L.xviii–xx,but also of the priestly Legislation,—yet it does not follow from this that *all* the laws of the Book of Origins, *in that form in which we now possess them,* are older than the Deuteronomistic Legislation.[216]   The possibility exists that they may have been reduced into order anew after the time of the Deuteronomist, and here and there changed and supplemented, so that he knew certainly of *a* priestly Legislation, and refers to it, xviii.2,xxiv.8, but not therefore of the same priestly Legislation, which we now have before us.

137. The Book of Origins may so much the more have undergone changes, since the Legislation, contained in it, was neither intended, nor suited, to be disseminated among the people, and, consequently, just by reason of its private character, admitted continually of being expanded and modified.   In this respect it is distinguished both from the Book of the Covenant and from the Deuteronomistic Law, which from the very first were intended for the people, and so were in their nature unchangeable, or at least could merely undergo insignificant modifications.   Whether, however, there exists sufficient reason actually to assume a later edition of the Book of Origins, after the Deuteronomist,—of which the *possibility* only appears from the foregoing,—is very difficult to decide, though such an edition is far from improbable.[217]

138. Our enquiry as to the exact points of time, at which the documents of the Pentateuch originated, ought to begin with the Book of Deuteronomy, because it seems possible to attain more certainty with respect to this.   The Deuteronomistic Legislation implies the existence of the Temple of Solomon,[218] and the reign of Solomon generally[219]; it is later than Jehoshaphat [220] and Hezekiah.[221]   On the other hand, it seems to have lain at the basis of Josiah's Reformation,[222] and must, consequently,

have been committed to writing, either in the early part of his reign, or more probably, under the reign of Manasseh.[223] With this definition of time agree also exceedingly well certain other particulars, besides those above-mentioned.[224] Moreover, the reign of Manasseh (695-642 B.C.) was in every point of view a fitting time to call into life such an attempt at the development and introduction of Mosaism, as we observe in the Book of Deuteronomy, and it explains fully at the same time the peculiar form of the Deuteronomistic Legislation.[225]

139. The Temple of Solomon existed from the year 1005 B.C. to 588 B.C. In that interval the Book of Origins was produced. Before the building of the Temple the necessary conditions for the production of such a work did not exist.[226] But it would seem, that already under Solomon's reign, or at least shortly afterwards, through some priest or Levite, the foundation was laid for the Book of Origins; and we have therefore to regard the historical narratives of Genesis, which appear to us to be derived from that Book and to belong to the oldest portions of it, as a product of the age of Solomon.[227] Certainly, by this original author, Solomon's contemporary, nearly the same subjects of Legislation were from the first treated as those with which the Book of Origins is occupied.[228]

140. But, after the condition of the people and the position of the priests became changed, and the religious and priestly ideas developed themselves, the necessity also was felt to fill up and modify the original Law-Book, and, in connection with this, the history also of the Mosaic time was more fully related (Chap. XIV). It has been already remarked [104] that critical investigation has not yet been sufficiently advanced, to separate the later additions from the original [of the Book of Origins]— much less to determine with perfect certainty the correct age of the one and the other. Yet the assertion seems by no means rash, that e.g. L.xvi,xvii, N.xvi,xviii,xxxi, belong to the later or latest portions of the Book of Origins, the editing of which in

its present form must be set later than that of Deuteronomy.[229] In general, in investigating the development of the priestly Legislation, we can only ascribe force to proofs derived from the laws themselves and their mutual comparison; inasmuch as the Prophets—as we have seen above, Chap. XXI—very seldom betray any acquaintance with the Legislation, and, consequently, afford us no help for determining the age of its parts.[230]

141. Inasmuch as the Jehovistic historical narratives contain a more fully developed tradition, and in general present themselves as of a later date than the Book of Origins—particularly than the portions which have been assigned above to a contemporary of Solomon, (comp. notes [227,97,122-129]) they cannot have been committed to writing until after Solomon and the division of the kingdom. The time of their being written falls, consequently, between the years 975 and 775 B.C., since Hosea and, after him, Isaiah and Micah give plain signs of knowing them, notes [194,195]. In the first part of this interval these documents in particular may have originated, which the Jehovist (the writer of G.ii.4b-iv) knew and used, while he himself may have lived about the year 800 B.C.

142. It is, however, not only possible, but even probable, (i) that some documents, which have been inserted by him, may have originated from a yet older date, and perhaps, even under David or Solomon, if not still earlier [231]; (ii) that also after the year 800 B.C. some of these Jehovistic or prophetical passages may have been written, which were afterwards inserted into the Pentateuch.[232] The later Elohistic narratives in Genesis, and the first chapters of Exodus, must be nearly contemporary with the Jehovistic, [123,125]. Whereas, on the one hand, it seems hazardous to define more accurately the exact time, to which each narrative or each group of narratives belongs,[233] on the other hand, the strongest reasons may be adduced for the interval, of two centuries and upwards, here indicated.[234]

143. The age of the Book of the Covenant, E.xx.22–xxiii,

cannot be determined with perfect certainty. Since, however, the author of the document used by the Jehovist, which regards the Book of the Covenant as Mosaic, E.xxiv.4,7, lived probably between 975 and 875 B.C., that Book itself must have originated much earlier, and already under the reign of David, 1055-1015 B.C., if not even yet earlier.[235] With this also agree very well the contents of this Book.[236] Against the notion, that Moses himself wrote it, there exist important objections, which, however, concern not so much the contents, as the form of the legal prescriptions.[237] Thus we must regard the Book of the Covenant as not only a very old, but also the most authentic, document concerning the Mosaic Institutions.

144. The laws, contained in L.xviii–xx, betray some marks of high antiquity.[238] But in their present form they must be younger than the age of Solomon, while they preceded the Deuteronomistic Legislation. Thus they fall between 975 and 650 B.C., probably in the second half of this interval.[239]

Lastly, E.xiii.3–16, with the remaining documents, used by the Jehovist, must have been composed between 975 and 875 B.C.[240]

145. We have said nothing as yet about the Decalogue. We possess it in two editions varying from one another, E.xx.2–17, D.v.6–18, neither of which, however, seems to contain the original Mosaic text.[241] Yet, though doubt may be justly entertained as to the genuineness of some, non-essential, additions, the strongest evidences may be brought for the Mosaic origin of the commands themselves, and for the order in which they are handed down to us.[242]

CHAPTER XXII.

THE COMPILER OF THE PENTATEUCH.

146. If we still possessed the documents, which the compiler of the Pentateuch had at his disposal, in their original extent, we should then be able to form without any difficulty a just idea of his labours. Now, on the contrary, we must not seldom have recourse to more or less probable conjectures, and leave alone some points entirely, as to which it seems to be no longer possible to come to any decision. It appears with sufficient certainty from the Pentateuch itself, that the compiler proposed to himself to form out of his documents a well-connected whole, and that he, consequently, allowed himself to be guided in his work both by the desire to secure such an uniformity, as was absolutely necessary, if such a whole was really to exist, and at the same time by the great reverence which he felt for the documents used by him, in consequence of which he left their peculiarities as much as possible untouched.

147. That it was, in fact, the purpose of the compiler to produce a well-connected work, appears from the Pentateuch itself most plainly. That different documents are inserted in it,— that it contains different passages at variance with each other,— has been shown above. Yet this does not conflict with the fact, that the whole has been laid down according to a definite plan, and is regularly developed (54) and note [68]. This plan is no other than that of the Book of Origins, Chap. XV, which the compiler has laid as the basis of his work, and into which he inserted the other historical and legislative documents in the most suitable manner and position. The mutual contradiction of many laws and narratives thus combined cannot have entirely escaped the notice of the compiler, though he thought them

probably capable of explanation; as in a later time the Jews, after the introduction of the Pentateuch by Ezra, regarded its different prescriptions as very well capable of being reconciled with each other. The application of a similar process of har- monising, or the supposition of its being possible, may be so much the more ascribed to the compiler, since he was certainly persuaded of the high antiquity of his documents and of the Mosaic origin of many of the laws inserted by him.

148. The effort of the compiler after uniformity reveals itself *e.g.* in the continuous use of the names Abraham and Sarah, (for Abram and Sarai), after, in G.xvii.5–16, the origin of these two names has been explained,[243]—but further and especially in the so-called archaisms of the Pentateuch. It has been observed, for instance, that the pronoun הוּא, and the substantive נַעַר,[244] are usually employed in the Pentateuch for both sexes, and that in place of הָאֵלֶּה is used הָאֵל.[245] Most probably, these peculi- arities occurred in some older laws or historical passages, and were introduced by the compiler for the sake of uniformity everywhere, or at least almost everywhere, unless, indeed, the later legislators and historians had already followed their pre- decessors in this respect. In no case are these few varia- tions[246] from the usual phraseology sufficient to prove the high antiquity of the Pentateuch above the remaining Books of the Old Testament.

149. Yet this aim after uniformity was also coupled in the compiler with a great respect for the documents adopted by him, and was not unfrequently sacrificed to it. This respect reveals itself in this, that he inserts his documents, as far as possible, *entire*, and leaves untouched their peculiarities in thought and phraseology. Nowhere does this appear more plainly than in Genesis. The compiler imparts here the Book of Origins as far as the history of Isaac in its entirety, and does not even omit parts of it, which after the more full accounts of the later sources might seem to be superfluous, *e.g.* in G.xii,xiii,xix; further, he

retains the Divine Names, used through the different documents, except, perhaps, G.xvii.1, where either he, or a later writer, has set 'Jehovah' in place of 'Elohim'[247]; lastly, he quotes his documents, as he had found them, without retouching their peculiar phraseology, or erasing their other characteristics.[248] That the later criticism, since the time of ASTRUC (1753), has been able to separate from one another the different documents, both of the Book of Genesis and of the Pentateuch as a whole, and to represent them in their original form, is, perhaps, the most satisfactory proof of the faithfulness, with which the compiler has executed his task.

150. Meanwhile it follows from the nature of the thing that the compiler, while he allowed himself to be guided by the principles above indicated, found himself compelled to make additions, here and there, to his documents, in order either to bring them into a proper connection with one another, or to clear up something or other, which seemed to need explanation. The additions of the last kind are comparatively few: perhaps, G.xx.18 gives the only example of them,[249] [but see G.xxi.1,] since the notices in Deuteronomy, which have all the appearance of glosses, ii.10-12, 20-23,iii.9,11,13^b,14,x.6-9, have proceeded not from the compiler, but from the Deuteronomist himself.[250] But, as regards the additions of the first kind, to these may be applied exactly what has been above remarked with respect to the activity of the compiler in general. It is extremely difficult to show with certainty, where the compiler's hand has been busy, because we no longer possess the authorities, with which it had to do, in their original form. Passages, such as G.v.29,xxxv.9,xxxvii.28, xxxix.1, E.vi.13-30, N.xvi,xxvi.9-11,[251] are well adapted to give us, at least, an idea of the way, in which the compiler carried out his difficult task.

151. From our enquiry as to the age of the different documents of the Pentateuch it has appeared,[229] that according to all probability some portions of the Book of Origins are younger

than the Deuteronomistic Legislation. From this it follows at once, that we cannot assume a double editing of the Pentateuch, one which preceded the Deuteronomist, another by which the Deuteronomistic Law was connected with the four Books, Genesis–Numbers.[252] Further, it follows from this that the compiler of the Pentateuch must be looked for in the same circle in which the Book of Origins arose and was gradually modified,—*i.e.* among the priests at Jerusalem.[253] Lastly, it appears—both from the age of the documents of the Pentateuch, as above established, Chap.XXI,.and the prophecies of Ezekiel,[300] —that the compiler completed his task very shortly before the beginning of the Babylonish Captivity, between the years 600 and 590, B.C.[254] In fact, if we start from these conceptions, the composition of the Pentateuch can be explained in a very natural way;[255] as, conversely, by this fact the accuracy of these conceptions is itself confirmed.

CHAPTER XXIII.

GENERAL SURVEY AND VALUATION OF THE RESULTS OBTAINED.

152. MOSES left to the Israelitish People the law of the Ten Commandments in their original form, perhaps also a few other ordinances, in writing. Further, he regulated, as far as possible, the religious, political, civil, and moral life of Israel,—not, how-ever, by means of written directions, of which, in fact, in that age·little need existed, since their use would have been but small. About the end of the time of the Judges, or under David's reign, the Book of the Covenant, E.xx.22–xxiii, came into existence, a collection of laws for regulating the civil and religious life of the people, which certainly agree for the most part with what Moses himself either had continued to maintain

or had first introduced into practice. About the same time a beginning may have been made of committing to writing old songs,
some of which date from the Mosaic time, (*the Book of the Wars of
Jehovah,* N.xxi.14,) and genealogies,—perhaps also some more
copious narratives about the patriarchal or Mosaic time.[143]

153. Not long after the completion of the Temple of Solomon,
a Priest or Levite wrote the origin and the settlement of the
Theocracy, beginning with the creation of heaven and earth, and
ending with the Conquest of Canaan through Joshua, and the
division of the land among the twelve tribes (*Book of Origins*).
His writing, in which especially the worship was described and
more minutely regulated, remained in the hands of the Jerusalem
Priesthood, and was by them continually modified and supplemented, in the same spirit in which it was begun, and in accordance with the necessities and requirements of the time. In
the interval, 975 B.C. and afterwards, arose small collections of
laws, comp. Hos.viii.12, of which we find one remaining in
L.xviii-xx, and the writing of history was also practised with
great zeal, chiefly by the Prophets. They did not confine themselves to preserving and collecting the older records, and committing to writing the existing traditions, but wrote the history
of the time treated of in the Book of Origins, or of some part
thereof, in a prophetical spirit,—a work which was quite in
accordance with this calling in Israel, and was, probably, completed chiefly in the prophetical schools.[144]

154. Yet, in spite of the combined activity of the Prophets
and the Priests of Jerusalem, the state of the people, viewed
from the religious and moral point of view, left still much
to be desired; and the conviction was confirmed, especially
through the reign of Manasseh, 696 B.C. and afterwards, that
a new and strong effort must be made to bring the Mosaic
principles into supreme authority. With this object some
Prophet, unknown to us, wrote, still under Manasseh, the
addresses and laws of Deuteronomy. Most earnestly he

warns the people no longer to allow idolatry, but to dedicate themselves wholly to the service of Jehovah, and to observe faithfully the Institutions of Moses. While he sets forward these last, he at the same time modifies them in accordance with the wants of the age, and lays special stress upon worshipping Jehovah at Jerusalem only. If already the earlier legislators, in the consciousness that they were writing in the spirit of Moses, and were building onwards upon the foundation laid by him, ascribed their laws to Moses himself, the Deuteronomist inspired with the same conviction, and in agreement with the ideas of morality then entertained, saw no difficulty in not only representing his addresses and laws as Mosaic, but even ascribing the writing of them to Moses himself. How well adapted the means chosen by him was to attain the end which he set before him, we learn from Josiah's Reformation, B.C. 624, which may be regarded as the triumph of the Deuteronomistic principles.

155. After the Deuteronomistic Legislation had been committed to writing, the Book of Origins still underwent some, not unimportant, modifications. Nevertheless, shortly after Joshua's Reformation, and still before the Babylonish Captivity, the documents of the Pentateuch were brought into the present form, and were combined into one whole by a compiler, who belonged probably to the Priests at Jerusalem, and at all events laid at the foundation of his work the priestly Book of Origins, and wrought in the spirit of the later portions of that Book. We owe to him most probably not merely the Pentateuch, but also the Book of *Joshua*, which is not only connected, in respect of its contents, in the closest manner with the Mosaic Books, but is also for the most put together from the same sources and in the same spirit: see Chap.XXIV,XXV.

156. In the above is already included, in point of fact, the answer to the two questions, *viz.* :—

(i) How far can a Mosaic origin be ascribed to this Legislation of the Pentateuch?

' (ii) What is the **value of the** historical notices contained in the Pentateuch?

But the following remarks may serve to give a more full reply to them.

157. If a law can only *then* be called Mosaic, when it has been committed to writing by Moses himself, only very few of the ordinances of the Pentateuch can deserve this name. But, inasmuch as the Legislation, comprised in the Pentateuch, contains, as a whole, the development of the principles expressed by Moses,—inasmuch as, for a great part, it is nothing else than a description, in a legislative form, of the usages and institutions called into life by Moses,[256]—it may throughout be regarded, in a wider sense of the word, as Mosaic. We must, consequently, admit that most of the laws originated after Moses, some even long after him,—that the Pentateuch itself contains ordinances, which conflict with the Mosaic institutions. But, at the same time, we hold it to be certain that no prescriptions are found in it, which would not tend to maintain the principles, and to carry out the proper plan, of Moses,—the forming of a people dedicated to the service of Jehovah alone,—in accordance with the lessons of experience, and the continually changing necessities of the age.[257] Compiled out of documents of different ages, the Pentateuch explains to us the course of development of some Mosaic ordinances and institutions.[258] Brought into its present form about the beginning of the Babylonish Captivity, it contains the final result of the whole development of Mosaism.

158. The historical writers, whose narratives are preserved to us in the Pentateuch, lived all without exception a considerable time after Moses,[259] and stood thus already far away from the Mosaic, and *à fortiori* from the patriarchal, time. They derived their accounts partly from written records, but largely from oral tradition. Sometimes they confined themselves to the reproduction of this tradition, just as they found it; but generally their (prophetical or priestly) point of view exercised no

unimportant influence upon the form and matter of their narratives.

159. From this follows the duty of submitting each account
to careful criticism,[260] which shall take into consideration—

(i) the age of the narrator, and the antiquity of his documentary sources, in case he appears to have made use of any such,—

(ii) the point of view of the narrator, in connection with the
form and matter of his account,—

(iii) the greater or less agreement of the tradition, which lies
at the basis of his narrative, with the accounts of other writers.
Such a criticism leads to the result, that the *chief points* of the
history of the patriarchal and Mosaic time are certainly assured
verities, but that, with respect to many details, an uncertainty
prevails, which, for want of other historical information, cannot
easily be removed.[261]

CHAPTER XXIV.

THE BOOK OF JOSHUA: ITS NAME AND CONTENTS.

160. THE Book of Joshua derives its name from the person,
whose deeds are related in it.   The view, that this designation
points out Joshua as the writer of it, finds no support in the
book itself,[262] and, besides, conflicts with analogy.   Other historical books also of the Old Testament, *e.g. Judges, Ruth,
Samuel, Kings, Esther,* bear the names, not of the writers, but
of the persons of whose history they treat.[263]

161. The Book of Joshua divides itself naturally into two
parts, i–xii and xiii–xxiv, of which one relates the conquest of
Canaan, the other the partition of the land, and the last institutions of Joshua.

162. In the First Part, we distinguish the preparation of the

people for the march through the Jordan, i,—the sending-out of
the spies, ii,—the crossing of the river, iii, iv,—the circumcision and
celebration of the passover, v. The series of conflicts is opened
with the capture of Jericho, vi, and of Ai, viii.1–29,—preceded
by the detection and punishment of Achan's crime, vii,—and
followed by the ratification of the covenant on Ebal and Gerizim,
viii.30–35. After the Gibeonites in a crafty manner had made
peace with Joshua, ix, the kings of southern, x, and then of
northern, Canaan, xi, underwent severe defeats, in consequence
of which their towns fell into the hands of Israel. These towns
are summed up in xii.

163. The Second Part, after an introduction, xiii, in which
the arrangements of Moses about the trans-Jordanic tribes are
recorded, describes the inheritance assigned to Judah, Ephraim,
and Manasseh, xiv–xvii. The progress of the partition of the
land is described, xviii, xix,—then the designation of the free
cities, xx, and the dwelling-places of Priests and Levites, xxi.
The return of the trans-Jordanic tribes to the district assigned to
them, with the consequences of it, are related in xxii. Then we
are made acquainted with the addresses delivered by Joshua to
the assembled people, with the renewing of the covenant consequent thereupon, xxiii.1–xxiv.28. The Book is closed with a
short account about the death of Joshua and Eleazar, and the
burying of Joseph's bones, xxiv.29–33.

CHAPTER XXV.

THE BOOK OF JOSHUA COMPILED FROM DIFFERENT DOCUMENTS LONG AFTER THE CONQUEST OF THE LAND.

164. If the result of our examination into the composition of
the Pentateuch awakens already the suspicion that the Book of

Joshua is just as little from one hand as it is contemporary with the events related in it, this suspicion is raised to certainty by a careful inspection of the Book itself. For the compilation of the Book out of more than one document may be urged—besides the express quotation from the 'Book of Jashar,' x.13,—

(i) The obscurity of some narratives, iii,iv,viii, which can only be explained from the fact that they are composed out of written documents, which are at variance with each other; [264]

(ii) The difference of view, which is observed to exist between the historical and the geographical parts of the Book, especially with reference to the extent and completeness of Joshua's conquests; [265]

(iii) The difference of phraseology. [266]

165. The idea, that this Book was written during the lifetime of Joshua, [267] or shortly afterwards, is at once irreconcilable with the difference of documents above indicated. Besides, as is generally admitted, the Book of Joshua supposes the existence of the Pentateuch and, perhaps, in its present form, (Chap.XXVI,) which in itself would be quite sufficient to contradict that idea. Lastly, it is contradicted both by the repeated use of the formula 'unto this day,' iv.9,v.9,vi.25,vii.26,viii.28,29, ix.27,x.27,xiii,13,xiv.14,xv.63,xvi.10, from which it appears that, between the lifetime of the writer and the events related in Joshua, there lay a considerable interval of time, [268]—and by x.13, from which passage, comp. with 2S.i.18, it follows that the author knew and used a collection of songs, which could only first have come into existence under or after David's reign. [269] The passages, to which appeal is made for the maintenance of the high antiquity of this Book, fail in the power of proof ascribed to them, or afford arguments only for the earlier origin of some portions of the Book, from which nothing can be inferred with reference to the whole. [270]

CHAPTER XXVI.

THE CLOSE CONNECTION BETWEEN THE PENTATEUCH AND THE BOOK OF JOSHUA.

166. THE close connection between the Pentateuch and the Book of Joshua appears in the plainest manner from the contents as well as the form. Not only is the story taken up in Jo.i.1, which was broken off in D.xxxiv,—not only are the actions of Moses, as lawgiver and leader of the people, everywhere implied, and frequently described in the very words of the Pentateuch,[271]—but it may even be asserted, that this latter is incomplete without the Book of Joshua, and is brought to a conclusion, as it were, by the help of that Book. Whereas, for instance, in the Pentateuch the settlement of Israel in Canaan is announced repeatedly, both in Genesis and in the other Books, and is regarded as the actual fulfilment of the Divine promises,[272] so, on the other hand, the Book of Joshua represents the conquest of the land as the realisation of the assurances of Jehovah to the Patriarchs and to Moses.[273]

167. Hence between the Pentateuch and Joshua there exists the same connection as between a prophecy and the account of its fulfilment. Add to this also—

(i) That the whole Book, especially the historical Part, is manifestly intended to exhibit the consequences, rich in blessing, of the faithful observance of the Mosaic prescriptions, in the example of Joshua and Israel fighting under his command; so that a *hortatory* tendency must be ascribed to it, and, indeed, one quite in the spirit of the Pentateuch, especially of Deuteronomy; [274]—

(ii) That some portions of the Book, especially all which has reference to the partition of the land, the designation of the free cities, and the dwelling-places of the Priests and Levites, xiii-xxi, can and must be regarded as prescriptions of the Law, with as much right as many a chapter of the Pentateuch, *e.g.* N.xxxiv.

168. These phenomena, regarded in themselves, are sufficiently explained on the supposition that the writer of Joshua not only knew and used the Pentateuch, but also wrought with the express object of supplementing it. Since, however, it is now certain that the Book of Joshua, as well as the Pentateuch, is compiled out of different documents, the suspicion arises that the connection and agreement between the two writings must be explained from the use of common sources. This suspicion is entirely confirmed by the phraseology, views, and ideas, which characterise the different parts of Joshua, compared with those of the documents of the Pentateuch. It follows from this, in fact, that a not unimportant portion of the Book is derived from the hand of the writer of Deuteronomy, Chap.XXVII, while another portion must have belonged to the Book of Origins, Chap.XXVIII. Finally, the whole composition of the Book makes it probable that the Compiler is no other than that of the Pentateuch, Chap.XXIX.

CHAPTER XXVII.

THE DEUTERONOMISTIC PORTIONS OF THE BOOK OF JOSHUA.

169. THE first twelve chapters of Joshua not only treat of one sole subject, the conquest of the land of Caanan, but are also so closely connected with each other that they must be regarded as the work of one and the same author, who, though he had before him written accounts,[264] yet so manipulated these that his narrative formed a well-connected whole. This appears not only from the continually-recurring use of the same phrases and

terms of speech,[275] but from the references made by one narrative to another.[276] A careful comparison of these chapters with
the Book of Deuteronomy leads to the conclusion that their
author is no other than the Deuteronomist, who, however, in
the composition of his narrative must have availed himself of
written documents much more than in Deuteronomy itself. Yet
also in the second half of Joshua passages are inserted from his
hand, as xxi.41–43,xxii.1–xxiv.28, it being understood that here
also, especially in xxii and xxiv.1–28, he does not narrate altogether independently, but attaches himself to written records.

170. The proof of this position is contained in the following
remarks :—

(i) The aforesaid chapters in Joshua are full of Deuteronomistic formulæ and terms of expression. These are met with
especially in those portions of the narrative in which the author
had an opportunity of bringing out his own proper style of writing,
e.g. in the transitions and in the addresses, e.g. Jo.i and Jo.xxiii.
They exhibit so very strongly the proper characteristics of that
style, that they cannot be explained from mere imitation.[277]

(ii) Again, the few expressions occurring in the above-named
chapters, which are looked for in vain in Deuteronomy,[278] are
either of so little significance, that they cannot be produced
to prove a difference of authorship,[279] or they can be explained by the writer's dependence upon written documents,
which appears also plainly, now and then, from the character of
the narrative itself.[280] This dependence is so little a proof
against the Deuteronomistic origin of 1–xii,xxi.41–xxiv.28, that
we should rather wonder if we did not observe it. It is, in fact,
nothing more than natural that the Deuteronomist—who, as we
have seen[218-225], lived under Manasseh's reign—knew and used
written records about the conquest of the land. Here and there
the phraseology appears to show that the Book of Origins also
belonged to the written records which he used.[281]

171. If it is once for all certain that Deuteronomy and

Jo.1–xii,xxi.41–xxiv.28 are from one and the same hand, it then becomes very probable that they also belong to the same whole, or, in other words, that the Deuteronomist wrote the account of the Mosaic Legislation and the conquest of Canaan by Joshua in an independent work. This conjecture is confirmed by the manifestly obvious purpose of the account of the conquest and of the last transactions of Joshua. The Deuteronomist evidently desired to sketch in him, and in Israel fighting under his command, an image of faithful observance of the Law, and to set in a clear light its consequences full of blessing.[282] How thoroughly this object is in agreement with the tendency of the Deuteronomistic Legislation itself [58,225], is at once obvious.

CHAPTER XXVIII.

THE PORTIONS OF JOSHUA DERIVED FROM THE BOOK OF ORIGINS.

172. THAT the Book of Origins also contained an account of the settlement of Israel in Canaan is in itself probable[81,83] (see Chap.XV), and is confirmed by the traces of the phraseology of that Book, which we observe in the Deuteronomistic portions of Joshua.[281] The prophetical part of Joshua raises this probability to certainty. What remains, in fact, in the Book of Joshua, after removal of the Deuteronomistic portions, is, for a large part, derived from the Book of Origins, —in particular, xiv–xvii,xviii.11–xix.51,xx.7–xxi.40, — while xiii,xviii.1–10,xx. 1–6, xxiv.29–33 must, not indeed entirely, yet certainly in part, have been taken over from the aforesaid Book.

173. It seems, in fact—

(i) That these passages are not from the hand of the Deuteronomist, inasmuch as they are characterised both by a different phraseology,[283] and by different ideas as to the extent of Joshua's conquests.[284]

(ii) That their contents agree entirely with the well-known legislative tendency of the Book of Origins, in which already, in an earlier place, the boundaries of Canaan, N.xxxiv.1–15, the partition of the land, N.xxxiv.16–29, the designation of the Levitical towns and free cities, N.xxxv, were previously written; to which prescriptions the definition of the territory of each tribe, Jo.xiv–xvii,xviii.10–xix.51, and the enumeration of the Levitical towns and free cities, Jo.xx.7, xxi.40, very naturally attach themselves[285];

(iii) That in the narrative itself the partition of the land is continually referred back to the directions of the Book of Origins[286];

(iv) That the peculiar phraseology of the Book of Origins recurs in the aforesaid passages, as well as the same kind of subjects that led to the use of it.[287]

174. Further, it is not only possible, but even probable, that the author of the Book of Origins, in the composition of his account about the partition of the land, availed himself of written documents,[288] and that, in particular, Jo.xvii.14–18,—perhaps also Jo.xiv.6–15,—is derived from such a document.[289] The same conjecture might be applied to those passages which the geographical part of Joshua has in common with the Book of Judges; comp. Jo.xv.13–19 with Ju. i.10–15, Jo.xv.63 with Ju.i.21, Jo.xvi.10 with Ju.i.29, Jo.xvii.12,13, with Ju.i.27,28, Jo.xix.47 with Ju.xvii,xviii.[290] Yet, for various reasons, it is probable that all these passages belong not to the Book of Origins, but have been inserted in the Book of Joshua by the compiler, and that he derived them, not from the Book of Judges which we now possess, but from one of the documents out of which that Book is composed.[291]

175. In connection with the result of our former enquiry as to the age of the Book of Origins, Chap.XIV,XXI, it is a very

important question whether the portions of the said documents, which we meet with in the Book of Joshua, must be assigned to the oldest or original portions of it, or to those afterwards added. This question cannot be answered with certainty. Against the high antiquity and, consequently, against the originality of the accounts about the partition of the land, xiv–xix, well-founded difficulties can just as little be alleged as against that of iv.19,v.10–12 [280,281]. On the other hand, the list of the Levitical towns, xxi.1–40 [42], is probably a later portion of the Book of Origins, as is the narrative, which lies at the basis of xxii.[292] We have thus to conclude that the second portion also of the Book of Origins, which is concerned with the conquest and partition of Canaan, was from time to time retouched and expanded, and so kept in agreement with the first part, which remains preserved to us in the Pentateuch.

CHAPTER XXIX.

THE COMPILER OF THE BOOK OF JOSHUA, AND THE CREDIBILITY OF HIS NARRATIVE.

176. ACCORDING to the usual views,[293] the Deuteronomist was not only the author of i–xii,xxi.41–43 [43–45], xxii.1–xxiv.28, but also the compiler of the whole Book of Joshua. Against this view, however, there exist various objections :—

(i) It is not probable that the Deuteronomist adopted into his work about Moses and Joshua the passages assigned above to the Book of Origins, inasmuch as they both fit in less appropriately into the plan of that work, and are more or less at variance with the accounts therein given. We find, in fact, in the Deuteronomistic passages of Joshua, not a single proof that they were designed by the writer himself to make one whole with the accounts of the Book of Origins ;[294]

(ii) xxiv. 29–33 is certainly not Deuteronomistic; if the Deuteronomist had been the compiler of the whole Book, he would not surely have left out the conclusion of his own work, and set in place of it another document; it is, at all events, more probable that another collector has done this ;[295]

(iii) In xiii,xviii.1–10,xx.1–6, phenomena present themselves which are simply and naturally explained by the supposition that the compiler, *distinct from the Deuteronomist,* combined thus with one another the documents in his hands, and worked them into one whole.[296]

177. If it appears from the above that we have every reason to ascribe the final editing of Joshua to a compiler distinct from the Deuteronomist, it follows also from this that his work was almost confined to merely taking over the documents which he had before him, and that he very seldom appears as an independent narrator.   Only in xiii,xviii.1–13,xx.1–6, he has worked freely the historical matter, and has added also besides, in xv,xvi,xvii,xix, some notes to his documents.

178. Since not only the Book of Origins, but also the work of the Deuteronomist, treated of the conquest and the partition of Canaan as well as the history of the Mosaic time, Chap.XXVII, XXVIII, it was very natural that the compiler of the Pentateuch, who knew and used both the aforesaid writings, should have followed this their example, or, in other words, should have added to the Pentateuch a Book of Joshua composed out of the same sources.   In point of fact there exist no difficulties of any importance against the conjecture that the compiler of Joshua is not different from the compiler of the Pentateuch.[297]

179. With respect to the credibility of this Book, some remarks have been already made,[282,291] which must be yet further extended.   The more limited, for instance, was the independent activity of the compiler, the more does the value of his writing depend on the character and antiquity of his documents.   Hence it follows that the Deuteronomistic portions can

by no means be put on the same line with the Book of Origins. The last-named, with exception of xxi.1–40 [42], comp. note[292], gives us completely credible and important contributions towards the physical and political geography of Canaan, without, however, our having any certain assurance that the locations of the tribes were *already in Joshua's time* exactly so defined, as the author here describes them on the basis of the state of things which he knew by his own observation.[298]

180. Just, however, as the priestly character of the Book of Origins has from the first acted unfavourably on the contents of xxi.1–40 [42], so must also the credibility of the Deuteronomistic narrative, i-xii,xxi.41 [43]—xxiv.28, necessarily be affected by the obviously hortatory object of the author. With the same freedom, wherewith the Deuteronomist treated of the Mosaic time,[225] he worked up also the historical traditions and documents about Joshua's performances.[283][274] Probably, others had already preceded him in sketching an ideal representation respecting Joshua's contemporaries, and some truth also lay at the foundation of it.[299] Yet it is so strongly coloured by the Deuteronomist, that not only its hortatory purpose plainly strikes the eye, but also its unhistorical character cannot be denied.[300]   Hence follows this rule: The Deuteronomistic narrative of the conquest of the land deserves most credence in those particulars where it depends manifestly on older documents; whereas, on the other hand, the particulars, in which the purpose of the whole comes out strongly, are also more or less suspicious.[301]

NOTES.

CHAPTER I.

(2)   [1] Δευτερονόμιον is the translation in D.xvii 18, Jo.viii.32, of מִשְׁנֵה הַתּוֹרָה *i.e.* properly, 'a *copy* of the Law.' But the LXX in both places understand a '*repetition*' of the Law,' [D.xvii.18, Καὶ γράψει αὐτῷ τὸ δευτερονόμιον τοῦτο εἰς βιβλίον, Jo.viii.32, Καὶ ἔγραψεν Ἰησοῦς ἐπὶ τῶν λίθων τὸ δευτερονόμιον νόμον Μωυσῆ,] in which sense also this inscription of the Book must be understood.

(3)   [2] It is well known that the different sections of the narrative begin usually with the formula, 'These are the generations (תּוֹלְדֹת) &c.' It appears in G.ii.4,v.1,vi.9,x.1,xi.10,27,xxv.12,19,xxxvi.1,9,xxxvii.2, and besides it occurs also in N.iii.1, R.iv.18. If we connect, as the contents allow, G.i.1–ii.3 with ii.4–iv.26, [as forming one complete section of the history,] and xxxvi.1–8 with xxxvi.9–xxxvii.1, then the whole book of Genesis contains ten *tholedoth*.

(5)   [3] Subscriptions of this kind occur, besides the places mentioned in the text, in L.xi.46,47,xiii.59,xiv.54–57,xv.32,33.

CHAPTER II.

(9)   [4] Consult, among others, Hengst.*Beitr*,iii.p.149–178,Häv.I.i.p.15–27,Del.p.23, &c. Riehm,p.106–116, Schultz,p.87–97.

(10)   [5] The Greek and Arabic translators—the only ones, who were able to express the article—omit it in E.xvii.14, and read בְּסֵפֶר, 'in *a* Book,' [not בַּסֵּפֶר, 'in *the* Book.'] In fact, this reading appears to deserve the preference above the Masoretic. If, however, the article here is to be retained, then it may be explained in the same way as in N.v.23, [where we read, with reference to the curses pronounced in the 'trial of jealousy' over a woman suspected by her husband of adultery, 'And the Priest shall write these curses in *the* book.'] The supposition, that mention is

here made of a book of larger extent, which Moses had already begun to write, is not in the least degree justified. Comp. D.xxv.17-19, from which passage we see the meaning of the words in E.xvii.14, 'Write *this* for a *memorial* in a Book.'

⁶ And *not* the Ten Commandments, which on the contrary, according to *v.*1, were written down by Jehovah Himself. Hence in *v.*28 Jehovah is the subject of the verb, 'and he wrote.' Comp. BERTH.p.90-99, KURTZ,ii.p.322-325, KNOB. E.L.p.327,328.

(11)   ⁷ So, in the main, RIEHM and SCHULTZ. On the other hand, it is maintained by HENGST.iii.p.153-166, KEIL,§33, and others, that Moses, according to D.xxxi.9, first wrote down all that precedes, and delivered it to the Priests. This 'delivery,' however, according to them, must have been only symbolical, so that he afterwards received the Book back, and recorded in it the account of the solemn act, which extends to xxxi.23. What then follows, from *v.*24 onwards, is an addition, written shortly after Moses's death, wherein first the final 'delivery' of the Pentateuch is recorded, *v.*24-30,—then the 'Song of Moses,' xxxii, with a note appended, *v.*44-52, —then the 'Blessing of Moses,' xxxiii,—lastly, the account of his death, xxxiv. But, irrespective of the difficulty which xxxiv.10-12[1] raises against this account of the matter, it is untenable for these reasons:—

(i) It is not proved and it is not probable, that the first 'delivery' of 'this Law' must have been symbolical;

(ii) There is no indication,—not even from the words in xxxi.24, 'Moses made an end of writing the words of this Law in a Book, *until they were finished,*'—that with this verse a different writer comes forward;

(iii) On the contrary, the language and style in xxxi.24-30,xxxii.44-47, are exactly the same as in the preceding chapters.

(iv) To this it must be added, that the passages cited above, which imply the previous existence of 'this Book' or 'this Book of the Law,' cannot be thus explained. ⁸

(12)   ⁸ The idea, that the formula 'this Law' must denote the whole Pentateuch (defended by SCHULTZ, p.91-93) is based upon the unproved assumption, that the Book of Deuteronomy never existed separately, nor ever can have existed apart from the rest. It is thus left out of sight that the second principal section, v-xxviii, is concluded with these words, xxix.1, 'These are the words of the Covenant, which Jehovah commanded Moses to make with the children of Israel in the land of Moab, *beside the Covenant which He made with them in Horeb.*' From this passage it follows,—not only that 'this *Covenant,*' xxix.9,14, is not the Covenant of Sinai, but that made in the land of Moab, [the Deuteronomistic Covenant,] but also—that the exactly corresponding expression, 'this Law,' denotes the Deuteronomistic Law. Accordingly, I do not hesitate to assume this reference—not only in the above-cited places, where the connection requires it, but also—generally, wherever the formula occurs,

---

1 Add also xxxiv.6 'But no man knoweth of his sepulchre unto this day.' *Ed.*

2 If, *e.g.* as HENGSTENBERG supposes, Moses wrote down the discourses contained in i.1-xxxi.8, only *after* he had delivered them, how can we account for his referring to 'the words of this Law, written in this Book,' &c., in the midst of these very discourses, as in xxviii.58,61,xxix.20,21,27,xxx.10. *Ed.*

xvii.18,19, xxviii.58,61, xxix.29, xxxi.11,12, xxxii.46. An objection to this has been drawn from xxxi.10–13, [where Moses commands that 'this Law' shall be 'read before all Israel,' 'at the end of every seven years, in the solemnity of the year of release, in the Feast of Tabernacles ;'] and it has been maintained that the Jews have always understood this direction, as enjoining the reading the *whole Thora*, not Deuteronomy alone. But—

(i) This does not appear from Neh.viii, for this simple reason, that the 'reading' there mentioned did *not* take place as here enjoined, at the *Feast of Tabernacles* (KEIL on HÄV.I.ii.p.26) :—

(ii) Still less does it appear from Neh.ix.3, (KEIL, as before,) since—even allowing that other portions also of the Pentateuch were then read, which, however, does not appear,—the Feast of Tabernacles mentioned in this passage is not said to have been kept in the *year of release*, of which alone mention is made in D.xxxi.10 ;

(iii) The authority of JOSEPHUS, *Ant.*IV.viii.12, in case it should be regarded as excluding our view, is entirely set aside by the Talmudical directions, which DELITZSCH produces, p.24,25;

(iv) Even supposing that the Jews had understood D.xxxi.10–13 as speaking of a reading of the whole Law,—as was very natural, after that the five Books were connected into one whole,—it would not at all follow, that this was the intention of *the writer himself* ; whereas his intention, with which alone we are here concerned, appears plainly enough from the passages above-quoted.

(13)   * The last-named supposition is considered by many to be at variance at once both with the character of the Bible and with the reverence due to it. We shall return to this point. Comp. VETH in the *Bijb. Woordenboek voor het Christelijk Gezin*,ii.592–593, and my remarks in the *Godg. Bijdragen* of 1856,p.63–67.

CHAPTER III.

(14)   ¹⁰ This is denied by HENGST.,p.173–178, who appeals to the context in order to show that this commendation rests on good grounds and is exactly in its proper place. This, however, may be granted, without its therefore following that it is becoming when placed in the mouth of Moses himself. Even KURTZ,ii.p.380–382, sees in N.xii.3 a proof that Moses did not write the whole Pentateuch.

(15)   ¹¹ According to the passages here quoted Amram, the father of Moses, was a grandson of Levi, and Jochebed, his mother, was Levi's daughter. See especially N.xxvi.59, (where the name of Levi's wife has dropped-out or has not been filled-in,) and E.vi.20, where Jochebed is called the aunt of Amram. Either these genealogies are extremely defective, which, however, would be strange if a contemporary, and, above all, if Moses himself, had recorded them, or the Israelites did not remain in Egypt during 430 years (see E.xii.40, according to the Masoretic text), or even during the half of that time (see LXX,Sam.Text). From the great number of the Israelites at the Exodus, E.xii.37, N.i.46, &c., in connection with G.xlvi.27, with

the genealogies above considered, and with the duration of the sojourn in Egypt, arise other difficulties, which are utterly inexplicable on the supposition, that the Pentateuch is the work of a credible contemporary. See COLENSO *On the Pentateuch*, Part I.

[12] In the second year after the Exodus, on the twentieth day of the second month N.x.11, Israel departs out of the wilderness of Sinai. Yet in this same year, xiv.34, falls the sending-out of the spies with its consequences, N.xiii,xiv. Now, if the 'first month' in N.xx.1,—'The Israelites came into the wilderness of Zin *in the first month*,'—is regarded as the first month of the fortieth year after the Exodus, then we are told nothing out of the thirty-seven years of the wanderings, except the rebellion of Korah, &c., and the confirmation of Aaron in the dignity of high-priest, N.xvi,xvii, with which event the laws in N.xviii are to some extent connected, but those in N.xv,xix, not at all. EWALD, however, BUNSEN, and, lastly, also BLEEK,p.163, 164,222,223, maintain that the 'first month' in N.xx.1, [where mention is first made of the people dwelling in Kadesh,]—both because no express year is named, and also on account of D.ii.14, 'and the space in which we came *from* Kadesh-Barnea, until we were come over the brook Zered, was thirty-and-eight years,'—must be regarded as the 'first month' of the *third* year after the Exodus. But, certainly, the death of Aaron, recorded in N.xx.22–29, falls in the *fortieth* year, N.xxxiii.38; so that, according to this view, between two consecutive verses of N.xx—*viz. v.*21, 22, or, perhaps, *v.*13,14,—an interval of *thirty-seven* years is not only passed by in silence, but is absolutely not even indicated. Does it not here appear most manifestly, that we have before us no narrative of contemporaries or eyewitnesses, but a very incomplete account of a writer, who lived long after Moses? This inference remains valid, whichever of the two explanations of N.xx.1 is assumed to be true. The difficulty is not removed but increased, if KNOB. *N.D.J.*p.102–103, and elsewhere, rightly maintains, that we have here to do with a discrepancy between the documents of the Pentateuch themselves; so that the author of N.xx.1 makes the Israelites *return back* to Kadesh, while according to D.i.46,ii.14, they stayed there once only, and that in the second year after the Exodus.

(16) [13] Comp. note [12]. From what is there said, it appears that the difference between the interpreters has, in fact, its foundation in the doubtful meaning of the text—if not in the mutual difference between the portions of the Pentateuch, which, naturally, in the process of being combined into one whole, must have given occasion to indistinctness of expression.

[14] Comp. N.xxxiii.40, a still more enigmatical notice. It does not appear how the King of Arad could hear that 'Israel came by the way of the spies,' N.xxi.1, when the people, according to N.xx.22, had already left Kadesh, and removed from the neighbourhood of Canaan. Also *v.*3, 'Israel utterly destroyed them and their cities, and [one] called *the place* Hormah,' is very obscure—in connection, especially, with N.xiv.45, D.i.44, Ju.i.17.

(17) [15] The first mention of 'Wars of Jehovah' could only occur after Israel had waged war against the inhabitants of the trans-Jordanic land, against the Canaanites and the neighbouring nations. The need of a collection of songs and narratives, referring to these wars, was not felt at the time, when the people were busied

in waging them, but at a later period, when they began to look back upon them with thankfulness. Hᴇɴɢsᴛ.iii.p.223–226, extends the idea 'Wars of Jehovah' by referring to E.xiv.14,25, 'Jehovah shall fight for you,' xv.3, 'Jehovah is a man of war,' xii.41, 'the hosts of Jehovah,' xii.51,N.xxxiii.1,' by their hosts'; and he supposes further that all events of this kind, during the march through the wilderness, were recorded in the order in which they followed each other, so that the whole collection arose by degrees. How improbable this is, is obvious.

CHAPTER IV.

(18) ᴹ From the above it follows that we shall not speak here of passages such as G.xxiv.34–48, comp. v.1–27, or G.xli.17–24, comp. v.1–8,—still less of such as D.i.6–iv.40, where Moses, in his first address to Israel, reminds them of the events in the wilderness, and so naturally, as a rule, repeats, what had been already mentioned in the previous books, especially in Exodus and Numbers. It must not be denied, however, that the variations in D.i.6–iv.40 are in some cases remarkable, and can only be explained in a very forced way on the supposition, that the three Books have one and the same author.

(i) We read, for instance, in D.i.20–23, that Moses, after their arrival at Kadesh, in the second year after the Exodus, gave command for the invasion of Canaan, but *upon a general request of the people* sent out spies first; while in N.xiii.1,2, it is recorded only that Jehovah commanded him to send out spies, [and in v.3, that he 'sent them by the commandment of Jehovah,'] without any mention either of the preceding command for the invasion, or of the request of the people.

(ii) In D.i.37,iii.26,iv.21, the fact is continually placed in the foreground that Jehovah was angry with Moses *on account of the Israelites*, by reason of their perverse conduct; whereas the cause of God's displeasure, according to N.xxvii.12–14, xx.12, lies only in the unbelief, or, it may be said, the impatience, of Moses. It is strange, at any rate, that no mention should be made of this just exactly in an address of Moses himself.

(iii) In N.xx.14–21, Israel asks twice for permission to march through the territory of Edom; and this request is twice very positively refused, and answered with a threat of avowed opposition: whereas in D.ii.4–8 there is given a Divine command, that Israel should refrain from warring with 'their brethren,' the Edomites, or troubling them in any way; they must buy from them meat and water, &c., which the Edomites, v.29, readily supplied. Even if, as Hᴇɴɢsᴛ. maintains, iii. 283, &c. a different fact is mentioned in D.ii.4–8 from that in N.xx.14–21,—*viz.* one which occurred on the *eastern* border of Edom, whereas N.xx removes us to the *western*,—it still remains very strange that in Numbers the *evil* deeds only, in Deuteronomy the *good* deeds only, of the Edomites are mentioned. Since, however, the Deuteronomistic Legislation, xxiii.7,8, betrays a favourable state of feeling with respect to the Edomites, it becomes highly probable that the narrator allows himself to represent the conduct of Edom otherwise than it has been exhibited in N.xx.

In other words, if, from the mere fact, that in D.i–iv events already mentioned are *repeated*, it by no means follows that in this passage we have another narrator, different from the author of Exodus and Numbers, yet the variations, by which the repetitions are marked, make it very improbable that they proceed from the same hand as the foregoing narratives.

If this conclusion is established, then the same judgment must also be pronounced about some other passages, *e.g.* about D.i.9–18, comp. E.xviii, and about D.x.6,7, comp. N.xx.23,xxxiii.31–33, although it may be admitted that the attempts to reconcile these [latter] passages, by Kᴇɪʟ.,§29, and the writers there cited, are not unhappy, and, if we did not know from other quarters the freedom of the Deuteronomist, might seem worthy of acceptance.

[17] We confine ourselves here, and in notes [18,19], to producing some plain examples; since here it is above all necessary to lay the foundation firmly, on which to build hereafter, Chap.XI. &c. Some of the double accounts are mere repetitions; yet by far the greater number are of such a kind, that one of the two excludes the other.

(i) This is true at once of G.ii.4^b–23 compared with G.i.1–ii.4^a. The second account of the Creation begins with the formation of the *man*, v.7, mentions then the creation of trees and plants, v.8,9, of beasts, v.19, and lastly that of the *woman*, v.21,22. It is, consequently, no mere supplement or recapitulation of the first, but an entirely new account, which sets out from different views. Comp. Hᴜᴘꜰ. p.109, &c. Bᴜɴs.i.p.cxlii–cxlvii.

(ii) In xi.10–17 we have the genealogy of Shem to Peleg repeated once more, although it has been already inserted in x.22–25.

(iii) After that the overthrow of Sodom and Gomorrah and the deliverance of Lot has been related at full length in xix.1–28, the same fact is again mentioned in v.29 briefly, but quite completely.

(iv) The origin of the name 'Beersheba' is twice explained,—first, xxi.31, from a covenant made by Abraham with Abimelech,—again, xxvi.32,33, from a like covenant made by Isaac with Abimelech.

(v) So, too, the name 'Bethel' is derived from two different facts,—first, xxviii. 10–19, from the vision, which happened to Jacob in his flight to Mesopotamia,—again, xxxv.15, from a theophany, which occurred after his return.

(vi) Jacob receives the name 'Israel,'—first, in the nightly 'wrestling' by the 'Jabbok,' xxxii.24–32,—again, after his return, at Bethel, xxxv.10.

(vii) Whereas the settlement of Esau in Seir is implied in xxxii.3–6,xxxiii.1–3,14 16, and, according to the context of these passages, is regarded as contemporary with Jacob's sojourn in Mesopotamia, we read in xxxvi.6,7, that Esau with all his house and his whole property, which he had acquired *in the land of Canaan*, went to Seir 'from the face of his brother Jacob; *for their riches were more than that they might dwell together; and the land of their sojournings was not able to bear them because of their cattle.*' If these words have any meaning, they imply that the settlement in Seir did not take place till after the return of Jacob.

(viii) In xxvi.34,xxviii.9, we have two accounts about the wives of Esau, which supplement each other, (see also xxvii.46.) But we have besides a third, xxxvi. 2,3, which differs from both the former. There have not been wanting attempts to reconcile these passages with each other, just as in the cases of the other passages above-mentioned. As an example I give the most important, that of Hengst.iii. p.273-278: to mention them all is superfluous, since, though differing much from each other, yet they all exhibit the same characteristics, and the contradiction of one involves that of all the others. The three wives of Esau are named—

xxvi.34,xxviii.9	xxxvi.2,3
Judith, daughter of Beeri the Hittite	Adah, daughter of Elon the Hittite
Bashemath, daughter of Elon the Hittite	Aholibamah, daughter of Anah, daughter of Zibeon the Hivite
Mahalath, daughter of Ishmael	Bashemath, daughter of Ishmael

The points of agreement and difference are well exhibited by Knob. *Gen*.p.278. Hengst., then, tries first to show that '*Anah* the daughter of Zibeon the *Hivite*' is the same as '*Beeri* the *Hittite*.' As usual, he supposes that 'daughter (בַּת) of Zibeon' is an error of transcription for 'son (בֶּן) of Zibeon.' And now Anah, the son of Zibeon we are told, *v*.24, 'found in the wilderness, as he fed the asses of Zibeon his father,' the *hot-springs* (הַיֵּמִם) E.V.' mules'; thence he acquired the name (בְּאֵרִי), *i.e.* 'man of the well.' The same Anah, however, is called a *Horite* in *v*.20,29, whereas in *v*.2 he is called a *Hivite*, and, supposing him to be the same as Beeri, he is called also a *Hittite*, xxvi.34. Yet even here Hengst. sees no discrepancy. It is generally assumed that in xxxvi.2, instead of (הַחִוִּי) 'the Hivite,' must be read (הַחֹרִי), 'the Horite. But even this conjecture, he says, is unnecessary. Anah was properly a *Hivite*, but is called *Horite* in *v*.20,29, because he belonged to the Troglodytes [people living in caves] = Horites [from חֹור, 'a cave']. And, whereas in xxvi.34 he is called a *Hittite*, this name must not be considered here as being the name of a particular *tribe*, but as the *general* name of all the Canaanites; comp. Jo.i.4, 1K.x.29, 2K.vii.6, Ez.xvi.3. Thus there remains no other difference except that the names of the three wives do not agree; *Judith* is called *Aholibamah*, *Bashemath* is named *Adah*, and, lastly, *Mahalath* becomes *Bashemath*. But what is more natural? In the East it is very usual for women to change their names, especially when they enter the married life: the alteration of all the three names proves clearly that this has been the case also with Esau's wives.

If this demonstration requires any contradiction, it may be noted as follows:—

(i) One who discovers 'hot springs,' can hardly on that account obtain the surname 'Beeri'; for בְּאֵר, *Běer*, is a (dug) *pit*, not a (natural) *spring*. The surname, therefore, does not at all agree with the fact, with which it is said to be connected.

(ii) Allowing that in xxvi.34 *Hittite* may be a general name, for which more accurately *Hivite* should be said, we are not at liberty to regard this last name as identical with *Horite*. *Horim* is always a Proper Name, and cannot be explained to mean 'cave-dwellers.' Horites and Hivites have nothing in common with each other: on the contrary, the first stand in the O.T. always in the same line with *Avim, Emim, Zamzummim*; and, just as these aboriginal inhabitants of Canaan must have disappeared before the Canaanites, so must also the Horim before Edom. Comp. G.xxxvi.20, D.ii.12,22. 'Hivite Horites' there have never been: the name involves a contradiction in terms.

(iii) Allowing that Esau's wives might have changed their names, can it then

· be assumed that *Mahalath*, Ishmael's daughter, at her marriage with Esau, took the very same name *Bashemath*, which Elon's daughter, now called Adah, bore before her marriage?

But enough : it is not necessary for our purpose to assume—however plain this also appears to me—that the double accounts are *irreconcileable*. Their points of *difference* show at once that they are *not from one hand*, [?] DBL.p.505 ; and that is all which concerns us here.

[18] HENGST.iii.346, says: 'We shall in this enquiry direct our attention less upon Genesis, especially upon the first eleven chapters of that Book, than on the other Books. It may be supposed that Moses found contradictions in the history of the older time, and, without removing them, repeated the tradition as he received it. On the contrary, where Moses relates what he himself has said, done, and experienced, *there* every real contradiction appears as an evidence against the genuineness of the record.'

[19] (i) The father-in-law of Moses is called 'Raguel,' in E.ii.18,—'Jethro,' in iii.1,iv.18,xviii.1,2, &c. (for 'Jether' in iv.18 must be thus read)—'Hobab,' [the son of Raguel,] in N.x.29. There has been no want of efforts to reconcile these accounts: see especially *Bijb. Woord.*ii.121,122. If, however, they had come from one hand, then the variation would not exist at all, or, at least, the way to an explanation would be plainly indicated.

(ii) After the name Jehovah has been revealed to Moses, and its meaning explained, in E.iii.14,15, there follows in vi.2–4 a second communication of the same name.

(iii) In xxxv–xl the building of the Tabernacle, according to the directions given in xxv, &c., is related at full length. But before this, xxxiii.7–11, mention is made of a *tent*, erected outside the camp, and called the 'Tent of Testimony,' [E.V. 'Tabernacle of the Congregation,'] exactly as the Tabernacle is called in xxxv. 21, &c. Some have, indeed, maintained that in xxxiii the tent of Moses is meant ; but this conjecture is not supported by the text. Comp. KNOB.*E.L.*p.321,322, and Chap.V of this work.

[20] (i) Aaron's death is related in N.xx.22–29, and a second time in xxxiii.38,39.

(ii) The idolatry of Israel, practised with the Midianitish women,—according to *v.*1, with the 'daughters of Moab,'—is related in N.xxv. Then Moses receives a command, *v.*16–18, to punish the Midianites for this, and the punishment actually takes place in xxxi.1–3. In the battle, the Israelites kill Balaam with the sword, *v.*8 ; and afterwards Moses reminds them, as of a well-known fact, that the Midianitish women, *according to the word* (? by the advice) *of Balaam*, had induced the Israelites to the practice of idolatry, *v.*16. Nothing is said in xxv of that 'word' of Balaam. On the contrary, the long circumstantial account about Balaam in xxii–xxiv is concluded with the words, '*and Balaam rose up, and went, and returned to his place*,' xxiv.25, comp. xxii.5,—which account leaves no room either for the advice to the Midianites, or for Balaam's death in the battle against Midian.

CHAPTER V.

0) [21] Comp. Raw.,p.81,82.

[22] We confine ourselves also here to producing and illustrating a few examples: see note [17].

(i) The origin, progress, and immediate consequences of the flood are related in G.vi.1–ix.17. That this narrative is compiled out of two different original documents, appears from the following facts.

(α) The corruption of mankind, and the displeasure of Jehovah at it, are recorded and explained in vi.1–8, and yet again afterwards, v.9–13. The difference between the two accounts appears not only from the repetition, but also from the very peculiar statement of the cohabiting of the 'sons of God' (i.e. the angels) with the 'daughters of men,' v.1–4, of which the other document, v.11,12, knows nothing.

(β) In vi.19,20, God commands that Noah should take with him into the Ark two examples of each kind of animal, a male and a female, as actually takes place, vii.8,9,14,16. On the other hand, in vii.2,3, the command runs differently; of the unclean animals he must take with him *one* pair, but of the clean animals *seven* pairs. This last, however, is not merely *not mentioned* in vi.19,20,vii.8,9,14, 15, but is even expressly contradicted.

(γ) At the end of the Flood, Jehovah, according to one account, viii.20–22, upon the occasion of Noah's sacrifice, swore by Himself never again to destroy all things living, nor to disturb the course of nature. According to the other account, ix.1–17, God blessed Noah, established a covenant with him, and promised solemnly that no second Flood should destroy the earth.

(ii) A second example is given us in the history of Joseph, G.xxxvii,xxxix,xl, as has latterly been shown, especially by Hupf.,p.65–71. Two accounts lie here at the foundation of the narrative. According to one, Joseph, by the advice of *Reuben*, was thrown into a pit, but, while his brothers ate bread, was [taken up and] stolen by *Midianitish* merchants, carried to Egypt, and sold to Potiphar, an eunuch of Pharaoh, who, being captain of the body-guard, was at the same time keeper of the prisoners, G.xxxvii.1–25ᵃ,28ᵃ,29–36. According to the other, Joseph, by the advice of *Judah*, was sold to *Ishmaelites*, who carried him to Egypt, and sold him to an Egyptian, in whose house he at first enjoyed prosperity, but afterwards, through the conduct of his master's wife, was thrown into adversity; and it was only in consequence of this that he came into the prison, G.xxxvii.25ᵇ–27, 28ᵇ,xxxix, (except some words in v.1). Only through these hypotheses can the difficulties be got rid of, which burden the story in its present form.

[23] (i) Manifest traces of different documents present themselves in E.xix. Certainly v.20–25 cannot be from the same hand as v.1–19. The statement that Jehovah 'came down,' v.20, is superfluous after v.18; nothing is said in v.1–19 about 'priests, who come near to Jehovah,'—much less about Aaron, who, according to v.24, was to climb the mount with Moses. Perhaps v.13ᵇ, which is now unintelligible, may have been borrowed from the same source as v.20–25.

(ii) In E.xxiv we remark also two accounts. In v.1,2, Moses—though according to xx.21 he is still upon the mount—receives the command to climb it with Aaron, Nadab, Abihu, and seventy elders, which command he obeys, v.9–11. On the other hand, v.3–8 originally followed immediately on xxi–xxiii, and the story is carried on in v.12–15. In v.3–8 Moses descends from the mount, which he had ascended in xx.21, concludes the covenant on the basis of the laws contained in xxi–xxiii, and has now, v.12–15, by Divine command, to climb the mount again with Joshua. On the contrary, v.12, 'Come up to me into the mount,' is not in its place after v.11, since Moses in v.11 is already *on* the mount.

(iii) The same remark applies to E.xxxi.18–xxxiv.35. It is sufficient to point to—

(α) xxxii.7–14, which verses contradict v.17–19, (where Moses is still unaware of what had occurred in the camp, although Jehovah had communicated it to him, v.7,8), and also v.30–32, (where he goes to deprecate the anger of Jehovah, although already, v.14, 'Jehovah repented of the evil which He thought to do unto His people,' and repented, too, in consequence of Moses' prayer, v.11–13);

(β) xxxii.25–29, which account scarcely agrees with v.30–34, (since, if the punishment had already taken place, it could not any more be *deferred*, v.34ᵇ, to the future);

(γ) xxxiii.12, where Moses says to Jehovah, 'Thou hast not let me know whom Thou wilt send with me,' [comp.v.14,15,] whereas in xxxii.34,xxxiii.2, God twice promises that He will send His angel before the face of Israel;

(δ) xxxiv.1–4, which verses evidently break the connection between xxxiii.23 and xxxiv.5–8.

(iv) Also in the Book of Numbers such examples are not wanting. For instance, the repetitions in N.xiv are, at all events, explained most simply, if we assume that v.26–35 are taken from another document than v.11–25. And it should be distinctly noticed that one of *these* documents does not mention Joshua among the spies, and names with commendation only Caleb, the son of Jephunneh, N.xiii.30,31,xiv.24, in opposition to which passages stand N.xiii.6,8,16,xiv.6,7,38, derived from the other document. For still further proof of discrepancy, see Knob.*N.D.J.*p.61, &c.

(v) So N.xvi (rebellion of Korah, Dathan, and Abiram,) seems to be based on two documents, which are here, as afterwards in xxvi.9–11, worked up into one single narrative. One of these contained the statement, that Korah, with two hundred and fifty Israelites, 'men of renown,' from the tribe of Levi as well as other tribes, made a claim to the priestly dignity, but suffered for their presumption, when he, with his whole company, was consumed with fire from heaven before the Tabernacle. The other account makes no mention of Korah, but only of Dathan, Abiram, and On, of the tribe of Reuben, who refused to pay respect to Moses, and, with all theirs, went down alive into the pit. It is difficult, with the narrative as it now lies before us, to show with certainty what has been taken out of the first account, what out of the second, and what again has proceeded from the hand of the compiler. But the general relation of the two traditions to each other appears plainly enough—

(α) from v.2–11, [16–22,35–50,] (Korah), v.12–15 (Dathan and Abiram, &c.),—

(β) from v.25–32 (Dathan, &c., but in v.32, the words 'and all the men who belonged to Korah' are from the hand of the compiler),—

(γ) from *v.*xvii.1–5, which verses show manifestly that Korah's rebellion had quite a different object in view from that of Dathan, &c., xvi.12–15.

It is remarkable also, that in D.xi.6 Dathan and Abiram are mentioned, but not Korah.

CHAPTER VI.

(22) [24] The result of such an enquiry makes no claim to the same objective certainty, as the facts mentioned in the former two sections. It seems, therefore, desirable to distinguish these well from the narratives now under consideration,—a point which has not always been kept in view by former enquirers. That *e. g.* the name 'Jacob' was only once changed to 'Israel,'—that, consequently, G.xxxv.10, proceeds from another hand than xxxii.24–32,—is incontestable; but it may be doubted whether G.xxi.22–34 is based on the same tradition as G.xxvi.26–33.

The most manifest examples [of the point to which this note refers] are the following:

(i) G.xii.10–20 comp. with xx.1–18. The points of agreement and difference between the two accounts are obvious enough. Is it likely that Abraham, after the lesson which he had received, xii, should have had recourse yet once again to the same means of escape?

Besides, the writer of G.xxvi.1–11, refers distinctly in *v.*1 to xii.10–20, but seems to have no knowledge of G.xx.1–18.

(ii) G.xxi.22–33, comp. with xxvi.26–33. For the original identity of the two accounts, among other arguments, the following may be urged:—

(α) The names, not only of the king of Gerar [xx.2], but also of his 'chief captain,' [xxi.22,32,xxvi.26,] are the same in both narratives. It is probable, therefore, that the same persons are named in each case. But then, on the other hand, between G.xx and G.xxvi there lies an interval of ± 80 years, comp. G.xxi.8,22,xxv.20,26,27;

(β) In both accounts we find given the explanation of the name 'Beersheba,' G.xxi.33,xxvi.33; in respect of this point, however, only one of the two accounts can be strictly correct. Yet, if either Abraham or Isaac is wrongly brought into connection with the origin of this name, it follows that in one of them the account of the covenant with Abimelech becomes doubtful also.

In connection with what has been already remarked about Beersheba (note [17.iv]), it is thus quite reasonable to suppose that both accounts are based on the same tradition. That one of the patriarchs had made a covenant with Abimelech in the. presence of Phichol, and that the name Beersheba was connected with the covenant, was the constant matter of the tradition. But doubt existed as to the point whether Abraham or, perhaps, Isaac, was the patriarch in question.

(iii) Out of the remaining books, we may here notice E.xvi, comp. with N.xi, and E.xvii.1–7, comp. with N.xx.1–13. It should be observed that the description of the manna in N.xi.7–9 is superfluous after E.xvi.13–15,—that both in. E.xvii.7 and in N.xx.13 the name 'Meribah' appears—once joined with Massa, once without any further definition,—that the 'unbelief' of Moses, N.xx.11,12, may at least be called strange, as following after E.xvii.1–7,—that the two accounts in Numbers betray no trace whatever of acquaintance with the former, quite similar, miracles related in Exodus, &c.

CHAPTER VII.

(24)   25 This appears at once—

(α) from the use of the word 'sea,' *i.e.* the *Mediterranean sea*, to denote the *west*,—
(β) still more plainly from the formula 'on the other side of the Jordan.'

This latter formula occurs repeatedly in the Pentateuch. It is sometimes used to denote the actual land of Canaan, which lay for the Israelites, so long as they had not yet passed over the Jordan, 'on the other side of the Jordan,' N.xxxii.19ᵃ, D.iii.20,25,xi.30. But it is usually employed to indicate the country which we also, taking our stand in Canaan, are wont to call the 'trans-Jordanic land, G.l.10,11, N.xxii.1,xxxii.19ᵇ,32,xxxv.14, D.i.1,5,iii.8,iv.41,46,47,49. How one and the same formula can have these two meanings—and often, indeed, without any further definition, such as 'eastward,' 'towards the sun-rising,' which are sometimes added,—is well shown by Hengst.iii.p.313–324. A distinction must be made between the individual stand-point of the writer or speaker, and the general or geographical stand-point. From the first of these may be explained the passages, where 'on the other side of Jordan' denotes the land of Canaan; from the second those passages, where the same formula indicates the trans-Jordanic region. Yet Hengst. has not drawn out the consequence, which follows naturally from his demonstration; *viz.* that, since this (so-called) geographical idiom must have formed itself in Canaan, and yet is the prevailing one employed in the Pentateuch, *the Pentateuch itself must have been written after the settlement of Israel in Canaan.* Comp. Riehm,p.111,n.1.

(γ) The name 'land of the Hebrews,' G.xl.15, used for the description of Canaan, could only have arisen after the Israelites had become the only, or, at least, the chief, inhabitants of the land, *i.e.* after the conquest under Joshua.

26 In Genesis we may notice the following passages: xix.20–22, comp. xiv. 2,8, explanation of the name 'Zoar,'—xxi.31,xxvi.31,33, of 'Beersheba,'—xxviii.19, xxxv.15, of 'Bethel.' Comp. further G.xxiii.2,xxxv.27, 'Kirjath-Arba, that is Hebron,' xxxv.19, 'Ephrath, that is Bethlehem,' and other like passages. It must be allowed that such particulars might also have been known in the wilderness. But the supposition is much more natural, that, when Israel was settled in Canaan, the recollection of their forefathers and their adventures was revived among them by the contemplation of their former places of abode, and gave occasion to the recording of the traditions, which were current about them. Besides which, it may be said to be at least doubtful whether the names 'Hebron' and 'Bethlehem,' —nay, even 'Ephratah,' comp. 1Ch.ii.19,51,54,—were already in use at the time of Moses.

27 Comp. D.i.1–5, N.xxi.20,24,26.

(25) [28] The classification here attempted of the so-called *anachronisms* of the Pentateuch—incorrectly so-called, since the name would only properly apply, if the Pentateuch, as a whole, *professed* to be the work of Moses or of the Mosaic age,—cannot, from the nature of the thing, be perfectly correct. Some passages may very reasonably be assigned to more than one class. Comp. generally, KEIL,§38, HENGST.iii.p.179–345.

(i) G.xii.6, 'And the Canaanite was then in the land,' comp. xiii.7, 'And the Canaanite and Perizzite dwelt then in the land.' At the time of Moses, when the Canaanites still dwelt permanently in the land, the remark would have been quite superfluous, and it would not have occurred to any one to make it. It is not true that, in order to see in this place an evidence against the Mosaic origin, we must translate, 'the Canaanite was then *still* in the land' (HENGST.p.185). On the other hand it is quite correct that the notice is properly introduced by its connection with the context both in xii and xiii (HENGST.p.185, &c.) But this is nothing to the purpose. Neither Moses nor one of his contemporaries could possibly suppose that his readers would forget for a moment, that 'the Canaanite was then in the land': he had thus no reason whatever to make the remark.

(ii) In E.xvi.31, N.xi.7–9, we find described the taste, appearance, and mode of cooking, of the manna. In the time of Moses, after that the Israelites, according to E.xvi.35, had eaten manna for forty years, this notice was not needed.

(iii) In E.xvi.36 we read, 'Now the *homer* is the tenth part of the ephah.' HENGST.,p.211–213, tries to make it appear probable that עֹמֶר, *homer*, is not the name of a *measure*, but of a vessel into which the Israelites gathered the manna, a sort of bowl or basin. From this it would follow that we have nothing here to do with a measure, which was in use in Moses' time, but was afterwards disused. Yet, supposing that *homer* denotes a bowl—in any case, however, a bowl *of a definite size*—what could induce Moses to describe the relative size of such a bowl, which was then in the possession of every one? Does not the description transfer us to a later time?

(iv) The same is true of N.iii.47, and similar passages, where the weight of the 'shekel of the sanctuary' is defined as 'twenty gerahs.' See note [29.ii].

[29] (i) In G.xiv.14, D.xxxiv.1, we find the name 'Dan,' which, according to Jo xix.47, Ju.xviii.29, was given to the town Laish (Leshem) in North Palestine, some while after the conquest of the land. Even KURTZ,ii.p.545, sees no chance of maintaining the Mosaic origin of G.xiv.14. HENGST.,p.194, and SCHULTZ,p.97, betake themselves to a miserable resource. In 2S.xxiv.6, forsooth, mention is made of *Dan-Jaan*; this place they would distinguish from Dan (=Laish), and identify with the town meant in G.xiv. Accordingly, the Dan here named must be a different one from the place, which is so called everywhere else, and, on the other hand, must be the same as a town, which is called—not *Dan*, but - *Dan-Jaan*! Add to which that in 2S.xxiv.6 also—as appears from the whole narrative—the usual, northerly, Dan is meant, however we may judge of the meaning of the addition *Jaan*. Comp. THEN.,p.256,257.

(ii) Repeatedly we find named in the Pentateuch the *shekel of the Sanctuary*, E.xxx.13,24,&c.,N.iii.47,50,vii.13,19,&c.,xviii.16, and sometimes the observation is added, that it was equivalent to 'twenty gerahs.' The appellation, 'shekel of the Sanctuary,' indicates certainly that another shekel was also known. How can we imagine the origin of this designation in the time of Moses? Does not the name, ' shekel of the Sanctuary,' imply that the Sanctuary had been already for some time in existence, and that the priests in attendance at it knew the true or full weight of the shekel, and still made use of it, even after that another' was in use among the people? If it is supposed that the ordinary shekel was only half as heavy as the ' shekel of the Sanctuary,' *Bijb.Woord*.iii.p.328, and thus was equivalent to the ' *bekah*,' E.xxxviii.26, yet still the above remark holds good.

³⁹ (i) The well-known formula, 'unto this day,' occurs frequently in Genesis, but refers there to practices or names belonging to the patriarchal time, of which it might be properly used as early as the time of Moses, G.xix.37,38,xxvi.33,xxxii.32,xxxv.20, xlvii.26. In Deuteronomy it occurs in ii.22 (with reference to the dwelling of the Edomites in Seir), xxxiv.6, (' no one knows Moses' grave *unto this day* '), but also x.8, ' at that time Jehovah separated the tribe of Levi, to bear the Ark of the Covenant of Jehovah, to stand before Jehovah to minister unto Him, and to bless in His Name, *unto this day*,'—where it sounds, indeed, somewhat strangely, yet, taken alone, would give no proof of later origin. This, however, seems certainly to be the case with D.iii.14, ' Jair the son of Manasseh took all the country of Argob . . . and called them after his own name, Bashan-havoth-Jair, *unto this day*.' Let it be observed that, according to the chronology of the Pentateuch, Israel was still, on the first day of the *fifth* month of the fortieth year, at Mount Hor, N.xxxiii.38, *i.e.* westward of the district of Edom, and began their march from that station on the first day of the *sixth* month, comp.N.xx.29,—further, that the march around the Edomite country, and the wars against Sihon, Og, and Midian, N.xxi,xxxi, could not have been completed in a few days,—that the settlement of Jair, if it occurred in Moses' time, could only have taken place after the termination of all these wars,—lastly, that Moses, D.i.3, is addressing Israel on the first day of the *eleventh* month! The latest apologists see, however, no difficulty even here. KEIL,§38,n.2, comp. also SCHULTZ,p.31,32, speaks of the settlement of Jair as ' indeed, a fact out of the last years (? days) of the march, but one which was yet not so near to the time of the discourses in Deuteronomy, that such a remark could not have been made even then,—especially if we consider that it is just immediately after their introduction that new names are maintained with the greatest difficulty.' There might then, in fact, he thinks, have been good reason for mentioning that the name *Havvoth-Jair* was still 'maintained' ! As to the incident itself, see (iii) below.

(ii) The conquest of Canaan is represented as a fact already past in D.ii.12, 'The Horim also dwelt in Seir beforetime ; but the children of Esau succeeded them, when they had destroyed them from before them, and dwelt in their stead, *as Israel did unto the land of his inheritance, which Jehovah gave unto them*.' But says HÄv.I. ii.p.32, &c. the formula ' land of his inheritance (possession),' does not here mean Canaan, but the trans-Jordanic land, and that, too, regularly: see D.iii.20,Jo.i.15, and comp.Jo.xii.6,7, where יְרֻשָּׁה 'possession' or 'inheritance,' is used, first of the trans-Jordanic land, and then of Canaan. What these two passages are to prove, is not clear. That the trans-Jordanic land was the ' inheritance ' of the tribes of Reuben, Gad, and half-Manasseh, is, no doubt, very plain. But in D.ii.12 it stands, ' as *Israel* did unto the land of his inheritance,' and ' the land of *Israel's* inheritance, which Jehovah had given him,' can hardly be any other than Canaan. Thus there remains nothing else to be done than either, with HENGST.p.240, to assume that the perfect in one half of the verse is a *proper*, and in the other half a *prophetical*, perfect (!), or to admit that the conquest of the land is here implied. SCHULTZ,p.29,30, is of opinion that the words quoted belong still to the address of Jehovah, which begins with *v.*9, and is carried on in *v.*13ª; thus he explains the use of the perfects in the latter part of *v.*12, which he interprets as *prophetical* perfects (*futura exacta*). But nothing is more plain than that the writer himself has made the remarks in *v.*10–12, as an explanatory parenthesis, and cannot have put into the mouth of God such historical information as, for instance, *v.*11. Besides, even if Jehovah were speaking here, that would give us no right to interpret just this one perfect, ['did,'] as referring to a *future* event, [while the other, 'dwelt,' at the beginning of the verse, refers to the *past.*]

(iii) Here, too, D.iii.11 comes into consideration, where we read that the 'iron bed' [? stone sarcophagus] of King Og, 'nine cubits long and four cubits broad, after the cubit of a man,' was kept at Rabbath-Ammon. Be it remembered that the death of Og had only just taken place, when Moses delivered this address. Is it likely that the bed of this king was all at once carried over to Rabbath-Ammon? Above all, is it probable that Moses, either in his address to the people, or afterwards, when he committed it to writing, mentioned these particulars? Have we not here before us an archæological notice of some one, who lived long after the time of Moses?

(iv) In D.xix.14ª, also, the conquest of the land is implied.

(v) In N.xv.32 reference is made to the sojourn of the Israelites in the wilderness, as to a time gone by.

³¹ (i) G.xxxvi.31, 'these are the kings who reigned in the land of Edom, *before there reigned any king over the children of Israel.*' That men in a sober genealogical table do not borrow definitions of time from an event still future,—that, consequently, this notice cannot have been written down before the time of Saul,—seems very plain. HENGST., however, p.202, &c. and others before and after him, judge otherwise. They see here a reference to G.xvii.16,xxxv.11, where Abraham and Jacob receive the promise that kings shall proceed from them. 'Before the time when this promise came to be fulfilled,' the writer would say,' Edom already had kings.' One feels, however, that a genealogy is a very unsuitable place for such fine allusions. Besides which, in G.xvii.16,xxxv.11, not a word is to be read about *Israel being governed by kings.* It is only said that Abraham and Jacob should have kings among their descendants; so that the promise to Abraham, at all events, received its fulfilment also in the appearance of the Edomitish kings.

(ii) In D.ii.23 we are told of the settlement of the Philistines in the Pentapolis, and the expulsion of the original inhabitants of these cities, the Avim. The strongest historical reasons lead to the conclusion, that this settlement took place not till after the conquest of the land by Joshua. Comp. STARK,p.125, &c. At the time of Moses, the Philistines did not yet live in Canaan, but between that land and Egypt, E.xiii.17.³

---

³ Does E.xiii.17 necessarily imply that they lived *between* Canaan and Egypt? May they not have lived in the Pentapolis, in the south-west of Canaan itself, so

(iii) In D.iii.14 we find the account about Jair, the form of which notice we have already considered in note ³⁹4. A careful examination of all the passages of the O.T., where *Jair* and the *Havvoth-Jair* occur, N.xxxii.41,41, D.iii.14,14, Jo.xiii.30, 1K.iv.13, 1Ch.ii.22,23, Ju.x.3,4,5, has brought me to the conviction,—

(α) That the *Havvoth-Jair, i.e.* the nomad-*villages* (kraals) *named after Jair*— (so is the expression rendered in the Greek, Latin, Chaldee, Syriac, and Arabic translations)—three-and-twenty in number, lay in Gilead, 1Ch.ii.22,23, 1K.iv.13;—

(β) That the ' threescore great cities with walls and brazen bars,' [named also in] 1K.iv.13, which belonged to the circle of Argob in Bashan, have nothing to do with the *Havvoth-Jair*, and, consequently, Jo.xiii.30 contains an inaccurate—perhaps, corrupt—datum;—

(γ) That also in D.iii.12–14 a confusion exists, which gives us reason to doubt as to the accuracy of the text;—

(δ) That there were not *two* Jairs,—one, a contemporary of Moses, the other, one of the Judges,—but one only, the Judge of that name, Ju.x.3–5, from whom the designation *Havvoth-Jair* must be derived;—

(ε) That, consequently, both in N.xxxii.41,42, and in D.iii.14, what really happened long afterwards seems to have been transferred erroneously to the Mosaic time; the fact being, that the writer in the Pentateuch, while narrating the assignment of the trans-Jordanic land to the tribes of Reuben, Gad, and half-Manasseh, mentions at the same time what important changes took place in later days in the partition of this district.   Comp. Then. on 1K.iv.13, Birth. on 1Ch.ii.22,23, and, on the other side, Hengst.iii.227–237, von Raumer,p.405–410.

(iv) Probably, we must come to a similar conclusion as to the conquest of the town Zephath, called afterwards Hormah, Ju.i.17, comp. N.xxi.1–3. At all events, the supposition that the town was *twice conquered*, and *twice received the name of Hormah*, has everything against it. And, if we must choose between the two narratives, then Ju.i.17 deserves certainly the preference for precision and clearness before N.xxi.1–3. Comp. above note ¹⁴.

(26)   ³² The proof of this position can merely be indicated here: a full development of it belongs more properly to a commentary upon these chapters.

(i) G.xlix. (comp. Diest., Land,) implies in *v.*10–12,13,15,20, the settlement of the tribes in the land of Canaan,—in *v.*5,7, the miserable condition of the Levites during the time of the Judges,—in *v.*8, perhaps, David's accession to the throne.

(ii) E.xv.1–18, may originally have been a genuine Mosaic song: particularly, *v.*1–12 contains nothing, that points of necessity to a later time. But the original passage was afterwards modified,—perhaps, in order to be sung by the congregation at the celebration of the Passover in the Sanctuary at Shiloh. This appears from *v.*13, especially from the words, ' Thou hast guided them (Thy people) in Thy strength unto Thy holy habitation,'—further, from *v.* 17, ' Thou shalt bring them in, and plant them in the mountain of Thine inheritance; a place, Jehovah, hast

---

that the shortest route from Egypt into the *Hebrew portion* of Canaan, would lie through the lands of the Philistines? It still remains true that historical reasons are against the supposition, that the Philistines lived here in the days of Moses; and thus it would follow that E.xiii.17, as well as D.ii.23, is of later date. *Ed.*

Thou made for Thee to dwell in; a sanctuary, Adonai, have Thy hands established,'—where manifestly the settlement in Canaan and the existence of a sanctuary, perhaps at Shiloh, is implied.[4]

(iii) D.xxxii.1–43 supposes not only the conquest of Canaan, but also the great prosperity of Israel under the rule of David and Solomon, and the apostacy of the people from Jehovah, which was consequent upon it. That the poet—who makes no claim whatever to be taken for Moses—does not *foretell* all this, but supposes it as partly already past, and partly still present, appears plainly from *v.*13–25. KAMPH. has rightly assigned the whole poem to the Assyrian period, *i.e.* to the year 770 B.C., or *afterwards.*[5]

(iv) D.xxxiii has very lately been considered thoroughly, at length, by GRAF. He comes to the conclusion, p.79–83, that the writer of D.xxxiii,—who, according to him, does not give himself out for Moses, but, on the contrary, in *v.*4 distinguishes himself as plainly as possible from the lawgiver—was a contemporary of Jeroboam II, and thus lived ± 800 B.C. It appears to me very probable that GRAF has herein judged rightly. But, independently of this, there can be no doubt of the later origin of the 'Blessing' on account of *v.*5, where mention is made of the introduction of the kingly form of government,—*v.*12, which implies the existence of the Temple at Jerusalem,—*v.*7, where the wish is uttered for the restoration of the unity of the kingdom,—*v.*8–11, which verses so picture the activity and the dignity of the Levites, that they place us at all events under the reign of Jehoshaphat, or *in a yet later time,*[6] comp. 2 Ch.xvii,xix; while, lastly, the poet gives [throughout] plain evidences of being acquainted with the 'Blessing of Jacob.'

(v) Lastly, as to the 'Blessings of Balaam,' comp. GEBB, HENGST., OORT. They imply, especially in N.xxiii.24,xxiv.9, a knowledge of the 'Blessing of

---

[4] Does any portion of this song date from the Mosaic time? It seems unlikely that additions should have been made, as is here supposed, to a genuine Mosaic Song,—additions, too, *v.*13–18, which differ in no respect in language and style from the previous portion of the poem. Perhaps, the *whole* Song dates from a later time; and, if that time was the age of David or after it, the references in *v.*17 would be—not to Shiloh, but—to Canaan, 'the mountain (mountainous land) of God's inheritance,' *Jerusalem*, 'the place which Jehovah had made for Himself to dwell in,' the *Tabernacle* or *Temple*, 'the Sanctuary which the Lord's hands had established'—unless, indeed, the three expressions are all used to express the holy land of Israel. [Since this note was written I have received Prof. KUENEN's last corrections, in which he notes on the above passage as follows:—' This seems to me now too conservative. I cannot deny that you have made the Mosaic origin of this Song appear much more doubtful.'] *Ed.*

[5] In P.III.798–801 I have given the reasons which have led me to assign this 'Song' to the Deuteronomist, and, therefore, to about the age of Josiah, ± 625, see P.III.865–867. *Ed.*

[6] In P.III.xvii–xix, especially (841,842), I have shown, as I suppose, that the 'Blessing of Moses' could not have been written till *after* the Captivity of the Ten Tribes, and have given reasons for concluding that it was written in the age of Josiah, or not long before it. *Ed.*

Jacob,'7 and in xxiii.21,xxiv.7,17, the existence of the kingly form of government in Israel. Comp. further, OOBT,p.41-81, and notes ⁹⁰⁻¹¹,²²².

⁸⁸ (i) The possibility exists only [? see notes below] with respect to D.xxxiii that
it is an interpolated passage, since not a word is said about this 'Blessing of Moses,'
either in what precedes, or in what follows. All the other passages, however, are
connected in the clearest manner with the narratives, of which they now form a
part, and may thus be, perhaps, as old as, or older, but certainly not younger, than
the narratives themselves. With G.xlix.1-27 comp. v.28 ⁸; with E.xv.1-18 comp.
v.19-21⁹; with D.xxxii.1-43 comp. xxxi.19,21,22,30,xxxii.44.

(ii) N.xxii-xxiv is, probably, a complete whole, not closely connected either with
what goes before or with what follows. But the contents of these chapters are
implied in D.xxiii.4,5.¹⁰

<hr>

CHAPTER VIII.

(27) ⁸⁴ The usual formulæ are, 'And Jehovah spake unto Moses, saying, Speak unto
the children of Israel, &c.' E.xxv.1,2,xxxi.12,13,&c.,&c.,—'And Jehovah spake
unto Moses, saying, Command Aaron and his sons, &c.,' L.vi.8,9,&c. Sometimes
Jehovah speaks to Moses and Aaron, L.xi.1,xiii.1,&c., or, after Aaron's death, to
Moses and Eleazar, N.xxvi.1. Other variations, also, occur; but they do not
change the main point, with which alone we are here concerned.

(28) ⁸⁵ Thus, for instance, the celebration of the Feasts is treated of in E.xxiii.14-17,
L.xxiii, N.xxviii,xxix,—the Passover, besides the above passages, also in E.xii.1-13,

<hr>

7 Comp. G.xlix.9; but the 'Blessing of Jacob' *may* be imitated from that of
Balaam, so that, as far as this point is concerned, the latter *may* be the oldest. *Ed.*

8 There is reason, as it seems to me, for believing that G.xlix.1ᵇ-28 *is* an interpolation, so that in the original narrative v.29 followed after v.1ᵃ,—'And Jacob
called unto his sons, and he charged them, &c.' *Ed.*

9 I believe that here also E.xv.1-19 is a later interpolation, and is, perhaps, a
mere amplification of the song of Miriam, v.20,21, in the original story. *Ed.*

10 Since, in my judgment, both the 'Blessing of Jacob' and the 'Hymn of Moses,'
are later interpolations, Prof. KUENEN's argument in the text does not appear to me
valid, so far as these two passages are concerned,—that is to say, the signs of a
later date, which are observed in them, do not prove that the *narrative*, in which
they are imbedded, is also of later date. And, indeed, Prof. KUENEN himself lays
no stress on it as regards the 'Blessing of Moses.'

But the 'Song of Moses.' D.xxxii.1-43, is undoubtedly a part of the same whole
with the context before and after, and the signs of later date in it prove the context also to be of later date. So D.xxiii.4,5,—and, therefore, Deuteronomy itself,
of which it forms an integral part,—cannot have been written by Moses; since it
refers to the story of Balaam, which betrays itself to be of later date than the time
of Moses. *Ed.*

21-28,43-51, N.ix.6-14,—vows, in L.xxvii, N.xxx, and the vow of the Nazarite in N.vi.1-21,—the sin-offering, in L.iv.1-v.13, N.xv.22-31,—the punishment of the Sabbath-breaker, in E.xxxi.14,15,xxxv.2, N.xv.32-36,&c. In short, we have only to read the three Books consecutively to perceive that nothing lay less in the purpose of the compiler, than to set forth a regular *system* of legislation.

⁵⁴ What laws must be brought under each of these three divisions, appears from the survey of the contents of the Books, which has been given in Chap.I. This is the place to note that, in point of fact, the ordinances are represented to have been issued in the same chronological order, in which they are delivered to us in the Pentateuch. With respect to many laws, *e. g.* E.xii,xiii,xx.22-xxiii,xxv-xxxi, this is at once manifest. The laws contained in Leviticus were revealed 'in the Tabernacle of the Congregation,' L.i.1, and, probably, while the people still remained in the wilderness of Sinai: see, *e.g.*, L.vii.37,38,xvi.1, (comp. x.1,2,) xxvi.46,xxvii.34. Also, with respect to the legislative portions of N.i-viii, no doubt can exist as to their falling, according to the view of the compiler, before the removal from Sinai. In N.ix.1 the first month of the second year after the Exodus is expressly named. The departure out of the wilderness of Sinai is related in N.x.11,12. In N.xv,xix, there is no reference to the time of the promulgation. On the other hand, N.xviii seems to imply the rebellion of Korah, &c., N.xvi,xvii. In N.xxvi.1,xxvii.2,xxxi.12,13,xxxii. 2,28, Eleazar is named, in token that the ordinances, there recorded, fall after Aaron's death. Eleazar appears already in N.xvi.37,39,xix.3,4, but only as the presumptive successor of his father, comp. N.xvi.41,42,43,46,47,xvii.3,xviii.1. Lastly, in N.xxxiii.50,xxxvi.13, we have the 'plains of Moab' expressly named, as the scene of the last-mentioned Divine revelations.

(30) ⁵⁷ I purposely speak only of such ordinances; for the historical question whether the first Passover was kept in this night, does not belong to this place. Independently, however, of that, the ordinances in question give the clearest signs of a later time. It is inconceivable that Moses, before even a Tabernacle or a worship existed, should have laid down the law, that on the first and seventh day of the Feast of Unleavened Bread there should be a 'holy convocation,' E.xii.16,—that then he should have spoken of the march out of Egypt as an event already past, *v.*17,—that then also he should have treated of the *strangers* and their obligations, *v.*19, and of the conditions, under which they might partake of the Passover, *v.*43-49. The same is true both of the law about the Unleavened Bread, xiii.3-10, and of the ordinance about the dedication of the firstborn, *v.*11-16.

(32) ⁵⁸ Three examples may suffice :—

(i) In N.xxviii,xxix, we find a circumstantial enumeration of all the offerings, which must be brought upon the great Feasts; in xxix.12-38, the offerings are prescribed even for every day of the Feast of Tabernacles.

(ii) L.xxvii contains directions about vows, and the redemption of objects dedicated to God; among other things, in *v.*1-8 is given the redemption-price of men and women of different ages

(iii) The law about leprosy and its cleansing, L.xiii,xiv, is very minute, and descends so much into details with respect to the different kinds, their more or less malignant character, the symptoms and the cure of the disease, that the author must have made a distinct and special study of that subject, unless, indeed, he availed himself of the long experience of a number of predecessors,—at all events, of priestly traditions about this point.

 Comp. Hengst.ii.p.415–502. That at the time of Moses the Israelites possessed a literature, is a matter subject to no reasonable doubt, and it is now generally admitted. Difference of views prevails, however, as to the extent, to which the knowledge of writing was spread in those days. While some think that not a few Israelites possessed a certain expertness in this art, others are of opinion that at that time it was still very little practised. The enquiry into this matter is the more difficult, since naturally the Pentateuch is our chief source for it,[11] so that nearly everything depends upon the authority which we assign to its testimonies, while this again is determined by the time of their being recorded. But then, in order to settle this last, we should desire, among other things, to know whether, and to what extent, the art of writing was generally spread in the days of Moses. The danger of reasoning in a circle here is thus very great, on which account we assign very little weight to the whole question, towards defining the age of the Pentateuch.

We add here simply a word for the confirmation of the above. We have already seen that Moses is very seldom presented as a *writer* in the first four Books of the Pentateuch, and that the first mention of a whole law-book from his hand occurs in the Book of Deuteronomy,—as, in general, the addresses and laws of Deuteronomy *lay much more stress on writing* than the first four books of the Pentateuch,—at least, they imply a much more general use of the art. Comp., besides the passages quoted in (10,11), N.v.23,xi.26, (if any weight be ascribed to the expression 'them that were written,') xvii.2,3, D.vi.9,xi.20,xvii.18,xxiv.1,3,xxvii.3,8, xxxi.19,22,24. This can hardly be accidental. We must make our choice between these two representations,—that of the first four Books, and that of Deuteronomy. How the choice must be decided, cannot be doubtful. We assume, with the Books of Exodus and Numbers, that *in Moses' time men wrote very little.*

Here, however, it may be objected:

(a) The Books of Exodus, Leviticus, and Numbers, although they seldom make mention of writing, yet contain a Mosaic Legislation, which, if it is really and entirely Mosaic, must have been written also by Moses, or, at all events, in his time.

Ans. In such a matter as this, it is plain, we can only lay stress upon direct testimonies. The silence of the author, about the writing down of all the Mosaic laws,

---

11 Our chief evidence, as Prof. Kuenen says, for the existence of the art of writing among the Hebrews in the time of Moses, must be drawn from the Pentateuch itself. If, therefore, it should appear that the *whole* Pentateuch is of later origin, such evidence as this cannot be relied on. There is no reason to suppose that the *Egyptians* were acquainted in that age with the art of writing by means of *letters*, which is the kind of writing here under consideration. From whence, then, could the Israelites have derived this faculty, while they were yet living in Egypt? Is it not more reasonable to suppose that they first acquired it, after a residence of some time in Canaan, from contact with the Phœnicians, *e.g.* in *Samuel's* days, and that it was actually taught, among other things, in his 'School'? *Ed.*

is more significant, than any inference which we might draw from the existence of these laws.

(β) In Egypt, the services of the Israelite slaves were regulated by 'officers,' chosen out of the people itself, named שֹׁטְרִים *shotĕrim*, E.v.6,10,14,15,19. We meet with the same name once again in the Book of Numbers,xi.16, and frequently in Deuteronomy,i.15,xvi.18,xx.5,8,9,xxix.10,xxxi.28. Now this name indicates 'writer,' and constrains us to suppose a pretty general acquaintance with the art of writing among the Israelites of those days.

Ans. But the original meaning of שֹׁטֵר is a different one, *viz.* 'to order,' comp. NOLDEKE, *Gesch. der Qorâns* (1860),p.13,n.1. Besides, who assures us that these overseers bore this name already in Egypt? Is it not very possible that a later name has been used to express a matter, which after Israel's deliverance out of Egypt no longer presented itself? And, even assuming that the word was so old, and always denoted 'writing,' does it in any way appear *what* and *how much* these officers wrote? We shall certainly adhere most closely to the truth, if we imagine their mode of action to be as simple as possible. The number of bricks delivered by each Israelite might have been registered by them, without any great dexterity in writing. The same remarks apply to the passages in Deuteronomy, as have been made about writing in general. Comp. VETH. in *Bĳb.Woord.*iii.300, &c.

(33) "We shall presently, note [41], consider more fully the distinction which is here made. Without further discussion, I will sum up those passages, which contradict each other, in the same order in which they occur in the Pentateuch.

There exists contradiction—

(i) Between E.xiii.13 (=xxxiv.20)—'every firstling of an ass thou shalt redeem with a lamb, and, if thou wilt not redeem it, then thou shalt break its neck,'—and N.xviii.15,16, L.xxvii.27. In N.xviii.15,16, it is prescribed that 'the firstlings of unclean beasts' shall be redeemed from the priest for five shekels of silver, 'from a month old.' The permission to give a lamb as the price of redemption in the case mentioned in E.xiii, or else to kill the ass-foal, is here distinctly excluded. Even KEIL, 1st ed. §26,n.1, admits this; but he ascribes the alteration to Moses himself, see note [41]. On the other hand, he denies that L.xxvii.27 can here be taken into account, because there 'mention is made of the *special case* of the firstling of the unclean beast being dedicated as a vow to Jehovah, when it must be redeemed with the addition of the fifth part to the value, or, if this does not take place, then it must be sold.' But this 'special case' could never have happened, since *all* the firstlings without exception belonged to Jehovah, and could not therefore be dedicated to him by a vow, L.xxvii.26. I the meaning of L.xxvii.27 had been rightly explained by KEIL, then this passage would be in direct contradiction with all which the Law lays down about firstlings. But, on the contrary, it runs parallel with N.xviii.15,16, except that *here* no mention is made of the addition of a fifth to the selling-price. KEIL has, accordingly, in his second edition, silently retracted this view. Comp. further KNOB. *E.L.*p.127,128.

(ii) In E.xx.24–26, we observe as follows :—

(α) Liberty is given to all Israelites to make an 'altar of earth' and to offer sacrifice upon it ;—

(β) It is expressly declared, (as, in fact, it was already included in the above

permission,) that altars might thus be built in more than one place, in these words—
' in all places where I record my name I will come unto thee and I will bless thee;'—

(γ) It is forbidden to ascend by steps to the altar.

This ordinance is at variance—

(α) With N.xviii.1–3, according to which even the Levites might not approach the altar,—

(β) With .L.xvii.8,9, where it is expressly commanded, that sacrifices shall be offered only at the Tabernacle,—

(γ) With E.xxvii.1, where mention is made of an altar three cubits high, to which certainly the ascent must have been made by steps, as appears, indeed, from the , provision of ' breeches to cover their nakedness,' made in E.xxviii.42.43.

We shall return hereafter to this important passage (note ²⁰⁰). Here I only observe that the true interpretation of v.24ᵇ is well exhibited by KNOBEL *in loco*.

(iii) In E.xxi.1–6 it is laid down that the Hebrew, who may have sold himself to another Hebrew as a slave, shall receive back his freedom after six years' servitude, and, if he does not wish to use it, shall be bound to his master by a symbolical action ' for ever,' *i.e.* for his whole life long. Of this manumission in the seventh year of service not a word is said in L.xxv.39–43 ; on the contrary, it is prescribed that the Hebrew slave shall do service until the year of Jubilee, and shall then obtain his freedom. The two are brought into agreement (KEIL *in loco*, HENGST.p.440) by assuming that L.xxv.39–43 was only applied in any case, where the Hebrew slave had not yet completed his six years' service in the year of Jubilee. But in this way the prescription, which sounds altogether general in L.xxv.39-43, would be confined to very few cases. Comp. SAALS.p.702,&c. whose own explanation is much more worthy of notice,—*viz.* that L.xxv speaks of an impoverished *Israelite*, while E.xxi speaks of *Hebrew* slaves, probably men of *mixed* origin, *e.g.* children of an Israelitish father and a Heathen mother, who stood much on the same line with the later proselytes. This distinction, however, seems very subtle and improbable, especially with an eye upon D.xv.12, where the Hebrew slaves are called *brothers*; and it is irreconcilable with the supposition, that both laws proceed from one author.

(iv) In E.xxiii.14–17 (=xxxiv.18–23) mention is made of *three* chief Feasts, which were to be annually celebrated, by the appearance of each male Israelite before the presence of Jehovah. On the other hand, in L.xxiii, N.xxviii,xxix, *seven* holy seasons (Sabbath, New Moon, Unleavened Bread, Feast of Weeks, New Moon of the Seventh Month, Day of Atonement, Feast of Tabernacles) are named, and for all these holy seasons alike a ' holy convocation '—*i.e.* a gathering of the people to the holy place—is prescribed. How this ' holy convocation ' is to be explained, is doubtful. From the laws themselves [in L.xxiii] it seems plain, that they were to be coupled with the discontinuance of work, both of *servile work* and of *all manner of work*, (although this last is only prescribed for the Atonement Day, L.xxiii.28,30,31, N.xxix.7,) and further with the offering of different sacrifices to Jehovah, comp. L.xxiii.2,4,7,8,24,27,35–37, N.xxviii.18,25,26,xxix.1,7,12, E.xii.16. It follows also from the commencement of both laws, L.xxiii.1,2, N.xxviii.1,2, that— not the priests only, but—*all Israelites* were concerned with this ' holy convocation,' on which account it is said continually to all Israel, ' it shall be an holy convocation unto *you*.' Hence I conclude that at the ' holy convocation ' *all the people*—whether *really*, or in *idea* (= in its representatives, the priests? or the inhabitants of the town where the sanctuary stood?), took part in the gathering. If this is true, then L.xxiii, N.xxviii, do not agree with E.xxiii; for here the three chief Feasts,—Feast of Unleavened Bread, Feast of Harvest, Feast of Ingathering,—are ranked distinctly, by the command to 'appear before the Face of Jehovah,' higher than the other Feasts, if these latter exist at all, of which, however, there is no indication in E.xxiii. For the rest, I willingly allow that our knowledge of the Israelitish Feasts, and the modifications which these most probably experienced in the course of ages, *is* still exceedingly defective. Comp. Ew. (*Alt.*) p.385–411, HUPF. (*Fest.*), KNOB. (*E.L.*) p.529– 541, and Chap.XIX of this work (103,104).

(v) In E.xxv.15 it is prescribed that 'the staves shall be in the rings of the Ark : they shall not be taken from it.' With this N.iv.5,6, seems to be at variance, where the covering of the Ark, and the '*putting-in the staves* thereof,' appears as one of the priestly duties. The matter is of little importance, and proves not so much that the two passages quoted are derived from different Legislations, as, probably, that the author of N.iv.6 speaks not as an eye-witness. KEIL directs attention to E.xxxvii.5,xl.20 ; but, strictly speaking, these two passages also conflict with each other, and do nothing towards removing the contradiction between E.xxv.15 and N.iv.6.

(vi) E.xxxviii.25–27 (comp.xxx.12–14) conflicts with N.i, inasmuch as in the former passage (i.e. *before* the *first day of the first month* of the second year, E.xl.17) it is implied that the census had already taken place, which according to N.i.1 was not commanded until the *first day of the second month* of the second year. KEIL (*in loco*) remarks that in E.xxxviii mention is made of a simple *counting* of the people, whereas in N.i we have a mustering and marshalling of all the men fit for war. But it is hard to suppose that Moses without any necessity should have directed the '*simple* (sic) counting' of 603,550 men twice,—and that the result should have been identically the same each time, although between the first and the second numberings there lay an interval of some months. Manifestly, E.xxxviii 25–27 is a *prolepsis*, which, however, makes the strongly-historical character both of E.xxxviii itself and of Numbers more than doubtful. Comp. note [66].

(vii) L.xxiii.18,19,—where the sacrifice at the Feast of Harvest is fixed at seven lambs of a year old, *one* bullock, *two* rams, for a burnt-offering, a kid of the goats for a sin-offering, and two lambs of a year old for a thank-offering—is at variance with N.xxviii.27–30,—where for the same Feast a sacrifice is prescribed of seven lambs of a year old, *two* bullocks, *one* ram, for a burnt-offering, and a kid of the goats for a sin-offering. BERTH., p.289, and with him also KEIL, and DEL., p.49, endeavour to get rid of the difference by the assumption, that the sacrifices mentioned in L.xxiii.18,19, belong to the loaves of first-fruits, while in N.xxviii.27–30 the proper offerings of the Feast are summed up. But were, then, the sacrifices, belonging to the loaves, *not* Feast-sacrifices? Did not the Feast derive its very character from the completed Harvest, of which the two loaves were the symbols? Besides, notwithstanding the discrepancy, the agreement between the two passages is so great, that we have manifestly before us in the one a modification of the sacrificial system prescribed in the other.

(viii) In N.iv.3,23,30,35,39,43,47, the time of service of the Levites is defined

I

as lasting from the *thirtieth* to the fiftieth year of life; in N.viii.24, on the other hand, it lasts from the *twenty-fifth* to the fiftieth year. Hengst.p.391,&c. attempts to remove this contradiction by the hypothesis, that N.iv speaks only of the carrying the Tabernacle and its belongings, during the march through the wilderness: whereas N.viii speaks of the duties of the Levites *generally*; they began to enter upon these in the twenty-fifth year of their lives; but they were not admitted to carry the tabernacle until five years afterwards. It is unfortunate that this explanation—adopted by Keil—is in direct opposition with N.iv.47,—'from thirty years old and upward even unto fifty years old, every one that came to do *the service of the ministry and the service of the burden*, in the Tabernacle of the Congregation.' The original expressions are unmistakeably plain, לַעֲבֹד עֲבֹדַת עֲבֹדָה יַעֲבֹדַת מַשָּׂא בְּאֹהֶל מוֹעֵד, 'to serve ministerial-work and carrying-work in the Tabernacle of the Congregation.' Nevertheless, Hengst.p.394, translates these words,— 'who came to do service—yea, service of carrying—*at* the tabernacle, &c.' In the like arbitrary manner is the plain meaning of v.19,24,27, perverted. If, indeed, throughout the whole chapter, *only* the work of carrying had been mentioned, then the formula בְּאֹהֶל מוֹעֵד, v.3,15,23, &c. might denote '*at* or *with reference to* the Tabernacle, &c.' But that is not the case; so that the simplest interpretation, '*in* the Tabernacle, &c.,' is certainly also the true one. Del.p.50, candidly admits the discrepancy.

⁴¹ Del.p.48-50, is of opinion that those, who think that they observe contradictions in the Legislation of the Pentateuch, show plainly that they are unacquainted with the method, according to which the passages in question should be treated, and which is applied, among others, by those who practise Roman jurisprudence. The *Corpus Juris Justiniani*, consisting of the *Digests, Institutes*, and *Codex*, is a whole, and is meant to be applied as such. Jurists, therefore, (see *e.g.* Savigny, *System des heutigen Römischen Rechts*, i.§43,&c.) follow this rule, that they resolve the contradictions, which present themselves, into mere *appearance*. This is done—

(α) By the *systematical* process, *i.e.* by assigning to each of the conflicting passages its proper domain, beyond which it ought not to be considered to apply; by which method Delitzsch reconciles *e.g.*L.xxiii.18 and N.xxviii.27, see note ⁴⁴·ᵛⁱⁱ;—

(β) By the *historical* process, *i.e.* by regarding only the *latest* prescription as being in force, and the older as abrogated, so that this latter is recorded as historical matter, and in order to elucidate the later prescription which has acquired force of law;—and in this way he judges as to the relation of Deuteronomy to Exodus, Leviticus, and Numbers, and as to N.iv comp. with N.viii, see note ⁴⁴·ᵛⁱⁱⁱ.

I do not believe that the Mosaic origin of the whole Legislation contained in the Pentateuch is made more probable by this analogy. The contradiction between the different portions of the *Corpus Juris* arises precisely from this, that it does not proceed, as a whole, out of one time or from one hand. If, therefore, the case really stands with the Pentateuch just as it does with the Corpus Juris, then by this very fact the gradual origin of the Legislation becomes highly probable. Add to which, that the examples, adduced by Delitzsch, do not recommend his method, and that he takes up together unlike cases. The 'systematical' reconciliation of L.xxiii.18 with N.xxviii.27 is unsuccessful; N.iv, comp. with N.viii, is not to be paired with N.xxvii.1–11, comp. with N.xxxvi; rather, it appears from this last passage, that, upon the occasion of an original ordinance being modified or amplified, reference is made back to it, which is by no means the case with N.viii.

Generally, I should consider Delitzsch's method very worthy of consideration, if we were still living under the Mosaic law, and were obliged to apply it. I should then much prefer it to Hengstenberg's arbitrary contrivances and perversions of the text. But our object is historical, and, consequently, it requires also to be pursued in a strictly historical way.

(34) ^{4²} The examples of such complementary matter—which occur very frequently in Deuteronomy, compared with Exodus, Leviticus, and Numbers—are comparatively rare in the three last-named Books, especially if we leave out of consideration here the laws which conflict with each other; see note ⁴¹.

(i) The law contained in N.xxxvi is expressly described in that passage as being complementary to the ordinance in N.xxvii.1–11; but at the same time these prescriptions are both derived from Moses, and are even both placed in the fortieth year after the Exodus.

(ii) N.v.5–10 is an appendix to L.v.14–vi.7, and prescribes that the recompense for an injury caused to a neighbour,—consisting in the restitution of the mischief done, with the addition of the fifth part of its value,—must be paid to the injured person, or his goël (avenger), or, *if the last also be wanting, to the priest.* It may serve to show that this complementary law did not proceed from the author of the former law in L.v, but from another writer, if we observe that here, v.8, the expression אֵיל הַכִּפֻּרִים, 'ram of the atonement,' occurs, which is not found in L.v, and for which in L.xix.22 we find אֵיל הָאָשָׁם, 'ram of the tresspass': comp. note ⁴².

(iii) N.xv.22–31 is a complement of L.iv.13–21,27–35. Here, however, it may not unreasonably be maintained that both prescriptions have proceeded from one author. The passage of Leviticus, for instance, speaks of *sinning in ignorance against a command*; while that of Numbers treats of the *involuntary neglect of a command.*

(iv) The following passages, also, may be compared: N.xix, especially v.11–22, comp. with L.xi–xv,—E.xii.43–50, N.ix.6–14, comp. with E.xii.1–13,21–28,— N.xxx comp. with L.xxvii.

(35) ⁴³ I confine myself here to producing some plain examples.

(i) The month, in which the Passover falls, is called in E.xiii.4,xxiii.15,xxxiv.18, 'the month of Abib'—month of ears; whereas in L.xxiii.5, N.xxviii.16, it is called 'the first month,' comp. E.xii.2,18,xl.2,17, N.ix.1, &c.

(ii) The phrase 'I am Jehovah' or 'I am Jehovah your God,' which is so common in some chapters of Leviticus, xviii–xxv, and N.iii, is entirely wanting elsewhere, e.g. in the Book of the Covenant, E.xx.22–xxiii.33.

(iii) The laws in the Book of the Covenant begin usually with כִּי or וְכִי which is followed by the verb and its subject, E.xxi.2,7,14,18,20,22,26,28,33,35,37,xxii.4,5, 6,9,13,15,xxiii.4,5. On the other hand many other laws commence with אִישׁ אֲשֶׁר נָפֶשׁ כִּי אָדָם כִּי אִישׁ, L.i.2,ii.1,iv.2,v.1,xiii.2,38,40,xv.2,5,16,33,xx (passim), xxii. 3,5,18,21,xxiv.17,19, &c. What Kurtz alleges, §27,n.13, to remove this difference, is only applicable to a few of the above passages.

(iv) The Feast, called elsewhere the 'Feast of Tabernacles,' L.xxiii.34, is called the 'Feast of Ingathering' only in E.xxiii.16,xxxiv.22. The Feast of Pentecost is called the 'Feast of Harvest' in E.xxiii.16, and the 'Feast of Weeks' in E.xxxiv.22; whereas in N.xxviii.26,comp.L.xxiii.15–21, it goes by the name of 'Day of Firstfruits.' Comp. further, generally, KNOB.*E.L.*,p.495,500,573,&c.

CHAPTER IX.

(36) " They are the following :—

(i) E.xii, institution of the Passover;

(ii) L.xxiv.10–23, punishment of blasphemy;

(iii) N.ix.1–14, delay of the celebration of the Passover on account of uncleanness;

(iv) N.xv.32–36, punishment of Sabbath-breaking;

(v) N.xxvii.1–11, xxxvi, succession of inheritance through daughters;

(vi) N.xxxi, division and dedication of booty.

All these laws—at least, in the form in which we now possess them—have never stood separately, but are in expression and form precisely adapted to constitute a portion of such an historical narrative, as that with which they are now connected. This appears especially plain with respect to E.xii, N.xxxi; but also, in regard to other passages, the above statement cannot appear doubtful.

" There exists a very close connection between E.xxv–xxxi.11, L.i–vii, (laws concerning the building of the Tabernacle and sacrifices), and E.xxxv–xl, L.viii,ix, (account of the building of the Tabernacle and of the consecration of the priests). With this last, again, L.x is very closely connected, except, perhaps, *v.*16–20 : comp. KNOB. *in loco.* This connection appears not merely from the agreement between the contents of the laws and the historical narrative, but also from the similarity of phraseology in both cases, and the numerous references to the Legislation, which characterise the narrative. See, however, POPPER.

Also in the Book of Numbers similar phenomena occur.

(i) The census in N.i gives exactly the same result as in E.xxxviii.26, note *44.vi*;

(ii) The laws about the Levites, N.iii,iv, are connected with L.x, comp.N.iii.4;

(iii) N.vii stands in immediate connection with E.xxv–xxxi, and the history closely connected therewith, E.xxxv–xl;

(iv) N.x.11–28 refers back to the ordinance about the erection of the camp and the order of march, N.ii;

(v) N.xviii (see especially *v.*3,4,7) is connected with the history of Korah's rebellion, N.xvi: see note *23.v*.

" (i) Thus, *e.g.*E.xxiv and xxxi.18–xxxiv.35 are connected, so that E.xxv–xxxi.17 is just as certainly inserted between the two historical passages, as, on the other hand, xxxi.18–xxxiv.35 breaks the connection between xxv–xxxi.17 and xxxv–xl. Not only in this last passage is the building of the Tabernacle related, as if nothing whatever had occurred after E.xxv–xxxi.17; but, besides this, in the historical passage, E.xxxiii.7–11, the existence of a Tabernacle is supposed, which according to E.xxxv,&c. has still to be built. In reply to this it may be said that in

E.xxv.16,21, Moses receives a command to lay up 'the Testimony, which Jehovah will give him,' in the Ark of the Covenant, as he actually does, E.xl.20 ; and this 'Testimony' is no other than the law of the Ten Commandments, which Moses, according to E.xxiv.12, was to receive on Mount Sinai. KNOBEL, *in loco*, denies this : but his view seems inadmissible ; comp. note [100]. But it will evidently be inferring too much from this one circumstance, to derive from it a proof that E.xxiv and E.xxv, &c. form part of one whole : all that can be concluded is, that E.xxv,&c. *so far as this point is concerned*, is introduced in the right place. Besides, this one detail is more than counterbalanced by E.xxv.9,40 [12],xxvi.30,xxvii.8 (comp.N.viii.4), where reference is made to what Jehovah had notified to Moses 'on the Mount,' as to something *already past*—though, according to E.xxiv.18, xxxii.7, Moses was still upon the Mount, while receiving from Jehovah these very directions about the Tabernacle, E.xxv.1–xxxi.11,[and would, therefore, if xxv,&c. formed part of the same whole as xxiv and xxxi.18–xxxiv.35, have been all along upon it.]

(ii) N.xv is not the least connected, either with N.xiii,xiv, or with N.xvi, whereas, on the contrary, N.xiii,xiv,xvi, follow each other,—at least, chronologically. We may the more reasonably regard N.xv as an interpolated passage, from the fact that *v*.2 in the present connection sounds like a sharp piece of unsuitable irony, [since they had just been condemned to perish in the wilderness, xiv.26–35].

(iii) The same judgment must be pronounced as to N.xxviii,xxix,xxx, which stand in no connection whatever with N.xxvii.15–23 and N.xxxi, while, on the other hand, these passages are immediately connected : comp.N.xxvii.13 with xxxi.2.

(iv) In like manner we must judge as to the whole of Deuteronomy in its relation to xxxii.48–52,xxxiv. Immediately after the two passages quoted above in (iii), we should expect the account of Moses' death, and not the contents of Deuteronomy. See Chap.X.

(37) [47] BAUMG., I.i.p.xci,&c. has adopted these. They are rejected, however, by most later critics, and expressly contested by KURTZ,ii.293,294,299,&c.

[48] The seven groups are the following: (i) E.xx–xxiii.19, (ii) E.xxv–xxxi.11, (iii) L.i–vii, (iv) L.xi–xvi, (v) L.xvii–xx, (vi) L.xxi–xxvi.2, (vii) N.x.11–xxxvi. We remark immediately that the last group is of much larger extent than the others ; but this is only in appearance, since all the historical passages and many loose laws are severed by BERTHEAU from the group, so that we obtain these seven 'series,' (α) N.xv.1–16, (β) and (γ) N.xix, (δ) N.xxviii,xxix, (ε) N.xxx, (ζ) N.xxxv. 1–15, (η) N.xxxv.16–34. Comp. note [50].

[49] BERTHEAU discusses the historical passages, p.297,&c., and comes to this twofold conclusion :—

(i) That the historical passages, separated from the laws, form no whole, and thus can never have existed separately, as a history of the Mosaic time, *i.e.* ' *the Historical has not existed without the Legislative,*' p.300 ;—

(ii) That the seven groups, which together compose a whole, formed according

---

[12] In xxv.9,40, however, the *participles* seem to express rather *present*, not *past*, time—' I (am) showing,' 'thou (art) shown.' Hence these verses appear to be discrepant with the others, xxvi.30,xxvii.8. *Ed.*

to a fixed plan, formerly existed separately, *i.e.* '*the Legislative has existed without the Historical; the Historical has been added to the Legislative already existing,*' p. 310. In what manner this has taken place, has appeared already in some measure, note ⁴⁹; but it must be here shown yet more definitely. To group (i) belongs the introduction, E.xix, the conclusion of the Covenant, E.xxiv.1–11, and an appendix, E.xxiv.12–18,xxxi.12–xxxv.3 ; to group (ii) belongs E.xxxv.4–xl; to group (iii), L.viii–x; groups (iv), (v), (vi), follow each other without interruption ; after (vi) the history is continued in L.xxvii–N.x.11. Finally, group (vii) has lost entirely its original form through the insertion of the historical pieces; N.x.11–xiv precedes the first ' series ' of its laws; between this series and the second and third N.xvi–xviii is placed ; after the third follows the historical section, N.xx–xxvii ; then we have the fourth and fifth series ; then the continuation of the history, N.xxxi–xxxiv ; and lastly the sixth and seventh series, N.xxxv.

(38)   ⁵⁰ Besides some passages of smaller extent, the following are severed from the groups as ' additional laws,' E.xx.22–26,xxiii.9–13,xxxi.12–17,xxxiv.11–26,xxxv.1–3, L.xxiv.1–23,xxvii, N.v.5–vi,viii–ix.14,xv.17–41,xxvii.1–11,xxxvi,—to which must still be added the half-historical pieces, E.xxxi.1–11, N.i–v.4,x.1–10,xxxiii.50–xxxiv, —lastly, also N.xvii.

How much there lies of arbitrariness in the separation of these laws, is obvious to every one. I point only to a few plain examples. Why are the laws in N.v.5–vi ' additional,' and those in N.xix not ? Bertheau cannot appeal to the *position* ; for N.xix stands between two of his historical passages, xvi–xviii,xx–xxvii, just as much as N.v.5–vi ; the laws in this passage, N.v.5–vi, are preceded by the usual preface, ' and Jehovah spake unto Moses, saying ' ; finally, its contents are at least as important as those of xix. In like manner we must judge as to N.xv.17–41 : from his point of view, Bertheau ought to have taken up into group (vii) at least v.17–31, but—then this group would have had a series too much. How difficult it is to sever the historical passages from the legislative, appears very plainly from this, that E.xxxi.1–11, as being semi-historical, is not reckoned to the group, so that it contained, forsooth, the commands about the erection of the Tabernacle, but not about the execution of these commands ; it appears also from the omission of N.xviii, a chapter of the highest importance, which cannot possibly be omitted in the Legislation,—at least can just as little be omitted as L.xxi,xxii,—but which, nevertheless, is dismissed from it by Bertheau ; it appears, lastly,—for I cannot name everything,—from L.xvi.1, where reference is made to L.x.1,2,—is made, consequently, to an *historical* passage,—*i.e.* to a passage, which, according to Bertheau, was added *afterwards* to the legislative.

⁵¹ The Pentateuch knows and names only one Decalogue, the well-known one which we find in E.xx.1–17, (the 'Ten Words,' E.xxxiv.28, D.iv.13,x.4). From this it does not at all follow that there are no other laws expressed in the form of ten commands ; but, if this form had been used *throughout* in the Books of Exodus, Leviticus, and Numbers, then, probably, this appellation would not have been given to the Decalogue alone,—then, also, most likely, some trace, or, at least, some reminiscence, of such a division would have been preserved in the Pentateuch. In the O.T., however, as in the Jewish tradition, we find nothing of this kind. Comp. Berth.p.xi–xvi, Jost,p.451–468.

Nevertheless, even in the absence of such a tradition, this hypothesis of Bertheau might be maintained as being quite simple and natural. Yet this is not the case. Here, also, I confine myself to a few examples.

(i) In E.xxi.12-27, the ten commands of the third series follow each other thus, (i) *v.*12, (ii) *v.*13, (iii) *v.*14, (iv) *v.*15, (v) *v.*16, (vi) *v.*17, (vii) *v.*18,19, (viii) *v.*20,21, (ix) *v.*22-25, (x) *v.*26,27. The ninth command ought evidently to be split into two, *v.*22,23, and *v.*24,25 ; the last two verses contain a general rule, which, by being connected with *v.*22,23, into one single command, partly loses its meaning. Bertheau can only here appeal to the absence of כִּי or וְכִי at the beginning of *v.* 24 ; but this particle is wanting also in xxi.3,4,5, and yet he sees here the commencement of three different commands. He had much better, therefore, have connected *v.*24,25, with *v.*26,27 ; since these last verses contain an exception to the rule set forth in *v.*24,25.[13]

(ii) E.xxi.26-32 forms one command: on the contrary, *v.*2-6 is split into five commands, and that, too, although the form of both sections, with a few unimportant variations, is quite the same.

(iii) E.xxiii.9-13 is to be regarded as a later addition to the Book of the Covenant, chiefly because it does not fit in to the ten-fold division, since all the other proofs of this its later origin are easily disposed of.

(iv) Again, it is strange that the small section, E.xxiii.14-19, is cut up into ten commands ; *e.g. v.*15ᵇ, 'and none shall appear before me empty,' is a separate command, though—supposing that it stands here in its place—it has no proper meaning except in connection with *v.*15ᵃ. Compare further Kurtz as above, note ⁴⁷.

⁴² Comp. Ew.ii.p.211-217. Bertheau seems to have been specially happy, p.197-216, in the division of L.xvii-xx, particularly in xviii.6-23 (first and second series). But even here there is no want of arbitrary displacement and splitting. Comp. further Bunsen's *Bibelwerk*,v.p.237, &c. 344, &c.

CHAPTER X.

(39) ⁴³ See above, note ⁹. Comp. especially xxix.1,—' these are the words of the Covenant, which Jehovah commanded Moses to make with the children of Israel in the land of Moab, *beside the Covenant which He made with them in Horeb,*'—and the formula ' *this* Law,' which distinguishes the Deuteronomistic Legislation from another, *i.e.* the Sinaitic.

(41) ⁴⁴ Very numerous are the references to what happened at Sinai and during the march through the wilderness. Comp. *e.g.* D.i.9-18 with E.xviii,—D.i.22-36 with N.xiii,xiv,—D.ii with N.xx, &c.—D.iii.26-28 with N.xxvii.15-23,—D.iv.9-11 with E.xix,xx,—D.vi.16 with E.xvii.1-7,—D.ix.8, &c. with E.xxxii, &c. especially *v.*10

---

[13] It appears to me that Bertheau's division might possibly be justified here. But, on the whole, his theory, however ingenious, seems very arbitrary and fallacious. *Ed.*

with E.xxxi.18, v.12 with E.xxxii.7–9, v.21 with E.xxxii.20, v.22 with N.xi, v.23 with N.xiii,xiv,—D.x.1,2,4, with E.xxxiv.1,2,4,28,29, v.22 with G.xlvi.27,—D.xi.3,4, with E.xiv,xv,—D.xxiv.9 with N.xii,&c.

Between some of these parallel passages, it is true, some discrepancy may be observed, see note [16]. But, on the other hand, the agreement,—sometimes, in minute details,—is so great, that we must assume the Deuteronomist to have had acquaintance with the preceding narratives, though he has here and there repeated their contents with great freedom.

Reference is made to a Legislation already existing in D.xviii.2, (comp. N.xviii. 20), D.xxiv.8, (comp. L.xiii,xiv,) D.xxvi.18,19, (comp. E.xix.4–6, L.xviii–xx,&c.), and to the Decalogue in particular in iv,v,x.

(42) [55] (i) This appears very plainly from D.v.6–21, comp. with E.xx.2–17. The edition of the Decalogue in D.v is later than that in E.xx. The reader may refer, among other points, to the insertion of the words, 'as Jehovah, your God, has commanded thee,' v.12,16,—to the additions, 'nor thine ox, nor thine ass,' v.14, 'that it may go well with thee,' v.16, 'his field,' v.21,—to the inversion of the order in v.21, which completely changes the original meaning of the word 'house'; for in E.xx.17 it denotes the house and all that belongs to it, so that v.17[b] sums up the different parts of the 'house'; whereas in D.v.21 the word denotes merely 'dwelling.' How Kurtz,ii.283, &c. can regard the edition of the Decalogue in D.v as the original, would be inexplicable, if we did not know that his business was to maintain the Lutheran reckoning of the Ten Commandments. Comp. on the other hand, Knob.E.L.p.197, &c.

(ii) Reference may also be made to D.vii.20,22, comp. with E.xxiii.28–30, and D.xvi.19, comp. with E.xxiii.8, where in each instance E.xxiii has the original,—to D.xv.12–18, comp. with E.xxi.2–11, which law is elucidated in Deuteronomy, comp. Hengst.iii.438, &c.—to D.xvi.1–17, where the three great Feasts are treated of, comp. with E.xxiii.14–19, L.xxiii,—the Deuteronomist having adopted the description of the Feasts first out of Exodus, [comp. 'month of Abib,' v.1, with E.xxiii.15,] and then again out of Leviticus: see note [43.4,iv]. Thus the third of these Feasts is called 'Feast of Tabernacles,' as in L.xxiii.34 ; but the origin of this name is not mentioned, it being understood as known already (from L.xxiii. 42–44).

[56] Del.p.25, &c. regards Deuteronomy, as well as E.xx–xxiii, as being a genuine Mosaic composition, and, on the other hand, he thinks that the middle three Books of the Pentateuch did not receive their present form until a short time after Joshua, and were only in part committed to writing in the wilderness. Hence it follows that, according to him, Deuteronomy is older than Exodus, Leviticus, and Numbers. We shall consider his view further on in Chap.XXI. Here I remark only that the different accounts, which are given in Deuteronomy, of some historical incidents (note[16] —which however, according to Delitzsch, were the *originals*,—are either not at all employed by the authors in Exodus and Numbers, or else are used in a very strange fashion, which is doubly surprising, if Moses himself recorded them in the form, in which we read them in Deuteronomy. It will presently appear, (note [41]), that the points of difference between the Legislation in Exodus–Numbers and Deuteronomy indicate a very different relation between the Books than is assumed by Delitzsch, as may appear in a measure already from the phenomena noticed above, note [55].

Of quite another kind is the view of the three other scholars above-named, which is developed at greatest length by GEORGE, p.13–75. He, for instance, assumes that the historical portions of the Pentateuch are the oldest, and that the Book of Deuteronomy was written in the age of Josiah, whereas most of the laws of Exodus–Numbers were first committed to writing in and after the Babylonish captivity. His proofs for this position are partly external, p.13–18, partly internal, *i.e.* derived from the comparison of the two legislations, p.18–75.

(i) *External evidence.* Jeremiah, who knows Deuteronomy well, and makes great use of it, knows, however, nothing of the Legislation contained in Exodus–Numbers,[14] as appears from vii.21–23, where he appeals to D.vii.6,xiv.2,xxvi.18, yet completely excludes the whole Law of Sacrifices, [as laid down in Leviticus and Numbers.]

Ans. But Jeremiah, as Hosea before him, vi.6, Isaiah,i.11–15, and other prophets, may have set the moral commands of the Law far above the ceremonial prescriptions, and regarded the former as the real foundation of the Covenant with Jehovah, without its following from this, that a ceremonial legislation did not yet exist in his time; he may even, in the passage quoted, have expressed his conviction that the prescriptions about ‘burnt-offerings and sacrifices’ were of later origin than the moral commands, without it following from this that Exodus–Numbers was committed to writing after Deuteronomy. See Chap.XX.

(ii) *Internal evidence.* This is connected with GEORGE's view as to the history of religious worship in Israel. He thinks, *e.g.* that no distinction was made between priests and Levites, or between high-priests and priests, until after the Babylonish captivity, and that the Mosaic Tabernacle never existed; also he is of opinion that the spirit and tendency of Deuteronomy transports us to a much earlier age than that of Leviticus. D.xxxi.14,15, is quite arbitrarily

---

[14] It is remarkable that Jeremiah, while showing the most intimate acquaintance with the Book of Deuteronomy, repeatedly using its favourite phrases and peculiar forms of expression, not only takes no notice of the sacrificial system, as laid down in Exodus–Numbers, but scarcely makes any reference to the *historical* portions of the first four Books,—never appeals to the accounts of the Creation, the Fall, or the Deluge, nor quotes a single incident in the life of Abraham, Isaac, or Jacob, only speaking of them once, xxxiii.26, generally and collectively, as the three patriarchs to whom Jehovah had sworn to give the land of Canaan, precisely as the Deuteronomist also does, i.8,vi.10,ix.5,27,xxix.13,xxx.20,xxxiv.4,—never mentions the names of Adam or Noah, nor even those of Moses, Aaron, or Joshua. These phenomena would be explained very easily, if Jeremiah really *wrote* the Book of Deuteronomy, as some suppose, see Part III, or if for some other reason he was specially conversant with that Book; but it seems hardly capable of explanation on the traditionary view. He was thoroughly imbued with the very language, as well as the sentiments, of the Deuteronomist: this is plain and admitted by all. He had also, it would seem, other portions of the Pentateuch in his hands, and was acquainted with some of the particulars contained in them. If, however, he possessed the whole Pentateuch, as we now have it, and regarded it as sacred and divine, how can we account for his remarkable neglect of the contents of the other books? *Ed.*

regarded as a later interpolation ; and no account at all is taken of D.xviii.2,xxiv.8. This whole criticism is very one-sided, and sacrifices everything to the priority of Deuteronomy.

The view of GEORGE, therefore, in the form in which he brought it forward, has been almost universally rejected. What amount of truth lies at the basis of it may be seen in Chap.XXI,XXIII. Here we are still occupied with showing the differences which exist between Deuteronomy and Exodus–Numbers, rather than with determining the true relation between the two Legislations.

(44) [37] Comp.D.xviii.2,xxiv.8. It is of much importance to keep this distinction in view, while the following points, also, are under consideration. The neglect of it will put us in danger of taking for discrepancy, what is easily explained from the different objects aimed at in the two legislations.

(45) [38] Out of the three preceding Books, comp.E.xxiii.20–33, L.xxvi.[15] The laws contained in these Books, vary in this respect from each other : whereas some are set forth without any assigned motive whatever, in the case of others the general or special reasons, which account for their being issued, are expressly named. In L.xviii–xx, for instance, this is very common. What occurs, however, in the other Books only here and there, as an exception, becomes the *rule* in Deuteronomy. The lawgiver passes over continually into the admonitory tone, connects glorious promises with obedience to his commands, fearful threats with the neglect of them, &c. It would be superfluous to produce examples of this. From note [39] it appears, further, that this phenomena *taken by itself* will not prove anything for difference of authorship : it is only in connection with the points which follow that it acquires significance in this respect. SCHULTZ,p.7, defines the object of the Deuteronomistic Legislation in the following words : ' Its purpose is throughout, especially by means of amplifying, auxiliary, ordinances, to conduce to this end, that the laws or insti- tutions of the previous Books, whose full validity is here assumed, may be carried out—not in any arbitrary kind of way, but—*according to their inner nature, their higher object, their idea,* in spite of all difficulties which may exist in Canaan or elsewhere.' To what extent this describes truly the relation of the Deuteronomistic laws to the foregoing, will appear below, notes [50,51]. Yet in general the distinc- tion between Deuteronomy and Exodus–Numbers is not incorrectly expressed in the words above transcribed. The hortatory tone of the Deuteronomistic Legislation, its greater earnestness, its being addressed to the whole people, have, no doubt, in view the dedication of the *hearts* of the Israelites to the service of Jehovah and their free-will obedience to His prescriptions.

(46) [40] There is pretty general agreement as to the difference in language between Deuteronomy and the preceding Books: see *e.g.* KEIL,§30,HÄv.I.ii.p.461,&c. While some think to explain the difference entirely by reference to the purpose and form of Deuteronomy, others are of opinion that it gives evidence of difference of authorship. In connection with the other proofs which lead to the same conclusion, this last ap- pears fully justified, especially from the fact that the language of Deuteronomy is so

---

[15] There is reason, as I believe, for supposing that both these passages are Deuteronomistic interpolations, P.III.566 : see notes 192a,iv. *Ed.*

uniform, that is, is distinguished by so many, continually recurring, formulæ, which are just as constantly wanting in Exodus–Numbers, as, on the other hand, many vivid expressions and ideas of these last are looked for in vain in Deuteronomy.

(i) We find the phrase '*burn out* (E.V. 'put away') the evil from among you,' · D.xvii.7,xix.19,xxi.21,xxii.21,24,xxiv.7, '*burn out* the evil from among Israel,' D.xvii.12,xxii.22, '*burn out* the innocent blood from Israel,' D.xix.13, 'from among you,' D.xxi.9, '*burn out* (E.V. 'bring away') the hallowed things out of the house,' D.xxvi.13, '*burn out* (E.V. 'take away') thereof for unclean use,' D.xxvi.14, —but in Exodus–Numbers *never*.

(ii) On the contrary the formulæ, 'and that soul (those souls) shall be cut off,' —'in their (your) generations,' ¹⁶—שׁיא שׁיא, 'every man,'—occur very commonly in the preceding books, but in Deuteronomy *never*.

(iii) Both חֹק and חֻקָּה, 'statute,' in the *singular*, occurs very frequently in Exodus–Numbers, E.xv.25,xxx.21, L.vi.11,15,vii.34,x.15, N.xviii.8,11,19, E.xii.14, 17,43,&c.&c.¹⁷—in Deuteronomy *never*.

(iv) On the other hand the synonymous words, 'statutes,' 'commandments,' 'judgments,' 'testimonies,' occur in Deuteronomy on every page combined with one · another in various ways, iv.1,5,8,14,45,v.1,31,vi.1,2,17,20,vii.11,12,viii.11,xi.1,32, xii.1,xxvi.16,17,xxvii.10,xxviii.15,45,xxx.10,16. In the foregoing books the same combinations occur a few times in L.xviii–xx, then in the subscriptions, L.xxvi.46, N.xxxvi.13, lastly, also in G.xxvi.5, E.xvi.28, L.xxvi.15.¹⁸ They are, consequently, much more frequent in Deuteronomy, and must, therefore, be regarded as a peculiarity of his style of writing.

(v) The formulæ, 'observe to do,' D.v.1,29,vi.3,25,&c. (15 times),¹⁹—'the good

---

¹⁶ In P.III.548 this formula should be added as one of the 'expressions common throughout the first Four Books of the Pentateuch, but never employed by the Deuteronomist': viz.—(xiv) 'in their (your, his) generations,' G.xvii.7,9,12,E.xii. 14,17,42,xvi.32,33,xxix.42, xxx.8,10,31,xxxi.13,L.iii.17,vi.18,x.9,xxii.3, xxiii.14,21, 41,xxiv.3,xxv.30,N.ix.10,x.8,xv.14,15,21,23,xviii.23,xxxv.29, comp.G.vi.9—*nowhere in Deuteronomy. Ed.*

¹⁷ In P.III.548.viii the numbers of references may be largely increased, as follows:— חֹק or חֻקָּה, *sing.*G.xlvii.22,22,26,E.v.14,xii.14,17,24,43,xiii.10,xv.25,xxvii.21,xxviii. 43,xxix.9,28,xxx.21, L.iii.17,vi.11,15,vii.34,36,x.9,13,14,15,xvi.29,31,34,xvii.7,xxiii. 14,21,31,41, xxiv.3,9, N.ix.14,14,x.8,xv.15,15,xviii.8,11,19,23, xix.2,10,21, xxvii.11, xxxi.21,xxxv.29—*nowhere in Deuteronomy. Ed.*

¹⁸ These exceptions may be Deuteronomistic, or, at least, later interpolations in the older story: see note ¹⁹. *Ed.*

¹⁹ 'Observe to do' occurs *twenty* times in Deuteronomy, *viz.*v.1,29,vi.3,25,vii.11, viii.1,xi.22,32,xii.1,32,xv.5,xvii.10,19,xix.9,xxiv.8,xxviii.1,15,58,xxxi.12,xxxii.46,— and *nowhere else in the Pentateuch*; 'observe' and 'do,' in the same context, occurs *ten* times in Deuteronomy, *viz.* iv.6,vi.17, (see *v.19*),vii.12,xiii.18,xvi.12,xxiii,23, xxiv.8,xxvi.16,xxviii.13,xxix.9,—and also in L.xviii.4,5,26,30,xix.37,xx.8,22,xxii.31, xxv.18,xxvi.3, but *nowhere else in the Pentateuch*.

There is thus, evidently, some peculiar relation between L.xviii–xxvi and Deuteronomy, of which we shall see other strong indications. Either these chapters

land,' D.i.[25,]35,iii.25,iv.21,22,vi.18,viii.[7,]10,ix.6,xi.17,[20] [comp. 'good mountain,' iii.25, 'good cities,' vi.10, 'good houses,' viii.12]—'which ye go over to possess,' with variations, D.iv.5,14,26,vi.1,vii.1,xi.8,10,11,29,xxiii.20,xxviii.21,63,xxx.16,18, xxxi.13,xxxii.47,[21]—'go after Jehovah,' 'go after other gods,' D.iv.3,vi.14,viii.19, xi.28,xiii.2,4,xxviii.14,xxxi.16,[22]—*never* occur in Exodus-Numbers.

(vi) So, too, the expression 'set before the face,' in the sense of 'give up,' 'place at the disposal' of a person, D.i.8,21,ii.31,33,36,vii.2,23,xiii.14,xxxi.5, comp. xxviii.7,25, is found *nowhere* in Exodus-Numbers; for the single example produced by Keil,§33,n.3, viz. E.xxx.36, is quite of a different kind.

(vii) The following phrases are also peculiar to Deuteronomy, some of which never occur elsewhere—not only in the Pentateuch, but—in the whole Bible:—

'putting forth of the hands,' D.xii.7,xv.10,xxiii.20,xxviii.8,20 ;

'work of the hands,' D.ii.7,xiv.29,xxiv.19,xxviii.12,xxx.9 [23] ;

'as the roebuck and as the hart,' D.xii.15,22,xv.22 ;

---

are due to the Deuteronomist, and, if so, they may have been written by him some years before he wrote Deuteronomy itself, P.III.811,—at a time when he, perhaps, may have only intended to retouch and vivify the older document which had come into his hands; and, therefore, may have adhered more closely to the style of the older writers, making use, now and then, of their formulæ : *e.g.* in L.xxvi.46 we have חֻקֹּת, 'laws,' in the *plural*, which we never find in Deuteronomy itself; and also 'Sinai,' for which we have *always* ' Horeb ' in Deuteronomy (see note [39.viii]), except once in the 'Blessing of Moses,' xxxiii.2, which may have been written under similar circumstances, P.III.811, as a complement of the older narrative. Or, else, these chapters, L.xviii-xxvi, must have been composed by some prophetical writer or writers out of the same circle as the Deuteronomist. *Ed.*

[20] This phrase is found also in E.iii.8,N.xiv.7, both which, from internal evidence, I assign to the Deuteronomist: see P.III.566. But, for Prof. Kuenen's argument, it is enough that the phrase was manifestly a *favourite* phrase with the Deuteronomist, but not with the other writers of the Pentateuch. *Ed.*

[21] Add from P.III.550.iii—D.i.8,iv.1,22,vi.18,viii.1,ix.1,5,x.11,xi.8,31,xii.29,xvii. 14,xxvi.1 ; comp.i.21,39,ix.4,23,xxx.5. *Ed.*

[22] Comp. also D.i.36.vii.4,xii.30 ; and note as follows:—

(i) The expression in D.xxxi.16, 'go a whoring after other gods,' occurs also in L.xvii.7,xx.5,6, which may be due to the Deuteronomist, (note *), and also in E. xxxiv.15,16,16, which, together with the context, E.xxxiv.5-26, I see reason for regarding as a Deut. interpolation ;

(ii) The expression in D.i.36, 'fulfil after Jehovah,' occurs in N.xiv.24, (? Deuteronomistic, pote[20]), and also in N.xxxii.11,12, and I see grounds for regarding N.xxxii as also a Deut. interpolation ;

(iii) The expression in D.vii.4, ' turn away from after Jehovah, occurs in N.xiv. 43,xxxii.15,—both, as above (ii,iii), perhaps, Deut. passages ;

(iv) Comp. D.xii.30 with E.xxiii.24,32,33 ('snare'), and E.xxxiv.12 ('snare'), 15,16 ; there is reason to regard E.xxiii.20-33, as well as xxxiv.5-26 (as above, i), as, perhaps, a Deut. interpolation. *Ed.*

[23] Add from P.III.552.iv—D.xvi.15,xxvii.15,xxxi.29. *Ed.*

*flocks (עֶשְׁתְּרֹת) of thy sheep,' 'increase (שְׁגַר) of thy kine,' D.vii.13,xxviii.4, 18,51; the latter expression occurs also in E.xiii.12 **24** ;

'Belial,' D.xiii.13,xv.9.

(viii) It is remarkable, again, that the scene of the Legislation is always in Deuteronomy called *Horeb*, D.i.2,6,19,iv.10,15,v.2,ix.8,xviii.16,xxix.1, while the name *Sinai* occurs only in xxxiii.2, in the so-called 'Blessing of Moses,' an interpolated passage.

As to the connection between the two names, see the *Bijb. Woord.* iii.348, where at the same time HENGSTENBERG'S attempt, to reason away the difference of the names, is set aside.

(ix) The verb אָהֵב, 'love,' is used to express the relation of Jehovah to Israel, D.[iv.37,]vii.8,13,x.15,xxiii.6,while in D.[v.10,]vi.5,vii.9,x.12,xi.1,13,22,[xiii. 3],xix.9,xxx.6,16,20, mention is made of Israel's duty to 'love' God: the last idea is met with in the rest of the Pentateuch only in E.xx.6 **25** (=D.v.10),—the former *nowhere.*

(x) Only the Deuteronomist knows of Israel's duty to 'cleave' unto Jehovah, D.iv.4,x.20,xi.22,xiii.4,xxx.20.

(xi) Only the Deuteronomist gives the admonition to 'circumcise the foreskin of the heart,' D.x.16,xxx.6 : comp., however, L.xxvi.41.**26**

(xii) First in Deuteronomy the idea, that Jehovah is *the only God*, is forcibly expressed, D.iv.35,39,vi.4,xxxii.39 ; whereas in Exodus-Numbers Jehovah's *might and exaltation over the other gods* is more prominently set forth, E.viii.10,ix.14,xii.12, xviii.11,xx.3–5. Comp. further, especially RIEHM,p.16-24.

Note, also, that this difference in language is in reality coupled with a difference in *ideas*, which fact is inconsistent with the view, that it may be explained merely out of the national character of the book. Besides which, most of the points of difference above noted are quite unconnected with that rhetorical character. See especially DEL.p.28,29, DE WETTE,p.211, and, on the opposite side, KEIL,§30. The points of agreement between Genesis–Numbers and Deuteronomy, produced by him, are very insignificant, and may be explained, wherever that is needed, from the fact of the Deuteronomist being acquainted with the former Books, of which we have more than once made mention above. We shall treat about the *archaisms* below, Chap.XXII.

(48) ** Nothing is more difficult than to establish a general rule, according to which the cases mentioned in the text (48–50) may be judged. Frequently critical feeling alone can decide here. This is especially true of the ordinances out of the Books of Exodus–Numbers, which do not occur in Deuteronomy. What has been remarked in (44) as to the purpose of this Book, explains completely why the laws, which concern only the priests and Levites, are not here repeated. It is more strange that the Deuteronomistic Legislation nowhere notices the Levitical cities, D.xviii.1,2,

24 It will be seen that E.xiii.12 agrees with E.xxxiv.19, but is at variance with L.xxvii.27, N.xviii.15,16 (see note ⁴⁰·¹). I see reasons for assigning E.xiii.12, like E.xxxiv.19 (note ²²·¹), to the Deuteronomist. *Ed.*

25 This passage also is very probably Deuteronomistic: see note. *Ed.*

26 L.xxvi.41 is, perhaps, a Deut. interpolation: see note **19**.

comp. note[61]; and that no mention is made of the solemn celebration of the New Moon and of the Day of Atonement, although the three Great Feasts, note[48-51] are treated of in D.xvi. Other omissions will be mentioned in note[61] since those' ordinances, which are not repeated, are continually replaced by others.

(49)   [61] (i) The variations of the Deuteronomistic Legislation with respect to the priests and Levites are so important, that they may be brought under different heads.

(1) *The distinction between the priests and Levites is not maintained so strongly as in Exodus–Numbers.*

In these latter the priests are called either *cohănim* or 'sons of Aaron'; the Levites are expressly subordinated to them, and excluded from all properly priestly duties, &c.: comp. N.iii,iv,viii,xvi–xviii, especially xvi.9,10,40,xviii.1–3. In Deuteronomy the state of things is manifestly different. The priests are frequently called, 'the priests the Levites,' D.xvii.9,18,xviii.1, [xxi.5,] xxiv.8,xxvii.9, [xxxi.9, comp. xviii.1–5,xxxiii.8–11,] as if the descent from the tribe of Levi was the chief thing, and as if this were the ground of the priestly dignity. In D.xviii.1 we even read, 'The priests the Levites,[27] *the whole tribe of Levi*, shall have no part nor inheritance with Israel,' where the distinction appears to fall away entirely, since 'all the tribe of Levi' stands in apposition with 'the priests the Levites.' Remarkable also is D.xviii.6–8, where the Levites without exception are regarded as competent to '*minister in the name of Jehovah, even as all their brethren the Levites*, (comp.v.1,) *who stand there before the face of Jehovah.*'

In Numbers, these expressions are never used of the Levites: there we read that they are to 'minister' to the *priests*, N.xviii.2, and to 'stand before the face' of the *priest*, N.iii.6, and of the *people*, N.xvi.9. Comp. also D.x.8,9, with N.vi.22,27,—and D.xxxi.9, where the bearing of the Ark of the Covenant is assigned to the *priests*, with D.xxxi.25,x.8, where the *Levites*, as in the foregoing Books, discharge this duty.[28]

In vain do Hengst.iii,p.401–404, Häv.I.ii.p.429,&c. and others, try to get rid of these facts. See especially Riehm,p.34–39.

(2) *The Levites [in Deuteronomy] do not live in the cities assigned to them, but are scattered about in the whole land.*

See D.xii.12,18,xiv.27,29,xvi.11,14, where mention is made to all Israel of 'the Levite, *who is in your gates*,' and D.xii.19,xiv.27,29,xvi.11,14,xviii.6,xxvi. 11–13, where they are placed upon the same line with 'the widows and orphans,' and commended to the charity of the Israelites.

(3) *The Deuteronomistic Legislation*, in distinction from N.xviii.21–32, *requires neither tithes for the Levites nor firstlings of all animals for the priests*, as laid down

---

[27] The E.V. has here made an important alteration of the text, by inserting 'and,' for which there is no authority in the original. *Ed.*

[28] The expressions, 'the Levites,' 'the tribe of Levi,' are here used by the Deuteronomist manifestly as synonymous with 'the priests the Levites,' xxxi.9, 'the priests the Levites, all the tribe of Levi,' xviii.1. In other words, with the Deuteronomist, 'priest' and 'Levite' are identical. *Ed.*

in N.xviii.15–19 and other passages, quoted above in note ⁴⁰⁴. Its definitions with respect to tithes, firstfruits, and firstlings, are as follows;

(*a*) The firstfruits—even of the 'fleece of the sheep,' of which the foregoing Books make no mention—belong to the priests, D.xviii.4, comp. xxvi.1–11;—

(β) The tithes of cattle are not mentioned, from which it must not be inferred that they were also not required;—

(γ) The tithes of the fruits of the field and the firstlings of clean cattle are to be brought to the holy place and there used at the sacrificial feasts, or, if the distance thither was too great, the Israelite might turn them into money at his place of abode, and procure for the price, at the place where the Sanctuary stood, the necessaries for the sacrificial-feast, to which also he was to invite the Levite, D.xii.6,17–19,xiv, 22–27,xv.19–23;—

(δ) The tithes of the fruits of the field must *in every third year* be collected in the place of abode of the Israelite, and left for the Levites, widows, orphans, and strangers, D.xiv.28,29;—

(ε) The firstlings of unclean animals seem not to belong to the priests; at all events, they are not mentioned, nor is anything said about their being redeemed.

How much all this varies from the prescriptions of the other Legislations is obvious. There is no want, it is true, of attempts to adjust the discrepancy·; but they must all without exception be regarded as unsuccessful.

It is maintained, for instance, that the usual tithes, N.xviii.21–32, are not *mentioned*, indeed, in Deuteronomy, but they are *understood*, and that here, consequently, *two tithes* are required.

Ans. But it is seen at once that in D.xviii.1–5 the revenues of the priests are summed up, and yet the 'tithes of tithes,' N.xviii.15–32, are not mentioned, and that the Levites, generally, appear as needy persons, which would be absurd, if they received the tithes, and even share besides in the sacrificial-feasts, and obtain a part of the (supposed second) tithes of the third year.

Again, it is maintained that the firstlings of clean cattle, even according to the earlier Legislation, did not belong wholly to the priests, HᴇɴɢsT. iii.406,407, Häv. I.ii.p.429,&c.

Ans. But this is in direct contradiction with N.xviii.15–18. One can hardly trust one's own eyes, when it is seen how unfairly this passage is handled, first by HᴇɴɢsTᴇɴʙᴇʀɢ, and afterwards by Kᴇɪʟ upon Häᴠᴇʀɴɪᴄᴋ. It is expressly said that the firstborns of men and cattle belong to the priests, *v.*15,—that they must not allow the firstlings of clean cattle to be redeemed, because they are holy, their blood must be poured out upon the altar, and their fat burnt, *v.*17; 'and *the flesh of them'*— so the lawgiver proceeds, *v.*18—'*shall be thine; even as the wave-breast and the right-shoulder, it* (the flesh) *shall be thine:*' in other words, as the priests are to receive the breast and right-shoulder of the thank-offerings, according to L.vii.28–34,x.14, 15,—(which passages, again, do not quite agree with what the law of Deuteronomy lays down, with respect to the priests' share of the thank-offering,)—so they are to receive also 'the flesh' of the firstlings. HᴇɴɢsTᴇɴʙᴇʀɢ explains this, as if they received in the case of the firstlings also only the breast and the shoulder, and he supports this interpretation by a number of sophisms. How entirely this is at variance, not merely with N.xviii.17,18, but also with *v.*16, E.xiii.12,13,xxxiv.19,20,—

all which passages declare plainly that the firstborns are not in part, but entirely, the property of Jehovah,—needs no demonstration. Since, then, it can hardly be maintained that the *firstborns* in N.xviii were a *different kind* of firstborns—though MICH. iv.107,108, is not deterred from making even this conjecture—analogy requires that we should not distinguish the *tithes* in Deuteronomy from those which occur in Numbers, or, in other words, that we abandon the hypothesis, in itself highly improbable, of *second tithes*. Comp. further, RIEHM, p.39–49.

The variations of the Deut. Legislation on these points are usually explained by the supposition that, at the time of the Deuteronomist, the demands of the earlier laws neither were, nor could. be, fulfilled, so that a modification of them, which at the same time was a relief for the people, was considered urgently necessary. We shall return, however, again to this point, Chap.XXI.

(ii) That the Deut. prescriptions about the form of government point to a later time, is shown by RIEHM, p.61–65.

(iii) Also the strong injunction to *worship Jehovah at one place* requires the same explanation, especially because the existence of the Temple at Jerusalem is manifestly implied, D.xii.5,11,14,18,21,26,xiv.23–25,xv.20,xvi.2,6,7,11,15,16,xvii.8,10, xviii.6,xxvi.2,xxxi.11. It is true, mention is made of 'the place, which Jehovah *shall* choose,' to put His Name there, or to dwell in. But, that this belongs to the *clothing* of the Deuteronomistic Legislation, and that, in fact, it is acquainted with the Temple, appears especially from xii.5, 'the place which Jehovah shall choose out of all your tribes,' and xii.14, 'the place which Jehovah shall choose in one of thy tribes.' In the case of these expressions, we must certainly think of a *fixed* place; the Tabernacle, with its continual change of place, 2S.vii.6, cannot here be meant. To the same conclusion we are led by the formulæ, 'make His Name to dwell there,' xii.11,xiv.23,xvi.2,6,11,xxvi.2, and 'put His Name there,' xii.5,21, xiv.24.

HÄV. I.ii.p.468, has rightly observed that Jeremiah, vii.12, uses the first of the above expressions in speaking of the Tabernacle at Shiloh. But, in the first place, Jeremiah, who had before his eyes daily the Temple at Jerusalem, might apply to a former Sanctuary a formula belonging properly to this Temple: in the case of the Deuteronomist, we can only suppose this, if we place him after Solomon. And, secondly, the other formula is usually employed with reference to the Temple, 1K. ix.3,xi.36,xiv.21, 2Ch.vi.20,xii.13. Add to this, that it is very doubtful whether Jeremiah,vii.12, is speaking of the Tabernacle, and not rather of a fixed Temple at Shiloh. Comp. GRAF, p.116,117.

(50) [63] The subjects which are regulated for the first time in the Deuteronomistic legislation, are (i) the kingdom, xvii.14–20,—(ii) prophetism, xviii.15–22,xiii.1–5, —(iii) the mode of making war, xx, (for the law in N.xxxi is quite of a different kind,) —and some others of less importance. RIEHM, p.57,&c.61,&c. How strongly the regulation of these particular subjects, especially of the kingdom and prophetism, argues for this Legislation having originated a considerable time after Moses, is plain. Add to which, that the law of the kingdom, xvii.14–20, in the first place, cannot have been in existence in Samuel's time, 1S.viii.6–22,xii and, secondly, is manifestly directed against excesses, which had been already begun by Solomon, and the repetition of which the lawgiver tries to prevent, see notes [172,174,210].

(51) (**) See above note *, and below note ***, and Chap.XXIII.

SCHULTZ, p.13,&c.33, &c. thinks that he has discovered yet another proof of the Mosaic origin of Deuteronomy in the *plan* of the book, *i.e.* in the arrangement of the laws in D.v–xxvi according to the order of the Ten Commandments. He thinks this discovery so certain, that he would account, p.2, for the inability of EWALD, RIEHM, and others, to express their views about Deuteronomy, through the fact that they have not remarked this order. It exists, however, only in his own imagination, as may here be briefly shown. The ten groups of laws, then, which are supposed to correspond to the Ten Commandments, are these: (i) and (ii) v–xi, (iii) xii–xiv, (iv) xv–xvi.17, (v) xvi.18–xviii.22, (vi) xix.1–xxi.9, (vii) xxi.10–23, (viii) xxii.1–29, (ix) and (x) xxii.30–xxv, with appendix, xxvi. Properly, nothing more is needed than this statement to convince us at once that the whole view is untenable. The perplexed and confused reasoning, whereby SCHULTZ tries to show the agreement between each command and the group corresponding to it, gives it not even an appearance of truth. It is already exceedingly artificial, that the laws about the ' avenger of blood,' xix.1–13, about carrying on war, xx, and about the cleansing of the ground which has been stained by blood, xxi.1–9, are regarded as a further development of the command, ' Thou shalt do no murder': and yet this instance is the most probable of all. Comp.D.xxi.10–21,22,23, with the command, ' Thou shall not commit adultery ': the direction, that the corpses of persons hung shall be removed before the evening, in order that the land might not be defiled, is to be regarded as a development of the law which forbids adultery ! Just as absurd it is that D.xxii.1–4,5–12,13–29,—(this division is SCHULTZ's, and so, too, the preceding groups consist each of three subdivisions,)—is brought into connection with the commandment, ' Thou shalt not steal ': read only D.xxii.5,6,7,8–11,&c. about ' battlements,' ' mixed seed,' ' fringes on apparel,' &c.! After these instances, it seems almost superfluous still to remark,—

(i) That the connection of the laws about unity of worship, xii, false prophets, xiii, and cleanness of food, xiv.1–22, (wherewith SCHULTZ, to favour the triple form, unites v.23–29,) whether with each other, or with the Third Commandment, D.v.11, is equally arbitrary ;—

(ii) That the comprehension of rulers (kings), priests, and prophets, under the Fifth Commandment, which prescribes reverence towards elders, is merely in appearance correct, while, further, the directions *given to the king himself*, xvii.14–20, have nothing in common with the Commandment ;—

(iii) That the uniting together the First and Second, but, above all, the Ninth and Tenth, Commandments is a plain proof of the writer's inability to maintain fully his system ;—

(iv) That the prescriptions answering to the Ninth and Tenth Commandments, xxiii.30–xxv, for by far the greatest part, do not even exhibit any appearance of agreement with these commands. What agreement, for instance, exists between the cleanness of Israel, xxii.30–xxiii.18, (if with SCHULTZ we take all these verses together,) and the Commandments, which forbid false-witness and coveting the property of another? or between the same Commandments and D.xxiii.19–25 ? and D.xxiv? and (N.B.)D.xxv.4,5–10,11,12,17–19?

(v) In conclusion, I point also to D.xix.15–17, which verses have, in fact, some

K

connection with the Ninth Commandment (against false-witness), yet do not appear in the *Ninth* group, but in the *Sixth*, which ought to stand in connection with murder.

A thoughtful perusal of D.xii–xxvi rather convinces us anew continually, that occasionally, indeed, like is annexed to like, but that yet the writer *very often* places, one after the other, prescriptions which have nothing in common with each other. A *System* of Legislation, in the proper sense of the word, is no more contained in Deuteronomy, than in the preceding three Books, note ⁵⁰.

CHAPTER XI.

(53) ⁴⁴ Thus do, *e.g.* EICHORN, iii, *passim, e.g.* p.160,&c. and with him JAHN, WELTE, and others. On the contrary, the authenticity of the *whole* Pentateuch is maintained by HENGSTENBERG, HÄVERNICK, and KEIL, though it is generally given up, even by DELITZSCH and KURTZ. What passages are regarded as glosses, may be gathered from Chap.VIII. It is the less necessary to spend more time over this, since the latest investigation has plainly shown that the few passages, which in this way used to be struck out of the Pentateuch, give by no means the strongest evidence against its Mosaic origin.

⁴⁵ It is only with reference to a few notices in Deuteronomy, that exegetical reasons lead to the supposition that they also are glosses. See *e.g.* D.ii.10–12,20–23,iii.9–11, and especially x.6–9, at least x.6,7. But it will appear below, note ⁵⁰, that such notices must be regarded in a certain sense, indeed, as glosses, but yet as *proceeding from the author himself*. Only x.6,7, seems to suit so little in this connection, that it cannot be ascribed to the Deuteronomist. Comp. however, KNOB. *N.D.J.*p.248.

What is stated in the text (53) requires, further, for strict accuracy, some explanation. The Pentateuch, *as it now lies before us*, is ascribed by the traditionary view to Moses. Every one, therefore, who regards any portion of it as dating from the time after Moses, gives up in fact the traditionary view. In that case, however, there exists no further reason why he, any more than others, should continue to *maintain* or *hold* that view, at least, *as far as possible*. Such a course is only reasonable, when the traditionary view is regarded either (for dogmatic reasons) as infallibly true or as thoroughly credible. Short and just is the remedy of de WETTE, i.188 :—'The assumption of glosses by EICHORN and others, also by WELTE, would only then be justified, if the earlier composition had been *demonstrated* from some quarter or other.'

(⁴⁶) 'Mosaic' betokens here—not only *instituted*, but also—*written* by Moses. The traditionary view, according to which Moses *wrote the whole Pentateuch*, must always be well distinguished from the tradition concerning Moses *the lawgiver of Israel*. This last is so old and so general, that we can properly assign to it much greater weight than to the former. Bleek, p.181,&c.(comp. also his former treatises quoted in that work,) has not kept in view this distinction, and,—certainly, on this account—has not recognised the rule in question. He draws attention, for instance, to the fact, that in the book of Exodus–Numbers different laws and collections of

laws occur, which concern the Israelitish people, so long as they continued in the camp
in the wilderness, and in which all reference is entirely wanting to later times and
circumstances, *e.g.* to their dwelling in towns and villages, to the kingly form of
government, &c. All these laws, he thinks, must also have been committed to
writing by Moses, or, at least, under his eye and superintendence. And this
seems to him so certain and manifest, that he accordingly builds upon it the
proposition, p.197, 'that we have no right to assign away from Moses any laws
and ordinances ascribed to him, unless it appears that they exhibit manifest
signs of later time and a character different from that of the incontestably
genuine Mosaic prescriptions.' Now we have already seen, notes ⁴⁰,⁴¹, that the
laws of the Book of the Covenant, in particular, vary very frequently from the
other ordinances; so that, even on the principles put forth by BLEEK, we must
make choice between these laws, which vary from each other, and cannot ascribe
them all equally to Moses. Hereafter, note ³⁰⁰, we shall show that the laws of the
Book of the Covenant are older and more original than the others, so that these
last, if for no other reason, cannot have been recorded by Moses. But we will go
yet further, and maintain that the rule itself, set forth by BLEEK, cannot hold good.

(i) As regards the fact, from which it starts, it is, indeed, undeniable, that
many laws suppose the wilderness, and contain no references whatever to later
times. BLEEK himself takes, as the most manifest examples of this, L.i–vii,xvi,
xiii,xiv, N.xix, L.xvii,xi,xii,xv, E.xxv–xxxi, N.x.1–8,i,ii,iv, and shows at full length,
p.183–197, that mention is made continually here of 'Aaron and his sons,' of the
'Tabernacle of the Congregation,' the 'Camp,' the 'Princes,' in a word, of all kinds of
circumstances and regulations, which existed in the Mosaic time, but not afterwards,
comp. *e.g.* L.iv.11,12,21,i.5,7,11,ii.2,10,iii.2,5,13,&c.xvi.10,21,22,26–28,xiii.46,N.xix.
3,7,9,14, &c. &c.

(ii) But these phenomena admit of being explained in two ways. They show
either that the author of these laws really lived and wrote in the Mosaic time,
or that he transports himself into that time, chooses, as it were, his station
therein, and puts forth the laws in the person of Moses, or, at least, of one of his
contemporaries. Which of these two explanations is the true one, cannot be
determined *à priori*. BLEEK considers it very improbable that a later writer
should have tried, still more that he should have succeeded in the attempt, to
transfer himself so completely to an earlier period. But why should that be so
improbable? Was it not rather necessary, if the laws put forth were to pass as
Mosaic? Besides, does not the Pentateuch—even according to BLEEK—give
numerous and incontestable instances of such a transference? N.viii, *e.g.* professes quite as much as the passages above-named, to be an ordinance out of the
Mosaic time, comp. *v.*9,11,13,19, &c. And yet BLEEK acknowledges, p.214,215,
that this chapter, particularly *v.*23–26, is irreconcilable with N.iv, see above,
note ⁴⁰⁻ᵛⁱⁱⁱ, and thus must have proceeded from a different time. Comp., also, as
to N.iii and the difference between this chapter and N.i,ii,iv, BLEEK, p.284,285;
yet mention is continually made in these chapters also of 'Aaron and his sons,'
of the 'Tabernacle of the Congregation,' &c.

But especially the Book of Deuteronomy comes here under consideration. That
it professes to have been written by Moses,—that the Conquest of Canaan is set forth

continually in it as *future*,—is obvious, and is admitted by BLEEK, p.307, and elsewhere. Yet he assumes, p.303—and on very good grounds—that the whole Book
was written under Manasseh. Does it not follow from this, that the circumstances
of the Mosaic time, the local colouring, &c., may very well belong to the *clothing*
of any particular law, and that we are thus not justified in deducing its age alone,
or chiefly, from this?

(iii) Besides, BLEEK, in order to maintain his views with reference to the Mosaic
origin of these laws, L.i–vii,&c. is obliged to have recourse to very improbable
auxiliary suppositions. He regards, for instance, E.xxv–xxxi as genuine Mosaic
p.193,194,&c. It cannot, however, escape his notice, that there exists a discrepancy between these chapters,—viewed in connection with E.xxxv–xl,—and
E.xxxiii.7–11 ; see note [464]. This gives him occasion to suppose that E.xxv–xxxi,
and especially E.xxxv–xl, are placed *too early*, and that in E.xxxiii.7–11 mention
is made of *another* 'Tabernacle of the Congregation,' which was not superseded,
until the later years of the march through the wilderness, by the splendid Tabernacle, described in E.xxv,xxvi,xxxv,xxxvi. For confirmation of this conjecture
he appeals to E.xxvii.21,xxix.42,44,xxx.36, where the name 'Tabernacle of the Congregation' is supposed to be already known, whereas that mentioned in E.xxxiii.7–11
is newly introduced,—' Moses took the Tabernacle, and pitched it without the camp,
afar off from the camp, and called it the Tabernacle of the Congregation ; '—further,
he points also to E.xxx.12,13,xxxviii.25,26, where—especially in the last-mentioned
passage—the census is supposed to have been already made, which proves that in
reality the building of the Tabernacle took place at a later time than we should
conclude from the present order of the laws and narratives. Here we find what
may be called the Achilles'-heel of BLEEK's whole theory. All along, the chapters
regarded by him as Mosaic, L.i–xvii, N.i,ii,ix, all suppose the completion of the
Tabernacle, in accordance with E.xxxv–xl, and are regarded as promulgated *in the
Tabernacle*, L.i.1,ix.5,23,x.7,9, N.i.1,ii.2,17, and before the march out of the wilderness of Sinai, L.vii.38, N.i.1,19. Now I willingly grant, comp. Chap.VIII, that BLEEK
has most excellent grounds for pronouncing this order of events and laws to be improbable, p.219 ; yet he ought not to have ignored that they are given exactly thus in the
chapters which he holds for genuine Mosaic. Rather, this difficulty ought to have
given him occasion to test again his view, as to the Mosaic origin of these chapters,
and, while so doing, to lay more weight upon the testimony of the history of Israel
and of the Israelitish worship (see below, Chap.XIX), to which, as it is, too little
weight has been ascribed by him,p.188,189, since he maintains the antiquity of L.xvii,
and only afterwards, p.297, in the enquiry about Deuteronomy, comes to his senses.
The connection between E.xxv–xxxi and xxxv–xl is so close, that we cannot hold
the first group for genuine Mosaic, and yet regard the statements of the second in
main-points as unhistorical. Rather, E.xxxviii.25,26, in connection with N.i, must
be regarded as a proof, that, in the laws marked off by BLEEK as Mosaic, we have
before us the work of an author, or of different authors, who transported themselves
into the Mosaic time, but did not live in it, and who just for that very reason—
although in general they knew how to keep well the local colouring—yet now and
then plainly betray that they stood far away from Moses and his time. Comp.
further, Chap.XIX,XX.

The ideas of BLEEK as to the Mosaic Tabernacle, E.xxv,&c. are closely connected with those of BUNSEN, *Bibelwerk*,PartII, *Bibelurkunden*,i,p.218,226,&c.247,&c. where, likewise, the chronology of the Pentateuch is given up, and is modified, quite arbitrarily, for the purpose of maintaining the credibility of the narratives and the authenticity of most of the laws. The whole method of BUNSEN, by which the duty of distinguishing between the genuine *documents* and the later, often incorrect, *edition* of them, is consigned to the subjective judgment of the critic, deserves just as little recognition as that of BLEEK.

(54) " VATER.iii,p.393–728, HARTMANN.

" See above Chap.I. From the survey there given, it appears at once that the Pentateuch is in fact put together after a definite plan, and forms a whole. This is shown at full length by RANKE,i.9–156, HÄv.I.ii.p.35–58, and others. From Chap.III–X it may be easily deduced in what sense *unity* can be ascribed to the Pentateuch. The great fault of RANKE is this, that he does not properly distinguish connection of the parts, and regular plan of the whole, from unity of authorship. The last may be denied, without on that account ignoring completely the other two points.

(55) " This is also the view of most later critics, *e.g.* of de WETTE, STÄHELIN, BLEEK, TUCH, KNOBEL, EWALD, HUPFELD, VETH (*Bijb.Woord.*ii.p.588,&c.) DELITZSCH, KURTZ. In the determination, however, of the original extent of the prime-documents, of their age, and of their mutual connection, they differ much from one another. Further, I use here the name, *document-hypothesis*, quite in a general sense, so that it includes also the so-named *supplement-hypothesis*, Chap. XVIII, which most of the above-named scholars advocate.

(56) " Our principle derives its best justification from its application, (see below Chap.XII,&c.) from which it will also appear, why *e.g.* the contradiction between two laws is not always a sufficient reason for denying that both belonged originally to one and the same document.

CHAPTER XII.

(58) " (i) The plural אֱלֹהִים, *elohim*, as well as the singular, אֱלוֹהַּ, *eloăh*, is derived from the word אָל, which is not used in Hebrew, but has in Arabic (*aliha*) the signification of *dread* (be astounded, tremble, comp. FLEISCHER's opinion in DELITZSCH, p.64,&c.). *Eloăh* is thus properly 'fear,' then the 'object of fear,' the 'person or thing feared;' comp. the use of פַּחַד, fear,' in G.xxxi.42,53, 'the Fear of Isaac;' and in the same sense is *Elohim* used. How the plural should be explained,— whether by it is indicated the abstract idea, (properly, *res tremendæ*, 'what is terrible,' then, quite indefinitely, *numen tremendum*, 'the Deity,') or whether it is a *pluralis majestaticus*, and so, perhaps, a real plural, and, consequently, a relic of an earlier polytheism—I leave undecided. It is enough that *Elohim*, by virtue of its original signification, is used to express the Deity in the most general way. When it occurs in the O.T. joined with a plural [verb or adjective,] it may be occasionally translated by 'higher being,' 'higher beings.' When joined with a

singular, as is usually the case, *Elohim* denotes '*the* higher Being' *par excellence*, i.e. God. Comp. NOORDBERGH in the *Jaarb. voor Wet. Theol.*vi.731–741.

(ii) The name יְהוָֹה, as is well-known, should be expressed יַהֲוֶה, *yahveh*, or, יַהֲוָה, *yahvah*; the Masoretic vowels, [by means of which the form יְהוֹהַ, *yehovah*, E.V. 'Jehovah,' is obtained,] belong properly to the word אֱלֹהִים, *elohim*, or, אֲדֹנָי, *adonai*, [which the Jews pronounce instead of יְהוָֹה, whenever it occurs in the Bible.] It must—at least, according to E.iii.13–15 — be derived from הָוָה, *havah* = הָיָה, *hayah*, 'to be,' and denotes, according to this etymology, 'He Who Is.' In this appellation there lies, perhaps, an antithesis to the 'gods, who are not,' the אֱלִילִים, 'idols,' L.xix.4,xxvi.1, comp. KNOB.*E.L.*p.30,31, and, probably, at the same time an indication of the *unchangeableness* or *eternity* of Him, who bears the name Jehovah: comp., besides HENGST.ii.226–250, and other writers, quoted by KNOBEL as above, also BUNSEN's *Bibelwerk*,i.p.lxxxviii,&c. who declares for the translation 'the Eternal,' chiefly on the ground of E.iii.13–15. In any case, Jehovah is the personal or proper name of God, and through this is manifestly distinguished from *Elohim*. Comp. further KEIL,§25, where at the same time the very extensive literature, concerning the two names and their signification, is—at least, for a great part of it—abandoned.

[72] (i) However often 'God' has to be expressed as an appellative, the Hebrews can only use *Elohim*, e.g. in the formulæ, 'God of Israel,' 'God of Abraham,' &c. 'my God,' 'your God,' &c. 'I will be to them a God,' &c.: *Jehovah* would here be quite unsuitable.

(ii) Generally, where the *divine* and the *human* are expressly compared with each other, or such a comparison is designed by the writer, he must also equally use *Elohim*. Comp. e.g. Ju.ix.9,13, G.iv.25 (*Cain* killed Abel, *God* gave me Seth in his place), G.xxxii.28, E.xxxii.16. (*divine* work and writing, not *human*), E.viii.19, &c.

(iii) Israel alone knows God as Jehovah: hence, when the heathen speaks of God, he must use Elohim. If this rule is a few times contradicted in the O.T., G.xxvi.28,29, 1S.xxix.6, 1K.v.7,x.9, we can only regard this as a slip of the writer, who has become so accustomed to the use of Jehovah, that the name flowed from his pen involuntarily.

[73] Whenever, e.g. an Israelite speaks to a heathen, then the use of Elohim is most natural, and, therefore, also the most usual: see, e.g.G.xx.13, where Elohim is even joined with the plural, xxxix.9,xl.8,xli.16,25,28,32,32. Elsewhere, whenever the *God of Israel* is contrasted with the *gods of the heathen*, the former can only be called Jehovah, 1K.xviii.21,36,37, Ju.xi.24, E.xii.12,xv.11,xviii.11.

[74] GES. *Thes.*i.97, says, that אֱלֹהִם simply, without the article, has the same force as הָאֱלֹהִם, with the article; and this name is used six hundred times, both in prose and in poetry, with hardly any distinction for יְהוָֹה,—and so, indeed, that either name seems to be employed at will, or the use of it commonly depends upon the nature of the formulæ, and some usage of the language, or the choice, use, and custom of the individual writers.' The correctness of this position appears, among other things, from this, that in some later Books of the O.T., e.g. in Ecclesiastes, the name Jehovah is purposely omitted,—and that in the collection of Psalms a large number of Psalms is found, in which the name Elohim occurs almost

exclusively, and in quite the same sense, and in the same formulæ, as Jehovah in other instances: compare *e.g.* Ps.xiv.2,4,6,7, with Ps.iii.2,4,5,6,—Ju.v.[3,]4,5, with Ps.lxviii.[5,]8,9,—[Neh.xiii.1ᵇ, with D.xxiii.3ᵃ,]&c.; see DEL.*Symb.adPsal.*p.7, &c.; lastly, it appears from the use of the Divine names in G.i–E.vi, of which more presently.

(59) ⁷⁵ See the complete list of these three classes of contents in KEIL, §25,n.3, and more accurately in DEL.p.63,64, where are distinguished *Elohistic, Jehovistic, mixed,* sections, and sections of *uncertain character.* It seems unnecessary to give here a general review of them, since in Chap. XIII,&c. the narratives will have to be considered one by one. As examples I select G.i.1–ii.3, (*Elohim* alone, 35 times), G.xviii.1–xix.28 (*Jehovah* alone, 16 times, *Adonai,* 6 times), G.xxiv (*Jehovah* alone, [as a *Personal* Name;] 19 times), G.vi.9–xi.29 (*Jehovah,* 7 times, *Elohim,* 15 times, *ha-Elohim, twice*), G.xxxiv,xxxvi,xxxvii,xl, (chapters without any Divine Name).

(60) ⁷⁶ The most eminent advocates of this view are HENGST.ii.181–414,—KEIL,§25, and KEIL on HÄV.I.ii.p.72–104,— formerly also KURTZ, *Beitr.* and *Einh.*—who, however, afterwards, *G.A.B.*ii.531,&c.541,&c. declared himself for the documentary hypothesis, in that form in which it was put forth by DELITZSCH,—NOORDBERGH (*Jaarb. voor Wet. Theol.* vi.727–755, *concerning the Divine Name Elohim, its conjectural origin, transition into that of Jehovah-Elohim, and the use made of it in the Pentateuch.*)

It is rightly remarked by all these writers, that *Elohim* and *Jehovah* are by no means synonymous, and, therefore, also could not have been generally used promiscuously, notes ⁷¹⁻⁷⁴. Yet between this last proposition and *their* view respecting the Divine Names in the Pentateuch there lies a wide chasm, which can only be filled up by artificial hypotheses. It does not, therefore, surprise us that all these writers—however agreeing in the result—yet differ far from one another in the demonstration itself: every one's ingenuity and (so-called) penetration has here free play. Their explanations are mostly of such a kind that they condemn themselves. I give only a few instances of this, derived from HENGST.ii.306,&c.

(i) In G.i.1–ii.3 *Elohim* is used, because the writer has taken in hand to set forth clearly in the light, how God reveals himself gradually to man as Jehovah,— 'how He passed by degrees, for human consciousness, out of Elohim into Jehovah.' Thus at the Creation only the general idea of God (*Elohim*) lies, of course, at the basis of all. But, it will be said, in G.ii.4–6 *Jehovah-Elohim* is used (*i.e.* according to HENGST. *Jehovah, who is Elohim*), and in that passage, too, the Creation is spoken of, note ¹⁷¹. Yet, 'the living, personal, self-revealing, holy, God meets us here. He appears as the loving provider for men, as the regulator of moral life, commanding and forbidding, as the inflicter of punishment, as the revealer of the prospect of the future restoration.' Perfectly true: but then, is not *Elohim* in i.26–29,ii.3, just as truly 'the living, personal, self-revealing God, the loving provider for men, who regulates their religious life,' ii.3?

(ii) G.vi–ix is discussed in p.324–336. Among other things, *Jehovah* is used in vii.1–5 because there mention is made of clean and unclean animals, which distinction has reference to the matter of sacrifices, and sacrifices, we know, were offered to *Jehovah,* not to *Elohim,* 'since this act of worship supposes the greatest activity of the conscious recognition of God, taking place with reference to a *personal*, not a shadowy (*verschimmenden*), God.' What shall we say then of G.xxxv.1–7, where Jacob 'built an altar unto *Elohim* ? '

(iii) Again, in G.vii.16[b], *Jehovah* is used, because *He* is the righteous and merciful: but what then of G.vi.11,12,13 ? The writer here wishes to show that God, who had already begun to reveal himself as *Jehovah*, G.ii–iv, is yet 'relatively' *Elohim*, inasmuch as more glorious revelations of His nature, as Jehovah, follow afterwards in the history of Abraham. In order, then, to make this plain, he begins by using several times the name Jehovah, G.vi.1–8, in order that it may appear that God was already 'relatively' Jehovah, and then there follows the repeated use of *Elohim*, G.vi.9,&c. which now cannot any more be misunderstood (!) The introduction, G.vi.1–8, shows plainly that by *Elohim* must be understood 'not the *bare* Elohim, but Elohim already in transition to Jehovah, —Jehovah, who yet in relation to the following, *i.e.* to G.xii,&c. is Elohim' (!)

That these Rabbinical subtleties condemn themselves is obvious. They are, consequently, modified even by KEIL—at least, to some extent. Yet how these can maintain that the name Jehovah occurs in the first part of Genesis, G.i–xi, merely in such narratives, as stand in distinct connection with the revelation of that salvation which begins with Abraham, is to me an enigma. See, *e.g.*G.iv.1,3, 9,&c. x.9,xi.5,9.

(iv) With just as little reason does he explain the fact, that Jehovah becomes more rare in the last chapters of Genesis, by means of this statement, viz. that *revelations* of God are less numerous here than in G.xii,&c. At all events, in G.xxxix—where, strictly speaking, no revelation is mentioned—Jehovah occurs *eight* times, ha-Elohim *once* : while in G.xlvi.2–4 it is precisely *Elohim* that reveals himself to Jacob.

Our conclusion as to the untenableness of these attempts agrees, generally, with that of DEL.p.34,&c. and the writers quoted by him, p.70,71, besides the advocates of the document–hypothesis above-named, note [m]. With respect to this, it is remarkable that KEIL begins his treatise with the declaration that all attempts made hitherto (1851), to explain the different use of Jehovah and Elohim, must be regarded as failures, and that DRECHSLER has himself rejected afterwards (in DEL.p.71,72), his former explanation, which essentially agreed with HENGSTENBERG's view.

[77] This view, so far as I know, has only met with one defender, viz. VAN WILLES; i.p.1–92. It starts with the very improbable supposition, that the narrators had before them the *ipsissima verba* of the persons, about whom the narratives are speaking. Further, it does not appear what gave the writers occasion to follow in the use of the Divine Names—not the custom of their time, or their own judgment, but—the example of the persons in question. Lastly, his whole hypothesis can only be maintained through very hazardous auxiliary suppositions.

(i) Thus, *e.g.* the author has used *Elohim*, when God appears in the narratives as *El Shaddai*. But why Elohim, and not Jehovah? See our answer to this question below, note [81]. So in G.xxii.11 the author has used Jehovah, because Abraham in *v.*14 employs this name. But in *v.*8 the patriarch had used Elohim; so that the narrative, as it were, 'outruns him.'

(ii) In G.xxiv Abraham uses the name Jehovah, *v.*3,7: upon his footsteps, then, follow the other speakers in the narrative, and the narrator himself in *v.*21,26,52. But how can Abraham's habit of speech have exercised an influence upon Laban, who—without having heard one word out of the mouth of the servant—says to him, 'Come in, thou blessed of *Jehovah,' v.*31? It seems unnecessary, however, to spend any more time on this hypothesis.

[78] DEL., p.34, allows for a moment the possibility that the writer of Genesis may have used, for the sake of variety, first one, and then the other, name, and explains in this way the use of Elohim in many Psalms; the same poets, who employ usually Jehovah, make use of Elohim in some of their songs. I admit readily that this explanation would have some appearance of truth, if the two names were always so interchanged as in G.vii.16,xxvii.27,28, E.iii.4,ix.28,xviii.1, xix.3, &c. But how is it to be explained from this point of view that in G.i.1–ii.3 *Elohim* is used 35 times [as a *personal* Name,] without a single Jehovah, and in G.xxiv *Jehovah* 19 times, without a single Elohim? DELITZSCH ends, consequently, with admitting that, what in the abstract might be considered *possible,* yet in this particular case cannot be *really* the case, especially because the different use of Jehovah and Elohim ends after E.vi, at least, never occurs again to the same extent as in G.i–E.vi. Concerning the *Elohistic Psalms* comp. the *Bijb.Word.*iii.151,152. According to my judgment, the use of *Elohim* in these Psalms must be ascribed to subjective motives. The Compiler—(according to DELITZSCH, the Author)—thought good to omit the name 'Jehovah' throughout, and to substitute for it Elohim.[29]

---

[29] Why should the compiler (or author) have omitted 'Jehovah,' more or less, just in these particular Psalms, (*viz.* all those of Book II and the 'Psalms of Korah' in Book III, (P. II.429), and not in the others? Above all, why did he allow 'Jehovah' to appear *occasionally*—though much more rarely than 'Elohim,' —in *some* even of these Psalms, as *e.g.* in Ps.lxviii (E.31,J.4,A.7)? It seems to me impossible to account for this phenomenon, in *all* the instances where it occurs, in this manner. According to my judgment, these Psalms must have been written at a time when 'Jehovah' was more commonly employed by the *author* (or authors) of them than 'Elohim.' But this might arise *either* from its having *recently become known,* and not yet become familiar, as a household word, to *him* (or them) at all events, and in that case, we must believe, also to the nation at large,—*or,* from its having gone, for some reason or other, comparatively *out of use,* either with the nation at large, or at least with the individual writer (or writers). This last is the case supposed by KURNEN, or, rather, by DELITZSCH; and it will account satisfactorily for the phenomenon in some of the *later* 'Psalms of Korah,' as Ps.lxxiv and Ps.lxxix, (P.II.435), which agree with the Books of Ezra and Nehemiah in using 'Elohim' more freely than 'Jehovah,' (P.II.436). But the name 'Jehovah' occurs in the names of *Jo*el and Ab*iah,* Samuel's sons, 1S.viii.1,2,—*Jo*nathan, Saul's son, xiii.2,—A*hiah,* Eli's great-grandson, xiv.3,—Zeru*iah,* David's sister, and *Jo*ab, her son, xxvi.6,—Adoni*jah,* Shephat*iah,* Jedid*iah,* David's sons, 2S.iii.4,xii.25,— *Jo*nadab, his nephew, xiii.3, —*Jo*nathan, xv.27,—Bena*iah, Jeho*iada, *Jeho*shaphat, xx.23,24,—another Bena*iah,* xxiii.30, *Jo*nathan, *v.*32, and Ur*iah,* the Hittite, *v.*39. These all lived in David's age, and the name 'Jehovah' was, therefore, certainly *well known* to David and his contemporaries. It, therefore, as I believe, Ps.lx

(61) [79] In order to arrive at certainty, as to the meaning of E.vi.2,3, we must above all things lay stress upon a distinction which is too frequently passed by. Hengst. ii.262,&c. Kurtz, §25,n.2, and others try to show that the name Jehovah existed long before Moses. In this they appeal to the form of the name (derived from the old הוה, for which afterwards היה came into use), and especially to some pre-Mosaic names compounded with Jehovah, as *Jochebed*, E.vi.20, N.xxvi.59, *Ahijah*, 1Ch.ii.25, *Abiah*, grandson of Benjamin, 1Ch.vii.8,—according to Hengstenberg, also *Moriah*, G.xxii,2. With Ew.ii.p.184, I should judge that only the name Jochebed [30] had any force as proof, and should thence deduce that the family or tribe, to which Moses belonged, already knew the name Jehovah, so that Moses did not invent it, which, indeed, by itself would be very improbable.

But this whole enquiry, however important it may be for the history, does absolutely nothing towards determining the meaning of E.vi.2,3. In explaining this passage the question arises, *What says the writer* about the age of the name Jehovah? If, now, it were well and clearly shown that Abraham knew this name already, (as Hengstenberg supposes to be shown by *Moriah*, G.xxii. 2,) it would not by any means follow that this might be gathered also from E.vi.2,3. Yet very little acuteness is necessary to see that many interpreters have thus reasoned, half unconsciously, from this passage.

A second remark, which is closely connected with the first, concerns E.iii.13-15. Some use this passage in order to show what the writer *must have meant* in E.vi.2,3. But thus the *unity of the Pentateuch*, about which the difference of opinion exists, is assumed as proved.

We must confine ourselves, therefore, to the actual words of the writer, whom we have before us in E.vi.2,3. And, in point of fact, it does not then appear difficult to find out its true meaning. Let this be noted:—

(i) According to v.2, *Elohim* speaks to Moses; it is thus Elohim, who before had appeared to Abraham as *El Shaddai*, and now makes Himself known as *Jehovah*. In other words, El Shaddai and Jehovah are two forms of revelation of Elohim, a

---

(E.5,J.O.) and Ps.lxviii (E.31,J.4,A.7) are really *Davidic* Psalms, that is, either written by David or emanating from his age, it seems to follow (as I have argued in P.II) that the name 'Jehovah,' though known in David's time, was *not freely and familiarly used* by the writer or writers of these Psalms, either the king himself or some other eminent and devout persons of his time. And, if this be true, it tends strongly, as I conceive, to *confirm* the indications, furnished by other independent phenomena, as to the comparatively recent introduction of this name. *Ed.*

[30] On this point I must at present differ from Prof. Kuenen. It appears to me highly improbable (i) that the name Jehovah should have been confined for some time to one family or tribe of Israel, (ii) that, if known to the family or tribe of Moses, we should find no trace of it in the composition of the names of any of his relatives in E.vi.16-25, except Jochebed, (iii) that the name Jochebed should have been omitted in the account of Moses' birth in E.ii.1, 'and there went a man of the house of Levi, and took a daughter of Levi,' if it was *known* to the writer of this passage. I imagine, then, that E.vi.20, N.xxvi.59, are *later* insertions: see P.II.305. *Ed.*

lower and a higher form of revelation, the last-named chronologically later then the first. From this it may be inferred at once that the higher was still unknown, at a time when the lower already existed. If Abraham, Isaac, and Jacob, knew God already as Jehovah, then the antithesis between the patriarchal and Mosaic time is entirely done away.

(ii) The somewhat strange construction, v.3ᵇ, וּשְׁמִי יְהֹוָה לֹא נוֹדַעְתִּי לָהֶם, 'and I, my name Jehovah, was not known to them,' (E.V. *by* my name Jehovah) = 'I have not made myself known to them,' is explained, according to HITZ.*B.d.K*.p.23, *Psalm.*i.41,42, from passages such as Ps.iii.4,(5),xvii.10,xxxii.8,xliv.2,(3),cix.2,cxlii. 1(2), where with one verb (here נוֹדַעְתִּי) a double nominative is connected, of which the one (here the pronoun 'I,' that lies included in the verb) denotes the proper subject, the other (here 'my name') denotes *that* part of the subject to which the action of the verb belongs. Thus we have Ps.iii.4(5), קוֹלִי אֶל־יְהֹוָה אֶקְרָא, 'I call unto Jehovah with my voice,' where it stands properly, 'I, my voice, call unto Jehovah.' So in the other passages. The sense of E.vi 3, therefore, can only be this: 'I was not known to them, as far as concerns my name Jehovah.'

(iii) According to the Hebrews, there exists a very close connection between the *name* and the *nature* of a person or thing. The name is not accidental or arbitrary, but the expression of the nature: the *not knowing God by the name Jehovah* is, therefore, equivalent to the *not knowing God's nature, as this expresses itself in the name Jehovah.* HENGST.ii.267-291, has shown this to superfluity. It is generally agreed, then, that God's nature, expressed in the name Jehovah, was first fully revealed to Israel in the Mosaic time, and that this is expressly taught in E.vi.2,3. If there exists, however, such a close connection between *nature* and *name*, then—we should say—the making-known of the name must belong to the same Mosaic time.[31] HENGST. rejects this conclusion, yet sees himself thereby compelled to recognise in the patriarchs an acquaintance with the *sound* Jehovah, while he denies to them insight into the meaning of this name. For the patriarchs, therefore, the name Jehovah was something involuntary and accidental—in opposition to the true nature of names among the Israelites, as HENGST. himself has already shown. But —it is objected—the patriarchs understood this name, if not entirely, yet at all events partially. I answer that E.vi.2,3, mentions nothing of this, just as there, generally, the knowledge of the *name* is not distinguished—much less severed—from the knowledge of the *nature.* If the patriarchs understood something of *the nature of God as Jehovah,* that was, according to our writer, just as much of it as was expressed in the name El Shaddai. Comp. further, besides the commentators, HUPF.*Q.d.G.*p.87,88.

[40] The author of E.vi.2,3, knew the name Jehovah, yet still held that Abraham did not know it. From this it follows at once that those passages of Genesis, where

---

[31] Prof. KUENEN has not, however, *proved* what is here assumed, as generally admitted, viz. that 'God's *nature*, as expressed in the name Jehovah, was first fully revealed to Israel in the *Mosaic* time,' from which he infers that the *name* was introduced also in the *Mosaic* age. According to the view which seems to me most *probable* for reasons summed-up in my Pentateuch, II.493, the 'name' may have really first been explained to Israel about the time of Samuel. *Ed.*

God names Himself Jehovah, xv.7, or where others use this name, v.29,xvi.2,5, 11,&c., are not from his hand. But whether he himself, when speaking about the patriarchal time, has omitted to use the name Jehovah, cannot be deduced from E.vi.2,3, but must be made out experimentally. We shall see, however, that he uses the name Elohim throughout, and that the examples of the use of Jehovah [in Elohistic passages] are so rare, that it may be reasonably doubted whether the reading is correct in the few places where it occurs.

[81] As regards the patriarchal time, see v.3,4, (where the appearances of God to Abraham, Isaac, and Jacob, the Covenant concluded with them, and the promises given to them, are mentioned); as regards the deliverance out of Egypt, see v.6, (where mention is made both of the fact itself, and of the miracles with which it was attended); lastly, as regards the settlement of the theocracy, see v.7,8, 'I will take you to me for a people, and I will be to you a God,' 'I will bring you in unto the land, concerning the which I did swear to give it unto Abraham, to Isaac, and to Jacob.'

(62)   [82] The propriety of this distinction needs not to be shown at length. It is very possible, and not at all improbable, that our author's ideas about the age of the name Jehovah were shared also by others, upon whose writings they might thus exercise the same influence as upon that of the writer, whose express testimony we have before us in E.vi.2,3. We shall see, however, that some critics, by giving one-sided and exclusive attention to the name Elohim and the omission of Jehovah, have become involved in all kinds of difficulties, which fall away of themselves, when—as the nature of the case requires—we regard the use of Elohim as only one peculiarity of our author, which only acquires weight and meaning in connection with the rest. As marks, to which special attention should be paid, the following expressions and sentiments occur in E.vi.2–9:—

(i) God appears to the patriarchs as ' *El-Shaddai*,' v.3 ;

(ii) God ' *establishes a Covenant* ' (הֵקִים בְּרִית) with them, v.4 ;

(iii) God promises to them the possession of Canaan, ' *the land of their sojournings, in which they sojourned*,' אֶרֶץ מְגֻרֵיהֶם אֲשֶׁר גָּרוּ בָהּ, v.4 ;

(iv) God ' *remembers His Covenant*,' v.5 ;

(v) God makes the Israelites go out ' *from under the burdens of the Egyptians*,' מִתַּחַת סִבְלֹת מִצְרַיִם, v.6,7 ;

(vi) God ' *redeems* ' (גָּאַל) them with outstretched arm and great *judgments* ' (שְׁפָטִים) v.6 ;

(vii) God promises that He will ' take Israel to Him for a people, and will be a God to them,' v.7 ;

(viii) God is said to ' *lift up the hand* ' = swear, v.8.

[83] It follows, for instance, as a matter of course, from the contents of E.vi.2,3, that our author in the sequel of his history has made use continually of the name Jehovah, after the reason, for which he omitted it, had ceased to exist, through the communication of this name to Moses. We purposely here direct attention only, generally, with a single word, to the possibility that the author of E.vi.2,3, may have treated of the history of Israel also *after* the conquest of Canaan, to which he refers in v.8. Comp. Chap.XXIV,XXV.

(64) [31] 'Then, in the time of Enos, was it begun to call upon the name of Jehovah.' If we compare xii.8,xiii.4,xxi.33,xxvi.25, there can be no doubt about the meaning of these words. With Enos began the 'formal and solemn adoration of Jehovah in word and act, *i.e.* prayer and sacrifice,' Del.p.217,218. That such an adoration involves acquaintance with the name Jehovah, follows most plainly from בְּשֵׁם, *i.e.* properly, 'making use of the name Jehovah.'

[32] Comp. *e.g.* Kml.,§25, Häv.I.ii.p.104, and elsewhere.

•

CHAPTER XIII.

(65) [36] The most important proofs are the following, comp. note[32]:—

(i) God reveals himself as 'El-Shaddai,' xvii.1,xxxv.11, as in E.vi.3 ;

(ii) 'Elohim,' xvii.3,9,15,18,19,22,23,xxxv.9,10,11,15;

(iii) 'land of sojournings,' xvii.8, as in E.vi.4;

(iv) 'establish (הָקִים) a Covenant,' xvii.7,19,21, as in E.vi.4, comp. 'give (נָתַן) a Covenant,' *v.*2;

(v) 'to be a God unto thee and unto thy seed after thee,' xvii.7,8, as in E.vi.7.

The two sections agree also with each other—

(vi) in the change of names, xvii.5,15,xxxv.10,—

(vii) in the similar promises, xvii.6,16,xxxv.11[b],—

(viii) in the use of the phrase פְּרֵה וּרְבֵה, 'fructify and multiply,' xvii.[(2 + 6)], 20,xxxv.11.

We remark also in G.xvii some particulars, which we shall turn to account presently, *e.g.*—

(ix) The phrase 'be perfect,' xvii.1 ;

(x) אֲחֻזָּה, 'possession,' *v.*8 ;

(xi) 'in their generations,' *v.*9 ;

(xii) accurate chronological data, *v.*17,24,25 ;

(xiii) *Ishmael's* existence is supposed to be known, *v.*18 ;

(xiv) 'on the selfsame day,' lit. ' in the bone of this day,' *v.*23,26 ;

(xv) In xxxv.9, the land, from which Jacob returns, is called 'Padan-Aram,' while, at the same time, his journey to that land is merely referred to with a single word, as a known fact.

Against the points of agreement between G.xvii and E.vi.2–9 may be alleged the use of the name *Jehovah* in G.xvii.1, which is the more strange since in the same chapter *Elohim* is named six times. Many interpreters are, therefore, of opinion that Jehovah is a mistake in copying for Elohim ; others see in xvii.1 the hand— not of the *author*, but—of the *compiler*. These conjectures are not in themselves absolutely necessary, since it does not at all appear from E.vi.2,3, that the writer of the Elohistic document must have *always* omitted the name Jehovah in the *narrative* also: see note[30]. Only then shall we be entitled to resort to them, should the investigation teach us that in G.xvii.1 the name Jehovah is an exception to a rule otherwise universally followed. As to the particle עוֹד, 'again,' G.xxxv.9, see note [247].

(66)   [97] DELITZSCH, KNOBEL, and HUPFELD, the three latest interpreters of Genesis, who recognise the existence of an Elohistic document, are agreed in this, that the greater and smaller sections, above indicated, must be assigned to him. In fact they agree both with the former passages, E.vi.2-9, G.xvii, xxxv.9-15, and with each other, in a striking and often surprising manner. The full proof is given by the writers referred to; but the most obvious points of agreement may here find a place.

(i) 'land of sojournings,' G.xxviii.4,xxxvi.7, as in E.vi.4, G.xvii.8;

(ii) 'establish a covenant,' G.vi.18,ix.9,11, as in E.vi.4, G.xvii.7,19,21;

(iii) 'fructify and multiply,' G.i.22,28,ix.1,7,xxviii.3, as in G.[xvii.(2+6)],20, xxxv.11;

(iv) 'Padan-Aram,' G.xxv.20,xxviii.2,5,6,7, as in G.xxxv.9;

(v) אֲחֻזָּה 'possession,' G.xxiii.4,9,20,xlix.30,l.13, as in G.xvii.8;

(vi) לְדֹרֹת עוֹלָם 'for perpetual generations,' G.ix.12, comp. לְדֹרֹת G.xvii.9;

(vii) 'after their (its &c.) kind,' G.i.11,12,12,21,21,24,24,25,25,25,vi.20,20,20;

(viii) 'was perfect,' G.vi.9, as in G.xvii.1.

(ix) The name 'Elohim' is used throughout in all these passages, G.i (35 times), v.1,1,24,24,vi.9,11,12,13,22,ix.1,6,8,12,16,17,xix.29,xxviii.4,—the name 'Jehovah' never.

(x) 'El Shaddai' occurs in G.xxviii.3, in the mouth of Isaac.

(xi) The chronological data in G.xvii, note [86-xii], are prepared-for, implied, or expressed, in the genealogies, G.v,xi.10-32, also in G.xxv.20,xxxv.28.

(xii) There not only exists between these sections mutually no contradiction, but they refer back to each other continually. I name here only some obvious instances of this: comp. G.i.26,27, with v.1-3,ix.6,— G.i.29, with ix.3,—G.xvii.8 with xxviii.4, xxxv.12.

(xiii) The genealogy in G.v is immediately connected with G.i.1-ii.3, and is carried on in G.vi.9,10,ix.28,29,xi.10,11,&c.

(xiv) All the above genealogies agree in form with each other, e.g. in the use of הוֹלִיד, 'beget,' G.v.3,6,&c. (19 [28] times), vi.10,xi.10,12,&c. (8 [27] times), for which יָלַד is used in G.iv.18,[18,18,vi.4,x.8,13,15,24,24,26,xxii.23,xxv.3];

(xv) They agree also in the accurate statements of the ages of the patriarchs;

(xvi) And in the use of the formula, 'and he begat sons and daughters,' G.v.4,7,&c.

(xvii) In the notices about the deaths of the patriarchs, G.xxxv.29,xlix.33, we observe also the use of גָוַע, 'give up the ghost,' 'was gathered unto his people,' &c.

Our proof gains no little in force when we notice that the above-indicated passages not only agree with one another, but are also distinguished manifestly from other accounts occurring in Genesis, to which point we shall return presently. It is sufficient here to refer to G.v.29. That this verse is rightly regarded as not belonging to the Elohistic document, appears (α) from the use in it of the word 'Jehovah,' (β) from the connection of this verse with iii.17, and consequently with the whole section, ii.4–iv. It is, for instance, impossible that this section should have proceeded from the author of G.v, not only because in it the names 'Jehovah-Elohim,' and 'Jehovah' occur continually, but also because, according to G.v.1–3, Seth is 'the *firstborn* of Adam,' and, consequently, the author of that register did not know the history of Cain and Abel, nor, therefore, that of the Fall, to which v.29 refers. This is already plain enough by itself: but add to this that G.i.1–ii.3 and G.v are certainly from one author (see above), while on the other hand G.i.1–ii.3 must have had another author (note[17.1]) than G.ii.4–iv. Such agreement of the most different proofs raises this conclusion—as to the existence of the Elohistic document, to which G.i.1–ii.3,v, but not G.ii.4–iv, belongs,—above all reasonable doubt.

(87) [86] G.vi.9–22,ix.1–17, imply the whole account of the Flood, and of Noah's going out from the Ark,—G.xvii.18, the birth of Ishmael,—G.xix.29, the settlement of Lot in the cities of the plain; G.xvii.19 refers to Isaac's birth, whose person also appears as already known in xxv.19,20, where also at the same time Abraham's death is implied; G.xxviii.1–7,xxxv.9–15,27–29, refer to Jacob's adventures in Padan-Aram,—G.xlvi.6,7, and the following passages refer to some account of Joseph's adventures; lastly, in E.vi.2–9, it is probable that Moses enters—not for the first time, but—as a person already known.

[88] DELITZSCH assigns to the E. document G.vii.11–16[a],17–21,24,viii.1–5(6–12?), 13–19; KNOBEL, vii.4,6,7,8[b]–24, except v.16[b],viii.1–13; HUPFELD, finally, vii.6, 11,13–16[a], 17–22,24,viii.1[a],2[a],3[b],4 (partly), 5,13–19.[32] It is, probably, impossible to decide here with perfect confidence. This seems to be certain, that vii.1–5 (including v.4, although KNOBEL severs it,) and viii.20–22, do *not* belong to the E. document. On the other hand, its forms of speech plainly appear here in vii.14, (comp. i.11, 12,21,24,25,vi.20,)—in viii.17, 'fructify and multiply,' note [87.1.11]—in the accurate chronological data, vii.6,12,&c.viii.13, (comp.xvii.24,25),—lastly in the use of *Elohim*, vii.9,16[a],viii.1,15,—not to mention other expressions, as שָׁרַץ 'swarm,' vii.21,viii.17, as in i.20,21,ix.7. This is not the place, however, to enquire into this more closely. I only note further that by removing the passages, in which the name Jehovah occurs, *all* the difficulties disappear, which have been treated of in note [22.1].

[89] By means of these verses the gaps, mentioned in note [88], are in a great measure filled up. They are not, however, on that account arbitrarily torn from the context in which they occur, but show most plainly the characteristic signs of the Elohistic document, which we have already learned to know.

(i) xii.5, perhaps also v.4[b], is derived from another source than what immediately precedes, since it contains, when compared with that, a tautology, and starts from another point of view. According to xii.1, comp. with xv.7, Abram goes

---

[32] I now assign to the Elohist (as will be seen in Part V,) vii.6–9,11,13–16[a], 18[a],19[b],21,22,23[b],24,viii.1,2[a],3[b],4[a](*not* 'and the Ark settled'),5,13[a],14–19. These results differ slightly from those stated in Part IV, but agree very closely with those of HUPFELD, who also has written to 'approve my reason for distributing vii.18[b], 19[a], to the Jehovist, but not v.20[a], and as to v.22 the case is doubtful'—nor does he assent to my assigning vii.8[a], 'of clean beasts and of beasts not clean,' to the E. document. The fact of two different hands being distinctly traceable in these chapters is certain: the difficulty is to assign exactly the parts due to each writer. *Ed.*

out of *Ur of the Chaldees* to a land *to him unknown* ; whereas, according to xii.5 (and *v.*4ᵇ), he comes out of *Charran*, and journeys to *Canaan*. But, that this other source is the Elohistic document, appears from xi.31, (where Abram's settlement in Charran is mentioned, and Canaan is named as the object of his journey, exactly as in xii.4ᵇ,5,) and also from the language, comp. xi.31,xxxi.18,xxxvi.6,xlvi.6.

(ii) For like reasons must xiii.6, and very probably, also *v.*11ᵇ,12ᵃ, be regarded as part of the E. document. The reason for Lot's separating from Abram, given in *v.*6, is in itself satisfactory enough, and by no means requires the further development in *v.*7–10. So, too, the words in *v.*11ᵇ, 'and they separated one from another,' are quite superfluous after *v.*7–11ᵃ, as also *v.*12ᵃ repeats the very same as *v.*11ᵃ. Add to this, that the place of Lot's settlement is here, *v.*12ᵃ, denoted by the general description 'Lot dwelt in the cities of the circuit,' as in xix.29, where we find both the same formula, 'cities of the circuit,' and the remarkable expression, 'the cities in which Lot dwelt.' The other accounts, on the contrary, name distinctly *Sodom* as his place of abode. To this also may be added the agreement in language between *v.*6 and xxxvi.7.

(iii) Quite in the same way it appears that xvi.3,15,16,[33] according to the unanimous agreement of DELITZSCH, KNOBEL, HUPFELD, belong to the Elohistic document.

(iv) xxi.2–5 stands in immediate connection with xvii : it is distinguished by the use of Elohim, *v.*2,4, and by accurate chronology, *v.*5, while *v.*2 is superfluous after *v.*1, and must, therefore, have been derived from another source. On the other hand it seems hazardous to regard *v.*6 also as part of the E. document. Such etymologies, as that which appears in *v.*6, have not yet been met with in the E. document ; and this is besides manifestly a variation from the E. account, xvii.17,19.

(v) In xxv the traces of the E. document are very numerous : *v.*7–10 refer back manifestly to xxiii, about whose E. origin there can be no doubt ; also the expressions in *v.*8 agree with xxxv.29,xlix.33. But *v.*11 also appears to have the same origin, as we see by the use of *Elohim* and the conformity with xxxvi.1, &c. xxxvii.1 ; HUPF.p.29–31. The same judgment must be pronounced about *v.*19,20. as appears both from the accurate description of Rebekah's descent (N.B. which would be superfluous after xxiv), and the use of Padan-Aram and of הָאֲרַמִּי *v.dv.xiv*.

(vi) In the middle of the diffuse account of Jacob's fortunes in Haran we find xxxi.17,18, a passage, which, as it now stands in the text, disturbs the course of the narrative, and anticipates the contents of *v.*19–21. It is therefore derived, probably, from another source than what precedes ; and, that this source is no other than the E. document, is shown by the comparison of xii.5 and the observations made above (i) on this verse.

(vii) In xxxvii.1 occurs 'land of sojournings,' an E. expression (note ᵍ⁴⁻ⁱⁱⁱ), while the whole runs parallel with xxxvi.8 (settlement of Esau in Seir).

(viii) xlviii.3–6 refers back manifestly to xxxv.9–15, and is most probably from the same author. Comp. HUPF.p.35,36.

---

[33] Add also xvi.1 (comp. 'Sarai did not bear *to him*,' with xvi.15,16,xvii.16,19, 21,xxi.2,3,5, and contrast the expressions in xviii.10,14),—see also 'Sarai, Abram's wife,' as in *v.*3, not 'Sarai,' simply, in *v.*2,5,6,8,—and ' a maid, an Egyptian, and her name, Hagar,' comp. *v.*3, ' Hagar, the Egyptian, her maid.' *Ed.*

(68) [81] In order to make the inspection easy, I give here a full list of the passages, which up to this point have been assigned to the E. document [34]:—

G.i.1–ii.3,	xii.4ᵇ,5	xxv.7–11,19,20	xlvii.28
v, except v.29	xiii.6,11ᵇ,12ᵃ	xxviii.1–7	xlviii.3–6
vi.9–22,	xvi.3,15,16	xxxi.17,18	xlix.29–33
vii (a great part)	xvii	xxxv.9–15,27–29	l.12,13
viii (a great part)	xix.29	xxxvi.1–9	E.i.1–7
ix.1–17,28,29	xxi.2–5	xxxvii.1	ii.23–25
xi.10–32	xxiii	xlvi.6,7	

If we read these passages continuously, for which BOEHMER's *Genesis* [86] may serve as help, we shall find the remark made in the text confirmed. It is in the history of Isaac that they first cease to make a connected whole. We miss at once *e.g.* the account of the birth of Esau and Jacob, which, however, must have existed in the E. document, since the sequel refers back to it.

But the opponents of the document-hypothesis indicate already, long before G.xxv, great gaps in our E. document, (whose existence they do not recognize,) and these gaps, according to them, are only filled up by the Jehovistic pieces. KEIL, §24,n.2, after KURTZ, *Einh.*, gives the following examples, which partly have no force whatever, and partly are not applicable to *our* view of the E. document.

(i) Between G.ii.3 and v.1,&c.,vi.9,&c. is wanting the history of the Fall, ii.4,&c. without which the corruption of the human race, vi.11,12, remains entirely unaccounted for.

Ans. But what gives us any right to suppose that the author must account for that corruption? Are not his expressions, vi.11,12, plain in themselves? Is no recognition of sin conceivable, without an explanation of its origin?

(ii) Between v.32 and vi.9 is wanting the intimation of the universality of the corruption, even among the Sethites, which, however, is implied by the universality of the Flood: in other words, vi.1–8 cannot be missed.

Ans. But the E. document knows only Sethites, and does not name Cain and his descendants; in vi.2,4, the 'sons of Elohim' are not Sethites, but angels; lastly, in vi.11,12, the general corruption of men is plainly enough outspoken. What need we more?

(iii) Between vi.22 and vii.11 is wanting the notice of the time, at which the Flood was to begin.

Ans. But—even allowing that vii.1–10 in its *entirety* was borrowed from other sources—what gives us right to expect such a notice? Through vi.9–22,vii.11–13, it becomes, at all events, unnecessary.

(iv) Between xi.32 (or xiii.18) and xvii is a gap.

Ans. But this is completely filled up by xii.4ᵇ,5,xiii.6,11ᵇ,12ᵃ,xvi.3,15,16.

(v) Between xvii.27 and xix.29 there is, again, a gap, by reason of which the last account becomes quite unintelligible.

[34] From the results of my own analysis, to be published in Part V, I assent entirely to this list, excepting only vi.15,16,xi.28–30,xxv.11ᵇ,xiii.11ᵇxxxi.17,l.12, —though I assign some other passages also to the Elohist. And let it be observed that TUCH, STÄHELIN, DELITZSCH, KNOBEL, HUPFELD, KUENEN, are '*almost unanimous,*' [93], in respect of the above. *Ed.*

Ans. But here also the connection is restored through xiii.6,11ᵇ,12ᵃ, and we have no right, to expect anything more than the short reference in xix.29 to an event generally known among the Israelites.

(vi) Between xxii.13 and xxii.19, again, we cannot do without that very account, *v.*14–18, which is declared not to belong to the E. document.

Ans. But xxii is no portion of the E. document, either in whole, or in part.⁹³⁻⁷

(vii) xxv.24 does not continue the account in *v.*20.

Ans. True; but this is, also, the first instance of any part of the E. document not being inserted in Genesis. Besides, *v.*24 also seems not to belong to the prime-document.

⁹³ One example must here suffice. Between xxviii.1–7 and xxxi.17,18, is wanting the account of Jacob's marriage with Laban's daughter, of the birth of his children, of the increase of his possessions. All this, it is true, is told in xxviii.10–xxxi.16: yet, that *these* accounts are not taken over from the E. document, appears plainly, *e.g.* from xxviii.1, &c, where Jacob's journey is by no means represented as a flight from Esau, (as is the case in xxxv.7=xxviii.12–22), and, in conformity with this, nothing is said of a blessing stolen by Jacob from Esau, xxvii. Other points of difference are noted below.

(69) ⁹³ Tuch, Stähelin, but especially Delitzsch, Knobel, Hupfeld, are almost unanimous with respect to the passages quoted in the above Table.⁹¹ The difference of the two first-named consists chiefly in this, that they pass by the portions of the E. document in xii,xiii,xvi; further, as will appear presently, they ascribe to it many sections, which later enquirers assign to other documents.

⁹⁴ Ilgen distinguishes in Genesis two Elohists, (*Eliel* I and *Eliel* II,) and a Jehovist (*Elijah*). To his second Elohist he assigns many sections, which according to my judgment also do not belong to the primary E. document. His view is communicated (in tables) by Vater, iii.700,&c. Hupfeld, *Q.d.G.*p.viii,&c. has often, independently of Ilgen, arrived at the same results.

(70) ⁹⁵ (i) x.1–7,13–32—(that *v.*8–12 is not Elohistic, is generally admitted)—is distinguished, among other things, by the use of יָלַד, 'he begat,' *v.*13,15,24–26, comp.iv.18, for which the genealogies in v, and xi.10–32, use הוֹלִיד. Again, the genealogy of Arphaxad, *v.*22–25, is given in the E. document, xi.10–19. Further, the comparison of the register, xi.10–32, shows that the author of the E. document treats expressly of the holy line (from Shem to Abram), from which it follows that a table of nations, such as is contained in x, lies beyond his plan. Add to this also that *v.*8–12 agree so entirely in form and style with what precedes and follows, that it seems impossible to regard the verses as an interpolated passage; if this does not belong to the E. document, then neither does the whole chapter. Such is the opinion of Tuch and Hupfeld; but Stähelin, Delitzsch, Knobel, judge differently.

(ii) In xxii.20–24 יָלַד is once used, *v.*23. This genealogy also has no reference whatever to the holy line, while it is not at all implied in xxv.20, but is rather in contradiction to the epithet 'the Aramæan' there applied to Bethuel, since, according to xxii.21, Kemuel was the father of Aram, and *brother* of Bethuel, and hence the last could not be called 'Aramæan.' Comp. further, Huff.p.57,58.

(iii) xxv.1–6 cannot belong to the E. document; since, according to this, Abraham was already 137 years old at Sarah's death, (comp. xxiii.1 with xvii.17,) and can thus scarcely have begotten six sons, see xvii.17. In addition to this we have יַלְדָה and a number of other peculiarities, set forth by HUPF. p.58,59.

(iv) In xxv.12–18, we have a genealogy of Ishmael, in which, probably, v.12,17, portions of the E. document, are included. But the broken connection between v.17, and v.16,18, raises at once the suspicion that these last two verses, and therefore also v.13,15, are taken from elsewhere. To this tends also the agreement of v.13ᵃ,16, with x.5,20,31,32.[35] See HUPF.p.59,&c.

(v) It is difficult to state anything certainly as to xxxv.22ᵇ–26. For the E. document may be urged the use of Padan-Aram (note ˢᵗᵈᵛ) in v.26, perhaps, also, the contradiction between this verse and v.16–18, [since Benjamin, according to these verses, was not born in Padan-Aram]; against it the circumstance, that the sons of Jacob are summed up once besides in E.i.1–5, which is certainly a part of the E. document.[36]

(vi) xxxvi.8(9)–43 agrees closely with xxv.12–18, and for this reason alone does not, [or does, see note [35]] probably, belong to the E. document. Besides, the insertion of so copious a passage about Esau's descendants, and especially about the Horites, v.20–30, and the Edomite kings, v.31–39, can hardly be reconciled with the uniform conciseness of this document.[37] As to v.2,3, comp. with xxvi.34,35,xxvii. 46,xxviii.8,9, see the following note. See further HUPF.p.61–63.

---

[35] I believe the whole passage v.12–17 to be Elohistic. KURNEN admits this with respect to v.12,17, but points to the 'broken connection between v.17 and v.16,18.' I see none between v.17 and v.16; while that between v.17 and v.18 is caused by the interpolation of v.18 from another source. As to the agreement in phraseology between v.13ᵃ,16, and x.5,20,31,32, be it noted as follows:—

(i) In v.13ᵃ we have 'and these are the names of the sons of Ishmael,' as in the E. passages, G.xlvi.8, E.i.1, 'and these are the names of the sons of Israel';—

(ii) The phrase in v.13ᵃ, 'according to their tŏlēdoth,' occurs, indeed, once in the J. passage, x.32; but the Elohist uses tŏlēdoth freely, ii.4ᵃ, v.1,vi.9,xi.10,27,&c. and in this very context, xxv.12,19;

(iii) The other formulæ in v.13ᵃ,16, viz. 'by their names,' 'by their towns,' 'by their castles,' 'according to their folks (אֻמֹּתָם),' are none of them used in x, though so many different phrases of this kind are used there, viz. 'by their lands,' v.5,20,31, 'after their families,' v.5,20,31, 'by (after) their nations,' v.20,31,32, 'after their tongues,' v.20,31,—so that the expressions in xxv.13ᵃ,16, would seem not to be Jehovistic;

(iv) In v.16, 'twelve princes' seems plainly to refer to the E. passage, xvii. 20. Ed.

[36] I hold that xxxv.22ᵇ–26 is Elohistic. Ed.

[37] I believe that xxxvi belongs entirely to the Elohist, except the account of the Horites, v.20–30. He seems to have a special interest in the descendants of Ishmael, xvii.20,xxv.12–17, as well as in those of Isaac, and may, therefore, have expatiated in this chapter upon the descendants of Esau, and especially on their having had kings among them long before Israel, v.31, in fulfilment, it would seem, of the promises specially recorded by himself as made to Abraham, 'I will make nations of thee, and

(vii) Lastly, as regard xlvi.8–27, this register agrees generally with the E. account in E.i.1–5, and uses besides the name Padan-Aram. Yet it is probable from v.26,27, that it is compiled, upon the basis of E.i.5, from the accounts in Genesis, (comp. v.12 with G.xxxviii,) and from other sources.[36] See Hupf.p.34, n.13.

Generally, Tuch, Stähelin, Delitzsch, and Knobel, ascribe these genealogies to the E. document, besides which, x.1–7,13–34, is wholly by Tuch, partly by Stähelin, and xxii.10–24 by Stähelin, ascribed to the Jehovist. In fact it is very natural that they should be ascribed either *wholly* or *not at all* to the E. document.[39]

(71)   [36] The proofs, which lead us to infer the different origin of these sections and

---

kings shall come out of thee,' xvii.6,—'she (Sarah) shall be a mother of *nations, kings* of peoples shall be of her,' v.16. By him, then, the collateral branches of Ishmael and Esau were regarded as being in some sense included in the fortunes of Israel.

But that v.9–19,31–43 is due to the Elohist, may appear thus:—

(i) v.10, ' *these are the names of the sons* of Esau,' v.40, '*and these are the names* of the dukes of Esau;' comp. xxv.13, '*and these are the names of the sons* of Ishmael,' xlvi.8, E.i.1, ' *and these are the names of the sons* of Israel.'

(ii) v.9,10, '*and these are the generations* of Esau . . . *these are the names of the sons* of Esau:' comp.xxv.12,13, '*and these are the generations of Ishmael . . .* and *these are the names of the sons* of Ishmael.'

(iii) v.40, '*and these are the names* of the dukes of Esau, according to their families, according to their places, *by their names* :' comp.xxv.13, '*and these are the names* of the sons of Ishmael, *by their names*, according to their generations.

(iv) v.40, 'according to their families, according to their places, by their names,' v.43, 'according to their habitations' : comp. the expressions in xxv.13, 'by their names, according to their tolĕdoth,' v.16, 'by their towns, and by their castles, according to their folks.'

(v) v.43, אֲחֻזָּה, 'possession,' an E. expression, (note [37.v]). *Ed.*

[38] I must demur also to this conclusion. Besides the points of agreement with the E. document above-noticed, we may note as follows:

(i) v.26, 'that came out of his thigh,' as in E.i.5, but *nowhere else in the whole Bible* : comp. however, a somewhat similar expression, 'come out of thy loins,' also in a decidedly E. passage, G.xxxv.11 ;

(ii) v.15,18,22,25,26,27, נֶפֶשׁ 'soul, person,' as in xii.5, xvii.14,xxxvi.6, but also in xiv.21;

(iii) v.27, 'all the souls of Jacob's house:' comp.xxxvi.6, 'all the souls of his house.'

(iv) v.26,27, seems to be referred to in E.i.5, 'and Joseph was in Egypt';

(v) v.12ᵇ, 'but Er and Onan died in the land of Canaan ; and the sons of Phares were Hezron and Hamul,' may have been interpolated after xxxviii was written ; and Hezron and Hamul may have been introduced to fill up the vacancies caused by the removal of Er and Onan, as dead, from the *original* list. *Ed.*

[39] There is internal evidence, which shows that x.1–7,13–14, and xxii.20–24, are Jehovistic, not Elohistic, passages: see P.IV,73, and (note [93·41]). They do not concern the *descendants* of Abraham. *Ed.*

those summed-up above,[91] are very numerous, but require more extensive exposition than can here be given. I confine myself on this subject to the indication of a few chief points, referring for the remainder to HUPFELD, but also to KNOBEL and DELITZSCH, &c. who, although they ascribe to all these passages an E. character, at the same time assume that the Jehovist, (who was, according to them, the compiler of Genesis), has derived them not from the 'grundschrift,' but from other sources.

(i) The necessity of recognising more than one Elohistic document appears especially from the history of Jacob, xxviii–xxxv.

We find at once in xxviii.10–22 a narrative, in which Elohistic portions seem to be inserted, v.12,20; although the use of Elohim in these places might, perhaps, be explained also as proceeding from the Jehovist,[40] from whom v.13–16 certainly comes. To this narrative reference is made in xxxi.13,xxxv.1, in which last passage the journey of Jacob to Haran is called his *flight from Esau*, in agreement with the Jehovistic account, xxvii.1–45. Further, in xxxii.24–32 the origin of the name Israel is explained, and in xxxii,xxxiii, the settlement of Esau in Seir is represented as a past event. Lastly, xxxv.5 refers back to xxxiv (the revenge carried out by Simeon and Levi on Shechem).

We saw, however, before, (note [87]), that xxviii.1–7,xxxv.9–15,xxxvi.1–8, belong certainly to the E. document. But, if so, then it must also be assumed that the passages of xxviii.10–xxxv.8, [which may seem at first sight to be Elohistic,] (with exception of xxxi.17,18,) cannot be ascribed to the E. document. For there is contradiction—

(α) Between [the E. passage] xxviii.1–7, (according to which Jacob betakes himself to Padan-Aram, in order to seek himself a wife,) and the passages where it is said that he fled from his brother Esau [xxxv.1,3] ;

(β) Between [the E. passage] xxxv.9–15 (origin of the names 'Israel' and 'Bethel') and xxviii.10–22,xxxii.24–32, (where the same names are derived, but in another manner, and at other periods) ;

(γ) Between [the E. passage] xxxvi.1–8, (settlement of Esau in Seir, *after* Jacob's return,) and xxxii, xxxiii, (the same fact, but *before* Jacob's return). Comp. above (note [17.vii]).

It may still be maintained, as *e.g.* it is by KNOBEL, that in xxviii.10–xxxv.8 there are (besides xxxi.17,18) yet other passages of the E. document contained. This, indeed, is possible ; but they cannot be pointed out,—at least, not by means of the language or other plain characteristics. We had better, therefore, adhere to the negative result, that the narratives in question, although for a great part [seeming to be] Elohistic, yet do not belong to the E. document.

(ii) If this, however, is once for all established, that *some* [seemingly Elohistic] accounts, contained in Genesis, do not belong to the primary document, we may then conclude without much difficulty that in xx.1–17, we see such a narrative, (*Elohim*, v.3,6,11,13,17,—on the other hand, *Jehovah*, v.18, in a note which can only be regarded as an explanatory gloss on v.17).

(a) Here, first, the chronology presents at once a difficulty; according to the

---

[40] Elohim might have been used by the Jehovist more freely than usual in this passage, because of the intention to derive the name *Beth-El*, 'House of Elohim,' v.19, comp. v.17,22. *Ed.*

E. document, xvii.17, Sarah is ninety years old, and is in a state of pregnancy; Abraham's journey, xx.1, seems thus in this document not to be in its place.

(β) Also the expression, 'from thence,' in *v*.1, presents another difficulty ; since no mention has preceded of any definite place at which Abraham was staying.

(γ) Again, Abraham is here called נָבִיא, 'prophet,' *v*.7, which, it is true, never occurs elsewhere in the whole narrative, but stands decidedly very far removed from that picture of his person and character, which the E. document, generally, exhibits.

(δ) Besides, we meet here with a number of sentiments and ideas, of which the primary document gives us no second instance, (*e.g.* revelation of God in a dream, the efficacy of prayer, &c.), but which, on the other hand, do occur again in the other sources. Comp. HUPF.p.48–52.

(iii) In close connection with the narrative just considered stands xxi.22–32, (*Elohim* in the mouth of Abimelech, *v*.22,23), wherein, among others, the formula כָּרַת בְּרִית 'cut a covenant,' occurs, *v*.27,32, for which the E. document says 'establish a covenant,' (note ⁵⁷·¹¹), [or 'give a covenant,' (note ⁹⁰·ⁱᵛ),] and, what is more, quite with the same meaning. (KEIL is not right, when (§27,n.7) he finds in the formula 'establish, &c.' the sense 'to *realise the promises contained in* a covenant,' in direct contradiction with G.xvii.7,21, E.vi.4, where we can only suppose the meaning to be, '*conclude* a covenant.') Hence this section, though also [in form] Elohistic, and finding its counterpart (note ¹⁷·ⁱᵛ) in the Jehovistic account xxvi.17–33, yet is not derived from the E. document.

(iv) The same is true of xxi.9–21 (the account of Ishmael's dismissal and earliest adventures). We have already (note ⁹⁰·ⁱᵛ) spoken of *v*.6, and what is there said applies also in part to *v*.7. In the E. document, xxv.8, Ishmael appears,—at least, at the time of Abraham's death,—to be living with Isaac, just as Esau, according to xxxvi.1,&c. does not settle in Seir till after his father's death. Besides which, we find here other traces of a later time, and the usual marks of the E. prime-document are wanting. See HUPF.p.52,53.

(v) Also xxii.1–13,19, cannot have been derived from this source, although the name *Elohim* appears in *v*.1,3,8,9,12. No instance of angelic appearances—this remark applies also to xxi.9–21—is met with anywhere else in the E. document. The very fact of the use of the name 'Moriah,' to whose apparent meaning reference is made in *v*.14, is a reason against the supposition, that the author of the prime-document is here speaking. Comp. HUPF.p.54,55.

(vi) With respect to xxv.24–34 again, as with respect to most of the above-named sections, DELITZSCH and KNOBEL are of the same opinion with HUPFELD. In the undoubted portions of the E. document there appear scarcely any etymologies, such as we find in xxv.25,26,30.⁴¹ Besides, in *v*.28 preparation is made for the

---

⁴¹ It deserves to be noticed, however, that the Elohist derives names *indirectly*, *i.e.* by playing upon them, without expressly saying, '*therefore* one called his name &c.,' *viz.* 'Abraham' = 'father of a great multitude,' xvii.5, 'Sarah' = 'princess,' xvii.15,16, 'Isaac' = 'he laughed,' xvii.17, 'Ishmael' = 'El heard,' comp.xvii.20, 'as for Ishmael, I have heard thee;' whereas the Jehovist's regular formula is 'therefore one called &c.,' xi.9,xvi.14,xix.22,xxv.30,xxix.34,xxxi.48,xxxiii.17,Lii,

account of xxvii, (which is certainly not Elohistic), as also in that chapter, v.36, reference is made back to xxv.29–34.

(vii) Lastly, as to what concerns the copious story of Joseph, xxxvii,xxxix–l, with the exception of the small portions indicated above (note [81]) [i.e. xxxvii.1,xlvi. 6,7,xlvii.28,xlviii.3–6,xlix.29–33,l.12,13, according to KURENEN,[82]] they cannot have been derived from the E. document, since—

(α) The usual characteristics of this document, its peculiar forms of speech, &c., are sought for there in vain ;

(β) It appears from the above analysis of xi–xxxvi, that the E. document contained only very short notices about the fortunes of *Abraham* and *Isaac*, and the same is true, most probably, also with reference to *Jacob* ; for which reason it is not very likely, that it should have narrated *Joseph's* history at such great length.

No doubt, it is true (note [29-31]), that Joseph's history is drawn from more than one source. But, that the E. document has been one of these sources, does not appear. We have, probably, here also to think of a second Elohist,—perhaps, the same, from whose manuscript a part of the history of Abraham and Jacob has been taken.

(viii) We must treat here separately about xxvi.34,35,xxvii.46,xxviii.1,8,9.

These passages are so closely connected with each other, and with xxviii.1–7,— and they exhibit so plainly the character of the E. document (e.g. the definition of time G.xxvi.34, comp. with xxv.20,)—that nothing seems more natural than to refer them to the primary document, as, in fact, all interpreters do, DELITZSCH alone excepted. Yet there exists contradiction (note [17,viii]), between these passages and xxxvi.1–8, which latter passage must as certainly be assigned to the E. document. We have thus to make our choice between two views :

(a) xxvi.34,35,xxvii.46,xxviii.8,9, have not remained in their original (Elohistic)

---

comp. also xxvii.36. The derivations in xxv.25,26, seem to be of the former kind, *viz.* שֵׂעִיר, 'Seir,' from שֵׂעָר, 'hair,' with a play also on עֵשָׂו 'Esau,' (comp. עֵשָׂו,עָשָׂה),xxxvi. 8, and יַעֲקֹב, 'Jacob,' from עָקֵב, 'heel.' It seems to me not unlikely that v.25,26, may be Elohistic, and if so, then probably, is v.24 also, in spite of its relations to l.3, 'the days are fulfilled,' and xxxviii.27, 'and behold twins in her womb.' *Ed.*

[42] I should add to these some other passages, *e.g.*, (α) xxxvii.2[a], (β) xlvii.7–10, (γ) xlvii.27[b], and, perhaps, one or two verses more.

(α) (i) 'these are the generations of Jacob,' as in ii.4[a],v.1,vi.9,xi.10,27,xxv.12, 19,xxxvi.1,9 ;

(ii) 'Jacob,' as in v.1, not 'Israel,' as in v.3,13.

(β) (i) v.7,10, Jacob 'blesses' Pharaoh: comp.xxviii.1 ;

(ii) v.8,9, 'days of the years of the life,' as in xxv.7,xlvii.28 ;

(iii) v.9,9, 'sojournings,' comp.xvii.8,xxviii.4,xxxvi.7,xxxvii.1 ;

(iv) v.9, מֵאָה 'hundred,' *as in* v.3,6,18,25,28,vii.24,viii.3[b],xi.10,25,xxi.5,xxv.7, 17,xxxv.28,xlvii.28; but מֵאָת is used in xvii.17,xxiii.1, which are assigned to the Elohist, and also in the non-Elohistic passages, vi.3,xxvi.12,xxxiii.19,l.22,26.

(v) In v.7 Joseph presents *Jacob* before Pharaoh, whereas in v.2 he presents five of his brethren.

(γ) 'fructify and multiply,' (note [81-31]). *Ed.*

form, and, consequently, as they now stand, do not belong to the E. prime-document (DELITZSCH);

(β) in xxxvi.2,3, the same names were inserted originally as in xxvi.34,xxviii.9; afterwards, however, when the genealogies in v.9–43 were combined with v.1–8, the names of the wives were adopted in v.2,3, as they appeared in the more ample genealogies, v.10,14,18,25. In other words, xxxvi.2,3, was *originally*, but *not in its present form*, a portion of the E. document, (KNOBEL, HUPFELD).

To recognise with TUCH and STÄHELIN the contradiction, and yet regard both passages as derived from the same source, seems impossible.[43]

Between the other two views the choice is difficult. But the strongest arguments are on the side of the second.

BLEEK,p.256, sees even now no necessity to assume more than one Elohist. Since, however, he produces no new proofs, his view must be considered as negatived by the preceding evidence. On the other hand, the use of more than one E. document in the composition of Genesis is recognised by VAIHINGER and BOEHMER.[122] The latter in his *Lib. Gen. Pent.* has had the whole text printed with four different sorts of Hebrew types, in order thus to make visible his views about the origin of the book.

(72) [97] A superficial comparison of the passages ascribed above (note [96]) to this Elóhist (or these Elohists) with the portions of the E. document makes it at once probable that *this last is older than the former document.* It is more simple and more concise; whereas the other Elohist (just as the Jehovist) descends more into particulars, and works out more fully the points merely touched upon in the E. document. See Chap.XVI. Generally, it has been remarked already,[97] that the view, which supposes that more than one writer, in treating the history of the patriarchal age, has abstained systematically from the use of the name Jehovah, has in it nothing improbable.

[96] The critical analysis of E.i.1–vi.1 has not yet been carried far enough, to allow us to separate with certainty the different documents from each other. According to KNOB. *E.L.*p.1,2,21,&c., the following passages, E.i.1–7,13,14,ii.23–25, belong to the E. primary document. But all the rest is not by any means from one hand. He thinks that he is able to discern in it three different authors. To the first he ascribes iii,iv.18,27–31, the last verses only in part,—to the second ii.11–22, iv.19–26,—lastly, to the third, (the Jehovist,) iv.1–17, and, probably, all that remains in E.i.–vi.1, after the removal of the above-named passages. He himself, however, admits that this division is by no means certain. Only this seems to be certain, that among the documents here employed there must have been included at least *one* Elohistic document: we infer this from the use of Elohim in i.17,20,21,iii.6,

---

[43] It seems to me *not* impossible to suppose that the discrepancy here may be due to the Elohist himself. The traditions may have been uncertain, about these long-past events; or he may have obtained fuller information about the traditions of the Edomites, when he wrote xxxvi, (which we ascribe almost *wholly* to him,) than when he wrote the former passages, and may never have corrected them—remembering always that a Hebrew skin MS. is not to be thought of as if it were an English book. *Ed.*

11-15. The difference of the documents appears from ii.18,iii.1,iv.18, [since in ii.18, 'Reuel,' or 'Raguel,' and in iii.1,iv.18, 'Jethro' or 'Jether,' is given as the name of the father-in-law of Moses].

 Comp. Ew. *G.V.I.* i.98,&c.

CHAPTER XIV.

74) ᵛᵉ Thus Hupf.p.85,86. That these passages belong to the B.O. (Book of Origins), appears, among other things,—

(i) From the accurate definitions of time, xii.40,41,xvi.1,xix.1; ⁴⁴

(ii) From the use of the formula, 'on this self-same day,' xii.41,51,⁴⁵ note ⁴⁶·ˣⁱᵛ;

(iii) From the uniformity of most of these passages to each other; ⁴⁶

(iv) From the connection in which they stand to each other: ⁴⁷

Since, however, the law of the Passover, E.xii.1, &c. implies the death of the Egyptian firstborns, and it is said already, E.vi.6, that Jehovah shall redeem Israel 'with an outstretched arm and great judgments,' we expect in the B.O. also a more or less circumstantial account of the way in which the Exodus out of Egypt took place. Yet with Hupfeld and Stäh. p.29,30, I judge that this account is not contained in E.vii–xi, whence it follows that it has been omitted in the compilation of the present narrative,—we may suppose, on account of its being not circumstantial enough. Knobel judges otherwise, and regards the following sections as portions of his 'Urschrift,' or primary-document—vi.2–vii.7, (so Stähelin), vii.8–13,19–22,viii.1–3,11 (from נְלֹא), 12–15, ix.8–12,35, xi.9,10, xii.1–23,28. See the development of this view, E.L.p.53–59. Even without further evidence, it is plain that the philological proofs can only be said to be satisfactory in the case of E.xii.1–23, (which I also regard as derived from the B.O., see below,) and to be not destitute of all weight in the case of E.vi.10–vii.7; whereas, on the contrary, in E.vii.8–xi.10 the peculiarities of the B.O. are entirely wanting. Yet I cannot assign to it E.vi.10, &c. The genealogy, v.14–28, exhibits in v.16,18,20, some signs of E. origin; but it is introduced in this place in a very clumsy way, so that we miss entirely the regular progression, which usually distinguishes the narrative of the B.O. Consequently, it is now doubtful also, whether vi.10–13,29,30, belong to the B.O., though, vii.1–7, as well, exhibits in every respect the character of it

⁴⁴ The definitions of time in xvi.1,xix.1, resemble those in G.vii.11,viii.4,14; but there is no instance as yet in the B.O., which at all resembles that in xii.40,41. *Ed.*

⁴⁵ This formula is, indeed, used thrice by the Elohist, vii.13,xvii.23,26; but it is also used in E.xii.17, which is *not* assigned to him by Kuenen; and, *if* xii.41,51, belong to the same hand as xii.17, it would be used also thrice by *this* author. *Ed.*

⁴⁶ There seems to me no obvious uniformity between xvi.1, xix.1, and xii.40,41, 51. *Ed.*

⁴⁷ xii.40,41,51, are not needed in the context. *Ed.*

(*e.g.* comp.*v*.4 with vi.6, *v*.6 with G.vi.22, and notice in *v*.7 the accurate definition of time).

In the sequel, also, of the narrative, according to KNOBEL, the accounts of the 'Urschrift' are not lost, but still exist in E.xii.37ª,40–42, xiii.20, xiv.1–4,8,9,15–18 (part), 21–23,27,xv.19,22,23,27,xvi.1,2,9–26,31–36,xvii.1, xix.2ª. Yet this whole division, comp. KNOB. *E.L.*p.111,&c.,135,&c.,157,&c., starts manifestly from the (unproved) supposition, that the narrative, as it is now read in Exodus, consists of two parts, the Elohistic 'Urschrift' and the Jehovistic 'additions,' according to which theory the accounts of the B.O. *must* here exist, and form a connected whole. If we confine ourselves, as the nature of the case requires, to the proofs derived from language and style alone, then at most some traces of the B.O. seem to be met with in xvi, (see especially *v*.32,33); yet they are not enough to enable us to assign the whole account to it, especially because both the introduction of the Sabbath is implied, *v*.22, &c., and also the existence of the Tabernacle, *v*.32, &c., both which are only prescribed *afterwards* in the B.O., E.xxv, &c.; from which it follows that, at all events, the place, which xvi now assumes, cannot be original. It seems, then, preferable, in the first instance, to regard only the few verses above indicated as parts of the B.O., while it will be shown below in what sense also E.vi.10–12,vii.1–7,xvi, may be brought to it.[43]

(75)   [141] That these passages belong together, is admitted, *e.g.* by STÄH.p.1–19, De WETTE,§151–153, VATKE,i.p.428,429, KNOB.*E.L.*p.ix, and *passim*—(except that KNOBEL does *not* assign to the *Grundschrift* N.iv.17–20,vi.22–27,xv.17–21,31–41) —also by Ew.*G.V.I.*i.p.115,&c., who assigns even *all* the laws of Exodus–Numbers, except E.xiii.1–16,xxxiv.10–26, to the B.O., though he at the same time admits that the author of that book has inserted some smaller *Codices* just as he found them, such *e.g.* as E.xxi–xxiii, L.i–vii,xviii–xx. At the same time EWALD assumes that some laws stand, at all events, in a wrong place; thus L.xxiv.1–9 should have been inserted after E.xxvii.20,21,—N.vii.89 after E.xl.38,—N.viii.1,2, after E.xxxix. 31,—N.v.5–vi after L.v, &c. No *proofs*, in the strict sense of the word, are produced for these positions.

(76)   [142] The full evidence for this position is given by STÄHELIN and KNOBEL. Here we may adduce a few examples, which speak very strongly. Comp., then, L.i.1 with E.xxv.22,xxix.42,xxx.6,36—L.i with E.xxix.15–18,38–42,—L.vi.8–13 with E.xxviii.42,xxix.28–32, L.iii, &c.—also N.iii.4 with L.x.1, &c.,—and, generally, N.iii,iv, with E.xxxv–xl, &c.

[143] In a comparison between the laws of Exodus–Numbers and the narratives of Genesis, we have naturally to consider, first of all, G.xvii, since this chapter, in respect of its contents, exhibits more than any other a legislative character. It is remarkable, now, that the peculiar phraseology, which occurs in G.xvii, recurs almost without exception in the laws above-mentioned. Thus we find:—

---

[43] I reserve expressing at present any definite judgment about these passages, and content myself, generally, with stating Prof. KUENEN's views about Exodus–Numbers, the criticism of this portion of the Pentateuch being very difficult, and my own results being not yet fully prepared for publication. *Ed.*

(i) 'a perpetual covenant,' E.xxxi.16, L.xxiv.8, N.xviii.19, as in G.xvii.7,13,19 ;

(ii) 'perpetual possession,' L.xxv.34, as in G.xvii.8; comp. also the passages, where 'perpetual statute' occurs, E.xii.14,17,xxvii.21,xxviii.43, &c., and 'perpetual priesthood,' E.xl.15 ;

(iii) 'in their (your, &c.) generations,' E.xii.14,17,42,xvi.32,33,xxvii.21,xxix.42, xxx.8,10,21,31,xxxi.13,16,xl.15, L.iii.17,vi.18(11),vii.36,x.9,xxi.17,xxii.3,xxiii.14,21, 31,41,43,xxiv.3,xxv.30, N.ix.10,x.8,xv.14,15,21,23,38,xviii.23,xxxv.29, as in G.xvii. 7,9,12 ;

(iv) 'be for a God,' E.xxix.45, L.xi.45,xxii.33,xxv.38, as in G.xvii.7,8 ;

(v) 'and that soul shall be cut off from his people,' (with slight variations), E.xii.15,19,xxx.33,38,xxxi.14, L.vii.20,21,25,27,xvii.4,9,10,14,xviii.29,xix.8,xx.3,5,6, 17,18,xxii.3,xxiii.29, N.ix.13,xv.30,31,xix.13,20, Jo.ix.23, as in G.xvii.14 ;

(vi) 'on that selfsame day,' E.xii.17,(41),51, L.xxiii.21,28,29,30.

Comp., further, STÄH.p.41–55, whose demonstration we may adopt the more readily, inasmuch as the agreement between his 'First Legislation' (i.e. the laws of Exodus–Numbers, which belong to the B.O.) and the Elohistic portions of Genesis, appears especially in those places of Genesis, which have above, Chap.XIII, been assigned to the B.O., and not to a younger Elohist.

(78) ⁱⁱⁱ The ideas here developed will be put yet more clearly in the light hereafter, when we exhibit the age of the different documents of the Pentateuch, Chap. XXI ; and then, at the same time, the opportunity will be given of comparing it with the views of others. A separation of the original portions of the B.O., from those which were subsequently added, seems to me, in the present state of the enquiry, impracticable. For instance, the later portions are throughout by no means joined loosely with the former, but are so intimately connected with them, by re-touching and reconstruction, that they now form really one whole. What critical acuteness is still able to effect in this, has been shown by HUPF. Fest. Among other things he proves that the two laws, about the Sabbath-Year and the Jubilee-Year, which are contained in L.xxv, do not date from the same time, and he ascribes to the latter of these laws L.xxv.8–10,14–16,23–25, a much greater age than to the former, L.xxv.1–7. Comp. HUPF. Fest. III.p.12, &c. It seems, however, at the same time that the author of this later law about the Sabbath-Year has added to that about the Jubilee-Year some particulars, v.11–13,17–22, through which the two laws make in fact one whole. Something of the same kind may be remarked with respect to L.xxiii. That more than one hand has been at work in it, is recognised by HUPFELD, Part II, as well as by KNOBEL in loco; though in separating the portions of different kinds they by no means agree, especially because KNOBEL allows himself too often to be guided by his partiality for the 'Complementary Hypothesis.' HUPFELD shows, as it seems to me, convincingly, that, at all events, L.xxiii.3,9–22,39–44, are not from the same hand as v.1,2,4–8,33–38. His de-monstration found an opponent in BACHM.p.102–138, whose objections against the positive conclusions in HUPFELD's demonstration are often satisfactory, but who in his contradiction of the negative result of the enquiries of his predecessor is obliged to have recourse to a long-exploded system of harmonising. Whereas HUPFELD (and with him KNOBEL) had deduced from L.xxiii.37,38,—'These are the feasts of Jehovah . . . besides the Sabbaths of Jehovah, and besides your gifts,'

&c.—this inference, that *v.*3, in which the Sabbath is mentioned, was unknown to the author of the subscription in question, BACHMANN answers, p.110, that true it is that from *v.*37,38, it follows that no mention of the Sabbath occurs in *v.*4–36, but by no means that it might not be mentioned, nevertheless, in *v.*3 (*sic*). Just as weak is the manner in which he adjusts the strange position of *v.*39–44, after the subscription, *v.*37,38, that closes this calendar of feasts. If the mind is once for all made up to find everywhere unity and harmony, it is not difficult to adduce also (so-called) reasons for it. Further, it appears plainly enough from the above that, in my judgment, the enquiry set on foot by HUPFELD and KNOBEL is by no means brought to an end.[49] Comp. also the remarks of the last-named on L.x.16–20,xxiv. 10–23,xxv.18–22, N.iv.17–20,vi.22–27,xv.17–21,31–41.

(80)   [105] Comp. notes[40,41,42,]50 and further KNOB. *E.L.*p.111,&c.(on E.xiii.3–16),—p.181,&c.

[49] It is obvious that much more labour must be spent in the elaboration of the criticism of these chapters, before we can pronounce with any degree of certainty as to their author or authors. In addition to the objections stated by the author himself in (78), against assigning them *all* to the Elohist, further difficulties, as I have said (note p. 40), seem to be raised by the consideration, that this author, throughout the passages assigned to him in Genesis, has not shown the slightest interest in any matters of a *priestly* character—has never mentioned 'priest,' 'altar,' or 'sacrifice,' or betrayed any *professional* acquaintance with matters of this kind. How, then, can we account for his going so deeply into the minutiæ of the priestly office, in the books of Exodus, Leviticus, and Numbers, as he must have done, if the passages, here assigned to him, really 'proceeded from him'? With respect to the E. characteristics, noted in [105], it may be observed that, though really Elohistic, they are not necessarily convincing in all cases where they occur, if considered only each in itself, and without reference to its occurring in the same context, in connection with *other* E. phrases, or to the general tone and tenor of the passage in which it is found. Supposing, for instance, for the sake of the argument, that Samuel was the Elohist, it is obvious that any Prophet or Priest of the same age, such as Nathan or Zadok,—especially, if trained under Samuel's teaching, and desiring to copy his example,—would be likely to use some of the same peculiar formulæ which their master had used; though the general character of their writings would, probably, be very different, and the subjects, which would be specially treated of, might differ, according to the peculiar tastes or occupations of the writer. And, in point of fact, we do find that these very phrases *are* occasionally used in passages, which cannot be assigned to the Elohist himself: *e.g.*

(i) and (ii) are weakened by the fact that we have 'perpetual mountains' in G.xlix.26, which is certainly *not* Elohistic, besides the same expression in D.xxxiii. 15, and 'perpetual arms' in D.xxxiii.27;

(iii) occurs in E.xvi.32,33, a later addition to the B.O. (82);

(v) occurs in L.xviii.29,xix.8,xx.3,5,6,17,18, admitted by KUENEN, note [105], to have probably only 'an *allied* origin' with the B.O., *i.e.* to have come merely out of the same circle of writers;

(vi) occurs in D.xxxii.48, which, according to KUENEN, note [105] 'perhaps, we must assign to the passages added *afterwards*' to the B.O. *Ed.*

[50] I do not see that the statement in the text is confirmed by these notes, unless

(on the Book of the Covenant,)—p.499,&c. (on L.xviii–xx),—p.572,573, (on L.xxvi). E.xxxiv.11–26 points so manifestly back to the Book of the Covenant, that it is certainly derived from it.

(81) [106] This is erroneously denied by KNOBEL, who maintains this view, p.263,264, that הָעֵדֻת, 'the Testimony,' is not the Decalogue, nor yet the Book of the Covenant, but the Elohistic Law (=the Law contained in the B.O.) in its entirety. This view is untenable. Generally, where the expression הָעֵדֻת occurs, it denotes the Testimony of Jehovah '*par excellence*, *i.e.* the Decalogue. The Ark of the Covenant is called the 'Ark of the Testimony,' because the law of the Ten Commandments was contained in it, E.xxv.22,xxvi.33,34,xxx.6,26,xxxix.35,xl.5,21,N.iv. 5,vii.89, Jo.iv.16; as, in fact, we read expressly in E.xl.20, that Moses deposited the 'Testimony' in the Ark. In order to be able to see here a mention of the entire Elohistic Law, KNOBEL is obliged to have recourse to a very unnatural *prolepsis*. Elsewhere we find mentioned the 'tables of the Testimony,' E.xxxi.18, xxxiv.29. The whole Tabernacle is frequently called the 'Tent (אֹהֶל) of the Testimony,' N.ix.15,xvii.7(22),8(23),xviii.2, or the 'Tabernacle (מִשְׁכָּן) of the Testimony,'E.xxxviii.21,N.i.50,53,x.11. And, that these names are given to the Tabernacle, because the Ten Commandments were contained in it, appears from L.xxiv.3, where mention is made of the 'vail of the Testimony,' because, no doubt, behind this vail was placed the Ark with the tables of the Law.

It is, therefore, not without reason that HUPFELD and EWALD regard the Decalogue, together with the Book of the Covenant, as a part of the B.O., that is, they suppose the author of the B.O. to have adopted both of them into his work. Thus we are naturally led to the hypothesis, that the Decalogue was *omitted from the B.O.*, when it was adopted by the compiler of the whole Pentateuch, and, perhaps, because he had already taken it over in the connection in which it now appears, E.xx.1–17. It was, perhaps, the compiler, who took over out of the B.O. the motive for the consecration of the Sabbath in xx.11: the comparison of G.ii.2,3, for instance, makes it very probable [?] that this motive was added to the Decalogue by the author of that book, just as the Deuteronomistic Legislator, D.v.14,15, connected another motive with the same command.

[107] For what reasons this supposition also may be made, will be first seen below, Chap.XVII,XXI. Comp. KNOB.,p.111,&c.,310,&c.

[108] It is true, there exists no contradiction between L.xviii–xx and the ordinances belonging to the B.O. Yet the prescriptions, contained in these three chapters, do not properly belong to a priestly Legislation, since they chiefly have reference to civil life. Perhaps, however, from the agreement in language, &c., which, in spite of this difference, exists between L.xviii–xx and the B.O., we may infer that they have an allied origin, *i.e.* they were committed to writing in nearly the same priestly circle, as that in which the B.O. arose. We cannot here decide with perfect certainty; see notes [212,239,240]. The reasons which compel us to assign the adoption of L.xxvi to the compiler of the Pentateuch, are discussed in Chap.XXII.

it is first assumed that certain chapters in Leviticus and Numbers *do* belong to the B.O., which have not yet been *proved* to belong to it, and which may, possibly, *not* belong to it. The whole question, as to the composition of the central Books of the Pentateuch, requires still further consideration. *Ed.*

(83) [100] Observe the expressions ' on the selfsame day,' D.xxxii.48, אֲחֻזָּה, ' possession,' v.49, ' be gathered unto his people,' v.50, and the connection between D.xxxiv.8,9, and N.xx.29,xxvii.18,23. Meanwhile, from these last parallel passages it follows that the two sections of Deuteronomy stand in connection with certain accounts in the Book of Numbers, with respect to which it cannot be maintained with confidence that they belong to the *original* portions of the B.O.[110] Perhaps, we must, therefore, assign these passages of Deuteronomy to the number of those added afterwards.

(84) [110] (i) N.x.11–28 (see the chronology in v.11, comp. N.ix.1,i.1, E.xl.2,17,&c.) is closely connected with what immediately precedes, and assumes the arrangement of the camp described in N.ii.

(ii) The sending out of the spies to Canaan and their return,—further, the forty years' wandering through the wilderness, which was the consequence of it,—is generally implied in the sequel, e.g. N.xx.22-29, (comp.xxxiii.33,39,) xxvi.63–65,xxvii.3. Since, however, in N.xiii,xiv, manifestly two accounts are fused into one whole, note [25], it is natural to see in one of them a portion of the B.O.: among others, xiii.4-16 seems to belong to it, as appears by the comparison of v.16, ' and Moses called Oshea, the son of Nun, Jehoshua,' with E.vi.2,3, (the well-known passage about the origin of the name Jehovah).

(iii) With respect to N.xvi,xvii, nearly the same remarks must be made. The contents of these chapters are implied in xviii,xxvi.9-11, xxvii.3. Yet, as has been already observed, note [25·v], N.xvi is not all from one hand : from the B.O. [?] is derived all in xvi, that concerns the rebellion of Korah, and, consequently, also the whole of xvii. Certainly, xvi.36–40 stands in direct connection with Korah's rebellion ; while xvi.41-50 not only expressly names Korah in v.49, but also, just as xvii.1-13, breathes so entirely the same spirit of partiality for the priestly dignity as the account of Korah's death does, that we can, perhaps, scarcely doubt as to their having had a common origin. Further, xxvi.9-11,—perhaps, also xxvii.3— points back already to the combined narrative now contained in xvi : from which it seems to follow, that the narrator of Korah's rebellion is not different from the compiler of the whole, or, in other words, that Korah and his conspiracy were inserted by the process of retouching an account of Dathan's rebellion already existing, and not the contrary, as de Wette, §153, and others suppose.[51] See Chap.XXII.

---

[51] The author appears to mean that the compiler of the whole Pentateuch inserted *from* the B.O. the story of Korah in an account of the rebellion of Dathan, *later* than the B.O., which account he found already existing, and so afterwards he refers in xxvi.9-11 to the compound story. But what makes it certain that the ' rebellion of Korah is derived from the B.O.' ? What prevents our supposing that it is *not* so derived—that it may come from that author, who has been already more than once recognized as making later additions to the B.O.—that *he*, and not the ancient Elohist, may have added the story of Korah to that of Dathan and Abiram, this latter being itself, as is admitted, a ' later account,' already added to B.O.,—and that the same writer also made the addition in xxvi.9-11 ? *Ed.*

(iv) N.xx.1–13 is implied in xxvii.12–14,—where also reference is made back to xx.22–29, and in this again, v.24, to xx.12,13; also in xx.24,26, xxvii.13, we have 'gathered unto his people,' and xx.29, יִגְוַע, 'expire.' Comp. also D. xxxii.48–52, xxxiv.1–9. All these phenomena indicate that N.xx.1–13,22–29, xxvii.12–23, are rightly referred above to the B.O. Let it be observed also that in xxvi.1,63,64, xxvii.2, Aaron's death is represented as a well-known fact.

(v) That N.xxv also stands in connection with the B.O., appears from the expressions ' give a covenant,' v.12, ' covenant of an everlasting priesthood,' v.13,— from the agreement between v.8 and xvi.48,—from the close connection between v.16–18 and N.xxxi, (a passage of legislative and historical contents [112], and between v.19 [E.V.xxvi.1ᵃ] and N.xxvi. KNOBEL, who formerly, E.L.p.496, denied that N.xxv belongs to the E. document, stated afterwards his opinion, N.D.J.p.149, that N.xxv.6–18 was derived from that document, but v.1–5 from another source.

(vi) That in N.xxxii, again, two narratives are worked into one whole, appears among other things from this, that in v. 33–42 mention is made for the first time of the half-tribe of Manasseh, whereas in the preceding we read only of Reuben and Gad. Traces of the phraseology peculiar to the B.O. may be observed in v.2,5,22,29,32 ; see de WETTE, §153, STÄH.p.39. Besides which, the settlement of the tribes in the trans-Jordanic country can hardly have been passed over in silence in the original B.O., much less in its later, more ample, historical portions : see N.xxxv.13–15, where reference is made to this settlement (of half-Manasseh, as well as of Reuben and Gad).

(85) [111] The account of the war against Midian, v.1–12, can only serve to prepare the way for (i) the prescriptions in v.13–20 with reference to the law of war, and (ii) the directions in v.21–54 respecting the division of booty, and to make the application of both in actual life plain by an example. · This object comes out especially in v.19,20,49,50, but throughout the whole chapter is unmistakable. It is possible that, in fact, in Moses' time a victory was gained over Midian. But it is inconceivable that 12,000 Israelites, v.4,5, killed *all* the male Midianites, v.7,8, without any one of them losing his life, v.49,—that, further, these same 12,000 men carried off a booty of 675,000 sheep, 72,000 oxen, 61,000 asses, and 32,000 unmarried girls, v.32–35, besides also the married women and boys, who, according to v.9, were carried away to the Israelitish camp, but were then, by Moses' command, put to death, v.17. The surprising minuteness, with which, in v.36–47, the partition of this immense booty is related, is easily explained from the above-mentioned object of the narrative, just as, in v.27–30, the dedication of $\frac{1}{500}$ of one moiety to the priests and of $\frac{1}{50}$ of the other moiety to the Levites.

[112] N.xvi,xvii, (especially the portions in which Korah's rebellion is related,) are designed to put clearly in the light the distinction between priests and Levites, and to warn earnestly against any assumption of the priestly privileges by the tribe of Levi generally. Let it be observed how much stress is laid on this point in xvi.5–11,40,47,48. On the other hand, in xvii.1–13, more weight is laid upon the maintenance of the prerogatives of Aaron, and, so far, of the whole *tribe of Levi*, v.3, to which he belonged, in opposition to the other Israelitish tribes.

CHAPTER XV.

(90)   ¹¹² In the passages of Genesis, which belong to the B.O.,⁹¹ no mention whatever
is made of sacrifices, nor of the distinction between things clean and unclean. It
is otherwise, *e.g.* in vii.2,viii.20–22.

   ¹¹⁴ How very much the whole view of the History in the B.O. is governed by
this law, appears also from the following particulars. In the first period, from
Adam to Noah, man lives only on vegetable food; not until the second age does he
use flesh, i.29,ix.3. The patriarchs from Adam to Noah—Enoch alone excepted—
attain an age of from 800 to nearly 1,000 years, v: the ages of the following line,
from Shem to Terah, still exceed in all cases, in some very much, two centuries,
xi.10,&c.: Abraham and his descendants do not reach 200 years, but approximate
continually more and more to the usual length of human life, G.xxv.7,xxxv.28,
xlvii.28,l.22, E.vi.16,18,20, &c. Since the credibility of these accounts is doubtful,
they give the stronger evidence for the position, that in reality the writer of the
B.O. did not merely take over what tradition gave him, but worked up its data to
a regular system.

(91)   ¹¹⁵ Comp.HUPF.p.79–100, to whose admirable demonstration I am much
indebted.

CHAPTER XVI.

(93)   ¹¹⁶ The full proof for this statement cannot be given here: consult the commentaries of TUCH, DELITZSCH, KNOBEL, and the often-quoted writings of STÄHELIN
and HUPFELD. For our present purpose it seems enough to indicate some main
points.

   (i) That ii.4^b–25 must be from another author than i.1–ii.4^a, has been already
shown above ¹⁷⁻¹. Now this second account of the creation, as well as iii, used
the compound name 'Jehovah-Elohim,' which the writer, however, uses no more
after the history of Paradise, and for which he employs in iv, &c., the simple
name 'Jehovah.' *Why* this is done, cannot be said with certainty: perhaps the
explanation of HUPF.,p.124,125, is the most probable, *viz.* that 'Jehovah-Elohim' is
meant to express the *full* name of God, which, according to this writer's view, was
peculiar to Paradise, and for which afterwards, 'Jehovah' and 'Elohim' were used.
But in no case can this difference between ii.4^b–iii and iv be admitted as
evidence against the unity of authorship of these chapters. This is sufficiently
confirmed both by the connection between the two narratives, and their agreement
in phraseology, and is, in fact, not doubted by most interpreters. Comp. *e.g.* iv.1
(the name *Eve*, not known to the B.O.) with iii.20 (explanation of the meaning of
the name),—iv.7^b with iii.16^b,—iv.11 with iii.17^b,—iv.16^b with ii.8 (the name *Eden*
never occurs in the B.O.), &c.

   At the end of iv we find the beginning of a genealogy of the line of Seth,
which, however, is broken off at Enos—(as to *v.*26 see note ⁸⁴)—yet out of which
manifestly v.29 is taken,⁸⁷ whether the Jehovist himself, when he adopted v into his
narrative, added to it *v.*29, or the editor of the Jehovistic genealogy left out the
Sethitic line, because it was identical with that of the B.O., and only borrowed
from it the aforesaid *v.*29. Comp. also SCHRAD.p.183, who, however, assigns iv.

25,26, to the compiler of Genesis; while BOEHMER [187] ascribes to the editor of the whole Pentateuch iii.20,22–24, and iv (throughout). Both these, however, admit that the writer of iv knew, and wished to supplement, the narrative in ii,iii.

(ii) vi.1–8 gives a very peculiar explanation of the corruption of mankind (comp. about the 'sons of Elohim,' v.2,4, among others, KURTZ, *die Söhne Gottes*, &c.) and a justification of God's decision to destroy them: the phraseology in v.5–8 agrees generally with the Jehovistic passages in vii,viii, which have been already considered [22-L99]: comp. vi.5 with viii.21,—vi.7 with vii.4, &c.

(iii) In ix.18–27 we find, besides 'Jehovah,' v.26, the use of the phrase ' he began,' which has already occurred in iv.26,vi.1, comp. x.8, and shows that it is the constant aim of the writer to explain the 'beginning' of all practices existing in his time: comp. iv.20,21.

(iv) xi.1–9 shows again all signs of the Jehovist,—in v.5,6,8,9, the name Jehovah,—in v.6, God's taking counsel with Himself, as in iii.22,vi.6,viii.21,—in v.9, etymology, as in iv.1,v.29,ix.27, comp.x.25,—the use of פּוּץ, 'separate,' in v.4, 8,9, as in ix.19,x.18,—and of שֵׁם, ' name'=renown, v.4, as in vi.4, &c.

(v) That xii.1–4ª,6, &c., and xiii.1–5,7–11ª,12ᵇ–18, are from another hand than xi.10–32, ... has been already shown.[90-L1l]. They are distinguished by the constant use of the name Jehovah, xii.1,4ª,7,8,17,xiii.4,10,13,14,18,—further, by the mention of altars built by Abram, xii.7,8,xiii.4,18, comp. viii.20,iv.3,4, whereas the B.O. knows of no sacrifices in the pre-Mosaic time; lastly, by the phraseology, *e.g.* ' call upon the name of Jehovah,' xii.8,xiii.4, as in iv.26, &c.

That xii and xiii belong together, follows also from xii.6ᵇ comp. with xiii.7ᵇ.

(vi) In xii.2,3, a form of blessing occurs, of which the conclusion, especially,— ' and with thee (*i.e.* making use of thy name) shall all nations of the earth bless one another,'—is very peculiar. It occurs four times besides in Genesis, with slight variations, xviii.18,xxii.18,xxvi.4,xxviii.14, and *always in Jehovistic sections*, see xviii.14,17,19,20,xxii.14–16,xxvi.2,xxviii.13,16,21. This is a strong argument for the common origin of all these passages,—the more so, as they exhibit no trace whatever of the blessing repeatedly addressed to the Patriarch in the B.O.,xvii.6, 16,xxxv.11. Also the other signs of the Jehovist are not wanting in these sections. Thus in xxvi.1 there is a distinct reference back to xii.10–20; there, too, v.20,21, 22, occur etymologies, as also in xxii.14,xix.30–38 (continuation and conclusion of the narrative in xviii.1–xix.28), and in the passages cited above in (iv); xix.30–38 breathes the same spirit as ix.18–27; xxvi.25ª is parallel with xii.7,8,xiii.4,7,18.

(vii) xv,xvi, except v.[1,]3,15,16, and the other larger and smaller sections named in the text, may here be passed over in silence. It is generally admitted, that they belong to the Jehovist, for which, in fact, the strongest evidence may be adduced, as is done *e.g.* by KNOBEL and DELITZSCH.

Towards the end of Genesis, from xxix on, the critical analysis becomes more difficult, and its results more or less uncertain. The reason of this lies in what has been already remarked [96] as to the later Elohistic passages, of which the narrative is here partly composed. These agree much more with the Jehovist than with the B.O., and are, consequently, not so easily distinguished from the Jehovistic sections. Nevertheless, we observe also in xxix–l manifest signs of the Jehovistic author, to whom we have assigned a great part of i–xxviii. That *e.g.*

M

xxx.24–43 is [? partly] from his hand, appears both from the use of Jehovah, *v.*24, 27,30, and from the way in which Jacob's crafty character is here indicated, in agreement with xxv.23–34,xxvii, and, lastly, from the discrepancy between these verses and the account in xxxi.4–16, which certainly proceeds from the younger Elohist. Comp. further the commentators, and as to the genealogical passages, see note [116].

(94)   [117] (i) xiv has once, *v.*22, the name 'Jehovah': yet it contains besides so much that is peculiar, (*e.g. v.*13, 'Abram the Hebrew,') that it cannot possibly have proceeded from the pen of the Jehovist already known to us. Nevertheless, it fits in extremely well in the connection in which it now stands; comp.xiv.13 with xiii.18, and observe in xv.1 the reference to the contents of xiv. On this account it is almost universally assumed that the Jehovist must have inserted this whole chapter into the most suitable place in his narrative.

(ii) A similar conjecture seems to be justified also with respect to xxxiv, to which xxxiii.18–20 belongs as introduction. See, among others, HUPF.p.186–188.

(iii) xlix.1–28 contains once, *v.*18, the name Jehovah: yet there exists no ground whatever for assigning the whole poetical passage to the Jehovist. That he adopted it into his narrative has of late been shown by HUPF.p.73–76, and admitted also by KNOB. *Gen.* p.355,356.[52]

[118] We have already spoken of these,[55] and at the same time have pointed out the peculiarities which forbid our supposing that these genealogies have been adopted without modification. The use of יָלַד, 'he begat,' in x and elsewhere, is a characteristic of the Jehovist, iv.18.

(95)   [119] In this respect the comparison of xii.1–3 with xi.26–32 [?xi.26,27,31,32, note [53]] is instructive. According to this last account of the B.O., the whole tribe, to which Abram belongs, with Terah at its head, travels to Haran, and from

---

[52] I would suggest that this important section, xlix.1[a]–28 may be due to the Junior Elohist, except *v.*18, which may have been added by the Jehovist, as a kind of *rest* for the dying Jacob, when he (HUPF. KNOB. KURN.) adopted it, and inserted it into the narrative. The following phenomena (among others) seem to point to the later Elohist:—

(i) *v.*2, קָבַץ, 'gather,' as in xli.35,48, which belong to E[2], (the later Elohist), comp. 'Elohim' in *v.*25,28,32,32,38,39,51,52;

(ii) *v.*4 refers to xxxv.21,22[a], an interpolation in the Elohistic story, which uses 'Jacob,' *v.*14,15,20,22[b],23,26,27,xlviii.3, and due to E[2], who uses chiefly 'Israel,' xxxv.21,22[a],xlviii.8,10,11,13,14,21;

(iii) *v.*25, 'Elohim of thy father,' as in xxxi,5,29,42,53,xlvi.1,3, passages due to E[2], comp. 'Elohim' in xxxi.7,9,42[b],50[b],xlvi.2,3.

(iv) *v.*24,25, comp. the heaping of expressions 'Mighty One of Jacob,' 'Tender' =Shepherd, 'Stone of Israel,' 'the Elohim of thy father,' 'the Almighty,' with xlviii,15, 'the Elohim before whom, &c.,' 'the Elohim who *tended* me, &c.,' 'the Angel who redeemed me from all evil.'

N.B. The language in xxvii. 28 agrees closely with that in xlix.25: the writer of the former of these passages may have imitated the latter. *Ed.*

thence, after Terah's death, to Canaan. Here, then, we have to do with an ordinary migration: it is only afterwards, xvii, that *Elohim* makes a covenant with Abram. On the contrary, the Jehovist mentions that Jehovah called Abram out of Ur of the Chaldees, comp. xv.7. According to him, therefore, the selection of Israel begins already at the time of Abram's journey to the land, which Jehovah will show him,—a species of religious, and, at the same time, purely prophetical, representation.

This instance stands by no means alone. The selection of Israel is also put strongly in the foreground in other narratives, particularly in what the Jehovist mentions about the privileges granted to that people above others, and the lot of those nations, with which Israel came into relation or had tribal connection. From this point of view must be regarded ix.18-27, the blessing of Shem and curse upon Canaan,—xvi.12, the future lot of Ishmael,—xix.30-38, the origin of Moab and Ammon,—xxv.29-34, xxvii.29,40, the exclusion of Esau from the rights of the firstborn.

[130] See especially the efficacy of the intercessory prayer of the righteous, God's almightiness and faithful care of His chosen, xviii,xix, comp. xviii.14,17,18,—xxii. 1-18, disapproval of human sacrifice, and, on the other hand, appreciation of an obedience, which is ready to sacrifice the dearest object before Jehovah,— xxxix.2,3, the pious blessed by Jehovah, and, through thought of Him, restrained from evil.

[131] Examples of this are xxii.16, the prophetical נְאֻם יְהֹוָה, 'saith Jehovah,'— xxv.22, the formula 'to seek Jehovah,' usually employed about consulting the (priestly or prophetical) oracles,—xxvi.5, the enumeration, quite in the style of the Deuteronomist, of the different portions of the law, ' my charge, my commandments, my statutes, and my laws,'—further, xii.3, and the parallel passages quoted above,[116-vi] especially, xviii.18,19, xxii.18,xxvi.4,5, from which it appears that the blessing, which the nations of the earth should wish for each other, is by no means of a merely material, but is rather also of a spiritual, kind, so that the prophetical idea of a final conversion of the heathen to the religion of Israel [53] is not, indeed, expressed in these passages, but yet is closely connected with the expectation therein uttered.

[132] It is sufficient to point here to the ideas of the Jehovist about the origin of sin, iii, and its propagation, both among Adam's immediate descendants, iv, and among mankind that was destroyed by the Flood, vi.1-8. Comp. also viii.21. Also the sketches of character in the Jehovistic narratives about the Patriarchs give evidence of close study of character, which we look for in vain in the accounts of the B.O. In both points is revealed plainly the further development and culture, and, consequently, the later age of the Jehovist.

(96) [133] In xx.1-17 Abraham is called נָבִיא, 'prophet,' v.7,—God reveals Himself in a dream,—great efficacy is assigned to Abraham's prayer. So, too, we observe in xxi.9-21,22-32,xxv.24-34, and in these portions of xxix-xxxiii, in which 'Elohim'

---

[53] It seems to me doubtful whether there is any reference in these passages, directly or indirectly, to a general conversion of the heathen to the religion of Israel. *Ed.*

is used, similar phenomena, which vary greatly from the simple narrative-style of the B.O. and, on the other hand, either actually occur, or find their parallels, with the Jehovist.

[124] First of all, in the persistent avoidance of the name Jehovah, which however, may, perhaps, be regarded as a sign of the author's acquaintance with the B.O.; again, according to HUPF. p.98, in the conception of Israel's relation to the nations, which it sets forth with less particularity than the Jehovist, and in the less sharp notice of sin.

[125] See HUPF. p.167–195. Especially instructive in this respect is the comparison of xx.1–17 with xxvi.1,2, and of xxxi.4,5, with xxx.31–43.[54] We shall return again below, Chap. XXI, to the consideration of the relative age of the primary documents of the Pentateuch.

CHAPTER XVII.

(97) [125] The Jehovist touches frequently in Genesis on the future settlement of Abraham's progeny in the land of Canaan, *e.g.* whenever he mentions the promises of Jehovah to Abraham, xii.7, xiii.15, xv.18, and Isaac, xxvi.3, and enumerates the tribes, which should be driven out by Israel, xv.19–21. The 'Blessing of Jacob,' xlix.2–28, taken over by the Jehovist, has also reference to this settlement; and Jacob's burial, l.1–11, proceeds from the same supposition. On these and other phenomena the conjecture is based, that the Jehovist must have related also the later events.

[127] The proof is already given in Chap. XIV (see notes [100,109-112]), so far as it is there shown that the here-mentioned Jehovistic passages, partly, do not fit into the plan of the B.O.,—partly, are at variance with the accounts therein contained,—partly, at all events, have no necessary connection with them. Comp. also notes [19,20,23,24]. Let it be observed further, that there exists discrepancy between E.xii.39. where the use of unleavened bread is explained in a natural way from the precipitate haste with which Israel left Egypt, and E.xii.1–28, where that use is derived from a command of Moses. Other proofs are considered below.

(98) [128] That, *e.g.* E.ii.18,21,iii.1,iv.18,xviii.1, N.x.29, (different names of the father-in-law of Moses,) are not derived from the same primary-document, has been already remarked.[19,1] We find narratives compiled out of two or more documents in E.i.8–ii.22, iii.1–vi.1,[96] xix,xxiv, and xxxi.18–xxxiv.35, see [22-111].

So in N.xiii,xiv, and in N.xvi, we remarked [22-1vw] the traces of two documents, which are now compacted into one whole; yet it seemed to us afterwards,[114-11.111] that one was from the B.O., or rather was a later addition to that Book, written

---

[54] Obviously, the view of Jacob's conduct, which we receive from xxxi.4–16, is very different from that given by xxx.37–43: in the former his increase in wealth is ascribed directly to God's special favour, in the latter to Jacob's cunning. *Ed.*

in the same spirit. Hence it follows that the above-named chapters are only assigned in part to the Jehovistic portions of the Pentateuch.

[129] We have treated of the prophetical character of the Jehovistic narratives in Genesis in the notes to Chap.XVI, especially in [119-121]. It appears as strongly in E.xxxi.18–xxxiv.35, especially in depicting the character of Moses, and in grand conceptions with respect to the manifestation of God to man;—further in the beautiful narrative of N.xi, where again the character of Moses, especially his unselfishness, comes forward in the clearest light; the wish, expressed by him in v.29, is purely prophetical. So in N.xii, especially v.6–8, Moses is expressly compared with other prophets; and it is indicated how high a rank he takes among the men of God, just as in D.xxxiv.10–12, where manifestly reference is made to this passage of Numbers. Also the expectation expressed in N.xiv.21 is purely prophetical. In like manner, the history of Balaam acquires, through the oracles placed in his mouth, a distinctly prophetical character, N.xxii–xxiv.

Other signs also of the Jehovist, which, however, for a great part, he has in common with the younger Elohist, recur in Exodus–Numbers, e.g. the etymologies, E.ii.10,22,xv.23,xviii.3,4, N.xi.3,34,xiii.24,xxi.3,16, the insertion of poetical and prophetical passages,[55] such as G.iv.23,24,xlix, E.xv, N.xxiii,xxiv.

L.xxvi is a prophetical address, in form and contents not unlike those of Jeremiah and Ezekiel, but full besides of peculiar turns and expressions, which the author of this prophetical passage has in common with no other, or, if any, with the author of L.xviii–xx. Comp. KNOB., E.L. p.572,573.

[130] As in G.xv.19–21 the Canaanitish tribes are enumerated, so also in E.iii.8,17, xiii.5,(xxiii.23,28),xxxiii.2,xxxiv.11, N.xiii.29. E.xvii.15ᵃ is parallel with G.xii. 7ᵇ,8ᵇ, and other places,—N.xvi.2 ['name' = renown] with G.vi.4,xi.4. In N.xiii,xiv, reference is made continually to E.xxxii,xxxiv: comp. e.g. N.xiv.11,12, with E.xxxii. 9,10,—N.xiv.13–16 with E.xxxii.11,14,—N.xiv.17,18, with E.xxxiv.6,7. Now N.xiv.11–25 makes manifestly one whole, and is from another hand than v.26–35, as, among other things, appears from this, that the last section is quite superfluous after v.11–25,—further, from the mention of Caleb alone, xiv.24, (as in xiii.30), whereas in v.26–35 Caleb and Joshua appear, v.30, (as in xiv.6,38). Hence we must probably regard N.xiv.11–25, with the verses belonging to it, as the work of the Jehovist [? or Deuteronomist], who makes free use here of the older documents, which he has laid as the basis of his narrative in E.xxxii–xxxiv. Other instances of Jehovistic phraseology are given by KNOB. E.L. and N.D.J. passim. They are, however, not so obvious as in Genesis, partly because the subjects treated of in Exodus and Numbers afford much more variety, but also, doubtless, because in Genesis much more extensive use is made of older documents than in Exodus and Numbers.

[131] This supposition applies e.g. to E.iii.1–vi.1,xix,xxiv,xxxi.18–xxxiv, and needs no further more extended proof after what has been remarked above.[128] Here

---

[55] Some of these poetical and prophetical passages appear to me to be due to the Deuteronomist, who, however, as distinguished from the older and younger Elohist, may be included under the name 'Jehovist,' or, more properly, may be classed as a 'Jehovistic writer.' Ed.

also, however, there remains always much that is doubtful. With respect to E.xxxi. 18–xxxiv I observe, see [52-liii], that xxxii.7–14 has come probably from that writer, who reduced the whole into its present form, *i.e.* it would seem, from the Jehovist [? Deuteronomist]. Comp. KNOB.*E.L.*p.313,&c.

What is said about the higher antiquity of some of his primary documents is applicable to E.xix.1, [2ª] : comp.xxiv.3–8.

[152] This is true, *e.g.* with reference to E.xviii, (according to Ew.,*G.V.I.*i.p.89,90, a very old memorandum), which is very loosely connected with xvii and xix,—further, with reference to N.x.29–34, and *v.*35,36,[56] (again very old and important fragments, which, however, have so little connection with what precedes and follows, that nothing can be settled with certainty as to their original connection,)—lastly, also with reference to N.xxi.1–3, comp. note[14].

CHAPTER XVIII.

(99)   [153] This is the point of view of *e.g.* ILGEN, VATER, HARTMANN, de WETTE, (*Beitr.* i,ii, and *Einl.* 1st ed.), and others. Some of these scholars, *e.g.* ILGEN and de WETTE, laid great stress upon the different use of the Divine Names, for determining the origin of the narratives ; VATER and HARTMANN were of another mind on this point. The first-named, accordingly, built on the foundation first laid by ASTRUC (physician of Louis XIV) in his work, *Conjectures*, &c.

[154] With the view of TUCH agree, generally, among others, BLEEK, STÄHELIN, de WETTE (*Einl.* later editions), SCHUMANN. It is contested by KURTZ, *Beitr.* and *Einh.*, who, however, afterwards, though hesitatingly, united himself with DELITZSCH, —by DRECHSLER, KEIL, and others.

(100) [155] Comp. TUCH, p.1, and, further, especially STÄHELIN, de WETTE, *Einl.*, Von LENGKERKE ; the last two distinguish the Deuteronomist from the Jehovist, with whom STÄHELIN identifies him.[57]

[156] Comp. especially the review of the composition of Genesis in DEL.p.842,&c., and KNOB.*Gen.*p.xvii,&c. (comp. p.xiii,&c. of the first edition). As to VAIHINGER see note[187].

[157] DEL. p.646, is of opinion, that, probably, in general, the 'prime-record' and its 'manipulation' may be distinguished from each other, but that it is impossible to indicate how many and what kind of written accounts were used or taken over, either by the author of the prime-record or by the supplementer.. Indeed, there still exists here great uncertainty, which ought to be less a matter of surprise than

---

[56] I very much doubt *v.*35,36, being part of the ancient document : see P.II.407, 408. *Ed.*

[57] May not the opinions of the two former be reconciled with that of the latter in some measure, by the theory that the Deuteronomist was distinct from the *Jehovist*, but yet was identical with the *compiler* of the whole Pentateuch, whom STÄHELIN supposes erroneously to have been the Jehovist ? *Ed.*

the agreement, which has been attained from the very first respecting many most important particulars. KNOB. *Gen,*1st ed.,p.xiii, had recognized, generally, that the Jehovist, here and there, followed written records ; but he now believes, 2nd ed. p.xvii,xviii, that he can show that he has used especially two older works, and, further, has, with greater freedom, himself narrated occasionally. To the first prime-document, *e.g.* he assigns G.xx.1–17, xxi.6–31 (except parts of *v.*1,14,16),xxiv. 61ᵇ–67,&c.,—to the second, G.xiv,xv,xxv.21–23,25–26ᵃ,29–34,xxvi (except *v.*2ᵇ,15, 16,18,24,25, as far as יהוה, 27,34,35), &c. He sees the hand of the Jehovist himself in G.ii.4ᵇ–iv.26,v.29,vi.1–8,&c. It may be observed that the first of these prime-documents agrees *generally* with the Elohistic passages, of which we have spoken.[96];[98]

VAIHINGER again takes another course (Art. *Pentateuch* in HERZOG'S *Real-Ency-clopädie,* xi.p.292–370, especially p.331,&c.). He ascribes to the Elohist all those passages which have been assigned above to the B.O., but also some, which we have thought it necessary to sever from them[98] ; the Elohist's work has been completed and extended by the Jehovist, who has used for this chiefly a document, which VAIHINGER, after EWALD, names ' the Book of the Covenants,' whose author (called the pre-Elohist) was about two centuries older than the Elohist or writer of the B.O. To this ' Book of the Covenants ' VAIHINGER assigns, among other passages, G.xii.10–20,xiv.1–24,xx.1–17,xxi.(6–21)22–34,&c.,—in a word, many of the sections which have been severed above [99];[99] from the B.O. as *later* Elohistic passages, whereas others of these sections, *e.g.* G.xxix.1–xxxii.4, he ascribes wholly or mostly to the Elohist. Lastly, VAIHINGER supposes also, p.359,&c., that the self-same ' Harmonist,' who united Deuteronomy with the first four books of the Pentateuch,—which were, according to him, the work of the Jehovist,—allowed himself to make, here and there, in the four books, alterations and transpositions, so that we no longer possess the work of the Jehovist or 'Supplementer' in its original extent.

Lastly, some mention must here be made of the critical analysis of Genesis by BOEHMER, comp. note [99].

He finds in it remains of three different documents (A, B, and C), which he believes to have been combined and filled up by a compiler (D). The oldest of these documents (A) dates from the time of David's reign at Hebron; the second (B) is Ephraimitic, and written under Joram, the son of Ahab ; the third (C) is also the offspring of the Northern Kingdom, and written under Jeroboam II ; the compiler —not only of Genesis, but—of the whole Thora, was a contemporary of Josiah.

If we now consider how the Book is distributed among these four writers, it appears that the first document (A) agrees with our ' Book of Origins,' see note [99], since it contains—

i.1–ii.3	xiii.6,11ᵇ,12ᵃ	xxviii.1–9
v (except *v.*29)	xvi.3,15,16	xxxi.18
vi.9–22	xvii.1–27	xxxv.9–15,27–29
vii.6–9,11,13–16ᵃ,18–21,24	xix.29	xxxvi.6–8,xxxvii.1
viii.1,2ᵃ,3ᵇ,4ᵃ,5,13–19	xxi.2,4,5	xlvi.6,7
ix.1–17,28,29	xxiii.1–20	xlvii.11 (partly), 27,28
xi.10–27,31,32	xxv.7–10,11ᵃ,17,20,26ᵇ	xlix.29,30,32,33ᵇ
xii.4ᵇ,5	xxvi.34,35	l.12,13

· The second document (B) agrees most with that of our Jehovist; from that, for instance, are derived ii.4,&c., the other part of the history of the Flood, sections such as xii.1-4ᵃ,6-20,xviii,xxiv,&c.&c.

The third document (C) agrees here and there with our younger Elohist; from it, for instance, are taken xx,xxi (a great part), important portions of xxviii–xxxv (see note ⁹⁶), and of Joseph's history, as xl (nearly all), and parts of xli,xlii,xlv, xlvi.

Very important, according to BOEHMER, has been the work of the compiler. Not only did he allow himself to make throughout slight modifications in his documents, e.g. in G.ii,iii, where he added continually 'Elohim' to 'Jehovah;' but also he himself wrote very important portions of Genesis itself, e.g. iii.20,22–24,iv (entirely), vi.1–3,4ᵇ, and in the sequel xix.30–38,xxii.15–18,xxxvi.29–43,&c.&c.

It must be left to the commentators on the Book of Genesis to pass a judgment upon this hypothesis.

(102)   ¹³⁸ Comp. HUPF. Q.G.p.163. According to him, we possess the Jehovistic docu-ment, from the beginning as far as Jacob's arrival at Succoth, G.xxxiii.17, still almost entire. The compiler has left out of it only the sequel of the genealogy of the Sethites (after iv.26), and so that of the Shemites (after x.25), the birth of Ish-mael, (after xvi.14), and of Isaac, xxi.1, and, finally, the first part of the history of Abraham's temptation, xxii.1–13. All these particulars had, probably, to be omitted because they were imparted by the compiler from other sources,—the first four from the B.O., the last from a later Elohistic document. I mention this here to show that the supposition of the existence of such a Jehovistic document is by no means an *absurdity*: its *probability* ⁵⁸ will appear below.¹³⁹⁻¹⁴¹

¹³⁹ (i) The second account of the Creation, ii.4ᵇ–iii, is a complete perfect whole, and so little a completion of the first, that it might be even more reasonably main-tained that the first completed the second.⁵⁹

(ii) The same is true of Abraham's history, G.xii,xiii, which deserves considera-tion here the more, since the Jehovist, in the treatment of it, inserts once only an older document, G.xiv, but generally relates independently. His narrative, how-ever, is by no means to be regarded as incomplete. Since, e.g. in the B.O.,G.xi.

---

⁵⁸ It appears to me not at all probable that the Jehovist recorded originally the line of the Sethites, of which iv.25,26,v.29, are fragments that have been left by the later compiler, while all the rest has been omitted, because supplied by the E. genea-logy in v. Did the Jehovist, who had so much to say about the doings of Cain, Lamech, Jabal, Jubal, Tubalcain, and something in connection with the birth of Seth, Enos, and Noah—make no remark worthy of being retained in the text, about *any* of the other descendants of Seth? It seems to me equally improbable that his Shemite line should have been in the same way broken off with Peleg, x.25, if he gave it originally in full. *Ed.*

⁵⁹ I cannot concur in this judgment. It appears to me that the second account may have been intended to complete the first in respect—not of the creation of all things, but—of the doings and fates of the first pair after their creation, of which the first account tells us nothing. *Ed.*

26–32, Abram's journey from Ur to Haran had been already mentioned, he must—supposing that he only wished to supplement—have described the continuation of this journey from Haran to Canaan; on the contrary, he removes us, xii.1, comp. with xv.7, to Ur of the Chaldees.[60]

(iii) So the narrative of Lot's settlement in Sodom, G.xiii, which is left, after separating the accounts borrowed from the B.O., is quite complete.[61] Comp. further HUPF. p.101–167. What is developed fully by him in the case of Genesis may be applied also to Exodus–Numbers.

(iv) E.iii.1,&c., is a complete account of the revelation of God to Moses and the making known of the name Jehovah—in no sense a supplementing[62] of E.vi.2, &c. (B.O.)

(v) So is it also with N.xi (especially v.7–10) comp. with E.xvi[63] (especially v.13,14).

(vi) N.xxii–xxiv, again, is a complete history of Balaam, and very far from being a completion of what the later portions of the B.O. relate concerning him.[64]

(vii) Even in N.xvi, although this chapter is partly Jehovistic, and partly derived from the prime-record, the Jehovist appears by no means as a supplementer; see [110-111] and further, Chap.XXII, especially [255].

[140] (i) The Jehovistic genealogy of the Sethites, G.iv.25,26, for instance, is incomplete, since it is only carried on to the second member, Enos. This is explained (TUCH, DELITZSCH, KNOBEL) from this, that the Jehovist had nothing particular to mention with respect to the other descendants of Seth, and so confined himself to taking over the genealogy given in the B.O., G.v, into which he merely introduced one remark, v.29. But how is it then to be accounted[65] for that the Jehovistic note about Enos is not introduced into the genealogy itself (between v.9 and v.10), but obtained a place *before* it, iv.26, and so that the explanation of the name Seth occurs not between v.3 and v.4, but in iv.25?

---

[60] But suppose that G.xv is due to the later compiler (the Deuteronomist?) It will be seen that xii.1 does not *mention* Ur of the Chaldees; though, *as it now stands*, the expression 'thy country' must naturally be referred to Ur. *Ed.*

[61] True; but the words of the Elohist in xix.29 may have served as a *text* to the Jehovist, and suggested to him to *supplement* the Elohistic story with a full account of the destruction of Sodom and Gomorrah. *Ed.*

[62] May it not have been inserted as *introductory* or *preparatory* to the account in E.vi.2–8? *Ed.*

[63] What if E.xvi was inserted—an *enlarged* edition of N.xi—to fill up what seemed a blank in the earlier history,—since they must have been in danger of perishing from want of food *before* they reached Sinai, as well as after leaving it? *Ed.*

[64] Does this passage belong to the Jehovist, or was it merely adopted and inserted by him? *Ed.*

[65] The birth of *Seth* is brought in very naturally in iv.25, as the continuation of the story of the death of Abel, and the banishment of Cain; then the birth of *Enos* as naturally follows. *Ed.*

It is much more probable, now, that a compiler retained the beginning of the Jehovistic genealogy, because it recorded a few particulars, which were not in the B.O., but omitted the sequel, because it was identical with it, so that merely an etymological note, v.29, needed to be retained of it. The position occupied by iv.25, 26, is very intelligible if a compiler had before him both documents: he then follows his account in the Jehovistic document up to the point, where this becomes identical with that of the B.O. It is, on the other hand, very unnatural, if the Jehovist was a supplementer or compiler; for he then would have dropped his proper task of supplementing, in order to come forward as an independent narrator.[66]

(ii) The same remarks apply to the genealogy of the Shemites, imparted in x.22, 24,25, but not carried farther than Peleg, so that Reu, Serug, Nahor, Terah (in the B.O.,xi.18–25) are left out. Did the Jehovist leave them out, because they were already given in the B.O.? But why,[67] then, does he mention Arphaxad, Salah, Eber, and Peleg, which also appear there, xi.10–17? It is much more probable that the generations between Peleg and Abram were enumerated by him before G.xii.1, but were left out by the Compiler, because he imparted them out of the B.O. The Compiler might do this, but not the Jehovist himself; for then he would have connected [superscript] his narrative with xi.26–32, which he does not do.[68]

In opposition[69] to these and such like examples, there stand, if I am not mistaken, as worthy of especial notice, only two[70] places of Genesis, xx.18, a Jehovistic elucidation of the foregoing (Elohistic) narrative, especially of v.17, and xxii.14–18, a Jehovistic supplement of the (Elohistic) narrative of the temptation of Abraham. But both these passages want the force of evidence, which is ascribed to them. Thus xx.18 may be just as well an explanatory note or gloss of the *compiler*. Again, xxii. 14–18[71] cannot lay much weight in the scale, since already in v.11 the name Jehovah occurs; while on the other hand v.11–13 is so closely connected with v.1–10, that we can hardly help ascribing them to one and the same author: v.1–10 is by itself incomplete, and there is great resemblance between v.2 and v.12. The whole section, v.1–19, has thus a mixed character, which can be explained just as well from the uniting of two parallel accounts, as from the supplementing of one account by another author (the Jehovist). And, even admitting that this last view is the most probable, then it would only follow that the Jehovist was the

---

[66] Certainly: for the reasons above given, this last seems to me the *most* natural explanation of the phenomenon in question. *Ed.*

[67] Because he wishes to come *through* them to *Peleg*, in order to introduce the notice in x. 25. *Ed.*

[68] This does not seem to me at all necessary: see note [69]. *Ed.*

[69] Rather, as it seems to me, these passages may be adduced in *confirmation* of *that* view of the Jehovist, which regards him as a *supplementer*, but one writing freely and, whenever he pleased, independently. *Ed.*

[70] Add also a third, xxi.1, a Jehovistic taking up of the E. story in xvii, after the long digression in xviii–xx. *Ed.*

[71] I believe that it may be shown that G.xxii.14–18 is due to the later Compiler or Editor, not to the Jehovist. But what is to be said about G.xxi.1? *Ed.*

editor of this one section,—by no means that he discharged this duty with reference to the whole Book of Genesis, or even to the whole Tetrateuch from Genesis
to Numbers. G. xxii.1–19 would then be simply parallel to E.xix,xxiv.[141]

[141] HUFF., p.101–103, assigns the greatest weight to this ground of proof. DEL.,
p.647,648, judges otherwise; yet he has not, in my opinion, deprived of force the
demonstration of HUPFELD. The most obvious instances of discrepancy between
the Jehovistic accounts and those of the B.O., are the following:

(i) G.iv.26, comp. with E.vi.2, &c., or, generally, the use of the name Jehovah from
G.i to E.vi.2, in opposition to the evidence of E.vi.2, &c., as to the age of that name;

(ii) G.ii.4[b],&c., comp. with G.i–ii.4[a], see note [17.i];

(iii) G.xii.1,&c. (comp. xv.7) comp. with G.xi.26–32, see notes [116, 130.ii];

(iv) G.xxv.1,&c. comp. with the chronology of the B. O., xvii.17, xxiii.1;

(v) G.xxvii.&c. (the history of Jacob's flight from Esau), comp. with xxviii.1–9,
xxxvi.6–8.

Other instances, taken from the Book of Genesis, have been already considered
in another connection, Chap.IV–VI.

DELITZSCH rightly observes that, independently of the question whether there
really exist contradictions between such passages, yet in any case the compiler,
assumed by HUPFELD, did not remark them,—from which he concludes that the
Jehovist also may have so judged, and may have thought to *supplement* the B.O.
by accounts, which appear to us, rightly or otherwise, rather to *contradict* that
book. Yet we feel that, what the compiler may—rather, must—have thought,
need not therefore have been regarded in the same light by the Jehovist himself.
The compiler had the two documents before him, held them both for true, and
applied therefore what, of course, seemed to him a *certain* process of harmonising.
The Jehovist, on the other hand, cannot have thought that what he himself wrote
down was simply supplementary of the prime-record,—that is to say, supposing
that he understood his own narratives, and the effect they were likely to produce,
which will hardly be denied. Let anyone just try to imagine that the Jehovist meant
to *supplement*[72] the first account of the Creation through what we read in G.ii.4[b]&c.
about the origin of men, trees, and plants. On the other hand, it is very natural
that a compiler applied to these two accounts the explanation, which for so many
years has been the prevailing one among Christians.

Further, what is here remarked about the Book of Genesis may be easily applied
also to Exodus–Numbers, comp. Chap.IV–VI, in which Books the 'supplement-
hypothesis' seems even to be oppressed with yet greater difficulties; see below,
Chap.XXI,XXII.

(103) [142] In order to make the review more easy, I sum here in order the different
documents, which we have learned to distinguish:—

(i) A, the Book of Origins, in which we observed older and younger portions,—
Chap.XIII–XV.

(ii) B, the later Elohistic and Jehovistic accounts of Genesis, Exodus, and
Numbers, to which last some laws (in E.xiii and E.xxxiv) and the prophetical
passage, L.xxvi, are attached, Chap.XIII,XVI,XVII;

---

[72] See note 59.

(iii) C, separate collections of laws, E.xx.23–xxiii, L.xviii–xx: see notes [44,106];

(iv) D, the Deuteronomistic Legislation, Chap.X.

[142] See Chap.XIX. It is self-evident that, in the consideration of this History, the result of the enquiry in the following chapters must be, now and then, assumed, since the Books of the O.T. are, usually, the only sources, from which the fortunes of the people and the development of their Religion can be learned.

[144] See Chap.XX. The remark made in the foregoing note is here also applicable. Further, it is obvious that the two parts of our enquiry are closely connected, and sometimes flow over into one another.

[145] With respect to the age of the documents of the Pentateuch, difference of view prevails quite as much as with respect to the activity of the compiler or compilers. STÄHELIN, who does not distinguish the author of the Deuteronomistic Legislation from the Jehovist, sees in this last the compiler also of the whole Pentateuch. But most regard the Deuteronomistic Legislation as younger than the laws contained in the Book of the Covenant, in L.xviii–xx, and in the Book of Origins, Chap.X, and distinguish, in consequence of this, the two editings above-mentioned, (e. g. KNOBEL, EWALD, de WETTE, VAIHINGER, and others). Those on the other hand, who (whether with DELITSZCH, or with GEORGE, VATKE,) ascribe to Deuteronomy a higher antiquity than to the first four Books, and especially to the laws recorded in them, assume, of course, only one editing of the Pentateuch. Further, it is obvious, and will appear more clearly below, Chap.XXII, that the last view may also coexist with a somewhat different judgment as to the relative age of the portions of our present Pentateuch.

CHAPTER XIX.

(105)   [146] The historians of the O.T. are far removed from the objectivity, which we observe e.g. in a chronicle. They are *pragmatical* historians, as a very superficial inspection of their writings shows, and as is, in fact, admitted by all. See, e.g. HENGST., *Beitr.*,p.20–22 (on the Book of Judges). Nevertheless, a distinction must be made here between the different Books. The Books of *Joshua* and *Chronicles* cannot be placed in the same line with *Judges, Ruth, Samuel,* and *Kings.* The tendency of the first two Books is more priestly or Levitical,—that of the last, more prophetical. Hence it follows that greater weight must be assigned, in the enquiry with which we are now occupied, to the evidence of the latter than to that of the former. It is the more important to remark this, because—as will be seen further on—these two classes of writings are, just with respect to this very point, more or less at variance with each other.

(108)   [147] In general, the remark applies here, that the division above made, from the nature of the case, can only be comparatively accurate. Some examples belong indifferently to the first class or to the second, &c.

[148] It is self-evident that the testimony of the Chronicles that Rehoboam

'forsook the Law of Jehovah,' 2Ch.xii.1, has not so much weight of meaning, as
the statement of the same writer, 2Ch.xvii.9, that Jehoshaphat sent out Levites
with 'the Book of the Law,' in order to instruct the people in it. The first does
not at all prove that in Rehoboam's time the Law was in existence: the writer must
of necessity have so expressed himself, even if he knew that the Law was first
written down *after* Rehoboam's time. But the second is a sufficient proof that,
according to the view of the Chronicler, Jehoshaphat possessed and knew the
'Book of the Law.'

Upon this subject in its whole extent the following books deserve especially to
be consulted: de WETTE, *Beitr.*I.223–265, and *Einl.*,p.161, &c., HENGST., *Beitr.*,
III.1–148, HÄv.,I.ii.p.493–543, KEIL,§34.

(109)   [149] HENGST., p.40,&c., denies the cogency of these instances, inasmuch as in
these cases the sacrifices were always offered in consequence of theophanies or
angelophanies, which, as something quite out of the common, might interrupt the
lawful order of things. Yet, supposing that with HENGSTENBERG we interpret the
phenomena in question quite objectively, how, then, is it to be explained, that God
commands or allows something, which is in contradiction with the Law given by
Himself? And, if these theophanies are regarded as subjective visions, how, then,
could, *e.g.* Gideon or Manoah think that they acquired thereby the right to act
against the express command of Jehovah who had appeared to them? Besides,
HENGSTENBERG passes by the fact, that in any case, Ju.xxi.2,4, (where 'Beth-el,'
*v.*2, is a proper name, [not 'House of God,' E.V.]) is in contradiction with
L.xvii.1–9, and thus—together with all the passages enumerated in (110,111),
affords an analogy, by which we have to explain Ju.ii,vi,xiii.

(110)   [150] HENGST. again, p.48–50, denies the cogency of these passages. In Eli's
time the Ark of the Covenant had fallen into the hands of the Philistines; and
although these had brought it back, it was not placed back again in the Tabernacle,
but removed from Bethshemesh to Kirjath-Jearim, 1S.v.11,vi,vii.1,2. Israel was
thus in reality, while under Samuel's government, devoid of a national Sanctuary,
from which circumstance the irregular state of the worship is naturally explained.

Ans. (i) Was not the carrying the Ark of the Covenant into the conflict an
unlawful act, and, just because it was so often repeated,[73] a proof that the prescriptions of the Pentateuch about the placing of the Ark, did not yet exist?

(ii) If Israel really supposed that they were without a common Sanctuary, and
so for a time forsaken by God, sacrifices would have been stopped altogether, as
e.g. was the case afterwards in the Babylonish Captivity. That Samuel offered at
more than one place, is certainly not a necessary consequence of the Ark having
been placed at Kirjath-Jearim, but must be explained from other causes, *e.g.* from
the absence of any prescription, which forbade such sacrifices.

[151] The author manifestly expresses this approval, when he appends to the
statement, 'and Saul built an altar to Jehovah,' the remark, '*this was the first
altar which he built to Jehovah.*' In this is involved (i) that Saul built also other

73 There is no distinct statement of the Ark being taken out into the battle-field
except in 1S.iv.3–11: but see Ju.xx.27,28. *Ed.*

altars besides this, (ii) that the writer saw nothing wrong in this, but, on the contrary, regarded it as an evidence of praiseworthy zeal. Comp. THEN. *in loco.*

[133] That the Tabernacle stood at Gibeon we know only from the Chronicler, 1Ch.xvi.38–40,xxi.29, 2Ch.i.3. The writer of the Books of Kings says of Gibeon 'that was the great high place,' 1K.iii.4, and he expresses undisguised disapproval of the sacrificing on high places, v.2,3. It is most probable that the Chronicler, who tries to expunge as much as possible the signs of unlawful Jehovah-worship, (notes [133,134]) seeks to account for the respect paid to this high-place at Gibeon, by explaining it as a consequence of the Tabernacle being placed there.

[134] 1Ch.xxi.28–30 deserves especial notice. What the writer of 2 Samuel had related in the most simple manner,—viz. David's sacrifice in the threshing-floor of Araunah,—seemed to the Chronicler so obvious a violation of the Law, that he considers himself bound to make excuse for it. Through the appearance of the angel David was so confused, that he could not betake himself to Gibeon! Certainly, even if the other instances were not plain enough, this testimony of the Chronicler would be quite sufficient to teach us, that facts had indeed occurred in direct contradiction to the express prescriptions of the Law.[74]

(111)   [134] According to the Chronicler, 2Ch.xiv.3,xvii.6, Asa and Jehoshaphat abolished the high-places, *i.e.* the worship of Jehovah on the high-places, from which it has been concluded that their continuing to exist was *against their sentiments*, and, generally, against the sentiments of pious Israelites, through the corrupt state of the people, generally, who did not trouble themselves about the Law. Yet the *same* writer records, 2Ch.xv.17,xx.32,33, that under both these kings 'the high-places were *not* taken away,' just as the writer of 1K.xv.14,xxii.43, who knew nothing of any doing away of the high-places by these two kings. We adhere to his testimony. The Chronicler ascribes to Asa and Jehoshaphat actions, which they ought *according to his judgment* to have performed, if they really *did what was good in the eyes of Jehovah*, 2Ch.xiv.2,xvii.1–4. He could ascribe this to them with the more good faith, since he could not imagine to himself any piety, which did not consist in obedience to the prescriptions of the Law. We believe with him that Asa and Jehoshaphat *would have* acted thus, *if* they had known the Law.

[135] In our review (109–113) no mention was purposely made of the sanctuary in the dwelling of Micah, Ju.xvii, and at Dan, Ju.xviii, and of the worship, which Jeroboam established, and all his successors maintained, at Dan and Bethel. Indeed, it has been justly remarked, that these facts, both on account of the character of the persons concerned in them, and on account of their peculiar nature, cannot serve as a measure of what was or was not allowed in the time in which they happened. The same is true of 1K.xviii.20,&c. (Elijah's sacrifice on Mount Carmel). This only is remarkable that Jehu and his successors, who had ascended the throne through prophetical influence, and were declared adversaries of idolatry, yet continued to maintain the worship of Jehovah at Dan and Bethel, and that Amos and Hosea were zealous, indeed, against the worship of the calves, but *not against the worship of Jehovah out of Jerusalem.*

---

[74] It might, perhaps, be said that in *v.*30 the reason is given why David did not *at first* go to Gibeon to enquire directly of Jehovah. But why should he have gone to Gibeon at all, when the Ark was at that very time on Mount Zion? *Ed.*

(113)   [186] According to Ju.xviii.30 the Levite in question was *a grandson of Moses*; that is to say, it is now generally admitted that the true reading is מֹשֶׁה, not מְנַשֶּׁה. Through the introduction of the נ the Masorites wished to show that Jonathan agreed rather with the spirit of Manasseh, Hezekiah's son, than with Moses. Is it probable that Moses' grandson would have acted thus, if his grandfather had left behind a complete written Law, in which such actions were strictly forbidden ? [75]

[187] According to 1Ch.vi.22–28,35–38, Samuel was descended from Kohath, son of Levi. But from 1S.i.1 we should rather assume that he belonged to the tribe of Ephraim.[76] Comp., however, what HENGST., p.60, &c., has produced, with respect to the credibility of the genealogies communicated by the Chronicler. Also from 1K.xii.31 we might infer that the writer considered the *Levites*, generally, as fitted to assume the *priestly* office; since Jeroboam is here censured because he had appointed priests, '*who were not of the sons of Levi.*' According to the Law we should have expected, '*who were not of the sons of Aaron.*' Comp. note [217].

[188] What Samuel points out as wrong in Saul, 1S.xv.10–35, is not that he had sacrificed, but that he had not waited the arrival of the Prophet, and so had transgressed the command of Jehovah, 1S.x.8. Comp. THEN. *in loco.*

(114)   [189] It is true, L.viii–x contains an *historical* record. But this does not do away with the fact, that Solomon might and ought to have brought the dedication of the Temple into conformity with that record, if he had known it. Yet, whereas in Leviticus, after their consecration to this service, viii, Aaron and his sons fill the chief part, ix, especially v.8–22, on the contrary in 1K.viii Solomon is the chief personage ; the priests and Levites perform only what is necessary, v.3–11 ; then Solomon dedicates the Temple to Jehovah, v.12–53,—blesses the people, v.54–61,—himself takes part in the sacrifices, according to the most natural interpretation of v.62,63,—and consecrates a part of the court, v.64, in order to be able to sacrifice there. If, in Solomon's time, the priests and Levites, upon the basis of the Mosaic Law, had already for many centuries possessed a distinctly prescribed qualification, the king could not possibly have placed himself so entirely in the foreground. It is remarkable also that the Chronicler brings out much more the

---

[75] This argument appears to me not to have very great weight.

(i) It is doubtful whether Moses is the true reading.

(ii) If it be, there is nothing to connect this 'Jonathan, the son of Gershom, the son of Moses,' with the Levite in xvii; and certainly, the introduction of his name in xviii.30 is most abrupt, if it really is meant for the name of that Levite. It must seem strange also that he has never been named before, if the writer of the story knew that the *Levite*, who has been so prominent a figure throughout these two chapters, was 'Jonathan, the grandson of Moses,' or was called 'Jonathan' at all.

(iii) v.30 has all the appearance of being an interpolation—comp. the repetitions in v.30ᵃ,31ᵃ, and see P.II.462–465, where I have suggested that this Jonathan (if we read Moses, instead of Manasseh) may have been a *descendant* of Moses, who was made priest at Dan, when Jeroboam established the calf-worship there. *Ed.*

[76] Elkanah is called 'an Ephrathite,' 1S.i.1, which seems to mean 'Ephraimite' comp. 1K.xi.26, 'Jeroboam, an Ephrathite of Zereda.' *Ed.*

activity of the priests and Levites, as if he felt that these must have been passed over in the older account, which he generally follows verbally. See 2Ch.v.11–13, vii.1–3,6.

[141] See especially THEN., K.p.151, &c., 350, where also the remarkable passage, 1K.ix.25, is compared with 2Ch.viii.12–16: nowhere, perhaps, does the effort of the Chronicler, to get rid of the traces of the unlawful Jehovah-worship, appear more plainly than here. The connecting Uzziah's leprosy with his entrance into the sanctuary in order to sacrifice there, is the work of the Chronicler, or of one of his predecessors, and can as little be regarded as historical, as the account of Jos. *Ant.*IX.x.4. Yet there exists no ground for doubting either the one fact or the other, viewed separately by itself. Comp. BERTH., *Ch.*p.376,377, and on 2Ch.viii. 12–16, p.296,297.

[142] (i) It is already in itself very improbable that there existed a law about Naziriteship before there were any Nazarites, or, in other words, that theory went before practice in this matter. This is the more obvious, when we consider that vows in general, and in particular that of the Nazarite, are in their nature *voluntary*, and do not require to be summoned into existence by a law.

(ii) Besides, N.vi.1–21 regulates what is spoken of as already *existing*. That the lawgiver wished to prescribe something new, to promulgate the hitherto-unknown Nazarite-vows, is a supposition which is contradicted by the form and contents of this law.

(iii) Lastly, Samson and Samuel were Nazarites *for their whole lives*. This law, on the contrary, supposes a temporary Naziriteship, *v.*4,5,6,8,12,13. An *original* practice would surely not have needed to be referred to at such full length as this.

(115)   [143] Compare on this passage, besides the commentators, RUTG.p.146–148. It appears to me that Jeremiah speaks neither of the Sabbatical year, nor of the year of Jubilee. He himself refers, *v.*14, to the law contained in D.xv.12. From this law, however, followed the obligation to manumit the Hebrew male and female slaves, in the case of those only who had had them in service during six years. But—as the prophet himself says, *v.*14ᵇ—the law in question had not been regarded, probably for a long time past. The number of those, who were bound, according to the law, to perform the vows indicated in *v.*8–10, was thus great,—so great that, in comparison with them, the few proprietors, who had not yet had their slaves in service during six years, did not come into consideration, and, therefore, were not mentioned by Jeremiah.

[144] From the first of these passages it follows that the beginning of the month was celebrated by a feast, which, however, had a religious character; for, when David did not appear, Saul thought that he was *not clean*, and on that account had withdrawn himself from the feast. Such a celebration of the beginning of the month was, besides, nowhere prescribed in the Law: mention is made of New Moons only in L.xxiii.23–25, N.x.10,xxviii.11–15,xxix.1–6. In Hosea and Isaiah the Sabbath and New Moon are named in one breath, and thus the celebration of the latter has a religious character.

(116)   [145] In Ju.xxi.19 the elders say 'Behold! there is a feast of Jehovah (not 'feast *to* Jehovah') in Shiloh from year to year.' Is it not implied in this that there was

only one such feast observed—I do not say, by Israel, but—*at the sanctuary of Shiloh?* HENGST. thinks, p.79–81, that the Passover-Feast is meant, especially on the ground that the dancing virgins, *v.*21, remind us of E.xv.20. But dancing, as an exhibition of gladness, is, probably, general enough to be used at every feast. That the expression 'from year to year' occurs also in E.xiii.10, can serve just as ,little to prove that the Passover-Feast is meant in Ju.xxi.19. On the ground of the passages to be explained presently (note [165]), I should rather think of the great Feast of Harvest (afterwards called the 'Feast of Tabernacles'), both in Ju.xxi.19 and in 1S.i.3. From this last passage, again, it appears plainly that Elkanah went up to Shiloh only once a year, 'to worship and to sacrifice unto Jehovah of Hosts.' His sacrifices were thank-offerings, and were coupled with a common feast. This also reminds us of the 'Feast of Harvest.'

[165] The Feast, celebrated by Solomon in the seventh month, 1K.viii.2, during twice-seven days, *v.*65, is called '*the* Feast,' *v.*2,65. From this alone we should infer that this Feast ('of Harvest' or 'of Tabernacles') was the only one that was then celebrated, *i.e.* by the whole people at the common sanctuary. (THEN., p.126,124, judges differently, according to whom *the Feast* is no other than the Feast of the Dedication of the Temple, and who, consequently, sees also in 2Ch.vii.8–10 only an incorrect tradition, and regards 1K.viii.65, *in fine*, as correct.)

We are led to the same result by 1K.xii.27,32,33. If in Jeroboam's time three High Feasts were celebrated at Jerusalem, then the transposition of the *third* feast only was but a half-measure, which must be considered as less likely to have been effective, since the Passover, which was connected with the Feast of Unleavened Bread, seems in the Law much more important than the other two Feasts,—see the copious directions in E.xii, N.ix.9–14, in opposition to which, however, may be set N.xxix.12–39,—and in any case possesses much more historical importance, on account of the reminiscence of the Exodus connected with it.

Here, again, all is explained by the supposition, that the feast-legislation was gradually developed, so that, even so late as the time of Jeroboam, only the Feast of Harvest was celebrated by the whole people at the Sanctuary, while the two other Feasts existed, indeed, but were celebrated either at home, or at the high-places. Perhaps, the custom of Solomon to sacrifice (*i.e.* to bring a formal sacrifice) thrice a year, which is mentioned in 1K.ix.25, gave occasion to transfer also the other Feasts to the common Sanctuary. As to 2Ch.viii.12–16, which passage is in direct contradiction with what is here supposed, see notes [166,166].

[166] The first three passages treat about the Passover-Feast, the last about the Feast of Tabernacles. Consult the commentators. Even when we take into consideration the exaggeration, which may lie in the words of the historian,—even when we take into account the fact, that the stress is laid upon the celebration of '*such* a Passover,' *i.e.* so generally or so regularly, and not upon the celebration itself,— it is still evident that here is a fact established, which is altogether irreconcilable with the supposition that the Pentateuch existed from the time of Moses,—and in contradiction also with the account in 2Ch.viii.12–16, that Solomon sacrificed 'according to the commandment of Moses,' which we were already, notes [168,163], prepared to reject as not quite historical. How can it be explained that David, Solomon, Asa, Jehoshaphat,—not to speak of other well-disposed kings,—celebrated the Passover either not at all or unlawfully, if they had before them the Book

N

of the Law, in which the celebration is commanded and described at full length?
Hengst., p.83, objects that 2K.xxiii.22 and 2Ch.xxxv.18 contain rather a *proof* of the
celebration of the Passover during the time of the Judges, which (N.B.), according
to him, must include also the reign of David and Solomon. The fact is, that the
historians believed that the celebration of the Feast, which, from their point of view,
was prescribed by Moses, *must* have been observed at least in the time of the
Judges, whereas they *knew* that this had not been the case under the Kings, for,
had they not *known* this, they would not have made the statement in question, which
for them was so full of offence. If any one however, prefers, with Hengstenberg,
to consider this *belief* as of more authority than the *historical statement*, on occasion of which the fact of their so believing is communicated, he is, of course, at
liberty to do so; only his proceeding is in a high degree uncritical.

If still further evidence is desired, reference may be made to Neh.viii.17, where
the historian refers to Joshua, the son of Nun—certainly, we may believe, not on
the basis of yearly records as to the celebration of the Feast of Tabernacles, but on
the ground of the conjecture, that Joshua, at all events, *must* have paid regard to
that, which, in the writer's persuasion, Moses himself had instituted.

Besides, the word פֶּסַח, 'Passover,' occurs only in one single passage of the
Prophetical Writings, Ez.xlv.21, while, *perhaps* [?], Isaiah,xxx.29, refers to the
celebration by night of this Feast. The author of Zech.xii–xiv, ($\pm$600 B.C.),
mentions the Feast of Tabernacles, xiv.16,18,19, as Hosea did before him, xii.9.
This silence affords no proof against the antiquity of the festival-laws: but it
follows that no appeal can be made to the Prophets against the evidence of the
Historical Books. The Prophets show only that feasts were celebrated, Hos.ii.11,
Am.v.21,viii.10,&c., which no one doubts. We have purposely not spoken here of
Jo.v.10,11, since this narrative, comp. notes [220-221], is not only connected in the closest
manner with the Pentateuch, but seems actually to have proceeded from the author
of the B.O.

(117)   [167] The writer of the Books of Kings imparts, however, an account, 2K.xii.16,
from which it appears that they were already known under the reign of Joash.
Besides, Hengst., p.86,87, is able to tell us that in the formula ' burnt-offerings and
slaughter-offerings (sacrifices, E.V.),' are included sin- and trespass-offerings. But
L.xvii.8, N.xv.3,8, to which he appeals, give no semblance of proof for his proposition. As soon as ever in the Law four kinds of sacrifices had been described, it
would, in fact, be very difficult to indicate these *four* kinds by mentioning only
the *two* names.

[168] It is well-known that Hengst., p.127–148, has tried to give a proof, that
Jephthah's daughter was not sacrificed, but consecrated to the Sanctuary, appealing
in support of this to E.xxxviii.8, 1S.ii.22, from which passages (comp. L.xxvii.1-8)
he would make it appear that there were women—even in the time of the Judges—
who devoted themselves to the service of the Tabernacle, and who—as Hengstenberg must, of course, assume also—remained in consequence of this unmarried.
Independently of the incorrectness of the interpretation of these passages, Hengstenberg's explanation is impossible, so long as it remains inconceivable that
anyone who says, ' I will sacrifice him as a burnt-sacrifice to Jehovah,' means only
to say by these words, ' I will *not* sacrifice him as a burnt-sacrifice, but consecrate

him to the Sanctuary.' Comp. BERTH. *in loco.* Meanwhile HENGSTENBERG has shown, p.129,&c., that Jephthah's vow, Ju.xi.30,31, is expressed in such terms, that he *must* have thought—not of an animal, but—of a human being. Hence it follows that his ideas about the worship of Jehovah were very rude and impure. It is self-evident that we must not ascribe this to *all* the Israelites. But still human sacrifices do not appear to have been wholly unusual, as appears (i) from 2S.xxi.1–14, [178], (ii) from G.xxii.1–19, which narrative has manifestly the intention of forbidding human sacrifices, and showing by what it is replaced, under purer conceptions of religion. Comp. also Mic.vi.7ᵇ. Besides, the legislative portion of the Pentateuch starts from the supposition, that human sacrifices were offered only to idols, L.xviii.21, xx.1–5, D.xii.31,xviii.10, which, no doubt, must have been the rule, and the offering of a human being in honour of Jehovah only a strange exception. But is even the 'strange exception' conceivable, if Israel possessed a copious written law, in which it was expressly forbidden ?

[178] (i) In D.xiii.13,14, mention is made only of the extermination of the inhabitants of any town, which had fallen away to idolatry.

(ii) On the contrary, in Ju.xx.21, the ban is applied to the inhabitants of Gibeah, who violated the duty of hospitality ,in a shameful way, and to the Benjamites, who had refused to deliver them up. According to HENGST., p.91, Israel had on this occasion interpreted the law 'according to the spirit, but not, on that account, arbitrarily.'

(iii) In Jo.vii Achan is punished, because he had appropriated to himself a portion of that which was put under the ban. There is nothing strange in itself in this. But, together with Achan, the *members of his family* were put to death, v.15,24,25,—in other words, the children were punished for the sins of their parents, in direct contradiction to D.xxiv.16, *i.e.* in contradiction to a direction, which was adopted into the Law at a *later* time, in consequence of the development of the moral consciousness in Israel. Hence it plainly appears that the death of Achan is historical [?], although the *clothing* of the story—as we shall see hereafter —must be to a great extent set down to the account of the historian.

[179] It will probably not need to be demonstrated that the words 'and David sought the face of Jehovah,' and again, 'and Jehovah said,' 2S.xxi.1, must be understood of David's consulting a priest or prophet, comp. 1S.xxiii.1–6, who answered what according to his conviction was God's will. But the answer contained in v.1,—as I read it, ' On Saul, and on his house *is* blood, בֵּיתוֹ דָּמִים (=בֵּיתוֹ)'— [E.V. ' for Saul and for his bloody house, בֵּית הַדָּמִים'], because he slew the Gibeonites'—*could not have been given* by the priest or prophet, if he had known D.xxiv.16, with which the utterance is directly at variance. Besides, in consequence of the passage last-quoted, taken in connection with E.xx.5,xxxiv.7, N.xiv.18, D.v.9,vii.9,10, Jer.xxxi.30, Ez.xviii, there arise important questions, which, however, cannot be answered here. There is manifestly a contradiction between David's act and N.xxxv.9–34, which starts upon the assumption that only the murderer himself is worthy of death, and not his descendants. That the idea of averting God's wrath by the death of Saul's seven descendants had not arisen with the Gibeonites only, but was also approved by David,—nay, is implied to have been, applauded by the oracle,—is, further, a proof, that the notion, which Jephthah

formed to himself of God's nature, stood not so entirely by itself [in Israel] as is commonly thought.

[171] It seems almost superfluous to produce examples of one or the other. See *e.g.* Ju.v.24–27,viii.7,16,17,ix,xii.1–6,xiii–xvi,xix. In itself, indeed, it may be very possible that the Law stood at an infinitely higher level than the spirit of the people, and in many respects this was, in fact, the case, both in earlier and later times. But now that we have once seen that the Law was gradually formed, it appears difficult to imagine to ourselves the Israelitish people as being in possession of a Legislation so fully developed and humane, while itself was still so rude and unformed. Let it be observed especially that those who filled the first places in Israel,—*e.g.* Samuel, Gideon before him, and David after him—stood in this respect, at all times, much lower than the Law. How can this be explained, much less excused, if they had the opportunity of forming themselves through the reading of the Law and in accordance with its prescriptions?

[172] It is evident at once on a superficial view that R.iv.1–10 does not agree in some sense with Lxxv, but is altogether discordant with D.xxv.5–10. Let the following points be observed.

(i) In the course of the action between Boaz and the *goel* (nearest of kin), not a word is said about any legal definitions.

(ii) In D.xxv.5–10 mention is made only of brothers, while in R.iv.1–10 a proper *levirate* marriage is not mentioned. Has not here also the Deuteronomistic Legislation adopted and legalized a custom, which had already gone partly into disuse, (the marriage of a childless widow *with the nearest blood-relative*), by laying down a certain definition, through which the *brother-in-law* took the place of the nearest blood-relative, so that, in default of any such, the marriage-obligation dropped altogether? [77] Is not this much more probable than the supposition, that Boaz and the Elders of Bethlehem had *extended* the prescriptions of the Law according to analogy (HENGST., p.101)?

(iii) The historian himself explains, *v.*7, a custom which existed 'in *former* time in Israel,'—which was, in fact, afterwards, *i.e.* after the more general spread of the art of writing, replaced by a written contract, comp. Jer. xxxii.6,7. What connection existed between this custom and the taking off the shoe, mentioned in D.xxv, cannot be determined with complete certainty. This much alone is plain, that the two customs are not the same, while that, which R.iv mentions, cannot have been derived from the prescription of the Law. See SCHULTZ,p.589,&c. KEIL,Comm.I.ii.p.502,&c.

[173] If the possibility of the people desiring a king had been foreseen by Moses, and a law had been given by him with a view to this, then both Samuel's displeasure and God's anger, 1S.viii.6,7, would have been misplaced, unless it be supposed that the law of the kingdom was provided in order to seduce the people to a desire which was at variance with God's will. Rather, it seems from the passage referred to that Samuel considered the divine government as incapable of

---

[77] Did not the Deuteronomist, rather, express in the form of a law the custom, which actually existed in his day, having taken the place of the old practice, which existed in the time of Boaz? *Ed.*

existing together with an earthly kingship. Gideon also is of the same opinion, Ju.viii.23, when he says to the Israelites, 'I will not reign over you, neither shall my son reign over you: Jehovah shall reign over you' (always מָשַׁל)—although SCHULTZ, p.55, thinks that Gideon, perhaps, really entered upon the kingly dignity, but, in accepting the offer of the Israelites, made use of this *prudent* language, in order not to awaken envy. Comp. as to the oldest ideas about royal sovereignty RÉVILLE, *Chants populaires d'Israel, Nouv. Rev. de Théologie*, ii.318, &c.

Hence it followed that only in later times could the idea have been entertained of defining the kingly right and duties, when at length it was seen that kings could not be dispensed with. At the nomination of the king not the slightest reference is made to D.xvii.14-20. The 'manner of the kingdom,' enunciated and afterwards written down by Samuel, has nothing in common with this law: if this law had been meant, then nothing would need to have been said about writing it, since it existed already in writing. Whoever wishes, may consult HENGSTENBERG's demonstration that 'this action sets forth the existence of the Pentateuch in general and especially of the law of the kingdom,' p.246–261.

[174] It is obvious, for instance, that Solomon's conduct conflicts in all main points with D.xvii.14-20,—comp. 1K.xi.3, Sol. Song,vi.8 (the great harem,)—1K.iv,v, &c. (the magnificent Court and the collection of gold and silver,)—1K.iii.1,x.26-29, (the trade with Egypt, particularly in horses). We have thus the choice between two cases. Either Solomon wittingly and willingly transgressed the prescriptions of the Law, which were known to him, without the people taking any account of it, for they, just as the historian, admired his greatness and love of splendour; or a *later* legislator warned the kings of his time against following a course, which, in fact, Solomon's example showed to be corrupting for religion and the people, nay, for the king himself. How our choice must be decided, is already in itself not doubtful, much less in connection with note [172]. Besides, let it not be omitted to observe that the author of the 'law of the kingdom' shows as plainly as possible that he knows Solomon's history, when he adds to the command, which forbids to take many wives, the warning, '*that his heart turn not aside,*' *i.e.* from Jehovah. Do not these words contain an unmistakeable reference to the fact stated in 1K.xi.4? Is it not absurd to suppose that Solomon not merely transgressed the Law, but in addition justified the anxiety of the lawgiver on this point by his own example?

[175] In 1S.xxx.21-25 mention is made of 'a statute and an ordinance,' which David established, and which continued also after his day, so that in the writer's time it was still observed, v.25—viz. that the booty made in war should be equally divided among those who took part in the conflict. N.xxxi prescribes that the fighting men should receive half of the booty, while the other half should fall to the share of the 'congregation,' v.27; and a certain portion of both halves was to be set aside for the priests and for the Levites, v.28-30. That David knew this ordinance is in the first place improbable: but it is quite inconceivable that David's own ordinance should have continued to be observed, if at the same time a [Mosaic and Divine] law existed, which varied from it in more than one respect. Comp. further, as to the priestly tendency of N.xxxi, note [111].

(119) [176] When we consider that David acts as if he had no knowledge of the Law (see the instances produced in (110–118)),—that, on the contrary, the *historian* knew

the Law and ascribed it to Moses,—we must without hesitation see in 1K.ii.3 merely words of the latter. Comp. Then. *in loco,* and on the other side, Häv. I.ii.p.516–518. As to 2S.xxii(Psalm xviii) see Hupf. *Ps.*I.p.360, &c. However we may judge as to the origin of this Psalm, (which is, most probably, not Davidic), this, at all events, is plain, that the expressions used in *v.*23 are by no means so definite as in 1K.ii.3.

[177] Comp. Berth. *in loco,* and as to the Chronicler's point of view see besides n.[133,134,135,140]. Nothing is more plain than that most of the addresses and conversations, communicated by the Chronicler,—at least, as regards their form,—are not perfectly authentic; and, in fact, they for the most part agree in language and style with the Chronicler's own words [elsewhere]. Hence it follows that we cannot be satisfied with his testimony when it stands alone, much less when, as is the case here, it is contradicted by the facts. Besides, the above passages are very indefinite in expression and treat not of 'the Law of Moses' or 'the Book of the Law,' but of 'the Law' merely, without further definition.

[178] What historical fact lies at the basis of this account, cannot now any more be made out. For the reasons above-stated [177], we can only see in it a proof that, *according to the Chronicler,* Jehoshaphat knew the whole Book of the Law. But we cannot acquiesce in that view, since the facts, recorded by the selfsame writer, forbid us to do so. What facts are here meant, appears out of our preceding demonstration. But with respect to the reign of Jehoshaphat himself the writer gives two accounts which conflict with 2Ch.xvii.9. One is 2Ch.xx.32,33, note [144]; the other is 2Ch.xix.4–11, from which passage it appears that D.xvii.8–13 cannot have been committed to writing till after Jehoshaphat's time, note [230].

(120) [179] As to the signification of the expression, 'the Testimony,' in the Pentateuch, see note [106]. It is, consequently, not improbable that in 2K.xi.12 also the Decalogue is meant.[78] It may, however, be inferred from D.xvii.18–20, that at the king's pleasure copies were made of other laws also, and that here a collection of this kind is meant, such as certainly already existed in the time of Joash.

[180] It is extremely difficult to arrive at certainty with respect to the 'Book of the Law' which was found by Hilkiah, on which account, in fact, the opinions of interpreters are very divergent. It seems best to collect the different traits which the oldest narrative gives us, and then to combine them as far as possible into one form. They are as follows: generally, where the Chronicler's account varies, mention is made of it.

(i) The contents of the Book were unknown to the king, 2K.xxii.10, &c., as appears from the overpowering effect, which the reading of it made upon him. If, as some suppose, it had been the Mosaic autograph, or the temple-copy of the Law, of which other copies already existed, and which was known to the people, then the re-discovery of it would have been only of importance for *antiquaries,* and the reading of it before the king would have been superfluous.

(ii) The book was of such an extent that Shaphan could read it to the king,

---

[78] For various reasons this does not appear to me *probable*—chiefly, because it may be shown, as I believe, that the Decalogue—at least, in its present form—is of later origin than the time of Joash. *Ed.*

2K.xxii.10 (differently in 2Ch.xxxiv.18,) and that he in his turn could bring it before the people, 2K.xxiii.3, 2Ch.xxxiv.30. From this it appears at once that the *whole* Pentateuch cannot be meant.

(iii) It is called 'the Book of the Covenant,' 2K.xxiii.2,3,21, a name which, again, forbids us to think of the whole Pentateuch.

(iv) It contained instructions about the Passover, 2K.xxiii.21, and severe threatenings against transgression of the directions contained in it, 2K.xxii.13, &c.

(v) It gave occasion to a thorough-going Reformation, the aim of which may be summed up in these words, *the up-rooting of idolatry and of the worship of Jehovah on high-places,* 2K.xxiii.

(vi) To this may be added, that Hilkiah makes mention of his discovery in these words, 'I have found the Book of the Law,' 2K.xxii.8—(the Chronicler says, 'the Book of the Law of Jehovah by the hand of Moses,' 2Ch.xxxiv.14, *i.e.* the Law given by Moses),—and that the historian himself, 2K.xxii.11,xxiii.24,25, employs the same or like expressions.

(vii) Let it be noticed also that the contents of the book were certainly unknown to the king, but yet that he did not regard the book itself as new, since the conviction, that *the fathers* had not acted according to that Book, distressed him, 2K.xxii.13.

If we now observe that Deuteronomy corresponds to the 2nd, 3rd, 4th, and, especially, to the 5th of the above characteristics, we are led to the conviction that either this Book in its entirety, or (as appears to us more probable on account of (ii) and (iii)) in part, was found by Hilkiah in the Temple. How it came there, we cannot, of course, determine. If, however, it is true—as will be shown below—that the Deuteronomist lived under Manasseh,[79] then his writing or a part of it may have been deposited in the Temple already ± 50 years [?] before Josiah's Reformation, and may have been only accidentally found there at this time. Or, if it be assumed that the Deuteronomist had written records before him—as, in fact, is possible,—then Hilkiah's Book may have been one of those prime-documents, from which it would follow that the work of the Deuteronomist, although already in existence, was not yet known or received: if it had been, then the deep impression, produced by the reading of Hilkiah's Book, would remain unexplained.

But we refrain from further conjectures about a subject, which will, perhaps, never be brought to perfect clearness. Our hypothesis agrees more or less with that of Then. K.p.419,420, and Hitz. p.90, of whom the latter shows at the same time that it entirely agrees with Jer.xi.1–17, a prophecy spoken shortly after Josiah's Reformation. Meanwhile it follows from 2K.xxii,xxiii, that *in the eighteenth year of Isaiah, the Pentateuch, which we now possess, did not yet exist,*—a result warranted by the whole enquiry in this section, and more fully confirmed in Chap. XX,XXI.

---

[79] In P.III (865–867) I have given reasons for supposing that the Deuteronomist lived—not in Manasseh's, but—more probably, a little later, in Josiah's time.

CHAPTER XX.

(121)   [181] Tuch, p.lxxxviii, considers it not allowable to derive such quotations out of one of the prime-documents, but thinks that we must regard them as proofs of the existence of the Books in that form in which we now possess them. But, on what ground he so judges, is not to be seen. Comp. de Wette, *Einl.*I.p.223.
   [182] Comp. the similar remark in [147].

(123)   [183] The passages from the writings of the Prophets before the Captivity, where the formula 'Law of Jehovah' is used, in order to indicate the *Mosaic Law* — perhaps, to be distinguished from the present Pentateuch, in which the primary documents, referred to by the Prophets, may be inserted — are in chronological order the following :—

   (i) Am.ii.4, 'They have despised the *Law of Jehovah*, and have not kept his statutes (חֻקִּים ;' the Prophet has his eye especially on idolatry, as appears from *v.*4'.

   (ii) Hos.iv.6, 'Because thou hast rejected knowledge, I will also reject thee, that thou shalt be no priest to me ; seeing thou hast forgotten the *Law of thy God,* I will also forget thy children,'—perhaps, a reference to E.xix.6, 'and ye shall be to me a kingdom of priests, and an holy nation.'

   (iii) Hos.viii.1, 'Because they have transgressed my covenant, and trespassed against *my Law,*'—comp.vi.7, 'They, like men, have transgressed the covenant.'

   (iv) Jer.viii.8, 'How do ye say, We are wise, and the *Law of Jehovah* is with us,' in our possession : see below, note [185].

   (v) Jer.ix.13, 'They have forsaken *my Law* which I set before them, and have not obeyed my voice, neither walked therein,' but, *v.*14, have become guilty of idolatry.

   (vi) Jer.xvi.11, 'They have forsaken Me, and not kept *my Law,*'—again with reference to the practice of idolatry.

   (vii) Jer.xxvi.4, 'If ye will not hearken unto Me, to walk in *my Law* which I have set before you, &c.'

   (viii) Jer.xxxi.33, 'After those days, saith Jehovah, I will put *my Law* in their inward parts, and write it in their hearts,'—where, it would seem, the existence of a *written* Law is implied.

   (ix) Jer.xxxii.23, Israel's forefathers 'obeyed not Jehovah's voice, neither walked in *His Law.*'

   (x) Jer.xliv.10,23, the Jews, refugees in Egypt, had not, any more than their fathers, 'obeyed the voice of Jehovah, nor walked in *His Law,* nor in His statutes, nor in His testimonies '—'which He had set before them and before their fathers.' Comp. also Zeph.iii.4, Jer.ii.8,xviii.18, which passages shall be considered presently, note [186].

   Among the above expressions there are some, (v), (vi), (vii), where 'Law of Jehovah,' if it does not exclusively, yet at least does also, indicate that instruction of Jehovah, which He imparts to His people by His Prophets; and to the last of these passages, Jer.xxvi.4, it is added in *v.*5, as a further explanation, 'to hearken to the words of my servants the Prophets, whom I sent unto you,' &c.

[184] It is remarkable that in Isaiah's time the formula, 'Law of Jehovah,' was still so far from being a standing formula for indicating the Mosaic Law, that (in the genuine prophecies, which alone are considered here) *it is never used in this sense.*

(ii) i.10, 'Give ear unto the *Law of our God*, ye people of Gomorrah,' which is parallel to, 'Hear the *word of Jehova h*(*i.e.* the Prophet's own preaching), ye rulers of Sodom.'

(ii) ii.3, 'Out of Zion shall go forth the *Law*, and the *word of Jehovah* from Jerusalem.'

(iii) v.24, 'They have cast away the *Law of Jehovah* of Hosts, and despised the *Word* of the Holy One of Israel,' where the latter expression, parallel to the former, signifies the *prophetical admonitions*, including, perhaps, the then existing moral Law.

(iv) viii.16, 'Bind up the Testimony, seal the *Law* among my disciples,' and *v.*20, 'To the *Law* and to the Testimony : if they speak not according to this word, it is because they have no light in them,' *comp.* *v.*1, &c., where the instruction given by Isaiah in Jehovah's name is indicated. ·

(v) xxx.9, 'This is a rebellious people, lying children, children that will not hear the *Law of Jehovah*,' where by 'Law of Jehovah' is meant the instruction of Seers and Prophets, as appears from *v.*10, 'that say to the Seers, see not, and to the Prophets, prophesy not,' &c.

In the writings of other Prophets also we find traces of the same phraseology, *e.g.* Mic.iv.2=Is.ii.3,—Jer.vi.10, 'To whom shall I speak and give warning that they may hear? . . . . Behold! the *word of Jehovah* is to them a reproach ; they have no delight in it,'—lastly, perhaps, also Hos.viii.12, where there should be written with Hitzig, אֶכְתָּב־לוֹ רִבּוֹ תּוֹרֹתַי, 'Though I write for him (Israel) my instructions by tens of thousands, they are regarded as those of a stranger.' Also Hitzig is of opinion that in the expression ' my laws,' both the *laws* and the prophetical oracles are included.

[185] Very numerous are the utterances of the Prophets, in which the moral Law is set far above the ceremonial Legislation, and obedience to the former above observance of the latter. See Am.v.21,22, Hos.vi.6, Is.i.11-15, Mic.vi.6-8, Jer.vi.20, vii.22,23,xiv.12. This, at all events, is plain, upon thoughtful consideration of these passages, that the Prophets did not ascribe a divine origin to the religious worship and its duties in the same sense as to the moral commands, which they themselves enjoin in accordance with the principles laid down in the Decalogue, and which are further developed in some collections of laws, *e.g.* L.xviii, &c. We are justified, therefore, in deriving from their utterances a proof, that they did not recognise the ceremonial Law, with all its special directions and prescriptions, as Mosaic, and thus did not know our present Pentateuch, in which their Mosaic origin is so clearly expressed. This is especially plain from Jer.vii.22,23, (comp. Is.xxix.13), where the Mosaic origin of the ceremonial Law is actually, in express terms, denied, but also from Is.i.11, where the observance of the practices, prescribed in the Law, is placed far beneath obedience to the prophetical admonition, *v.*10, and Mic.vi.6-8, where the Prophet, after having rejected external observances, *v.*6,7, expresses the command of God, *v.*8ᵃ, in his own words, *v.*8ᵇ. In connection, again, with these utterances those passages are very remarkable, in which *law* and *priest* are named close to one another, and, apparently, not merely because

the priest possessed and applied the Law, but also because it is, as it were, priestly
territory, and the ground on which he moves in his quality of priest. See Zeph.iii.4,
—Jer.ii.8, where the priests are described as 'handling the Law,'—viii.8, where it
is said of the 'Law of Jehovah' that '*the false pen of the scribe has made it for
falsehood,*' *i.e.* that the copyists of the (priestly) Law,—whom also we must
certainly seek among the priests,—through the multiplication of the number
of their copies, had led the people to consider that it was not necessary to attend
to the prophetic word, and so to deceive itself: comp. Hitz. *in loco*; but others
explain it, '*The lying pen of the scribes has falsified it,*' *i.e.* has inserted in the
Law new and spurious passages;—xviii.18, 'Then said they, Come and let us devise
devices against Jeremiah; for the *law* shall not perish from the *priest*, nor *counsel*
from the *wise*, nor the *word* from the *Prophet*.' Comp. also Ez.vii.26,xxii.26, Hag.ii.
12, Mal.ii.6–9.

(124)   [186] We have already considered these Prophets, notes [182-185]. Especially, in
Jeremiah we remark plain references to the Law, though almost exclusively to
Deuteronomy. To bring forward proofs of this is almost superfluous, since the
matter is obvious, and is, in fact, generally acknowledged. Jer.xi.1, &c., is a very
clear instance.

[187] It is generally thought very conceivable and natural that the Prophets, though
acquainted with the Law and living under its authority, should yet have concerned
themselves little about its prescriptions, and should have maintained their
independence in respect of it. They were, it is said, Prophets, men of the Spirit,
Hos.ix.7, and, consequently, not subject to the letter of the Law. Yet it is not
considered withal that the Law itself does not permit such independence in respect
of its prescriptions. See D.iv.2,xiii.1,&c.xxvii.15–26,xxviii.15–19. The (so-called)
legal bias, which characterises Judaism, did not arise *in spite of the Law*, but
rather was really called forth through it into life. It arose, however, only after
the Captivity, while at the same time the prophetical system died away; comp.
note [191]. Does there not lie in this a proof, that the Law was brought into the form,
in which, as a legislative codex, it might regulate the civil and religious life of the
Israelites, not many ages, but only shortly, before this time? Comp. further,
Hävernick's opposition to this view, I.ii.p.551–556.

(125)   [188] Ezekiel was a priest, and has more points of contact with the injunctions and
the spirit of the priestly law than any of his predecessors. Comp. v.6,7,xi.12,xx.
13,16,21,24, &c. That he, however, was very far removed from a slavish subjection
to the Law, may appear from xl–xlviii. Comp. on this point Herz., i.p.126–8.

[189] Comp. Is.lvi.1–8,lviii,lxvi.6–24, &c. In the use of the formula 'Law of
Jehovah' he follows Jeremiah. Comp. Is.xlii.21,24,li.4,7, and above, notes [184,185].
A *Book of the Law* is not mentioned by the later Isaiah, nor intimated by any
other Prophet, earlier than Dan.ix.11,13.

[190] See Hag.ii.10–19. In Zechariah the references to the Law are few: but this
is partly connected with the bearing of his prophetical activity upon the future of
the theocracy, and with the visionary form of his oracles. In vii.12 he distinguishes 'the Law' from 'the words which the Lord of Hosts hath sent through
His Spirit, by the former prophets.'

[191] Comp. as to the Scribes and their activity, among others, Herzf. i.24–36, and elsewhere. The subjects, with which Malachi is occupied, stand for a great part in close connection with the Law and its neglect by the priests and by the people. Thus in i.6–ii.9 he treats of the negligence of the priests with respect to the sacrifices, and the precepts which relate to them; and in iii.7–12 of omission in the bringing of tithes. Also the description in ii.6–9 of the high destination of the priests and Levites is remarkable. It is certainly not accidental that these and the like subjects are treated by the Prophets before the Captivity either not at all, or only by way of exception. Compare further note [187], where the justness of the conclusion derived from these phenomena is sufficiently confirmed.

(126) [192] Hengst.i.359,&c.,Häv.I.ii.p.549,550,Keil,§34,n.14, are of a different opinion. In order to put the reader in a position to form a judgment of his own, I give here a note of the passages, which they regard as parallel. From this it will be seen that the agreement of one or two words is often sufficient in their eyes to set the imitation of the Pentateuch by Joel above all doubt,—that, on the other hand, the possibility that a writer of the Pentateuch may have known and imitated Joel, is never at all taken into consideration,—finally, that some passages are quoted merely for their sound, where the agreement disappears on closer inspection, e. g. Joel ii.3,17. The passages are ii.10 (? i.10) = D.xxviii.51,—ii.2 = E.x.14, —ii.3 = G.xiii.10,— ii.13 = E.xxxiv.6,xxxii.14, — ii.17 = D.xv.6,— ii. 23 = D.xi.13,14, —ii.30 = D.vi.22. After giving these demonstrations, I consider myself relieved from the necessity of mentioning all the so-called references to the Pentateuch in the following Prophets.

[193] Let it be observed that Amos, in order to set in a strong light the great bodily size and strength of the Amorites, ii.9, employs two comparisons, of which no trace appears in N.xiii.27–33, as, on the contrary, the images here employed are not used by Amos; further, that Amos shows, indeed, a knowledge of the forty-years' sojourn in the wilderness, ii.10,v.25, but mentions at the same time particulars about it, v.25,26, which he cannot have derived from the Pentateuch. On the other hand, there is agreement even in expression between iv.11 and G.xix.29 (Book of Origins); yet it confines itself to the use of the word הפך (the proper word for expressing the overthrow of Sodom,) and of 'Elohim.' It remains thus at the least doubtful, whether Amos has drawn his knowledge out of the Pentateuch, and so much the more, since he also elsewhere gives signs of being acquainted with the history of the surrounding nations, which he certainly drew, not from written sources, but from tradition, vi.2,ix.7. Comp. also vi.5.

Yet Hengstenberg, Beitr.ii.83–122, assumes also a very great number of places, where Amos is supposed to show a knowledge of the Pentateuch. Let any-one read his demonstration, and judge for himself. Some appearance of truth seems to belong to his view as to Amos iv.4, in which he sees an irony, to be explained from D.xiv.28,xxvi.12, where the tithes of the third year are prescribed, so that the prophet means to say, 'Bring liberally the tithes (required in the three years) on the three days!' But he forgets to observe that the tithes mentioned in Deuteronomy have just this peculiarity, that they are not brought to the Sanctuary, but are consumed in each man's dwelling-place. Besides, Hengstenberg remarks rightly that what he calls the citations out of the Pentateuch are mostly borrowed from *Deuteronomy*. In other words, it is very natural that the most prophetical Book of the Law should show also most agreement with the writings of the Prophets. Only then, however, when men have made up their minds beforehand to see citations everywhere, can it be inferred from this phenomenon that Amos knew Deuteronomy.

[194] This is the more probable, since the accounts vary from the narratives of the Book of Origins: comp. above, note [20] and Chap.XVI. Especially, Hos.xii.4,5, is manifestly derived from G.xxxii.24, &c. Comp. also HENGST. *Beitr*.ii.48–83, HÄv.I.ii. p.544, &c. Assertions like these, that Hos.i.11,ii.15, contain a quotation from E.i.10, D.xvii.15,—that Hos.ii.8 is a citation from D.vii.13,xi.14, &c.,—are not capable of refutation, but, however, are utterly insufficient to persuade anyone, who does not regard it *à priori* as certain, that Hosea had so taken up the Pentateuch into his memory, that he could not name the most common things, *e.g.* corn, new wine, and oil, without borrowing from Deuteronomy. Here is one proof more: Hos.ix.4 contains 'almost a verbal reference to D.xxvi.14.' If the two passages are closely compared, it will be seen that they agree in one point, *viz.* in this, that bread eaten in time of mourning was unclean, and thus was not fit for sacrifices: comp. Jer.xvi.7. Whence does it appear that Hosea borrowed this feeling just exactly from Đ.xxvi.14? There too it is simply *understood as already existing*, and is by no means prescribed, and has, in fact, passed over into Deuteronomy from the popular persuasion, in which the prophet also shared. Be it observed also that of the three cases here named, only one appears in Hosea. Is that an 'almost verbal' reference?

* [195] Upon Micah see HÄv. I.ii.p.550,551. Of the citations quoted by him only one deserves notice, Mic.v.7 = D.xxxii.2. But the author of that Song may even have imitated Micah, or finally both may have derived the expressions common to them from elsewhere. On the other hand, it is not correct to say that Mic.vi.5 must refer not only to N.xxii–xxiv, but also (in the words 'out of Shittim') to the following chapter, N.xxv! and it is truly ridiculous to see in Mic.vii.17 a reminiscence of G.iii.14, as if Micah could never have seen a living serpent!

In Isaiah, iii.9 points plainly to G.xix.5, as does xii.2 to E.xv.2. Other parallelisms are given by HÄv.p.551, and the writers produced by him: but they are deficient in any proper power of proof. That, *e.g.*, Is.xxx.9 is derived from D.xxxii.6,20, is certainly asserted, but cannot be shown, and, from the absence in Deuteronomy of the characteristic expressions, מְרִי and פֶּחָשׁ, is even improbable.

[196] We have no right, for instance, to insert after 'ye shall flee' the word רְבָבָה 'ten thousand,'—a word which Isaiah could not have omitted, if he had had it before his mind. It stands thus: 'One thousand shall ye flee at the battle-cry of one, at the battle-cry of five (the Assyrians).' Is this a citation from D.xxxii.30, L.xxvi.8? On the contrary, in these passages the image, presented by Isaiah, is more fully worked out, and, so to speak, spun out, and, on the other hand, the characteristic גְּעָרָה, 'battle-cry,' is left out. If, therefore, not the tradition, but the actual fact, is to be of force, we have here just the very contrary of a quotation from the Pentateuch.

[197] Reference is made to Nah.i.2 = E.xx.5,xxxiv.14, N.xiv.17,18. But the

epithets of Jehovah, which occur in these passages, are very common, and lived certainly in the mouth of the people.

So reference is made to Hab.iii.3 = D.xxxiii.2 : and, in fact, Habakkuk may have known the so-called 'Blessing of Moses,' see note [82-47] ; but this does not follow with any certainty from this and other passages.

[198] Comp. LAND,p.6.7. The passages, which agree, more or less, with Deuteronomy, are summed up by KEIL,§34,n.14.

[199] This appears from the passages quoted by de WETTE, *Einl.*§162[b], and taken over by KEIL, but not less from the survey made by KUEPER, although this writer has generally heaped together places of some, and of no, significance. In fact, the only passages, where according to him the laws of the B.O. are used by Jeremiah, are—

Jer.ii = N.v.11–31, comp. p.7,8, where, however, the agreement is unimportant—

Jer.vii.29 = N.vi.5,&c., which absolutely proves nothing—

Jer.xxxii.27 = N.xvi.22, where the characteristic הָרוּחֹת, 'the spirits,' is just exactly wanting in Jeremiah,—

Jer.vi.12,viii.10 = N.xxxvi.7,8 (*sic*),—Lam.iv.15 = L.xiii.45 ; yet the cry of the leprous, alas ! in Palestine needed not to be learned out of the Law. What consequences follow from this remark, will appear below.

[200] See, besides de WETTE and KEIL, especially ZUNZ, p.160,161, and below notes [217,225,227].

(127) [201] As will be shown below in Chap.XXIV–XXVIII. See also Chap.XIX, Part II.

[202] Especially, the Book of Judges comes here into consideration, because in this the writer comes more into the foreground than in Ruth. Whether Ju.i.20 contains a reference to the Pentateuch, may be doubtful : on the other hand, such a reference appears in Ju.iii.4. In general, we observe a great agreement between Ju.ii.1–3,ii.11–iii.7(words of the compiler), and different passages of the Pentateuch, which may be found summed up in BERTHEAU and other interpreters. See also BERTHEAU, *R.u.R.*,p.xxiii–xxv, but also BAUR, i.377,n.5, who tries to prove that the writer of Ju.i.1–ii.5 did not know the Book of Deuteronomy, but probably did know other parts of the Pentateuch.

[203] Anyone may satisfy himself as to this by comparing the following passages, quoted by KEIL, §34,n.7 : 1S.ii.13 = D.xviii.3,—xii.3 = N.xvi.25,xxxv.31,&c.,L.v.23, xx.4,—xii.14 = D.i.26,43,ix.7,23,xxxi.27,—2S.vii.22–24 = D.iv.7,x.21,xiii.6. Much more weight may, in fact, be assigned to the use of the formula, 'to serve Jehovah with all his heart,' 1S.xii.20,24, comp. vii.6, which is very common in the Book of Deuteronomy, iv.29,vi.5,xi.13,xiii.3,xxvi.16,xxx.2,6,10. Yet it is also possible that it is derived from Joel ii.12. To this it may be added also, that the Law is never expressly quoted, and that the writer, as we have seen in Chap.XIX, mentions, without any appearance of objection, actions of Samuel, Saul, David, which were in direct contradiction to the Law.

[204] Some examples are given by de WETTE, *Einl.*§162[b]. See also 1K.vi.12,13, ix.4,xi.33,34, where, among other things, occurs the heaping up of the words, 'statutes,' 'ordinances,' 'commandments,' &c., which is so common in Deuteronomy.[58,17]

(128)　²⁰⁸ Gen.p.14,15. The relation of the Pentateuch to the literature generally, is discussed by him in p.10–15, its relation to the history in p.6–10.

(129)　²⁰⁶ Thus in Job xxxi.33 a reference is seen to G.i–iii; but כְּאָדָם does not denote *as Adam*: comp. Hirzel *in loco*: in Cant.vi.13 is a reference to G.xxxii.1,2, which appears to need no contradiction. On the other hand, 'tree of life,' Prov.iii.18,xi.30,xiii.12,xv.4, may be explained as really a reference to G.ii.9,iii.22. So Hoikstra, *Godg.Bijdr.*,1856,p.882,883, has shown from Job xxxi, that the writer of this Book knew the Decalogue. On the other hand, the references in Job xxxi.11 to L.xviii.17, in Job xxxi.8–12 to D.xxii.22, in Job xxxi.26–28 to D.xvii.2–7, appears to me—not quite certain, but—far from improbable.

²⁰⁷ The Psalms devoted to the recollections of the fortunes of the people, Pa.lxxviii,xcv,cv,cvi,cxiv, and others, employ throughout expressions borrowed from the Pentateuch, and are very generally recognised as post-Exilic. The same is true of the alphabetical Psalm, cxix, which mentions the Law in every verse, and eulogises it throughout.

CHAPTER XXI.

(132)　²⁰⁸ Consequently, the weight of this evidence depends chiefly on the lifetime of the writer, who is here speaking, which will be treated of below.²⁸¹ It will also appear below ²³⁷ why we assume, on the authority of this writer, the high antiquity certainly, but not the Mosaic origin, of the Book of the Covenant.

²⁸⁰ The judgments expressed in the text must here be briefly justified with respect to each of these ordinances, and the more so, since it is not attended to by Stähelin and Knobel, (comp. their oft-quoted writings, and in reply, Ewald, Hupfeld, Riehm).

(i) E.xx.24–26, see above note ⁴⁰⁻⁶¹. That the freedom here allowed to the building of altars and to sacrifices is entirely in accordance with the practice which prevailed among Israel during many ages, and that the centralisation of worship was first attempted by Hezekiah, and carried out under Josiah, has been shown in notes ¹⁴⁹⁻¹⁶¹.

(ii) E.xxii.29ᵇ,30, contains prescriptions about the male firstborns of man and beast. Whereas in other laws, E.xiii.13, L.xxvii.27, is expressed the duty, to give to Jehovah also the firstborn of an ass or, generally, of unclean animals, the Book of the Covenant speaks only of cattle and sheep. Is not this the original direction, while the other is an expansion of this, introduced chiefly (in particular L.xxvii.26,27, N.xviii.15,16, comp. note ⁴⁸⁻¹) in the interest of the priests?

(iii) E.xxii.29ᵃ, comp. with xxiii.19ᵃ. The direction here given is so short, that different views may be taken of its relation to N.xviii.12,13,xv.17–21. Yet here also the originality appears to lie on the side of the Book of the Covenant, in which the duty to give up the firstlings is expressed in quite a general form, and nothing is said definitely as to the destination of these firstlings—for the priests? for sacrificial feasts? Comp. D.xiv.22–27, where something similar is laid down about the tithes.

(iv) E.xxiii.12. The motive here added to the command for observing the Sabbath is more natural and original than that which is adopted out of the B.O. in E.xx.11 (comp.G.ii.2,3,) while D.v.14ᵇ,15 is a fuller expansion of xxiii.12.

(v) E.xxiii.10,11. Comp. on the passage Hᴜᴘғ.*Fest*.iii.p.10,11, where, as it seems to me, he has shown that mention is not made here of the land lying fallow in the seventh year, but of leaving the produce of the seventh year to the poor and the wild beasts: the pron. suff. in תִּשְׁמְטֶנָּה, 'thou shalt let *it* rest,' and נְטַשְׁתָּהּ 'thou shalt let *it* lie still,' referring not to אַרְצֶךָ 'thy land,' but to תְּבוּאָתָהּ 'its produce.' If this is so, then probably it will not need to be proved, that this law is—not only more excellent, but also—more original than L.xxv.2–7. That D.xv.1–5 implies the Book of the Covenant is generally admitted.

(vi) E.xxiii.14–17. Comp. above note ⁴⁰·⁴ᵛ. From the remarks there made it appears at once that this Feast-Legislation is older than that of the B.O. Let it be observed also that the Book of the Covenant certainly knows of a 'House of Jehovah,' xxiii.19, and also once speaks of 'Jehovah's *altar*,' xxi.14, [see also xx.26], not of his *altars*; but that at the same time the freedom of worshipping Jehovah also without the 'House' is recognised, xx.24–26. Whenever, then, in the passage, with which we are now concerned, mention is made of the appearance of men *before the face of Jehovah*, xxiii.15ᵇ,17, this need not be understood necessarily of a pilgrimage to 'the House of Jehovah;' it may also very well denote an assembling (of the inhabitants of one place, or of many places lying near each other) at one of their numerous altars, or, to use an expression borrowed from the historical books of the O.T., *at one of the high places*. If this conjecture is correct,—and it is very much supported by (115,116)—then it appears yet more plainly, that this law must be older than the B.O., which only knows of the 'holy convocation' at the common Sanctuary, and than the Deuteronomistic Law, which transfers all the Feasts to Jerusalem.⁶¹·¹¹².

(vii) E.xxii.31. It seems to be beyond all doubt that this prescription cannot have been formulated thus, when the fully-developed Legislation of the B.O. about things clean and unclean, L.vii.24,xi–xv, already existed. We have here manifestly before us a law, out of which at a later time this so intricate a system has been developed. The Deuteronomistic law, xv, stands in this respect on the same line with the B.O.

(viii) E.xxi.2–11. That this law is older than D.xv.12–18, is generally allowed, note ⁸⁸·¹¹. Yet also L.xxv.39–43 is later, as appears both from the nature of the case, and from the connection between the last-named law and that about the Sabbatical Year; see (v) above. Moreover, Jeremiah,xxxiv.13,14, includes this law expressly among the old ordinances, and no testimony of this kind can be produced for L.xxv.39–43.

²¹⁰ The words in question appear to refer to E.xiii.3–10, where mention is made of *mazzoth*, v.6, and of the month Abib, v.4, just as in E.xxiii.15, (comp. also 'for in it thou camest-out from Egypt' with E.xiii.3,4,8,9). Yet it seems scarcely possible to regard E.xiii.3–10 as the older, E.xxiii as the younger, law. E.xiii. 3–10 is most closely connected with v.11–16, and is certainly from the same hand, as appears most plainly from the agreement in phraseology. This second law, however, contains in v.13 a direction, which is certainly later than the similar

prescription, E.xxii.29ᵇ,30. Comp. notes ⁶⁹ᴸ¹²⁴ᵈ. Consequently, E.xiii.3–10 must be younger than the Book of the Covenant. We have thus, with respect to the reference in question in v.15, the choice between two views : either the author of the Book of the Covenant refers back to an older law, which is lost, or the words ' as I commanded thee ' are not from his hand, but proceed from the Jehovist, who adopted both E.xiii.3–16 and the Book of the Covenant into his manuscript, and in this last refers to the prescriptions formerly imparted by him. This last view seems to me the most plausible, and must also be applied to E.xxxiv.18.

(133)   ²¹¹ E.xxxiv.19,20ᵃ, is out of xiii.12,13 ; all the rest out of E.xxi–xxiii. Comp. Knob., E.L. p.326, &c.

²¹² The commands contained in L.xviii–xx are almost all of a moral nature, and directed partly against idolatry, and the corruption of morals clearly connected therewith, partly against marriages in forbidden degrees, &c. : xix.2 may be regarded as the *thema*, which is developed in these chapters. Most of the prescriptions are of such a kind that they may have arisen in more than one age of the Israelitish history : and hence it is that the determination of this age is attended with so many difficulties. The above statement rests on the following observations. L.xviii–xx agrees sometimes in its phraseology in a remarkable manner with the B.O. : see especially xviii.29,xix.8 (xx.17,18), and other examples in Knobel,p.500. Hence it follows that the writer knew, if not our present B.O., yet at all events an earlier edition of it. But then he must have lived after the author of the Book of the Covenant, which, as we have seen above, must have preceded the Book of Origins. On the other hand, we have to regard him as one of the predecessors of the Deuteronomist, who takes over his commands just as much as the prescriptions of the Book of the Covenant. Comp. *e.g.* D.xviii.10,11, with L.xviii.21, xx.27 (E.xxii.18),—D.xxiv.17 with L.xix.33 (E.xxii.21–24,xxiii.9),—D.xxii.30 with L.xviii.8,xx.11,—D.xxvii.22 with L.xviii.9,—D.xxvii.21 with L.xviii.23,xx.16 (E.xxii.19), &c. &c. In what sense L.xviii–xx may be said to be contemporary with the B.O., will appear below. As to E.xiii.3–16, comp. note ²¹⁰.

(134)   ²¹³ Comp. notes ⁹⁷,¹²²⁻¹²⁵.

²¹⁴ So, for instance, Ew. thinks, *G.V.I.*i.p.73,131, that G.xiv is one of the oldest pieces of Genesis, although he, rightly, does not assign it to the B.O., but supposes it to be adopted by a later narrator. A like supposition is certainly justified also with respect to other documents adopted by the Jehovist, although we cannot wholly assent to the views of Ewald and Vaihinger, note ¹⁸⁷. But we cannot here enter into further details about them.

(135)   ²¹⁵ Thus it is not improbable that E.xii.39,xviii, N.x.29–34,35,36,[?] are older even than the oldest pieces of the B.O. Comp. Ew.p.83,&c., where attention is directed also to N.xxi and the fragments there preserved from ' the Book of the Wars of Jehovah ' and to various other narratives.

(136)   ²¹⁶ This is, however, the most common view, maintained, among others, by Bleek, Stähelin, de Wette, von Lengerke, Ewald, Riehm, and, it would seem, also by Hupfeld. It was formerly also my own view, which I still prefer to the contrary views of von Bohlen, George, Vatke, note ⁵⁶. Gradually, however, the

conviction has settled in my mind, (i) that there is more truth in the views of these last, than is recognised by the defenders of the former view, (ii) that the Book of Origins, *as we now possess it*, cannot have the high antiquity, which, for instance, BLEEK, de WETTE, and EWALD assign to it. When it once became plain to me (comp. Chap.XIV) that, in point of fact, cogent reasons plead for a repeatedly renewed manipulation of the B.O., it was very natural also, on the ground of this result, to make trial of another view of the relation between that Book and Deuteronomy, a view which lies about midway between those hitherto put forward.

(137) [217] Here is the place to exhibit clearly the peculiar nature of the difficulties with which we have to contend. The investigation in Chap.XIX has taught us, that many ordinances of the priestly Law have probably never been acted on, *e.g.* that about the Great Day of Atonement, and about the Sabbatical Year and the Year of Jubilee. The question now arises, whether, perhaps, other prescriptions also of the B.O. may not have existed only in theory, and may never have been carried out in practice? This may be said, for instance, with reference to N.xxxi, comp. note [175], and especially with reference to the regulations as to the income of the priests, N.xviii. It is, at least, remarkable that, for example, *tithes* are merely once mentioned, Am.iv.4,—setting aside what the *Chronicler* says about the reign of Hezekiah, 2Ch.xxxi.5,6,12, and what the book of *Nehemiah* relates about the period after the captivity, x.37,38,xii.44,xiii.5,12. Now, as is well-known, the requirements of the Deuteronomistic Legislation vary, in more than one point, from those of the priestly laws, just exactly in respect of the priests and their revenues, note [61]. How is this variation to be explained? (i) Does the Deuteronomist moderate the demands of the priests in the interest of the people, so that they who followed his directions brought less than they formerly used to do? (ii) Or was the priestly Law not at all obeyed, and so the Deuteronomist required the less, because the more was seen to be unattainable? (iii) Or did the priests, *after* the time of the Deuteronomist, heighten their demands, because what was assigned to them by him did not suffice for their necessities?

The same questions may be put with reference to the distinction between priests and Levites, which in Deuteronomy is not made at all,—at least, is not maintained so sharply as in the B.O., *e.g.* N.xviii, (comp.xvi). (i) Were the Levites, at the time of the Deuteronomist, no longer distinguished from the priests? Was, consequently, the priestly Law in his time *no longer* carried out in its full extent? Or was the sharp distinction between priests and Levites introduced first *after* the the time of the Deuteronomist, just as the power for sacrificing was not from the very first, but only by degrees, assigned exclusively to the priests? [101,102]

Already, in former days, and lately also by ORTH, (*La tribu de Lévi et la loi*, in the *Nouv. Rev. de Théol.* iii.384–400, comp. iv.250–360) the answer has been sought to these questions in the sketch given of the new Temple by Ezekiel, xl–xlviii. Frequently, this prophet declares that in that Temple only the descendants of Zadok (comp. 1K.ii.35,27, 1S.ii.27, &c.) should discharge the priestly office, Ez.xl.46,xliii.19,xliv.6–16,xlviii.11. Yet he gives also reasons for this direction, xliv.6, &c.;—because the Levites had been guilty of idolatry, and had led the way for the people in it, therefore shall they fill the lowest offices, *v.*10–14, while the Zadokites alone shall be priests and draw near to Jehovah. He thus

O

justifies historically the exclusion of the Levites from the priesthood. This would
have been entirely superfluous, if the prescriptions of the B.O. had been then
generally known and introduced: since, according to these prescriptions, only the
descendants of Aaron could make any claim to the priestly dignity, and the Levites
were excluded from it *by their birth*: comp. N.xviii.3, &c. Ezekiel, therefore,
supposes manifestly the state of things which we know from Deuteronomy,
especially from xviii.6–8; yet, while he changes this for the future, he does not
refer to the Mosaic Law, which he yet might have done if he had possessed that
edition of it, which we now have before us. From all this ORTH infers that the
Legislation of the Books of Exodus–Numbers is later than Ezekiel, and probably
originated in the Babylonish Captivity. We cannot assent to this opinion, comp.
n.[226,227]; but we consider it not improbable that some truth lies in it, namely
this, that the *latest modification* and the *final redaction* of the B.O. falls in a later
day than the Deuteronomistic Legislation; so that the latest directions, contained
in that book, were in Ezekiel's time not yet introduced, and were not at all or
very little known even to the Prophet himself. In this way it is explained that the
Prophet does not appeal to it, but thinks it necessary to justify historically his
directions about the Levites.

(138)   [218] Comp. note [61,62], where the different passages are named which here come under
consideration. It is true, it may be always maintained that the Deuteronomist
may have expressed himself thus, if he had lived before the building of the
Temple. It remains, however, still noticeable that in all these places without exception mention is made of 'the place' in the *singular*, whereas the writer, if he
had been thinking of the Tabernacle moving about hither and thither, might also
—rather would more properly—have used the plural. Let it be considered also
that the 'Blessing of Moses,' D.xxxiii.12, certainly knows of the 'dwelling' of
Jehovah, lying in the territory of the tribe of Benjamin.

.   [219] Comp. notes [173,174]. That, in fact, the 'law of the king,' D.xvii.14–20, was
written after Solomon, and with the distinct purpose to prevent such errors as his,
appears especially plain from *v*.17,—in particular from the words, 'and his heart
turn not away.' It is altogether inconceivable, that Solomon carried his disobe-
dience to the Law so far, that he not only sinned against its prescriptions (*i.e.* took
many wives), but also justified by his conduct its anxiety for the possible consequences of this transgression. On the other hand, it is very natural that a later
legislator should enforce his warning by briefly pointing to the mournful consequences, which its neglect by Solomon had drawn after it. Let it not be forgotten
that it was just the act of marrying *strange* women, which might give occasion to
the practice of idolatry, and actually had given it to Solomon, 1K.xi.1–6. A
legislator, therefore, who knew nothing of Solomon, would not write, 'he shall not
take to himself many *women*, that his heart may not turn away'—but he must
necessarily have added, 'not many *strange* women.' Whereas, for anyone who
knew Solomon's history, the simple 'women' was perfectly plain.

    [220] This follows from 2Ch.xix.8–11, comp. with D.xvii.8–13. That both these
passages are parallel, appears from this, that both treat about a Court of Justice
at Jerusalem, 2Ch.xix.8, D.xvii.8,10, composed of priests, Levites, and laymen,
2Ch.xix.8, D.xvii.9,—a court of appeal in a certain sense, which decided about

such matters as were too difficult for the local judges, 2Ch.xix.10, D.xvii.8—at whose head stood the high-priest in spiritual things, a layman in temporal matters, 2Ch.xix.11, D.xvii.9,12, 'and (or) to the judge.' Further, it is obvious that D.xvii.8–13 supposes the existence of this Court of Justice at Jerusalem, and does not by any means *institute* it. This appears most plainly from the actual words of the legislator, *e.g.* from v.9, 'which shall be in those days,'—further, from the whole form of the law, which has the object of admonishing people to submit to the judgment of this Court, v.10–13, which is only intelligible if the Court was already in existence. Hence also it arises that in 2Ch.xix.8–11 Jehoshaphat institutes something *new*; in doing this he does not appeal, any more than the historian, to a prescript of the Law, of which his institution was a consequence ; the Court of Justice at Jerusalem was *created* by Jehoshaphat. The last fact allows of no other conclusion than this. The law, laid down in D.xvii.8–13, and, consequently, all Deuteronomy, in which the unity of authorship is generally admitted, originated after the reign of Jehoshaphat,—probably even long after Jehoshaphat ; for the Court of Justice instituted by him needed no longer the sanction of the legislator, but was so entirely inwoven into the habits of the people, that its existence could be simply taken for granted. Schultz, p.47, &c., finds himself compelled to do violence to the plain meaning of the whole ordinance, in order to be able to deny its close connection with 2Ch.xix.8–11 : his explanation needs no formal refutation.

[221] Both the Reformation of Hezekiah, 2K.xviii.4, and that of Josiah, 2K.xxii, xxiii, had in view the abolition of idolatry and the centralisation of worship. Both, therefore, in their tendency, are in accordance with the Deuteronomistic Legislation. This Legislation preceded the Reformation of Josiah, note [222] : did it also precede that of Hezekiah? This question must be answered negatively :—

(i) Because the oldest account of Hezekiah's Reformation, 2K.xviii.4, makes absolutely no mention of its legislative foundation, quite differently from the case of Josiah, 2K.xxii,xxiii ;

(ii) Because Hezekiah's contemporaries, Isaiah and Micah, give no signs of knowing the Book of Deuteronomy, notes [196,195]—which would be inexplicable, if it had exercised so important an influence in their lifetime ;

(iii) Because it is in itself much more probable, that practice—in part unsuccessful—should have preceded theory, than that the latter should have preceded the former. See the further development of this idea in note [225].

[222] Comp. note [160]. Let it be observed also at the same time that Jeremiah, who came forward as Prophet five years before Josiah's Reformation, gives plain signs of knowing the Book of Deuteronomy, note [189].

[223] This is the view of Ew. *G. V. I.*iii.682–689, Riehm,p.78–106, Bleek,p.292,&c., with whom others, as de Wette, Vatke, George, mainly agree : and the view of those, who set the composition of Deuteronomy in the early part of Josiah's reign, does not differ materially from this. Veth, *B.W.*ii.597, sets it under Ahaz or Hezekiah.

[224] They are the following :—

(i) In D.iv.19,xvii.3, warnings are given against the practice of a certain kind of idolatry, the worship of the host of heaven. No mention whatever is made of this idolatry, in the *genuine* prophecies of Isaiah, (it is otherwise in Is.xxiv.21,23, xxxiv.4), but it is certainly named by Zephaniah, i.5, and Jeremiah, viii.2,xix.13, xxxiii.22. The writer of the Books of Kings mentions its being done away by Josiah, 2K.xxiii.4,5, and he speaks yet once again of it, in a regular survey of the religious condition of the Kingdom of the Ten Tribes, 2K.xvii.16. From all this it follows that a warning against idolatry under Manasseh's reign was very suitable.

(ii) The so-called *Song of Moses*, D.xxxii.1-43, is probably older than the Book of Deuteronomy, and was ascribed by the Deuteronomist—though erroneously—to Moses, and on that account adopted by him. But this Song itself belongs to the Assyrian period, as both the contents, *v.*21-27, and the style indicate. Consequently, the author of this Book must himself have lived nearly about the time, in which we have above placed him. RIEHM, p 89-105, brings under discussion yet other particulars.

[223] In this enquiry we start with the historical accounts about Manasseh, 2K.xxi.1-18, 2Ch.xxxiii.1-20. They agree in this, that Manasseh practised idolatry in a shameless manner, polluted the Temple at Jerusalem, undid the work of his father Hezekiah, and withal shed much innocent blood. It appears further that there was no want of Prophets under his reign, who raised their warning voice on account of all these abominations. One of them was the author of Deuteronomy. Manasseh's conduct must have affected the more painfully him and those of kindred spirit, since it so sharply contradicted the tendency of Hezekiah. But just on that very account he felt himself aroused to make an attempt at a fundamental improvement of the religious state of things. To this end he could only direct himself to *the people*, not to the king, whose hostile feelings against the Theocracy was known to him. Thus, then, he proceeds in the admonitory and legislative addresses of his work. That he has put them in the mouth of Moses is certainly not to be commended according to our ideas of morality. Yet we are not at liberty to judge a contemporary of Manasseh by our ideas. Rather we must, on the ground of Deuteronomy, admit that such a *pia fraus* could be coupled in those days with a high degree of religious development. Let it not be forgotten also that a *powerful* attempt must have been ventured, if it was desired to succeed in a task which Hezekiah, supported by Isaiah, had only been able partially to complete. The form of the Deuteronomistic Legislation, however, was excellently fitted to attain the proposed end. The writer might the rather have chosen it, because he was conscious that he was aiming at nothing else than the maintenance of what Moses himself had called into life. Only *then* would he have abstained from the use of such a form, if he had believed that he was living under the authority of the letter of a Law written by Moses. Yet, although he knew the existing collections of laws—whose authors had already allowed themselves the same freedom in the use of Moses' name,—he was just as little a slave of the letter as *e.g.* Isaiah or Micah, notes [184,185], so that he considered that he was only making use of his good right, when he placed after the priestly Law or other law-books his own writing, which was in fact derived from them. See further Chap.II, and RIEHM,p.106-116,126-136. The latter makes the remark that in Deuteronomy, the expression 'beyond Jordan' means *Canaan*, when Moses is *speaking*, but the *trans-Jordanic* land, when Moses is *spoken of* in the third person. From this he infers that the writer of Deuteronomy wishes in this way to distinguish

himself from Moses. But the rule here laid down is not carried out in D.iii.8, where Moses is speaking, and yet the trans-Jordanic land is meant. RIEHM, however, sees in the last words of D.iii.8 a mere note, which, in the writer's view, is not spoken by Moses. This is, indeed, probable,—at all events, it is not set aside by D.xi.30 (KEIL on HÄv.I.ii.p.33); since, just as it is natural that Moses, speaking in the trans-Jordanic country, should mention to the Israelites where Mount Gerizim lay in the actual Canaan, so it is unnatural that he, also speaking in the trans-Jordanic land, and to the Israelites, about the land of the kings, whom they had slain a few days before, should have added, D.iii.8, 'that was beyond Jordan, from the river of Arnon unto Mount Hermon,' and what follows in v.9. The remark of RIEHM is not without importance in connection with Chap.II, and shows that in that Chapter the person of the narrator is, not without reason, distinguished from Moses.

Conjectures as to the sources from which the Deuteronomist may have drawn, may be found in BLEEK, 309,&c. Nothing can be determined with certainty about them. The Deuteronomist naturally knew the existing collections of laws, of which some certainly are now lost. Yet of these he made free use, and allowed himself to be guided, at all events, just as much by what he observed in actual life, and by the necessities which it presented.

(139) [226] Before this time the worship was still in an unregulated state, and the priests and Levites wanted a common centre for their activity. Also first under David friendly relations were formed with neighbouring nations, especially with the Phœnicians. Before the last years of David's reign Israel lived in continual wars with foreigners, and there was no proper unity of the people. First under Solomon peace prevailed, and prosperity and civilization increased. When it is considered that to the B.O., among other things, belongs also the cosmogony in G.i.1–ii.4ª, and the genealogy in G.v, it will not be difficult to believe that such a work could not have originated, at all events, before Solomon. It must, it would seem, have been composed either *under* or *after* him.

[227] For this determination of time may be urged the following reasons :—

(i) In G.xvii.6,16,xxxv.11, it is promised to Abraham and Jacob, that *kings* shall proceed from them. These promises could not inspire interest in the Israelite, and be regarded by him as the announcement of a joyful future,—and as such they undoubtedly are given—in the time of the Judges, or under Samuel (comp. 1S.viii.); it would only happen under David or Solomon. Also G.xxxvi.31 should here be taken into consideration, if it had not appeared to us, that the document to which this notice belongs, cannot be referred to the B.O., notes [93-vi]. From this, however, it follows only that this document also—one of the sources of the Jehovist, note [231]—was written after the introduction of the regal form of government, and probably not long after.

(ii) Very soon after the building of the Temple, and the settlement of the priests at Jerusalem, the need must have been felt of a fixed regulation of their operations, which is exactly given in the B.O., and certainly in the first edition of it. Solomon's reign was also, in the domain of politics, devoted to the organisation of things already existing, 1K.iv, and so was an example for the imitation of the priests of Jerusalem.

(iii) The great revolution in the arrangements of worship, which was brought to
a completion through the building of the Temple, must of itself have given occasion
to the writing, and so at the same time to the maintenance, of the Mosaic Institutions,
especially of those, which otherwise would have been lost. A diffuse description,
like that which we find in E.xxv–xxxi,xxxv–xl, can hardly be explained, except under
the reign of Solomon. Let it not be forgotten to remark at the same time that the
Temple of Solomon was in many respects built after the model of the Tabernacle,
so that the description of this last—which Solomon's contemporary knew through
personal inspection—was at the same time a rectification of the institution of the
Temple.

To these proofs Ew. adds, i.p.101,102, yet a fourth derived from 1K.viii.1-11,
which account, according to him, belongs to the B.O., though not in the form in
which we now possess it, mixed up and interpolated by a later writer. This opinion
is based upon the phraseology of these verses, which, according to Ewald, agrees in
a remarkable manner with that of the B.O. He points to the use of אֵסֶף, v.1, to
the formula 'all the congregation of the children of Israel, that were assembled
unto him,' v.5, to the agreement of v.7,8, with E.xxv.13,14,20,xxxvii.9, N.iv.6,&c.,
and of v.10,11, with E.xl.34,35. Since, however, Ewald himself must allow that,
in opposition to these points of agreement, there exist also important variations,
(e.g. v.1,2,3, and especially v.9), I should rather explain this agreement as arising
from an imitation of the Pentateuch, than from identity of authorship. On the
one hand, however, it is certain that the writer of 1 Kings knew the Pentateuch;
on the other hand it is very natural that, in his description of the dedication of
the Temple, he employed expressions derived from E.xxv,&c. Besides, the writer
of the B.O. would not have omitted to give the month in which the Temple was
dedicated; yet the datum in v.2 is certainly not from his hand, (Ew.p.101, note 1):
we have therefore to suppose that his note of time has been omitted and replaced
by another—which is certainly less probable than the supposition that a later
writer is using in v.2, and elsewhere, his own phraseology, but in v.5,7,8,10,11,
that of the B.O. well-known to him. Further, Ewald proceeds rightly from the
supposition, that the writer of the B.O. carried on his work farther than to the
death of Moses, as we shall see below, Chap.XXV–XXVIII.

²²⁸ This follows partly from the nature of the case, partly from what has been
reasoned out in the foregoing note ²²⁷·¹⁴·¹⁸. A work, to which G.ii.2,3 belonged, must
from the first have contained the institution of the Sabbath. On account of G.xvii
(institution of circumcision) it treated also, probably, about the rights of the members of the covenant-people, in distinction from strangers, &c. But, however
certain this may be in general, it is just as difficult to show in detail what subjects
were treated in the first edition of the B.O., what, on the contrary, remained for a
later recension of it.

(140)   ²²⁹ The Great Day of Atonement, L.xvi, seems to be an institution of a later
time, the extreme consequence of the whole system of purification, which is elaborated
in the B.O. Further, here, v.29,31, as elsewhere in the B.O., L.xxiii.27,29,32,
N.xxix.7,xxx.13, the formula 'humble his soul, is used to indicate *fasting*.
Credner seems to remark justly, p.149, that this is an expression of a later time,
implying that the practice of fasting had been corrupted into a mere mechanical act,

and directed against this corruption. Other writers use the verb צוה, *e. g.* Joel i.14, ii.12,15, Ju.xx.26, even Jeremiah, xiv.12,xxxvi.6,9 ; the later Isaiah is the first who repeats the formula of the B.O., Is.lviii.3,5,10 ; comp. also Ps.xxxv.13. It must be admitted, however, both that this ceremony fits in well with the whole organism of the book, comp.E.xxx.10, L.xxiii.26,27,xxv.9, N.xxix.7,8, and that the silence of the whole O.T. about this duty may be partly explained from its more or less private character, on which account it is not quite certain that the impression, which we receive on reading the ordinance, does not deceive us.

L.xvii, and especially *v.*1-9, has the same centralising aim as the Deuteronomistic Law. This last seems even not to be acquainted with the contents of these verses, to judge from D.xii.8,9. At all events it is almost inconceivable that the Deuteronomist should have placed in the mouth of Moses this explanation, that the unity of worship did not yet exist in the wilderness, if he had known, or at least, had supposed, that it was introduced in L.xvii under a threat of death for every transgressor.

With reference to N.xxxi comp. note [111]. A priestly tendency,—in the less favourable sense of the word,—such as we observe in this law, is alien to the original B.O.

N.xvi,xviii—in which last chapter we observe especially the directions, which make sharp the distinction between priests and Levites—belong together. They have been considered already in note [217]. That their final redaction must be set later than that of Deuteronomy is confirmed by D.xi.6, where the writer shows that he is not acquainted with the part taken by Korah in the rebellion of Dathan and Abiram : comp. notes [23.v.116.111]—nor, consequently, with the ordinances, which are brought into direct connection with Korah's rebellious undertaking.

[218] One single example may make clear my meaning. The verb שׁרע in the sense of *explain, make clear,* is very common in Aramaic, (and is found in the Aramaic of the Bible, Ezr.iv.18), and it is also, though rarely, used in the latest Hebrew writings, Neh.viii.8, comp. with Esth.iv.8,x.2 ; (Prov.xxiii.32 and Ez.xxxiv.12 are of another kind). Yet the same word is used in the above sense twice in the B.O., L.xxiv.12, N.xv.34,—in sections, therefore, L.xxiv.11-23, N.xv.32-36, which agree with each other in other points, and certainly also in this, that they do not rest upon pure historical tradition, but answer a question of law in a historical form. I do not hesitate to set these two sections among the later portions of the B.O. This judgment is confirmed, as regards L.xxiv, through the breach of continuous connection between *v.*17-22 and what precedes and follows— as regards N.xv, through the proximity of *v.*37-41, which, if only on account of the spirit which they breathe, must be assigned not to Solomon's age, but to a much later time. GRIGNR, p.20,&c., distinguishes also by the phraseology older and younger portions of the Pentateuch, and brings the latter even down to the time after the Captivity.

(142) [221] Comp. above notes [214.215]. As regards G.xiv, it appears from *v.*14 that this chapter was written after the conquest of the land by Joshua, and after the settlement of the Danites in Laish, Ju.xvii,xviii. It may, however, have originated in the time of the Judges, or, if Salem in *v.*18 is Jerusalem, under David's reign. Whether it is really so old, must be decided by the analytical criticism of this chapter, &c.

[223] The history of Balaam, for instance, N.xxii–xxiv, was first used by Micah, vi.5. It is therefore possible that it was not committed to writing till after 800 B.C., since Micah's prophecy falls not before 725 B.C. EWALD endeavours to make it probable, i.144–148, that it was in fact written about 750 B.C. Comp. his *Jahrbücher der Bibl. Wissenschaft*, viii.p.1–31, and, further, OORT, p.82, &c.

[223] No one has bestowed more care upon this than Ew.i.130,&c. Besides the B.O. and its sources, i.81–129, he sees in the Books of Exodus–Numbers remains of three narrators, whom he names the ' third, fourth, and fifth narrators of the primary history.' The *third narrator*—not different from our later Elohist—is the author, among other passages, of G.xx,xxix–xxxi, and of a great deal of the history of Joseph : he lived in the 10th or 9th century, in the Kingdom of the Ten Tribes, p.130–133. The *fourth narrator*, nearly agreeing with our Jehovist, is the author of G.ii,iii,xii,&c., and lived about the end of the 9th, or in the beginning of the 8th, century, p.133–141. Finally, the *fifth narrator*, from whom, among other passages, N.xxii–xxiv has proceeded, wrote about 750 B.C., p.141–153, and was the compiler of the first four books of the Pentateuch. I should be unwilling to deny that there lies much of truth in this conception. But in many particulars it does not admit of demonstration ; on which account it seems to me preferable to define nothing more than has been defined above.

[224] The limits of this interval are, as we have seen, accurately marked on both sides. *Not before* 975 B.C., *not after* 775 or 750 B.C., could the prophetical narratives have been committed to writing. If, now, we enquire whether, in point of fact, this time agrees with the spirit and with the form of these narratives, the question may be answered without any doubt in the affirmative. Setting aside special expressions, which point to a definite time, *e. g.* N.xxiv.17–24, the following phenomena of a general kind come here to be considered.

(i) The agreement between the ideas and expectations of the Jehovistic and later Elohistic narratives, and those of the older Prophets, Joel to Isaiah and Micah, is so striking, that it can only be sufficiently explained from their having been contemporaneous. Examples have been produced already, notes [119–121,122]. It is almost superfluous to produce parallelisms out of the Prophets : with G.xii.3 and the parallel passages, N.xi.29,xiv.21, comp. Joel ii.28–32 ; with the passages quoted in note [119], comp. Joel iii, Am.i,ii,&c.

(ii) Narratives, such as N.xii, E.xxxiii,xxxiv, imply a general acquaintance with prophetism, and point to the endeavours to distinguish the different degrees of prophetic Inspiration and divine Revelation. This also directs us to the above-named age.

(iii) Attempts, such as G.ii,iii, to explain the origin of sin, proceed from very advanced considerations about man and his moral position, and must be regarded as a fruit of that striving after *wisdom*, which first became domesticated in Israel through Solomon, and only after his time became thoroughly penetrated with religious principles : *Bijb. Woord.* iii.619,620. So, too, G.iv,x, and other genealogical passages imply an advanced intercourse with strange nations, which just began in Solomon's reign. If we had time to go into details, it would not be difficult to increase much the number of these proofs.

(143)   [225] It cannot be maintained that the interval between David's reign and the first

century after the division of the kingdom is not sufficient to allow of the idea originating that Moses was the *writer* of the Book of the Covenant. In an age so ancient, with the entire absence of all critical science, an interval of fifty years was in every respect sufficient for this; and according to our calculation the interval indicated may have been yet more considerable. If this is so, then it appears to me that the age of David was more fitted to originate a work like the Book of the Covenant, than the confused period of the Judges, in which the consciousness of the unity of the people was so little developed. Ew.i.90,91, thinks that his 'Book of the Covenants,' to which also E.xxi–xxiii belongs, was written under Samson's judgeship. But his proofs of this are far-fetched.

²²⁶ From E.xxiii.14–17 a later origin might be derived: but see note ²²⁹·ᵛⁱ and CREDNER, *der Prophet Joel*, p.215–217. Further, in the whole Book of the Covenant not a single direction occurs, which we cannot conceive to have originated either under David's reign or shortly before it. This will appear still further from note ²²⁷.

²²⁷ It is obvious that the Legislation of the Book of the Covenant is intended for an agricultural people, settled in Canaan. Yet, as has been already shown above, Chap.VIII, this in itself is no evidence against the Mosaic origin of the Book. Only Moses, while still encamped with Israel at Sinai, could not suppose that the people was already settled in Canaan, and ground his prescriptions on this supposition. This, however, is what we find almost throughout in the Book of the Covenant. It is true E.xxiii.20–33, comp.xxi.13, supposes the conquest to be yet in the future. But that this is an assumed, and not the actual, standpoint of the lawgiver, appears plainly from all the rest. We have only to read attentively xxi.2,33,xxii.5,6,31,xxiii.10,11, 'thy land,' 'thy vine,' 'thy olive-tree,' *v.*12, 'and the stranger,' without any further definition, *v.*19, 'thy land.' It is noticeable also that in xxiii.16 not only the dwelling in Canaan is supposed, but also the existence of the Feast of Harvest and the Feast of Ingathering: the Feasts are not prescribed in this passage for the first time, but the Legislation starts from the supposition that they already exist, and admonishes the people to keep them. This appears plainly from the use of the *article* in the expression here used—'*the* Feast of Harvest,' '*the* Feast of Ingathering,'—which cannot here be explained from any previous mention having been made of these Feasts, as, of course, might be the case 'with the Feast of Unleavened Bread' in *v.*15; see however above, note ²¹⁰. Also the reference to the sojourn in Egypt, xxii.21,xxiii.9, is more natural on the supposition that a later writer is speaking, than when Moses—not yet fifty days after the march out of Egypt—is regarded as so expressing himself. This remark applies still more to xxiii.15, 'for in this month (Abib) ye marched out of Egypt.' Let it be observed, meanwhile, that all these objections touch not so much the Mosaic origin of these commands, as the view that Moses wrote them in this form.

(144) ²²⁸ Let attention be paid to the repeated 'I am Jehovah your Elohim,' L.xviii.2, 4,21,30,xix.3,4,10,12,14,25,28,31,34,36,xx.7,24, which occurs also in the Decalogue, E.xx.2,—further, to the brevity and plainness of most of the prescriptions. See Ew.ii.166,205,&c. comp. 25,&c.

²²⁹ Comp. note ²¹². From the passages there quoted it appears that the author

of L.xviii–xx knew the B.O., if not in its present form, yet in a former recension, as is shown afterwards also by L.xix.21,22. Further, there may be noticed in these chapters a certain approximation to the Deut. phraseology, *e.g.* in the formula, 'my statutes and my judgments,' xviii.26,xix.37,xx.22, which is further enlarged by the addition of one or two synonymous words by the Deuteronomist,—in the connection 'observe and do,' xix.37,xx.8,22, for which Deut. says, 'observe to do,' comp. note ᵃʳ. These remarks lead us to the conclusion that the compiler of these chapters lived after 975 B.C., and stood nearer to the Deuteronomist than to the age of Solomon. The reader needs scarcely to be reminded that from the want of distinct historical allusions complete certainty is here unattainable.

[240] Comp. our remarks upon the age of the Jehovist and the antiquity of his sources. Let it be observed also that in E.xxxiv.19,20ᵃ, there *appears* an acquaintance with E.xiii.12,13, and that the last-named prescription, 'the ass, which is not redeemed, shall have his neck broken,' must be older than the prescriptions of the present B.O. with reference to this point, which latter manifestly contain a modification, in the interest of the priests, of the former (purely religious) ordinance: note [241].

(145)   [241] As to the variation of the two texts, comp. note [264] and KNOB. *E.L.*p.195,196. In general, the text in Exodus is certainly more original than that of Deuteronomy. Yet it does not follow from this that the first is in its entirety Mosaic. Rather must E.xx.11 be regarded as an addition out of the B.O., comp. G.ii.2,3, and the genuineness of the motives in *v.*5ᵇ,6,7ᵇ,12ᵇ, may justly be doubted, KNOB.p.196. It is, in fact, in itself very probable, that the fundamental law of the Theocracy was formulated as briefly as possible, especially since it was engraven on stone. Further, it is not natural that the first Table should have contained so many more words than the second. Lastly, it appears both from D.v and E.xx.11, that the later legislators regarded it as not unlawful, to expand and recast the original commands. It is very reasonable, therefore, to suppose such a recasting also in the case of the passages above-mentioned. Comp. also, as to the division of the Decalogue, KNOB., p.197,&c., and the writers quoted by him,—further, Ew.ii.205–217,—KURTZ, *G.A.B.*ii.284–291, and note [45],¹ above.

[242] For the Mosaic origin of the *Ten Commandments themselves*—setting aside the additions indicated in note [241]—may be adduced—

(i) The great unanimity with which the writers of the Pentateuch give testimony to that fact—comp. E.xix,xxxiv.28,xxv.16,21,xl.21, (see note [166],) D.v, see 1K.viii. 9,&c.;—from which it may be inferred that the Commandments were generally ascribed to Moses, a fact which must naturally exercise great influence upon our judgment.

(ii) The custom of later legislators, to combine ten commands in one group,—a custom which seems to imply the existence and the high antiquity of the Decalogue, comp. note [81].

(iii) The contents of the Ten Commandments themselves, which made them, in point of fact, excellently well adapted to regulate the religious and moral condition of Israel. The principle on which it is based is plainly expressed in *v.*2; the Commandments themselves contain nothing superfluous, and leave nothing essential untouched; the Decalogue is therefore, in fact—what it ought to be, if it proceeded from Moses,—a short collection of principles, which are more fully developed in writing by the later legislators in the documents which have been preserved to us. Further, it is well known that the authenticity of the command forbidding the use of *images* in worship, E.xx.4, D.v.8,—to be well distinguished from that forbidding the worship of *other gods*,—is more doubtful than the genuineness of the other prescriptions. For instance, reference may be made on this point to the prevalence of image-worship during the time of the Judges, and in the kingdom of the Ten Tribes,—especially to Ju.xviii.30 (comp. note [136]), also to 2K.xviii.4. But this important question can only be treated in a complete history of the Israelitish worship. Compare further (157), about the Mosaic character of the whole Legislation.

CHAPTER XXII.

(148) [243] The name Abram occurs repeatedly in G.xi.26–xvii.5; after xvii.5 it is replaced by Abraham, eight times in xvii (B.O.), but also in xviii (J.) thirteen times, &c. Sarai also never occurs after xvii.15. The case is somewhat different with the names Israel and Jacob: for Jacob is also frequently used after the accounts of the change of name, xxxii.29,xxxv.10,—*e. g.* in xxxiii.1,10,17,18,&c., xxxv.14,15,20,22,23,&c. This, however, must be explained from the fact that the two names of Jacob existed also together at the same time in the current phraseology, while, on the contrary, Abram and Sarai had dropped out of use.

[244] The feminine form הִיא ('she') occurs *eleven* times, G.xiv.2,xx.5,xxxviii.25, L.ii.15,xi.39,xiii.10,21,xvi.31,xxi.9,N.v.13,14; the fem. נַעֲרָה occurs once, D.xxii.19.

[245] For example, G.xix.8,25,xxvi.3,4, L.xviii.27, D.iv.42,vii.22,xix.11. But, on the other hand, there are found innumerable passages, where אֵלֶּה or הָאֵלֶּה appears; אֵל without the article, if I mistake not, is never found in the Pentateuch.

[246] It is true a great number of other words and phrases are produced, which occur only in the Pentateuch, *e. g.* by Keil, §15, n.2–7. But it is altogether unproved, and, further, unprovable, that such words and expressions are older than those elsewhere employed. Keil, indeed, assures us that they are almost all 'antiquated;' but this opinion is based only upon the supposed Mosaic origin of the Pentateuch. In opposition to these phenomena stands, further, the undeniable fact that the number of the Mosaic Books, *generally*, does not differ from that of the Prophets of the 8th or 7th century B.C. The difference would have been much greater if the interval between the last-named and the Pentateuch had really amounted to about seven centuries, as the tradition maintains.

(149) [247] Comp. note [88]. What has been there set forth more or less doubtfully may be here expressed with more certainty, now that we have seen that in the indisputable portions of the B.O., reaching from G.i to E.vi, the name Jehovah occurs *once* only, viz. in the passage here in question. Whether, further, the use of Jehovah

must be ascribed to the compiler, or to a copyist, will probably remain always uncertain. The ancient translations agree with the text; but the error may be older than the Alexandrian translation. According to Tuch, xviii.1 or xii.7 gave occasion to the change.

²⁴⁸ In order to understand rightly the significance of this, compare what has been observed in Chap.XVIII, and especially in note ¹⁴¹, in judging the 'Supplement Hypothesis.' The greater the temptation for the compiler to bring his documents into agreement with each other, the more we are bound to thank him that he has not done this: his work has thereby lost, perhaps, artistic excellence, but possesses thus greater importance for the historical inquirer.

(150)   ²⁴⁹ Comp. as to this passage note ¹⁴⁸, where at the same time some other points are produced, which may tend to throw light on the labours of the compiler. Most of the elucidating notices which occur in the Pentateuch must be ascribed, not to the compiler, but to the original narrators [?] themselves. Thus it is, e.g., with geographical explanations, such as G.xxiii.2,xxxv.27,xiv.7,8,&c.—with historical remarks, as N.xiii.22,—with archæological illustrations, as E.xvi.36, N.iv.47, xviii.16,&c. In fact there exists no reason whatever, in the case of these and similar passages, for withdrawing them from the writers of the narratives or laws in which they occur. These, however, lived—as we have seen—long enough after the Mosaic and pre-Mosaic time to have had occasion to make such remarks, and so much the more if (as frequently happened) they drew their narratives not only from tradition, but also from written documents.

²⁵⁰ Comp. note ⁶⁵, where also the reasons are assigned why, perhaps, D.x.6,7 must be excepted from the passages named in the text: comp. further, Ew.I,p.169. In style and language lies the manifest proof that the notices in question come from the Deuteronomist himself. It is not probable, however, that he intends to put them in the mouth of Moses—rather we must regard them as glosses from his own hand upon the discourses which he himself had recorded. Comp. as to a similar phenomenon, Scholten, p.35,&c.

²⁵¹ (i) The original text of the B.O. in G.v.28ᵇ had certainly 'and begat Noah,' comp. v.6,9,12,15,18,21,25. For this the compiler wrote 'and begat a son;' because in point of fact he wished to adopt in v.29 an etymology of the name 'Noah' out of the Jehovistic document, which was expressed in such a form, that the mention of the name Noah could not precede it.

(ii) In G.xxxv.9 the particle עוֹד ('again,') is introduced by the compiler. Just as necessary as this may be said to be, now that there stands before it in v.1–8 the account of another theophany to Jacob after his return from Padan-Aram, so impossible it is that the author of the B.O. should have placed it here, inasmuch as the theophany here related was in his narrative the first after Jacob's return.

(iii) With respect to G.xxxvii.28,xxxix.1, comp. note ²³·¹¹. The manner in which in the two verses in question, the two accounts are combined, shows plainly that the compiler saw no contradiction between them, or, in other words, that he set out with the supposition that both accounts were purely historical.

(iv) As to E.vi.10–30 comp. note ¹⁰⁰. That vii.1 (the designation of Aaron as the prophet of Moses) stands in the closest connection with vi.12 (the lament of Moses that he is 'uncircumcised of lips') is at once obvious. E.vi.13–30 is, consequently, an interpolated passage, and very probably interpolated by the compiler: the historian himself can never have thought of disturbing in such a way the regular course of his own narrative. The compiler, however, derived the details contained in *v.*14–25 from a full [?] register of the family of Jacob: what had reference therein to Reuben and Simeon he cuts short in *v.*14,15, and then imparts extended information about the tribe of Levi, especially about Moses and Aaron, their forefathers, and the descendants of the last-named, *v.*23,25, while he treats more briefly the other Levitical families, *v.*17,19,21,22,24. All this is not accidental. He who interpolated at this point this genealogy wished (i) to make known to the reader Moses and Aaron, their descent and their forefathers, (ii) to name by anticipation the descendants of Aaron, who in the sequel of the narrative, L.x, N.xxv, would play a more or less important part. In that case, however, the insertion of this genealogy can only be ascribed to the compiler. This appears also, further, both from *v.*13,26,27, where preparation is made beforehand for the communication of this genealogical list,—from *v.*26,27, where it is, as it were, again summed up,—and from *v.*28–30, where the compiler, by repeating the contents of *v.*10–12, takes up again the thread of the narrative.

(v) For N.xvi comp. notes [29,110], as also for N.xxvi.9–11. Thus far it is plain, that the three verses last-named were introduced after the two narratives, which lie at the basis of N.xvi, had been combined into one, whether the compiler of N.xvi was also the writer of N.xxvi.9–11, or the last-named found N.xvi already in its present form among his sources. Against the identity of the compiler of the narrative and the author of N.xxvi.9–11 may be urged the contradiction which exists between xvi.32 and xxvi.11. It is possible, however, that the formula, ' the men which *belonged* to Korah,' must be understood so as to include only Korah's dependents and not his sons. In that case there would exist no reason for seeing in xxvi.9–11 another hand than that of the compiler of xvi.

(151) [232] It is true, the possibility remains that the B.O., *as it existed at the time of the Deuteronomist—i. e.* without the laws and narratives, which could only have been written after his time, note [239]—was already combined into a whole with the other then-existing documents. Yet this is not probable. The Deuteronomistic Legislation itself is much more intelligible, if we assume that it originated in a time when, indeed, different writings about Moses and the Mosaic Legislation were in existence, but when no complete collection of them existed. Add to this that the later portions of the B.O. are not merely appended to the earlier, but are, in fact, incorporated into a whole with them. This seems to show that even after the Deuteronomist the B.O. had an independent existence, so that it may have undergone a new editing or an entire recasting.

[233] It is only such a writer that can be supposed to have introduced the latest modifications of the priestly Legislation. Let it be noted also that the modifications almost all betray a priestly tendency, so that the priests had an immediate interest with regard to them, to fuse them into one with the other records, and so raise them to the rank of a generally valid law-book.

[234] Let it be noted that the compiler must have lived some years at least after the Deuteronomist,—that he appears to have known laws and narratives, which did not originate till after the Deut. Law,—lastly, that (as has been shown above,

note [199]) even Jeremiah cannot by any means be thought to have known the
Pentateuch in its present form. From all this follows naturally of itself the
definition of time given in the text. Here also it should be noticed that *the entire
exclusion of the Levites from all priestly duties*, which in the present Pentateuch is
represented as a ‑Mosaic ordinance, N.xviii.3,7, &c., cannot have long existed at
the time of Ezekiel (notes [217-229]), and thus certainly cannot for any considerable
time have been inserted in a recognised law-book. Everything consequently binds
us to fix the final editing of the Pentateuch as near as possible to the Babylonish
Captivity. We should, in fact, have to decide for either the time of the Captivity
itself, or the time after the Captivity, rather than ascend higher than the date
above given, 600–590 B.C.

[245] However difficult it may be, we will, however, endeavour to set before our eyes
a connected view of the work of the compiler, since by that alone can the assertion
expressed in the text be justified. We shall here assume as known what has been
observed in the text, as to the principles by which he was guided. He laid, then,
the B.O. as the basis of his work, and followed throughout the chronological
guidance afforded him by that document. In the first half of Genesis, i–xxv, he
imparted the B.O. in its entirety, and confined himself to filling up its blanks
from a younger Elohist and the Jehovist. In the second half of Genesis he left
out, here and there, this and that passage out of the B.O., as often as his other
sources supplied him with the selfsame particulars, but at greater length; then
also he had at his command, besides the B.O., the writings of the Jehovist and one
or more younger Elohists. Sometimes he inserted their narratives without making
any change in them, *e.g.* xxvii.1–45,xxxviii; sometimes he saw himself compelled
to combine these with one another into one narrative, *e.g.* xxix–xxxii,xxxvii,xxxix,
&c. The same method was followed by him with respect to the accounts which
had reference to the call of Moses, the march out of Egypt, and the journey of
Israel to Sinai, E.i–xviii. Here also he adhered to the order followed by the B.O.;
but he filled up the short notices of that document with the more ample narratives
of others, especially those of the Jehovist, who, as we have seen above, Chap.XVII,
in the treatment of this part of the History, made still more use of ancient
documents than in Genesis. When, however, he approached the Sinaitic Legislation, the compiler departed so far from the custom which he had hitherto followed
as to leave out the account of the B.O. about the utterance of the Ten Commandments, and to replace it by the Jehovistic narrative, in which also the Book of the
Covenant was inserted, E.xix–xxiv; only he introduced in the Decalogue, E.xx.11,
an addition, which he had found in the B.O. (note [199]). After E.xxiv the compiler
dropped for awhile the thread of the Jehovistic narrative, in order to insert the
directory of worship, which according to the B.O. was imparted by Jehovah to
Moses on Sinai, E.xxv–xxxi, while he introduces the sequel and conclusion of the
Jehovistic narrative concerning the events at Sinai, xxxii–xxxiv—(N.B. xxxi.18
in its present form is an interpolation of the compiler: comp.xxxii.15,16,)—
between the commands about the building of the Tabernacle, xxv–xxxi, and the
account about the carrying out of the same, xxxv–xl. Nothing is plainer than that
xxxi.17 and xxxv.1 originally followed each other.

When, thus, a commencement had been made of imparting the ordinances,
represented by the B.O. as Sinaitic prescriptions, the compiler had only to advance

forward upon the path on which he had entered. From L.i. to N.x.27 he follows the steps of the B.O. : only he inserted at the most suitable place two documents derived from elsewhere, *viz.* L.xviii-xx, a collection of laws and prescriptions concerning chiefly civil and domestic life, and L.xxvi, a prophetical threatening against transgressing the Mosaic ordinances. At the end of xxvi he probably found already the subscription, *v.*46, from which it seems to appear that this chapter once made the conclusion of a collection of Sinaitic laws. Perhaps xviii-xx belonged to this collection, though these chapters are older than the prophetical address contained in xxvi. On the other hand, xxvii.34 appears to be from the hand of the compiler, and to be intended to separate the preceding directions from the genealogical information in N.i, &c. It is possible, however, that the said subscription (just as xi.46,47,xiii.59,xiv.54–57,xv.32,33) was already added to L.xxvii in the B.O. After N.x.28 the editor placed some accounts derived from Jehovistic sources, N.x.29–xii.16 ; then he combined the account of the B.O., touching the sending-out of the spies, with the narrative of this Jehovist on the same subject, xiii,xiv, which might the more easily be done, inasmuch as both accounts were fashioned on the same model, since the tradition that the Israelites had wandered about forty years in the wilderness was quite strong in the time of Amos : comp. Am.ii.9,10,v.25, and above note [192]. After N.xiv a collection of laws out of the B.O. found its place, N.xv. Then the compiler took over out of a Jehovistic document the account of the rebellion of Dathan and Abiram, and combined into a whole with it a narrative of the B.O. about Korah's rebellion, N.xvi. From the same source he subjoined xvii.1–xix. The historical narrative was continued, first by an account of the B.O., xx.1–13 ; yet, perhaps, a Jehovistic passage is inserted, *v.*14–21, to which the conclusion of the account derived from the B.O. well attaches itself, *v.*22–29. With respect to the war against Sihon and Og the compiler gives only Jehovistic notices, N.xxi, probably because they were more circumstantial than those of the B.O. Also N.xxii–xxiv is Jehovistic, with exception, perhaps, of xxii.1, which may be derived from the B.O., as is, very certainly, the conclusion, xxv–xxxi, partly of historical, partly of legislative nature. N.xxxii gives us a new example of the combination of two narratives. For a great part that chapter is derived from the B.O. : yet *v.*33, as the form of this verse shows at once, is not from the same hand as *v.*1–32. It is possible, however, that N.xxxii, in its entirety, is a later recasting of the original narrative in the B.O., so that to that, and not to the compiler, must be ascribed the breach of continuity between *v.*1–32 and *v.*33. N.xxxiii.1–49 is an old document inserted, *v.*2, in the B.O., and from that derived by the compiler : *v.*50–56 belongs not to this document, but either to the B.O. itself, or to a Jehovistic narrative ; the compiler inserted it here in order to make the transition to the latest Mosaic ordinances, which he derived from the B.O., xxxiv–xxxvi.12. Upon this must have followed the account of Moses' death, comp. N.xxvii.12–23. But, after the Deuteronomist had chosen his point of view in the eleventh month of the fortieth year after the Exodus, D.i.3, and, in fact, in the land of Moab, D.i.5, it was now the time to insert that part of *his* work which had reference to Moses ; for the Deuteronomist, as we shall hereafter see, treated also certainly of the history of Joshua. Without making any change, it would seem (see, however, KNOB. *R.D.J.* pp.205,231,256,257,305,324,325) the compiler took over from it D.i.1–xxxii.47, *i.e.*

all the addresses put into the mouth of Moses, together with the 'Song,' regarded
by the Deuteronomist as Mosaic. After that he placed the announcement of
Moses' death from the B.O., D.xxxii.48–52, which must have been connected
originally with N.xxxvi.12. Thereupon xxxiv.1–9 ought to have immediately
followed. But in the compiler's time a poem was in circulation, which originated
under the reign of Jeroboam II (note ²⁴ʳ), and was erroneously ascribed to Moses.
Whether already, before the compiler's time, this poem was regarded as a collection
of blessings, uttered by Moses before his death, or whether the compiler in v.1
expresses his own opinion, in either case he considered that here was the place to
insert that passage, D.xxxiii. Now followed out of the B.O. the account of Moses'
death, xxxiv.1–9, to which was attached a glorification of the services of the
Lawgiver, v.10–12, which the compiler either himself wrote down, or derived from
a Jehovistic biography of Moses. The Deuteronomistic narrative of Moses' end is
therefore omitted. We here conclude our sketch of the compiler's work. That we
owe to him also the Book of Joshua, and how he went to work in the composition
of it, will appear in Chap.XXIV,XXV.

CHAPTER XXIII.

(157)   ²⁵⁴ This is true, in the first place, of the Book of the Covenant, comp. note ²⁷,
but also, incontestably, of many other laws, e.g. with reference to sacrifices, the High
Feasts, &c.

²⁵⁷ This is true, e.g., of the prescriptions about Holy Places and Holy Persons.
From Chap.XIX,PartsI&II,we have seen that the right of every Israelite to sacrifice,
as well as the liberty to do so elsewhere than at the common Sanctuary, must have
been maintained by Moses, which is very easily to be reconciled with the building
of a Tabernacle, and the assignment of Aaron and his sons to exercise the priestly
office therein. Also the Book of the Covenant, which knows of a ' House of Jehovah,' maintains this right and this freedom, E.xx.24–26. Comp. note ²⁰⁴. On the
other hand, the liberty to sacrifice elsewhere than at the common Sanctuary is
revoked, L.xvii.1–9, and in the Book of Deuteronomy, passim,—especially xii.1,&c.
The descendants of Aaron are regarded as exclusively fitted for priestly duties both
by Ezekiel, xliv.10,&c.xlviii.11, and in the B.O., N.xviii,xvi ; while even in Deuteronomy the line of distinction between Priests and Levites is not drawn so sharply.
The history teaches that these most important modifications of the original Mosaic
institution were not introduced arbitrarily, but must be regarded as the result of
experience. It had shown that both the worship on the 'high places,' and the
participation of the Levites in its formalities, were an inducement to idolatry, and
that an end must be put as well to the one as to the other, if the worship of Jehovah
was to become alone dominant in Israel.

²⁵⁶ Comp. the examples of laws conflicting with one another, which have been
produced in notes ⁴⁶,⁶¹,²⁰⁰ and elsewhere. It cannot always be assumed that the
laws here mentioned were also introduced into practice ²¹⁷. But this is of less
consequence to the matter before us, since in any case they show the tendency,

in which, according to the judgment of their composers, the modification and development of the existing laws ought to take place.

(158) [259] *How long* after Moses the historians in question lived cannot be certainly determined—(i) because their own lifetime admits of being only generally but not accurately determined—(ii) and chiefly, because the opinions of the learned as to the year in which the Exodus out of Egypt falls, still differ very much from one another. While, for instance, most chronologists, on the ground principally of 1K.vi.1, place that event in the year 1492 B.C., it is placed by LEPSIUS and BUNSEN, according to Egyptian reckoning of time, in the year 1312 or 1320 B.C.—a difference of 180 or 172 years. The interval between Moses and the oldest writer of the B.O., which according to the usual view amounts to ± 500 years, is reduced by these two scholars to ± 320 years. This is not the place to judge their views. The credibility of the datum in 1K.vi.1, viz. that 480 years elapsed from the Exodus to the building of the Temple, is certainly not confirmed by the fact that $480 = 12 \times 40$.

(159) [260] It is self-evident that no rule is here laid down for historical criticism in general, but that the only object is to indicate the points which must be taken into account in criticising in detail the narratives of the Pentateuch.

[261] The complete development of these ideas would be here out of place. I confine myself therefore to a few examples.

Our enquiry has taught us that all the writers of the Pentateuch agree in this point, that Sinai is known as the Mount of the Legislation. But with respect to the extent of this Legislation, and the manner of its publication, our accounts are not in accordance with each other—(see as to E.xix,xxiv, note [28-bll]—as to E.xxv.16, 27,xl.20, note [108]—from which it follows that the B.O. also places the publication of the Decalogue at Sinai, but at the same time that the record about that matter is lost—comp., further, D.iv.9,&c.); while it appears besides that the later legislators, in assigning to Moses the ordinances recorded by themselves, went to work with great freedom. Hence it follows that the fact of the Legislation itself, no doubt, is placed above all suspicion (comp. also Ju.v.5); but the circumstances under which it took place are no longer known with certainty. Further, the accounts respecting the Sinaitic Legislation do not merely contain the record of the current traditions about it, but they are manifestly written either in a priestly or in a prophetical spirit, so that we learn therefrom *first of all* the later (priestly or prophetical) interpretation or view of the labour of Moses, and only *in the second place* that labour itself. It is, however, by no means accidental that, according to. the (priestly) B.O., the lawgiver, when at Sinai, is entirely or almost entirely occupied with the regulation of religious worship, down to the minutest particulars; whereas the laws preserved by the prophetic narrators, especially that of the Book of the Covenant, concern, it is true, religious worship also, but yet, throughout by far the greatest part, stand in connection with domestic and social life. Yet the greater justness of the prophetical view of the Sinaitic Legislation does not guarantee by any means the historical character of the descriptions contained in E.xix,xx,xxiv, since these accounts vary much from each other in details, while there is great agreement between them on the main point—(viz. Jehovah, through Moses as mediator, the

P

Lawgiver of Israel, and the Founder of His Covenant with that people). In proportion as that main-point itself is more purely prophetical, in the same degree is it also more probable that we have here before us its historical *clothing*,—based always on the ground of tradition.   To what extent this opinion is confirmed through the connection between the aforesaid chapters and E.xxxii–xxxiv, appears from note [234], comp. note [22-iii].

As to what regards the patriarchal time, the accounts contained in G.xii–l differ not only in minute points, but in many important main-points, from one another, *e.g.* with reference to the antiquity of the name Jehovah—the manner of worship —Jacob's journey to Haran—his whole relation to Esau—Joseph's being brought to Egypt, &c.   Besides which, other insurmountable difficulties arise through the connection of the chronology of the B.O. with the accounts derived from other sources: comp. *e.g.* Knob., *Gen.*pp.232,233, and notes [88,98] above.   Add to which that the priestly and prophetical authors, even in the treatment of this age of the history, do not belie their own standpoint, and that their representations are influenced by their own peculiar convictions : comp. *e.g.* Chap.XV,XVI.   Must not the consequence be deduced from all this, that both the description of the patriarchal time viewed as a whole, and that of each particular account, remains doubtful, so long as its truth is not expressly confirmed by careful comparison with the historically-guaranteed narratives about later times, sometimes also by analogy ?   What is said above, then, as to the certainty of the *main-points* of this history, must be understood of the Mosaic age in a *still narrower sense*.

In the above, purposely, nothing whatever has been said about G.i–xi, the history of the creation of the world down to the time of the patriarchs.   These chapters, in fact, cannot, in the present state of the enquiry, be regarded any longer as purely historical records about the origin and the earliest history of mankind, however at the base of some accounts—*e.g.* G.vi–viii, even G.xi.1–9—certainly something real must lie.   The two accounts of the Creation, G.i.1–ii.4[a], ii.4[b], &c., however high a value may be ascribed to them from a religious and ethical point of view, cannot be regarded as expressing actual reality, both by reason of the Semitic or even Israelitish character which they betray, and by reason of their mutual contradictions, and because they are irreconcilable with the most certain results of modern science.   All this may be urged also against the historical truth of G.v–xi.   Further, the chronology which is derived from these chapters is untrue, as, among other things, the investigations of Egyptologists have shown.   The genealogies, from which the reckoning of time is derived, are—in spite of their historical form—no historical documents, as, among other things, appears from this, that the lists of the Sethites, G.v, and the Cainites, G.iv.17,18, are composed of the same names, with exception of variations, which are easily explained from the difference of tradition and the theories of the writers.   In the genealogy of the Shemites, G.xi.10, &c.—as also in G.x—appear *lands*, *e.g.* Arphaxad [= Arrapachitis], *towns* (Reu, Serug), *events* (Salah, Eber, Peleg), as names of historical personages ; further, the Elohistic and Jehovistic accounts contradict each other in main points, [22,97,91], &c.   All these phenomena—and so many others, which meet us in reading G.i–xi—lead of necessity to the conclusion that in the first portion of Genesis we have preserved Semitic reminiscences of various kinds, songs, *e.g.* G.iv.23,24, and legends handed down orally for a long time by the Israelitish people, and afterwards worked out in the Israelitish spirit, *e.g.* G.ix.25–27, xi.9—valuable documents, consequently, of the modes of thought and ideas of Israel in the 10th–8th century B.C., but almost useless for the history of earlier times. Who can venture to ascribe historical certainty to the acute conjectures, *e.g.*, of Ew.*G.V.I.*i.342–381?

CHAPTER XXIV.

(160)   [262] For the contrary view appeal is made to Jo.xxiv.26. But 'the words,' which Joshua wrote in the Book of the Law of God, cannot possibly be our Book of Joshua: a document is spoken of, which was designed for the perpetuation of the covenant renewed as in Jo.xxiv. Comp. 1S.x.25.

[263] The Books of *Ezra* and *Nehemiah* form no exception to this rule. It is obvious also that the custom of giving titles to books according to their contents is quite in accordance with the *unpersonal* character of Israelitish historiography. In the narrative itself the person of the writer scarcely ever appears. This being the case, it would be strange if his book had been named after him.

CHAPTER XXV.

(164)   [264] As regards iii,iv, comp. iii.12 (an account which manifestly comes too early), with iv.1ᵇ,2, (where not the least reference is made, as might be expected, to iii.12, though, probably, such reference *is* made in 'the twelve men' of iv.4): see also iv.1,10, (repeated mention of the crossing of the whole people),—iv.11 & 15–18, (repeated mention of the stepping of the priests out of Jordan),—iv.21–24, (which is superfluous after *v.* 6,7.)

In viii also different accounts must have been used, as appears from *v.* 3, &c. comp. with *v.*12, &c,—further, from the break of connection between *v.*30–33 and what precedes and follows.

[265] While, for instance, in x.40–42,xi.16–23,xxi.41–43,xxiii.1, mention is made of a conquest of the whole land and an extermination of all its inhabitants, it appears from xiii.2–5.xv.63,xvi.10,xvii.14–18 that a considerable portion of Canaan remained in the power of the original inhabitants, and was either first conquered afterwards by the separate tribes or not conquered at all. That this contradiction finds its ground in the reference made in the first class of passages to the promises of the Pentateuch, KEIL, *Josh.*§43,*n.*2, is nothing to the purpose. It remains still true that this reference, with the idea therewith connected as to the completeness of the conquest, is wanting in the other passages, which would hardly have been the case if they were from one and the same hand.

Especially worthy of notice is the contradiction between x.36–39,xi.21,22 (conquest of Hebron and Debir and subordinate places, and *complete* extermination of *all* the inhabitants—'he left none remaining,' x.37,39—and ' of *all* the sons of Anak,' xi.21–22,) & xiv.12,xv.13–17, where both Hebron and Debir appear as inhabited by the sons of Anak, who were not driven out till afterwards, partly by Caleb, partly after Joshua's death by Othniel, comp. Ju.i.10,11. KEIL,*Josh.*pp. 198–199, supposes, after HÄVERNICK, that the conquests of Caleb and Othniel took place after Joshua's death, when the Anakim, formerly driven out, had made themselves again masters of Hebron and Debir.

Ans. (i) According to xiv.12, already in Joshua's lifetime—nay, six or seven years after the death of Moses, v.10,—the Anakim were in possession of Hebron; whereas nothing is said in this passage about their being driven out, much less about their being exterminated;

(ii) We are not at liberty to do violence to the plain meaning of the words x.37,39,xi.21,22; in which passages, beyond all doubt, the extermination of *all* the inhabitants of Hebron and Debir is related, even twice over. That this is not probable is admitted: yet it remains indisputable that the writer says it.

Also xxiv.23,26 hardly agrees with what is said as to the religious condition of the people while fighting under Joshua. In order to be persuaded of this, see KEIL's demonstration of the contrary, pp.405,406.

²⁶⁶ This subject is considered in Chap.XXVII,XXVIII. Here I call attention only to this, that in the historical portions of Joshua, i–xii, the original names of the Canaanitish towns are never named in connection with the later usual forms; whereas this is almost the regular practice in xii, &c., *viz.*xiv.15,xv.8–10,13,15,25,60, xviii.13,14,28,xix.8,13.

(165)   ²⁶⁷ Even KEIL, *Einl.*§44,*n.*5, observes that not only the account of Joshua's death, xxiv.29–33, but also xiv.14,xv.13–19,63,xix.47, as having reference to events which took place after Joshua's death, are irreconcilable with the idea that the book was written while he was still living. He sees, however, in the writer, on account of v.1,6, a younger contemporary of Joshua.²⁶⁷

²⁶⁸ Some of these passages leave us quite in uncertainty as to the lifetime of the writer,iv.9,v.9,vii.26,viii.28,29,x.27,xiii.13. The rest are appealed to for evidence that they must have been written before the introduction of the kingly form of government. They are considered below,²⁷⁰.

²⁶⁹ KEIL and others assume that the here-named 'Book of Jashar' was formed by degrees, so that, in later times, even a dirge of David's could be inserted in it. But we cannot conceive such a mode of origination for it: at all events, it conflicts with all analogy. See, further, note ¹⁸.

²⁷⁰ They are the following:—

(i) Jo.v.1,6,—where, especially in v.1, an Israelite speaks, who has passed over the Jordan with Joshua. But the reading in the text, עָד־עָבְרֵנוּ, 'until *our* passing-over,' is in the highest degree uncertain, and seems to be only an erratum, which originated from the eye wandering off to iv.23: in favour of the Keri reading, עָד־עָבְרָם, 'until *their* passing-over,' may be quoted, besides many manuscripts, all the ancient translations. It would also be very strange if the writer, just in this one passage, gave himself out for an eyewitness, but everywhere else spoke of the Israelites in Joshua's time in the third person.

(ii) From Jo.vi.25 it just as little follows that Rahab was still alive in the writer's time, as from xiv.14 that Caleb was still alive. Rather, in both passages mention is made of their *descendants.* The remark that these were still settled among Israel (had Hebron in possession) has a meaning, whereas it was a matter of entire indifference for the reader whether Caleb and Rahab were still living when our Book was written. It appears, however, positively, from the testimony of the Book itself, that it was written after Caleb's death; since xix.47, comp. with Ju.xvii,xviii, shows that fidelity to the worship of Jehovah had already made way for apostacy, which according to xxiv.31, occurred only after the death of the elders who had outlived Joshua. With these, however, Caleb at all events must be reckoned; he was, consequently, already dead when our Book was written. But the explanation of xiv.14, which follows of necessity from this, must, according to analogy, be applied also to vi.25.

(iii) Jo.ix.27,—from which passage it is supposed to appear that the narrative was written both before the foundation of Solomon's Temple, which is set forth in the last words as still future, and before the reign of Saul, who exterminated the Gibeonites, 2S.xxi.2.

Ans. (a) That Saul did not entirely exterminate the Gibeonites appears precisely from 2S.xxi.2ᵃ. Further, it is probable that they belonged to those Canaanites who discharged duties at the building of the Temple, 1K.ix.20,21 1Ch.xxii.2, 2Ch.ii.17,18, and whose descendants still appear after the Captivity Ezr.ii.43,55,58, Neh.vii.46,57,60.

(β) The formula 'unto the place which Jehovah shall choose' is Deuteronomistic [δ¹·¹¹¹], and, if only on this account, can prove nothing for the antiquity of the narrative. Besides, even if the writer lived after Solomon, he could hardly have expressed himself otherwise; if he had written 'which Jehovah *chose*,' then he would have excluded the time preceding the building of the Temple.

(iv) The naming 'Sidon the Great,' Jo.xi.8, xix.28, does not at all show that our Book was written before the time of David, that is, before Tyre got the superiority over Zidon. Was, then, the circumstance [of Zidon's greatness] so insignificant, that it could only have been known to a *contemporary* writer?

(v) In Jo.xiii.4–6 the district inhabited by the Zidonians is regarded as Israelitish territory, and a conquest of it is foretold; and after David, who made a covenant with Hiram, this expectation could no longer exist.

Ans. Certainly, after the time of David (such an expectation could no longer *arise*; but it remained, nevertheless, a fact, that it had once existed, and *theoretically* Israel still laid claim continually to that part of Canaan which was inhabited by the Phœnicians. Kᴇɪʟ forgets also, Josh.p.xxxiv,xxxv, that *v.*2–7 are not words of the writer, but are placed in the mouth of Jehovah, so that nothing can be properly inferred from them, from his point of view, with respect to the writer's lifetime.

(vi) Jo.xv.63, comp. Ju.i.21, must have been written after the conquest of Jerusalem, mentioned in Ju.i.8, but before the capture of that city by David, 2S.v.

Ans. We shall see below that xv.63 is most probably a note, taken over by the compiler out of the same document, which lies at the basis of Ju.i. It may, in point of fact, have been written before David's time. But this is not necessary; at all events, under David's reign, and long afterwards, Jebusites were still living in Jerusalem, 2S.xxiv.16,18, 1K.ix.20,21, Ezr.ix.1,2, Zech.ix.7,—a fact which a later writer might very well regard as a consequence of the inability of Benjamin (or Judah) to drive out the Jebusites shortly after Joshua.

(vii) Jo.xvi.10, comp. Ju.i.29, must have been written before the conquest of
Gezer by the Egyptian king, 1K.ix.16: at all events, this latter is said to have
slain the inhabitants, so that from that moment the payment of tribute must have
ceased, and so ' the dwelling of Canaanites in the midst of Ephraim.'

Ans. But if the Canaanites at Gezer had already paid tribute to Israel before
the time of Solomon, then Pharaoh would have done but a slight service to his
son-in-law, when he conquered this town and slew the inhabitants. Probably, the
Philistines were originally lords over Gezer, 2S.v.25, 1Ch.xiv.16,xx.4, and thus
Pharaoh's conquest was regarded as a victory over them, the hereditary foes of
Israel. Probably, the slaughter of the inhabitants must not be understood in such
a sense that no Canaanite whatever survived: on the contrary, it is precisely the
survivors who appear here as tributaries. The note in question, therefore, places
us rather *in* the time of Solomon than before it.

CHAPTER XXVI.

(166)   [271] We confine ourselves in the notes on this section to producing some examples:
the more full development of what is here set forth is given in Chap.XXVII,
XXVIII.

Moses is spoken of as lawgiver and leader of the people in i.7,13–15,iv.10,12,
viii.31–35,ix.24,xi.12,15,20,23,xii.6,xiii.8,xiv.2,&c.,xvii.4,xviii.7,xx.2,xxi.2,8,xxii.2–9
xxiii.6. It is remarkable that the name *Moses* occurs in Joshua 34 times, on the
contrary in Judges only 4 times, in 1&2S. only twice.

[272] See *e.g.* G.xii.7,xiii.15,xv.18,xvii.8,xxvi.3, &c.,—further, E.vi.4, and, in
general, all the laws, which are expressly said to have been given with a view to
the approaching settlement of Israel in Canaan, *e.g.* L.xviii.3,24,xxv.2, &c., &c.
Comp. above notes [21,23,234] and Chap.XXIII.

[273] See *e.g.* Jo.xi.23, xxi.41–43, and elsewhere.

(167)   [274] Jo.i.3, &c., 6, &c., 17,18,iii.7,10,iv.14,v.2, &c., ix.14ᵇ,xi.15–20,xxii, &c.

CHAPTER XXVII.

(169)   [275] See below [277]. In the list there given of Deuteronomistic formulæ lies at the
same time the evidence of the uniformity of the phraseology, which characterises
i–xii, and xxi.41–xxiv.28.

[276] Comp.ii with vi.17,22,25,—iii.7,i.17,18, with iv.14,—ii.10 with iv.23,—vi.18,
where preparation is already made for vii, especially for *v.*26 ; vi,viii are implied
in ix, as are vi,viii,ix in x; comp. xi.19 with ix,—xii.7 with xi.17. Generally it
may be asserted that no single narrative can be missed out of i–xii, except,
perhaps, viii.30–35, which section, moreover, through its phraseology, appears
manifestly to be from the same hand as the rest, though its being placed between

viii.29 and ix.1 might awaken the suspicion that it is an interpolated passage. However, this also is explained from the connection of these verses with D.xxvii. With this remark, again, the use of different accounts concerning the same fact by the author of i–xii, to which attention is drawn above, [264] is very intelligible. This only may be regarded as certain, that there are good grounds for assigning i–xii to *one sole author*,—not to a compiler,—still less to more than one author.

70) [277] Our object will be best attained if we enumerate the Deuteronomistic formulæ in the order of the passages in which they occur for the first time in the Book of Joshua. When whole verses from Joshua and Deuteronomy agree with each other, or are even similar in contents, we have simply indicated them beside one another :—

(i) Jo.i.1–9 = D.xxxi.1–8 ;

(ii) Jo.i.3 = D.xi.24 ;

(iii) 'be strong and of a good courage,' Jo.i.6,7,9,18,x.25 = D.xxxi.6,7,23 ;

(iv) 'make to inherit,' Jo.i.6 = D.i.38,iii.28,xix.3,xxxi.7 ;

(v) 'observe to do,' Jo.i.7,8,xxii.5,xxiii.6 = D.v.32, see note [50·v] ;

(vi) 'on the right hand and on the left,' Jo.i.7,xxiii.6 = D.v.32,xvii.11,20, xxviii.14 ;

(vii) 'be not afraid (do not fear), neither be thou dismayed,' Jo.i.9,viii.1,x.25 = D.i.21,29,xxxi.6,8 ;

(viii) שׁוֹטְרִים, 'officers,' Jo.i.10,iii.2, [viii.33,xxiii.2,xxiv.1] = D.i.15, &c., see note [50] ;

(ix) 'judges and officers,' Jo.viii.33,xxiii.2,xxiv.1 = D.xvi.18 ;

(x) Jo.i.11 = D.iii.18, &c., see note [50·v] ;

(xi) Jo.i.12–15 (comp. with iv.12) = D.iii.18–20 ;

(xii) 'make to rest,' Jo.i.13,15,xxii.4,xxiii.1 = D.iii.20,xii.10,xxv.19 ;

(xiii) 'rebel against the voice of,' Jo.i.18 = D.i.26,43,ix.23 ;

(xiv) 'utterly destroyed,' with reference to Sihon and Og, Jo.ii.10 = D.ii.34,iii.6 ;

(xv) 'the heart melted,' Jo.ii.11,v.1,vii.5 = D.i.28,xx.8 ;

(xvi) 'in the heavens above and on the earth beneath,' Jo.ii.11 = D.iv.39 ;

(xvii) 'the Priests the Levites,' Jo.iii.3,viii.33 = D.xvii.9,18, &c., see note [61.i] ;

(xviii) the Priests, (not the Levites) bearers of the Ark, Jo.iii.6,8,13,14,17, iv,vi.6,12 = D.xxxi.9 ;

(xix) 'so as to leave none (left) escaped, Jo.viii.22,x.28,30,33,37,39,40,xi.8 = D.iii.3 (comp. ii.34,N.xxi.35) ;

(xx) Jo.viii.29,x.26 = D.xxi.23 ;

(xxi) Jo.viii.30–35 = D.xxvii ;

(xxii) אָז with imperf. Jo.viii.30,x.12,xxii.1 = D.iv.41 ;

(xxiii) הִשְׁמִיד, 'destroy,' Jo.vii.12,ix.24,xi.14,20,xxiii.15,xxiv.8 = D.i.27,ii.12, 21,22,23, and *passim* ;

(xxiv) 'the place which Jehovah will choose,' Jo.ix.27 = D.xii.11, &c., see note [61.iii] ;

(xxv) 'Jehovah fighting for Israel,' Jo.x.14,42,xxiii.3,10 = D.iii.22 ;

(xxvi) 'every breath,' Jo.x.40,xi.11,14 = D.xx.16 ;

(xxvii) 'many days,' Jo.xi.18,xxiii.1,xxiv.7 = D.i.46,ii.1,xx.19 ;

(xxviii) Jo.xii.4 = D.iii.11 ;

(xxix) 'cleave unto Jehovah,' Jo.xxii.5,xxiii.8 = D.iv.4, &c. (note ⁴⁸,—the formulæ there enumerated recur, many of them, in Jo.xxii.5,xxiii.10,11,13,15,16, *e.g.* וְשָׁמַר 'take heed to yourselves,' 'love Jehovah,' 'the good (ground) land';

(xxx) Jo.xxiv.9,10 = D.xxiii.4,5 ;

(xxxi) Jo.xxiv.11 = D.vii.1 ;

(xxxii) Jo.xxiv.12 = D.vii.20 ;

(xxxiii) Jo.xxiv.13 = D.vi.10,11 ;

(xxxiv) Jo.xxiv.17 = D.vi.22,xxix.16 ;

(xxxv) Jo.xxiv.20 = D.xxviii.63.

Upon a careful reading of Deuteronomy and Joshua it will be seen that in the above list only the most obvious points of agreement are inserted. It teaches at the same time—what cannot appear from a mere enumeration like this—that the style of Joshua, especially in the addresses, Jo.i.xxii–xxiv, agrees entirely with that of Deuteronomy.

²⁷⁸ These are summed up by KEIL, §42,n.4, Josh.p.xxvii, &c., DE WETTE, *Einl.*§.170. They are the following:

(i) יְרִיחוֹ, 'Jericho,' Jo.ii.1,2,3,iii.16, &c. (27 times)—not יְרִחוֹ, as in N.xxii.1, xxvi.3,63, &c.;

(ii) שֵׁמַע, 'report,' Jo.vi.27,ix.9,—not שֹׁמַע, as in G.xxix.13, E.xxiii.1, N.xiv.15, D.ii.25.

(iii) קַנּוֹא, 'jealous,' Jo.xxiv.19,—not קַנָּא, as in E.xx.5,xxxiv.14, D.iv.24,v.9, vi.15.

(iv) יְרֹא, 'fearing,' Jo.xxii.25,—not יְרָאָה, as in D.iv.10, &c.;

(v) 'mighty men of strength,' Jo.i.14,vi.2,viii.3,—not 'sons of strength,' as in D.iii.18 ;

(vi) 'His blood be on his head,' Jo.ii.19, comp. Ez.xxxiii.4,—not 'his blood be on him,' L.xx.9,11–13,16 ;

(vii) In Joshua are wanting all the so-called archaisms of the Pentateuch. The following also are peculiar forms of expression in Joshua:—

(viii) 'Lord of all the earth,' iii.11,13 ;

(ix) 'treasury of Jehovah,' 'treasury of the House of Jehovah,' vi.19,24.

DE WETTE notices these signs of later phraseology in Joshua :—

(x) אוֹתְכֶם, xxiii.15, אוֹתִי, xiv.12, אוֹתָנוּ, xxii.19 ; but he himself points to L.xv.15,24, where similar phraseology occurs ;

(xi) נְכָסִים, 'riches,' xxii.8,—only besides in 2Ch.i.11,12, Eccl.v.19(18),vi.2 ;

(xii) The grammatical peculiarities in xiv.8,x.24.

²⁷⁹ With reference to many of the phenomena above noticed, this must be more definitely shown. As regards the archaisms of the Pentateuch, since the continued use of these must be ascribed to the compiler, Chap.XXII, it is natural to suppose that he confined them purposely to the Thora, in which they had once been legitimated by custom. The *scriptio plena* and *defectiva* in יְרִיחוֹ & יְרִחוֹ (for which should be read, probably, יְרֵחוֹ) must certainly be laid to the account rather of the Masoretes than of the original authors of the books. So too much weight cannot be assigned to the difference between שֵׁמַע & שֹׁמַע, since it concerns only the vowels, and just as little to קַנּוֹא & קַנָּא (קַנֹּא?). The infinitive יְרֹא occurs, besides Jo.xxii.25,

only in 1.S.xviii.29: the use of this form cannot in any case be reckoned as a sign of the development of the language. Just as little can the formula 'his blood be on his head,' which is only somewhat more common than the expression of the Law, 'his blood be upon him.' Between the expressions 'sons of strength' and 'mighty men of strength' there exists a difference of meaning: the first means 'men fit for war, warriors,' the second 'valiant warriors.' Since, further, the Pentateuch knows the word גִּבּוֹר, 'mighty man,' G.x.8,9, and applies it already to Jehovah, D.x.17, the absence of the last-named expression must be regarded as accidental.

[289] We must probably judge thus as to the expression 'Lord of all the earth,' Jo.iii.11,13, and 'treasury of the house of Jehovah,' Jo.vi.19,24; but the comparison of 'the Lord Jehovah,' E.xxiii.17,xxxiv.23, 'House of Jehovah,' E.xxiii.19, and 'treasury,' D.xxviii.12, teaches how little weight can be assigned to these few expressions. Also in iii,iv, (& viii) other evidences occur for the use of written records.[254] So, too, the definitions of time must in iv.19,v.10, have been derived by the Deuteronomist from another document than that from which, e.g., v.2–9 is taken. This appears from the following phenomena:—

(i) From the absence of accurate definitions of time in the account of the conquest, from which usage these two verses strangely depart; comp. e.g. Jo.xi.18,xxiii.1, xxiv.7.

(ii) From the contradiction between these two verses and v.2–9. The formula 'at that time,' v.2, in this connection refers back to iv.19; so that only on the eleventh day of the first month could a beginning have been made with the circumcision; and according to v.10, it must have been already finished on the fourteenth day. But this is a complete absurdity, if we take into account the great number of Israelites who were all uncircumcised. It is much more probable that v.2–9 originally stood in no connection with iv.19 and v.10.

(iii) In v.10 the words 'and the children of Israel encamped in Gilgal' are quite superfluous after v.8, where mention is already made of the people 'abiding in their places in the camp.' Comp. further notes [281,282].

[281] Most probably the two verses just discussed, iv.19,v.10, together with v.11,12, were derived from the B.O. In favour of this view may be adduced, besides the accurate definitions of time, the expressions 'the first month,' iv.19 (to which 'the month,' v.10, refers back), 'on this selfsame day,' v.11, קָלוּי='parched corn,' v.11 (as in L.ii.14),—also the agreement between v.12 and E.xvi.35. No clear traces of the B.O. appear anywhere else in the first portion of Joshua. From this, however, it does not by any means follow that this Book mentioned nothing else about the whole conquest, except the passage through the Jordan and the celebration of the Passover. It is not only possible, but even probable, from the analogy of what has happened in the Pentateuch, that the narrative of the B.O. has been obliged, on account of its conciseness, to make room for the more ample accounts derived from the other sources.

Also a narrative of the B.O. appears to be at the basis of Jo.xxii. This appears from מַטֶּה, 'tribe,' v.1,14, 'all the congregation of the children of Israel,' v.12, 'prince,' v.14,—also from v.9,19,29, where reference seems to be made to xviii.1. The more full development of this last evidence must be reserved for note [296].

KNOBEL's attempt, N.D.J.pp.605,606, to indicate the sources from which the

Deuteronomist drew in Jo.i–xii seems not at all satisfactory. See KUENEN, in
Godg. Bijd. (1862) pp.353,354.

(171)   [202] Comp. Chap.XXVI and the passages cited in note [274]. This tendency of the
narrative is especially visible in i.16–18, where the trans-Jordanic tribes, as in the
name of all, express the feeling of the true Israelite towards the theocratic leader:
and so in iv.14 (comp. iii.7) we read that the conduct of the people corresponded
to this declaration.

Not less remarkable are those portions of the narrative, which at the first glance
seem to conflict with that faithfulness of the people towards the Mosaic Law, which
is usually placed in the foreground. In vii the transgression of the one man,
Achan. is punished by the defeat of the whole people at Ai, in order that the
purity of Israel may be the better preserved: see especially *v.*11, &c. In ix the
people neglect to consult Jehovah, which is mentioned expressly as exceptional
conduct on their part, *v.*14[b]; immediately they are punished for it, as appears
from the sequel of the narrative. At the same time this would serve (i) to account
for the Gibeonites being preserved, in contradiction to the Divine command for
the extermination of the inhabitants of Canaan, and (ii) to set in clear light the
faithfulness of Joshua and of the princes of the people to the oath which they had
taken, *v.*18, &c.

Further, xxii deserves attention. The great zeal of the Israelites for the
maintenance of the unity of worship, see *v.*16, &c. *v.*22, &c., is in any case surprising; and inasmuch as the history of the time of the Judges, nay, even that of
the following centuries till the time of Hezekiah, testifies so plainly to the contrary,
it is most probably not historical. We, certainly, do not wander far from the truth
if we assert that the writer was more concerned with warning his own contemporaries against a sin, of which they were continually guilty, than with giving them
a completely correct account of the religious condition of the people under Joshua.
We are the more justified in this opinion, since the practice of idolatry is
manifestly implied in xxiv.14,15,23. (What KEIL, *Josh.*p.402, produces in order
to explain *v.*14,15,23 serves only to show that these passages do not agree with
the point of view assumed by him, and, consequently, he cannot allow them to have
the meaning, which, however, they plainly express.) It is possible that the
Deuteronomist is here following closely his sources, and that as a consequence of
this must be explained the contradiction which exists between the whole contents
of xxii and the verses quoted from xxiv. Yet this contradiction seems very
difficult to be understood, if it is not well observed what is the proper point of
view of the writer both here and in xxii. A warning against idolatry is just as
suitable in his mouth, and just as well adapted to the necessities of his contemporaries, as an exhortation to the maintenance of the one national Sanctuary.
Hence he omits neither the former nor the latter, without troubling himself as to
whether his historical picture contains in this manner elements conflicting with
each other.

Again, xxiv.26 also, where mention is made of a 'Sanctuary of Jehovah' *at
Shechem*, conflicts with xxii, and must be explained from the dependence of the
writer on his sources. The conjecture of THASIUS, pp.152,341, KEIL, and others,

that the place is meant where Abram (according to G.xii.6,7) first sacrificed in Canaan, is not probable. Yet, notwithstanding, it remains a fact that it is here called 'the Sanctuary of Jehovah,' and that is exactly what, after reading xxii, we should in nowise expect. As to the inferences to be drawn from the above, with respect to the credibility of the narratives generally, comp. Chap.XXIX.

CHAPTER XXVIII.

(173) ²⁸³ Comp. notes ²⁸⁶,²⁷⁷. The Deut. formulæ therein enumerated are entirely wanting in the geographical portion of Joshua,—among others also the expression, 'the Priests the Levites,' for which 'the sons of Aaron, the Priests,' is used in xxi.19; see also notes ²⁸⁶,²⁸⁷. Here also I observe that of the two words which denote *tribe*, the one, מַטֶּה, is *never* used in Deuteronomy, *very seldom* in the Deuteronomistic portions of Joshua,vii.1,18,xxii.1,14,—(and there, probably, derived by the Deuteronomist from his authorities)—but, on the contrary, is employed in the geographical passages *passim*, e.g. xiii.15,24,29,xiv.1–4,xv.1,20,21,xvi.8,xvii.1,xviii.11,21,xix.1, 8,23,24,31,39,40,48,51, &c., just as in the B.O., e.g. N.i, &c., while שֵׁבֶט is *very usual* (18 times) in Deuteronomy,—in the B.O. *less usual*, e.g. E.xxviii.21,xxxix.14, N.iv.18.xviii.2,xxxii.33,—in the Deuteronomistic passages of Joshua, again, *passim*, e.g. i.12,iii.12,iv.2,4,5,8,12,vii.14,16,—on the contrary, in the *geographical portions* it occurs *comparatively rarely* (e.g. in xxi.16, and in the mixed passages of which we shall speak more fully in Chap.XXIX, *viz.* xiii.7,14,29,33,xviii.2,4,7).

²⁸⁴ Comp. note ²⁶⁵.

²⁸⁵ This is so obviously manifest that it seems not to require any further development. If the Pentateuch, or, at all events, the B.O., had been Mosaic, we should then of necessity suppose that prescriptions are imparted in it, the carrying out of which could only be related first by a later writer. Now, however, that it is certain that the oldest portions of the B.O. could not have been committed to writing before the time of Solomon, it is also most probable that, together with the prescriptions themselves, is mentioned also the performance of them, which had then taken place. Let it be noticed also that the designation of *definite* towns as free cities and Levitical towns, and so, too, the description of the territory of the separate tribes, belongs to the *Legislation* just as much as the direction that there should be six free cities and forty-eight Levitical towns, or that Canaan should be divided by lot among the tribes. It may thus be rightly asserted that the B.O. would be incomplete if it did not comprise, besides the *general* directions in N.xxxiv,xxxv, the *special* prescriptions also contained in Jo.xiv, &c.

²⁸⁶ Comp. Jo.xiv.1,xvii.4,xix.51,xxi.1, where Eleazar appears as Joshua's assistant in the partition of the land, with N.xxxiv.17.. The 'princes' here named, v.18, &c., are mentioned likewise in the above-cited passages of Joshua: comp. also Jo.xvii 3–6 (Zelophehad's daughter) with N.xxvii.1–11,xxxvi; comp. finally the two chapters, Jo.xx,xxi, (see xiv.3–5), with N.xxxv.

Also in Joshua the same expressions are used as in Numbers, e.g.:—

נָחַל, 'make to inherit,' in Piel, Jo.xiii.32,xiv.1,xix.51, N.xxxiv.29, for which in Jo.i.6 and in Deuteronomy, ²⁷⁷,¹ᵛ, הִנְחִיל, is used.

מִגְרָשׁ, 'suburbs,' Jo.xiv.4,xxi.2,3,8,&c. N.xxxv.2,3,4,5,7, L.xxv.34,—

בִּשְׁגָגָה, 'unawares,' Jo.xx.3.9, N.xxxv.11,15; comp. v.6,9 with N.xxxv.12,25,28.

Further, in Jo.xx also there occur formulæ derived from D.xix.1–10, e.g., בִּבְלִי־דַעַת, 'ignorantly,' D.xix.4, Jo.xx.3, 'and not hating him yesterday and the day before,' D.xix.4,6, Jo.xx.5, which are not used in N.xxxv, on which account it has been assumed in the text that Jo.xx.1–6 is, indeed, in part, but not entirely, derived from the B.O. (by the compiler of Joshua, comp. Chap.XXIX).

[227] Besides the proofs already produced [228,229], here is to be noticed the use of קִנְיָן, 'substance,' Jo.xiv.4, L.xxii.11,— מַחֲצִית, 'half,' Jo.xxi.25, E.xxx.13,15,23, N. xxxi.29,30,42,47, and elsewhere in the B.O.,—lastly, and especially, the whole style, which agrees both generally with the manner of the B.O., and particularly with N.xxxiv.1–12. To this must be added also the custom of concluding the enumeration of the towns of the different tribes with a subscription, Jo.xvi.8,xviii.20,28, xix.8,16,23,31,39,48, of which examples are found also in Leviticus and Numbers.

(174)   [226] It may be thought that the author, who cannot have lived before, and probably lived after, Solomon's reign, [225,229] must have drawn the *whole* account of the partition of the land from older records. It is, however, much more probable that he went to work in this part of his work just as in the rendering of the Mosaic institutions [227,258],—that is, that he described the territory of each tribe as it existed in his own time, but as it had existed also, with slight modifications, since the conquest. From this he derived the right to ascribe to Joshua the designation of the boundaries of each tribal territory.

[228] Upon xvii.14–18 comp. Ew. *G.V.I*.ii.p.315, &c., where the proofs are produced, which may be adduced for the high antiquity of these sections.

xiv.6–15 is related to N.xiii,xiv, in respect of form as well as contents. Comp. 'follow wholly after Jehovah,' v.8,9,14 with N.xiv.24, (N.xxxii.11,12, D.i.36), and 'bring him word again,' v.7, with N.xiii.26, (D.i.22,25, Jo.xxii.32). The narrative, however, which is contained in N.xiv,xv, is composed of two documents,[159] of which one is Jehovistic; probably these two formulæ are actually out of this last. Hence it follows, immediately, that very different judgments may be formed as to the origin of Jo.xiv.6–15. These verses may have been adopted already into his work by the author of the B.O., supposing this not to have been the original writer, Solomon's contemporary, but one of the later manipulators of the Book. But they may just as well have been taken over by the compiler of Joshua from a Jehovistic record, which contained also the conquest of the land. These two views differ less from one another than may appear at the first glance. We shall, in fact, see presently (i) that the geographical portion of Joshua cannot have belonged in its whole extent to the *Solomonic* B.O., and (ii) that the compiler of Joshua himself was one of the Jerusalem priests or Levites,—so that the distance between him and the author of the geographical passages is not so great as we might now imagine.

[290] Among these similar passages is not included Jo.xxiv.28–31, comp. with Ju.ii.6–9. This last passage, in fact, has been taken over by the compiler of Judges from Joshua. This supposition cannot be applied to any of the other parallel passages, as has been convincingly shown, among others, by BERTH, *R.u.R.*pp.xxiv, xxv, and in the commentary on Ju.i; comp. note [291]. As regards Ju.ii.6–9, BERTH. p.55, &c., is of opinion that it is from the same author as Jo.xxiv.28–31; and he in general regards the compiler of Judges as being identical with that of Joshua. But

it would be very strange, if the compiler of the Pentateuch and Joshua brought also into its present form the Book of Judges, that he should have made no attempt to get rid of the contradictions between this Book and the Thora.

[291] With reference to these similar passages, three views may be adduced, which may also be held with modifications. It may be thought, for instance,—

(i) That the compiler of Judges (or author of Ju.i) took them from Joshua (Stäh.p.102);

(ii) That the compiler of Joshua (or the author of the B.O.) derived them from the Book of Judges (Maur, *Commentary,* Häv.I.p.57, &c., in part also Bertheau);

(iii) That the compiler of Joshua (or the author of the B.O.) took them from the same source, from which they were taken into the Judges (Keil.)

Against the *first* view stands the difficulty, that the passages in question in Ju.i occur together and in a good connection ; while in Jo.xiv–xix they are scattered here and there, and are so little connected with what precedes and follows, that they might be absent without any damage to the narrative. Further, the relation between Jo.xix.47 and Ju.xvii,xviii is decidedly opposed to this view.

The *second* view is negatived by the observation that the Book of Judges in its present form supposes the existence of Joshua, both by its whole contents, and especially by i.1,ii.6–9. Hence it follows that the Book of Joshua cannot possibly be younger than Judges, but must be perhaps older or contemporary with it ; in no case, therefore, can we suppose a borrowing from Judges.

There remains, therefore, only the *third* view, which has found a defender, among others, in Keil, *On the Parallel Passages in the Books of Joshua and Judges, Rudelbach u. Guericke's Zeitschrift,* 1846,p.3, &c. It does not differ much from the opinion of Bertheau,[290] according to which the passages in question were inserted first in the Book of Joshua, when it was no longer regarded as forming one whole with the Book of Judges. The original connection between Judges and Joshua seems to me very doubtful. What Bertheau, consequently, upon this ground ascribes to a later hand, I think must be assigned to the compiler of Joshua ; but he cannot have made use here of our Book of Judges, which did not then exist, but drew out of the same source, which was also in the hands of the compiler of Judges. Why the insertion of these passages is assigned to the compiler of Joshua and not to the author of the B.O., appears from what has been remarked above in judging of the first view : they are too little connected with the account of the partition of the land by Joshua, to allow of our ascribing their insertion to the actual author of that account.

(175) [292] Objections may, in fact, be brought against the credibility of xxi.1–40 [42], which appear irreconcilable with the notion of the high antiquity of that chapter.

(i) It is strange that the towns of the priests, *v.*4,10–19, should fall just exactly in the territory of Judah, Benjamin, and Simeon, *i. e.* in the later kingdom of Judah, close to the Temple. Just as probable as it is that after the division of the kingdom the descendants of Aaron settled down gradually in Judah, so unmeaning and unnatural would this settlement have been in Joshua's time.

(ii) It is not less strange that to 'the priests, the sons of Aaron,' not less than thirteen towns, *v.*4,19, with meadows for cattle belonging to them, are assigned. Aaron had, after the death of Nadab and Abihu, L.x, only *two* sons, Eleazar and Ithamar, E.vi.23. N.xxvi.60,61. During the conquest Eleazar was still alive, though his son Phinehas was already in the prime of manhood, N.xxv.7,8, Jo.xxii.

How is it possible that Aaron's descendants at the partition of the land were numerous enough to people *thirteen* towns, whether entirely, or in part, as Keil supposes? Nothing is more plain than that here a later state of things is transferred to Joshua's time. This, however, could not have been done so easily in Solomon's days as long afterwards; for which reason we assign this anachronism rather to a later manipulator than to the first author of the B.O.

In connection with these phenomena another question also presents itself. We observed above [217,229], that some prescriptions of the B.O. existed only in theory, and were never carried out in practice. Must we, perhaps, think thus as to the Levitical and priestly cities, especially the former? The manner in which the Levites are treated in the Book of Deuteronomy [1.1], gives rise to this suspicion, and what is above said, with reference to the complete credibility of Jo.xxi, does not tend to dismiss it. Here, however, is not the place to dwell further on this point.

As regards Jo.xxii, if the account of the B.O., which we find therein retouched by the Deuteronomist,[281] agreed in main points with the present narrative, it must have belonged, by comparison of L.xvii.1-9, to the later portions of the B.O.[229].

CHAPTER XXIX.

(176) [283] Maintained by De Wette, *Einl.* §168-170, and the writers there cited.

[284] Upon the contradiction between the historical and the geographical portion, see note [268]. It might be supposed that the Deuteronomist either did not remark this contradiction, or did not consider it incapable of solution. But this supposition is not probable, and ought only then to be adopted, if it appeared plainly, from the actual words of the Deuteronomist, that he himself had inserted the geographical portions. But this does not by any means appear. In Jo.i.6 it is only said that Joshua should *make* Israel *inherit* the land; this promise was already fulfilled when Joshua, according to xi.23,xii.7, gave the land to Israel as an *inheritance* or *possession*. There is, however, one passage in the Deuteronomistic portion which seems to point to the partition of the land by lot, viz. Jo.xxiii.4. But this shows only that the Deuteronomist had knowledge of this partition, and that also the *partial* extermination of the Canaanites was not unknown to him. Of the one and the other he made mention, in order to connect therewith the admonitions against intermarrying with Canaanites. But it does not follow from this that he must have inserted in his work the copious accounts contained in xiv-xxi. Hävernick also remarks, II.i.p.25, that xi.23,xii.6,7, are quite sufficient for the object of the author of i-xii, and that xiii-xxi appear as a kind of episode. According to him xxiii.1 points back—not to xiii.1, but—to xi.18,23.

[285] xxiv.29,30 appears to be derived from the B.O., by reason of the accurate definition of time in *v.*29, and the connection between *v.*30 and xix.49,50.

*v.*32 stands in connection with G.l.24-26, E.xiii.19, that is, with a later Elohistic and a Jehovistic account. That the document from which it, as well as *v.*31,33, was derived must have been the work of the Deuteronomist does not in any way appear. Further, the origin of short notices of this kind cannot be pointed out with certainty; and thus this second ground of proof obtains significance and force only in connection with the third.

[286] These phenomena are the following:—

In xiii appear plain traces of the B.O., but also of Deuteronomy. Thus v.2–6 seems to be derived from the B.O., on account of its contents, which do not agree with the Deuteronomistic view of Joshua's conquests ; also the phraseology in v.6—compare N.xxxiv.2,3, but also Jo.xxiii.4—points to that document. Yet v.1—comp. Jo.xxiii.1,2,G.xxiv.1—and v.7 (where שֶׁבֶט, not מַטֶּה, occurs,²⁸³) show that the compiler, whoever he may have been, has not inserted the account of the B.O. unchanged, but has retouched it. Now v.8–14 is attached to v.7 very awkwardly ; undoubtedly, עִמּוֹ, v.8, means properly, with that half of Manasseh, *which was to be settled on this side of Jordan*, since this had been spoken of in v.7 : yet it must signify, according to the writer's view, the *other* half, settled in the trans-Jordanic land. The writer is manifestly employed in naming the dwelling-places of the trans-Jordanic tribes. But the Deuteronomist in the preceding chapter, xii.1–6, and the author of the B.O., in N.xxxii.33–42, had already said all that was necessary about this. It is therefore probable that another writer is here speaking, *i.e.* a compiler, distinct from the Deuteronomist. He derived his matter, both for v.8–14 and for v.15–33, partly from the two passages aforesaid, partly (and especially v.15–32) from the B.O., that may very well have mentioned *in this connection* the boundaries and towns of the trans-Jordanic tribes, *though not in this form.* This last appears, among other things, from v.29, (שְׁבָט, and the whole involved construction), and v.30,31, (comp. with D.iii.14, see note ³¹·¹¹¹). On the other hand, v.21,22, point back manifestly to N.xxxi.8 (B.O.) ; v.14,33, are almost verbally derived from D.xviii.1,2, and must so much the more certainly have been introduced here by the compiler, inasmuch as the same idea, though in other words, is expressed also in xiv.4, (comp. N.xxxv.1–8, Jo.xxi.1, &c.) Such repetitions justify certainly the supposition, that we have before us in xiii a summary out of different sources, composed by a compiler, sometimes in an awkward fashion.

Also in xviii.1–10 we find the peculiarities of the B.O. mixed throughout with those of Deuteronomy : in v.2,4,7, שֶׁבֶט,—in v.7 great agreement with Jo.xiii.14,33, and Deut. ideas about the Levites, ' for the Levites have no inheritance in the midst of you, *because the priesthood of Jehovah is his* (Levi's) *inheritance,*'⁶¹·¹—v.10 מַחְלְקֹת, 'divisions,' xi.23,xii.7. On the other hand, we have in v.1, וַּיִכָּבֵשׁ, ' he subdued,' N.xxxii.22,29, and ' all the congregation of the children of Israel,' one of the very common formulæ of the B.O. ; again, in the sequel, xix.51,xxi.2,—also in the mixed passage, xxii.9,12, comp. note ²⁸¹,—the removal of the head-quarters to Shiloh, xviii.1,8–10, is continually understood. Both these phenomena, again, are readily explained on the supposition that an account of the B.O. retouched by the compiler of the book lies before us in xviii.1–10.

We have already spoken of xx.1–6.²⁸⁶

²⁹⁷ From the identity [of form and contents] it should follow, comp. Chap.XXII, that the Book of Joshua also was brought into its present form shortly before the Babylonish Captivity, by a Jerusalem priest or Levite. Although for this view no certain proofs can be alleged, yet on the other hand there exist against it no serious objections, so that it may be regarded beforehand as admissible. In this we differ from MASIUS, SPINOZA, c.viii,ix, CLERICUS, MAURER, HERZFELD, i.287, who set the Book after or in the Babylonish Captivity. It is true, it must be allowed to HERZ.ii.25, that passages, such as i.8,v.15 seem to place us at the time of the Captivity ; yet they give us no sufficient certainty. If, further, on the ground of these passages, HERZFELD's view is to be preferred, then this must lead to some

change being made in the whole idea which we have formed of the origin of
Joshua. The activity of the compiler would then not be confined to merely collecting existing records; it must have included a new retouching of them. Such a
retouching must then be assumed to have taken place in i.8,v.13, &c., and especially
in xxii.7,8,[278] and xxiii, comp. note [294]—in which passages ideas and expressions
are met with, which are connected in the closest manner with those of Deuteronomy, yet at the same time may seem to be somewhat further developed,
or which, *e.g.* those of xxiii, seem to imply the contents also of the geographical
portions, which is by no means the case with the other Deuteronomistic passages.
But, indeed, it cannot be thought strange that with reference to such subordinate
points no certain statement of opinion can be ventured.

(179)   [296] Comp. here note [298]. It might be inferred from Jo.xviii.9 that, at least, the
conclusion of the account about the partition of the land was composed from *contemporary* records. But let these points be observed :—

(i) xviii.1–10, at least in its present form, proceeds from the Compiler.

(ii) The 'book' there mentioned was in any case something quite different from
the document contained in xviii.11–xix.51. At most this last might be a product
of some manipulation of that 'book;' but then the manipulator may have modified
the contents according to the state of things, which he knew in his own time.

(iii) This possibility assumes a high degree of probability, if we consider that
the accurate discrimination of different times is by no means congenial to the spirit
of the Israelitish historian. This will be seen if we compare 1Ch.vi.54–81 with
Jo.xxi.9–42; it will be plain that the Chronicler has set the names of towns, which
were usual in his own time, in place of the elder, and perhaps also has modified
here and there what in his days had undergone change. MOVERS, *Text der Chron.*
p.65,&c., attributes many of these variations to mere changes of letters.

(180)   [299] In Jo.v.10,xxii (partly from the B.O.), xxiv.31, we find already the same idea,
as to the religious feeling of Joshua's contemporaries, which we find in the
Deuteronomistic narrative. Comp. Ew., *G.V.I.*ii.305,&c.

[300] It is sufficient here to point to passages such as i.8,&c., where the piety of
Joshua and his contemporaries is distinctly set forth as piety *according to the Law*,
i.e. resulting from the consideration and practice of the Mosaic Thora. The historical truth of this picture stands or falls with the Mosaic origin of the Pentateuch, especially of the Book of Deuteronomy. See, further, note [282].

[301] Thus it is probably not a matter of doubt whether or not a true historical
reminiscence lies at the basis of vii.25 [160],xxiv.14,15,23,26 [292]. On the other hand,
(to name also an insignificant detail), no stress can be laid on the fact that the
bodies of the King of Ai and of the five kings of Southern Canaan were taken down
from the tree before sundown, Jo.viii.29,x.27; since the writer manifestly wishes to
make it appear that the prescription of the Law, D.xxi.22,23, was accurately
followed. The case is the same with this particular as it is with the whole description of Joshua's observance of the Law: comp. note [300], and (119,120,127).

LONDON : PRINTED BY SPOTTISWOODE AND CO., NEW-STREET SQUARE.

CPSIA information can be obtained
at www.ICGtesting.com
Printed in the USA
LVHW080830031119
636174LV00011B/611/P